A
PASSIONATE
PREFERENCE

A
Passionate
Preference

The Story of the
North Carolina
School of the Arts

LESLIE BANNER

Incorporating interviews from the North Carolina
School of the Arts Oral History Project, as compiled by
Douglas C. Zinn.

 Down Home Press, Asheboro, N.C.

Down Home Press
P.O. Box 4126
Asheboro, N.C. 27204

FRONTISPIECE

Photo by Bruce Roberts
(Archives of the North Carolina School of the Arts)

CONTENTS

ILLUSTRATIONS

ACKNOWLEDGMENTS

THIS HISTORY would not have been possible without the generous support of James H. Semans, M.D., who first dreamed of seeking listeners for the story of the North Carolina School of the Arts; nor would anyone have heard that story without the complicity of forty-four willing raconteurs who paused to look back, with affection, emotion, and verve.

As with any lengthy research project, this one is indebted as well to innumerable people who took a moment to make a suggestion or track down a reference, answer a question or point the way; but a special mention of thanks should go to Bruce Stewart, NCSA's first dean of students, who shared his research and notes on the school's origins; to John Le Doux, NCSA archivist, who not only contributed his chronology to this project but his expertise and boundless patience as well; to Betty Masten, also of NCSA, who graciously discovered and organized some twenty years of the school's press releases; to Dennis Rowe, the project's research assistant, who grew into a marvel of organization and accuracy; and to Peggy Ellis, manuscript typist and bulwark, who remained calm, correct, and interested under provocation.

Finally, any piece of work done within range of Mary Semans carries something in the heart of it which is owed to her.

L.B.
D.Z.

PREFACE

OVER MANY YEARS the citizens of North Carolina have established a splendid record of growing support and enthusiasm for the performing arts. Public-spirited corporations, private donors, concerned citizens in many towns and cities and the General Assembly of our state have given life and continuity to outdoor drama, the state symphony, summer music camps, drama festivals, community theater, art shows, folk festivals, and many other means by which the creative spirit of our people and the will to achieve have been nourished and given expression.

A different, major, and decisive step forward in this ongoing effort of our state is the subject of *A Passionate Preference: The Story of the North Carolina School of the Arts*. Leslie Banner's story of the origins of this unique and audacious educational enterprise is essential reading to interested citizens. Indeed, her work is a splendid account of the movement from an idea to the reality of bricks, mortar, faculty, students, and strong community support. This account is of especial interest to the student of political science in following the resourcefulness and sustained effort of John Ehle, cultural aide to Governor Sanford, and of the astute strategy developed by Governor Sanford himself in achieving the enactment of legislation providing for the school. Clearly, the state and all who are interested in the performing arts as a major element of our cultural life acknowledge with profound gratitude the thought, energy, and effort that John Ehle and Terry Sanford expended over those early months of debate and advocacy. Without their intelligent and forceful direction, the school never would have been established, and it is fitting that the following pages record their personal and professional contributions to this great undertaking.

Leslie Banner faithfully identifies also the substantial role played by the civic leaders of the state and especially by Gordon Hanes, Philip Hanes, Smith Bagley, and others in Winston-Salem in finding a home for the school. She reminds us of the role of the press and civic groups in keeping our people alert to the importance of great music, drama, and dance. Her story is made all the brighter by the pages devoted to the impact of other persons, especially Vittorio Giannini. His great spirit, his abiding enthusiasm, and his utter unselfishness in bringing teacher, student, classroom, stage, and rehearsal hall into a unity of commitment and activity represent a great personal triumph and give us profound admiration for his life's work. The man and the idea were well met.

Vittorio Giannini enjoyed the support, strength, and great goodwill of those two indefatigable cultural leaders of North Carolina, Mary and Dr. James Semans. The international programs of the school are the direct result of their joint efforts and their combined determination that the students understand that the performing arts know no geographical boundaries. With other important civic and cultural leaders in North Carolina, Mary and Jim Semans envisioned the splendid role a school of performing arts could play in our state. When called upon, they characteristically set about to provide appropriate leadership and strong support. They, too, must be counted among the founding spirits of this institution along with members of its Board of Trustees and the officers and members of the foundation of the school.

Governor Sanford and his cultural associate, John Ehle, brought many important ideas to fruition during their exciting four years of stewardship. The North Carolina School of the Arts represents a signal achievement because talented and worthy young people now have there the opportunity for creative self-fulfillment. Leslie Banner's story should remind all thoughtful citizens of the responsibility we have today to enrich, enhance, and improve this manifestation of public will: that the youth of North Carolina find in the school of the arts a glorious chance to realize the best that is within them.

William Friday
Chapel Hill, North Carolina
September 1985

INTRODUCTION

LOOKING AT the young people of North Carolina in the early 1960s, it was apparent that there was considerable artistic talent, as doubtless there had been over the generations, that would remain untapped, untrained, and, quite frequently, never recognized. A school for the arts in the midst of these young people would certainly raise the awareness of their abilities and the rich potential of the artistic spirit. So one purpose of such a school was discovery—discovery by the individual and by those who might be of help in developing that latent talent. There is not any question that the North Carolina School of the Arts has served that purpose. Because of the school, there are hundreds of young people today who have achieved fulfillment in their lives because they discovered and developed their artistic talents.

Identification and discovery are only the beginning. Encouragement and training are necessary. In the 1960s there was a need in North Carolina for a place that set the climate for the special kind of training and learning in which artistic talent can burgeon and grow. But what is that? Gauguin, Helen Hayes, José Limon, Mary Lou Williams, and Leonard Bernstein followed no common path.

Most people with whom John Ehle and I talked at the time felt that the academic setting of a university or college campus was not likely to be the best growing climate for artistic talent. It is not for me to denigrate academic structure as the means for education; the point is that pedagogy may not have been developed with artistic talent and the training needs of artists in mind. There is a vast difference between intellectual achievement and artistic achievement, although surely the two combined are advantageous in the case of the creative artist. The conclusion after several years of contemplation and discussion was that academic structure could very well stymie the artistic spirit, which demands more room for creativity and self-development, which needs deliberate encouragement to experiment, to look foolish, and to grow, and which needs hours of practice each day as well as tough, hard rules and routines. We would need something different.

We decided we needed a faculty of successful artists. Although there were artists on several existing campuses, no campus had professional performers representing the full range of all performing arts.

Also, students in music and dance and, to a lesser extent, acting, need an early start, earlier than our colleges and other residential campuses provided. I am sure there is much we do not know about creativity and artistic talent, but it can be identified at an early age, and there is much evidence that the earlier the better, especially for the dancer and the musician, and perhaps for all artists. Certainly, the germination comes too early to wait until the child has finished college, then goes off to a conservatory.

It is the sound and proven approach of secondary and college education to ground well in the liberal arts, as broadly as possible, the budding businessman or businesswoman, the geologist, lawyer, physician, professor, and engineer, but for the performing artist, something different is necessary—sooner and distinctly—a greater demand for specific commitment and rigorous, repetitious training in an art.

For these reasons, I ruled out placing our greenhouse for the arts on a college campus. A difference of opinion was expressed by the faculty of the Woman's College, now the University of North Carolina at Greensboro. A number there felt, with considerable justification, the right to be proud of their music and art and drama departments. With that I could have no quarrel. The final argument was that they were already doing those things, and doing them extremely well in my opinion; but we were missing something, looking for something else as we thought about talented young people who never knew the extent of their talents.

I did not come to this conclusion arbitrarily or single-handedly, but after much discussion with an array of people. Along with all of these discussions, I was drawn away from my idea that we could satisfy our needs with a conservatory, my model being Juilliard, where college graduates or high school graduates might prepare for artistic apprenticeship and study. That, generally, would be too late for us. Furthermore, established conservatories had some entrenched flaws, and if we were to build a new institution for all the performing arts, and for children as well as young adults, which we hoped would be a new kind of institution, we did not need to follow a pattern, because there was no pattern, not even Juilliard.

What kind of a setting was ours to be? How could we mix junior high school with high school, college, and even postbaccalaureate studies? Certainly it would be no orthodox structure. So a new structure was put together, and it seems to have worked very well for twenty years.

There is another aspect beyond the unorthodox age and class structure—that is, the nature of instruction and administration for such a school. It is obvious that the Ph.D. is a distinguished research degree, but it carries burdens that must be overcome by the professor who desires to be a teacher of young artists. That seems heresy, on its face, but it is not. One's own education always has to be overcome by the truly good teacher; the reservoir of knowledge and intellectuality and academic methodology must yield to the needs of the teacher's students. That is true for the history teacher and the math teacher and the chemistry teacher. It is so in a peculiar and demanding degree for the teacher of young artists. Consequently, a learned background not properly translated is worse than no learned background at all, when it comes to teaching.

A faculty of professional performing artists proved to be ideal for teaching aspiring artists. Some of them have no degrees at all; one dean at the school did not finish high school. Mary Lou Williams, the jazz pianist and composer, was a friend of mine and taught at Duke University. I doubt that she had a baccalaureate degree. I never asked. It made no difference. She was an inspirational teacher because she understood the artistic spirit, *was* the artistic spirit.

Having agreed on a structure, having settled on a teaching philosophy, we confronted more hazardous challenges: How do you infect a school with unorthodoxy? How do you ensure its permanent commitment to the unbridled and focused artistic spirit? How do you organize a school in an unorthodox manner and build a faculty of professional performers, one that will flourish in a self-renewing manner?

By good luck, we started with a consensus candidate for president of the new institution, the unanimous and enthusiastic choice of all of those many who had struggled for the activation of a new idea. Vittorio Giannini was a brilliant choice. I have not to this day asked whether or not he had a doctorate. I had seen him in action and had heard even more about him. He understood the artistic spirit. He *was* the artistic spirit. He knew that the development of artistic talent is not a matter of the usual pedagogic principles. He knew the hard work involved, as well. Giannini knew this, both intuitively and by experience, so he was the ideal arts school administrator. No one understands the fragile partnership of discipline and freedom better than a successful composer. No one knows better that authoritarian discipline can stifle the creative talent. Art without self-discipline is less than it otherwise would be. Freedom, too, is poisoning if it dismisses self-discipline. Freedom to think, to grow, to chance, to dare, is a part of the shaping of artistic talent. So is hard work at one's craft. So is acceptance of the demand for excellence. Freedom as aimless loafing, or freedom to think and dream the artist's fantasies, can hardly suffice on its own. The student/artist, under the hand of a master artist, experiences the difference, recognizes the challenge, does the endless labor, sets free the creative urge, and develops and learns. What Vittorio Giannini did is recorded in this book. It was a smashing success.

Being an artist is hard work. Rigorous training, repetitive practice, adherence to exacting standards are essential objectives of the teaching at the North Carolina School of the Arts. My conviction is that an accomplished performing artist, regardless of formal education, knows all of this better than anyone else, and furthermore, likely knows how to impart such understanding to the student/artist better than anybody else.

It is also true that all concerned with the deliberations were insistent that there be built into the concept of the school of the arts curriculum an enduring commitment to education in the liberal arts for each artist. Whatever the art form, whatever the free spirit, whatever the talent, all of that will be enhanced by the general comprehension and understanding and compassion and sense of direction that come from studies in literature, history, languages, mathematics, science, psychology, philosophy, religion.

The school of the arts, as designed, had certain vulnerabilities because it was a stand-alone institution with its own Board of Trustees. The school was responsible only to its Board of Trustees, which in turn was legally responsible to the appointing authority, the governor, and beyond that—harder to pin down—responsible to the concept that made it a school. In the early 1970s it was proposed, at the time when other state institutions were being brought together under the umbrella of the University of North Carolina, that the North Carolina School of the Arts also become a campus of the University of North Carolina. I confess that I viewed this idea with both pleasure and fear. I was pleased that the institution would have a strong parent, would be insulated from the political vagaries. My fear was that in time, in such a structure, it would be forgotten that it was never intended, and should never be, that this institution should fit a pattern by which other sister institutions, eminent ones, would be measured. That was and remains a valid fear. A university system needs a bureaucracy, but bureaucracy is the deadly foe of the arts. If finally the bureaucracy swallows up the unique unorthodoxy of the school, all of those who had a part in the creation of the North Carolina School of the Arts made a mistake when they chose not just to strengthen the several departments at the Woman's College. That would not have been a bad decision. It would have been less costly. It would have been a good and useful and worthwhile endeavor, but it would not have been the North Carolina School of the Arts. Now, I suppose, my plea, even my prayer, is that we should not ever lose sight of the need for the remarkable difference: the early identification and training of students of high school age and even earlier, the faculty of professional performing artists, an administration in the style of professional performing artists, and the freedom from traditional academic forms.

I would like to scratch on the wall, somewhere at the North Carolina School of the Arts, neatly and in artistic style of course: "This institution is unorthodox and heretical."

Terry Sanford
Duke University
January 1986

THE
ORAL HISTORY
PROJECT

"ALL HISTORY was at first oral," retorted Dr. Samuel Johnson during a breakfast conversation with the philosopher-historian, William Robertson.

Dr. Johnson was commenting on how convenient it would be for Robertson to interview the survivors of a Whig-Jacobin uprising of some thirty years before. Although written history often supplies us with the origin and conclusion of events, oral history has the advantage of bridging the space between, providing details that might otherwise have been lost. Although the traditional source for the historian's research has been the manuscript, oral history has been used by many of the great historians of the past, including such well-known figures as Boswell and Macaulay. Today, with our emphasis on the spoken form of language, the role of the oral historian in preserving past and present events has become even more important. And with the tape recorder, the oral version of events can be stored with greater precision than even the relentless Boswell achieved.

The North Carolina School of the Arts Oral History Project was the brainchild of Dr. and Mrs. James H. Semans. The commitment and energy of the Semanses has been, and continues to be, the mother lode of innumerable projects, this one especially close to their hearts. They realized the importance of recording the events that led to the development and fostered the growth of the NCSA. Interviews were conducted with a former governor, several legislators, former school administrators, artists, and spiritual and financial supporters.

Because the school is only twenty years old, most of its supporters are still with us, although the Oral History Project has witnessed the deaths of Giorgio Ciompi and Ben Roney. Fortunately, both of these beloved individuals had been interviewed for this project. This is one of the many factors that made the Semanses see the need to record the origins of one of the country's finest training facilities for the performing arts.

The interviewing process always included a standard set of questions that were posed to every interviewee. The purpose of these questions was twofold. First, the answers made it possible to evaluate certain topics with some degree of consistency. Also, the individual's response could be compared with those of the entire group interviewed. Second, because memory is a selective process and the most powerful memory selection takes place immediately after an event occurs, the interviewer is able to ascertain which events had been most important to the interviewee. These answers also set the tone for the remainder of the interview(s).

Inquiries were also tailored to individuals depending on their role and special involvement with the North Carolina School of the Arts. Specific questions, however, were only the beginning. Spontaneity was a common occurrence. The tape recorder was turned on and off several times—often the interviewee wanted to respond without the recorder running. This is understandable because personalities were involved. Some individuals felt it was important for the interviewer to know the facts but did not want to commit themselves on a tape.

The interviewer must be flexible enough to allow a person to expand, direct, and offer whatever information he or she deems to be important. Although certain questions will resurrect events that may be only tangentially related to a specific event, all information is valuable. After all, it is much easier to edit materials than it is to elaborate on a limited amount of information.

Most of the interviews were conducted in the homes or offices of the interviewees. Although this format is not crucial for the collection of information, it is a more comfortable way for people to be interviewed and makes it easier for them to comply.

I have fond memories of every interview. I will never forget the delightful afternoon that Dr. James Semans and I spent with the grande dame of dance, Agnes de Mille. After a wonderful lunch in her New York City apartment, Miss de Mille answered our questions with the esprit for which she is noted. Her responses made it seem as if the events had occurred the previous day.

Unfortunately, time constraints prevented an all-inclusive interview schedule for everyone involved with the school, but a representative group of individuals participated. Although ours is by no means a complete list, a balance of viewpoints was collected.

A total of forty-four individuals were interviewed for the Oral History Project. These interviews were collected over a period of three years. The project began with an eloquent interview with Hugh Cannon and concluded with an insightful and whimsical exchange with Robert Hickok.

I began the project with a limited degree of knowledge regarding the development and early history of the North Carolina School of the Arts.

Throughout the project, I have not only learned the raw historical facts, but the image of the family became very apparent in the oral testimony. This devotion and familiar feeling that penetrates all levels of the school's activities sets it apart from many performing arts training facilities.

It is a rare opportunity to be involved in a project that elicits as much interest and unmitigated enthusiasm as did the Oral History Project. As Hugh Cannon so beautifully stated during his interview, "the school is a creature of each one of us." The excitement and dedication of each person I interviewed have left an indelible impression upon me.

Leslie Banner has integrated the oral testimony collected for the project with extensive written sources to present a readable and factual account of the origins of the North Carolina School of the Arts. She has synthesized these materials not only in an erudite manner but also with great skill and accumulating affection.

Douglas C. Zinn
November 11, 1985

A
PASSIONATE
PREFERENCE

*The time for a young artist to begin to be an
artist, to have a passionate preference for art
come over him, is somewhere between fifteen and
twenty-five. . . . The tenderest thing you can
have as patron of the arts is a sense of that,
almost unexpressed in the young person . . . his
first passionate preference.*

ROBERT FROST

THE STERNEST THING

N 1960 Terry Sanford was elected governor of North Carolina on an education platform and a promise to raise taxes. For months he campaigned across his home state with one message: "Quality Education is the rock upon which I will build the house of my administration." [1] And he told voters frankly the price was likely to be high. If this forthright demand for more money for education seemed an audacious and foolhardy election strategy to his opponents (who of course attacked his expensive Quality Education Program as "Pie in the Sky"), Sanford had ready the sorry statistics to justify his call for a "New Day": North Carolina ranked forty-eighth in the nation in the percentage of its population who were high school graduates and forty-first in literacy. It was forty-fifth among the fifty states in the amount spent to educate each child, and in the entire decade of the 1950s, the salaries of North Carolina teachers were raised less than those of teachers in any other state. [2]

With political acumen (what some might call good sense), Sanford called on women all over the state to support him in his bid to improve opportunities for their children. In spite of the strong push provided North Carolina Republicans by then vice-president and presidential candidate Richard Nixon, "High Tax Terry" was elected with a 122,000-vote majority. [3] Less than four months later, the sandy-haired, stocky young governor (he was only forty-three) was back on the hustings looking for public support, this time for his controversial tax on food.

On March 6, 1961, Governor Sanford explained to the North Carolina General Assembly that a food tax was the only feasible way to raise the additional revenue needed to get the Quality Education Program going. He asked for a budget of $100 million, with $50 million to be derived from the new tax. On March 9 Sanford addressed voters in Smithfield, North Carolina, explaining that he understood he was asking even the poorest to make a sacrifice, but it was the fairest way and the surest to avoid an even greater deprivation: "If we tax bread, we will also be taxing cake; if we tax fatback, we also will tax caviar; if we tax corn meal, we also will tax filet mignon. No one is going to go hungry because of this tax. But the children of North Carolina will go thirsty for quality education if we do not enact this program for better schools"[4] During Terry Sanford's four-year administration, the forty-fifth state in per capita income nearly doubled its financial support for public education.[5]

The implications of these appropriations for the school of the arts lay not in the sums themselves (of which the school would eventually receive only a tiny percentage), but in the character of the man whose leadership had sparked major changes in North Carolina's educational system and who had gained national attention by making education the creative thrust of his administration. During his four years in office, Terry Sanford was invited to speak on his experiments in education in thirty states and at Harvard and Yale universities. He was twice elected, by his peers at the Southern Governors Conference, chairman of the Southern Regional Education Board (SREB), which recognized Sanford as providing "prolific and great ideas" at a time when the educational establishment was lagging in creative development.[6] Perhaps most impressive—at least in demonstrating the extent to which Governor Sanford was willing to reach back for the first causes of failure in the schools—was the anti-poverty program that grew out of his efforts to provide an environment that would permit every child to learn. With the help of aides, most especially John Ehle, he established the North Carolina Fund in 1963, an innovative attempt to break the cycle of poverty. The Ford Foundation granted $7 million of the $11 million raised to begin the project, and the White House watched the plan's progress closely. Eventually, the community action plan in Lyndon Johnson's Anti-Poverty Program, VISTA, and the Job Corps were patterned on the North Carolina Fund.[7]

Governor Terry Sanford did not propose simply to pour money into the public schools; he had a concrete, populist agenda that addressed the needs of every citizen of the state, from college loans and scholarships for the state's very young teachers and doctors and lawyers, to training for the mentally retarded, rehabilitation and job skills for the prison population, and expanded opportunities for the black race at a time when the great civil rights advances were yet to be won. From such a position it is no very great leap to the assumption that a ballerina from Kinston or an oboist from Raleigh also has the right to state support for professional training. Behind his drive for specific action in every area of education lay a liberally conceived philosophy of government. Terry Sanford believed the proper business of a government to be "lifting the level of civilization by broadening the opportunities in life for its people." The chief tool for conducting this business he saw as education defined not in terms of chalk dust and

1. *"Quality Education is the rock upon which I will build the house of my administration." Governor Terry Sanford with North Carolina schoolchildren (Duke University Archives).*

school bells but in its visionary sense as "the means for the fulfillment of the human spirit and fruitful use of all talents." Thus by Sanford's very definition of government, the state would be required to support the arts as part of its duty to its citizens.[8]

At this time the Kennedy White House was leading the nation in acknowledging the importance of the arts in a people's life. Indeed, the efforts of North Carolinians had been acknowledged early on in the administration when the First Lady, through the good offices of Henry Hall Wilson, invited the young musicians of James Christian Pfohl's Transylvania Music Camp, in Brevard, North Carolina, to give the first in her series of Young People's Concerts. Wilson, an administrative assistant to President John F. Kennedy, had played the oboe in the very first session of Pfohl's summer music camp. When Pfohl heard about the proposed concerts, he contacted Hugh Cannon, Governor Sanford's administrative director, who called Wilson (Cannon had played the drums for Pfohl). Wilson arranged the invitation, and R. J. Reynolds Tobacco Company paid the Transylvania Symphony's travel expenses (the company's treasurer had played the trumpet for Pfohl). On August 22, 1961, Pfohl conducted his orchestra in the White House Rose Garden. President Kennedy, representing his wife, made a short speech of appreciation for the work in musical training being done with young people all over the country. Although the president could not stay for the concert, he promised to keep his office door open. Terry Sanford also welcomed the youngsters, and during the concert Henry Hall Wilson was called to the podium to conduct "Stars and Stripes Forever." That night, the Transylvania Symphony dined with the North Carolina congressional delegation and Governor Sanford, who was impressed with the number of talented students from North Carolina and troubled when they told him they were planning to leave the state to get the conservatory training they needed.[9]

In spite of President Kennedy's open-door cultural policy, however, and efforts by lobbyists and individual members of Congress—not to mention the high visibility of anything that concerned Jacqueline Kennedy—federal support for the arts remained primarily moral. Before 1964, no action was taken beyond the appointment of a White House adviser on the arts.[10] During these years when the political climate of the nation was opening to the arts but the federal pocketbook remained closed, Terry Sanford was ready to do more than just entertain new ideas. In fact, it is the impetuosity with which he supported these ideas that is perhaps the most vividly recalled characteristic of his administration.

Governor Sanford could not afford to be cautious because under North Carolina law he could not succeed himself. As a longtime observer of the state's political scene has noted, "one-term governors who are activists tend to go for broke," and in a sense, Sanford did just that. His former administrative director Hugh Cannon somewhat wryly admits that "a number of the Sanford programs simply were done with such speed that . . . [they] later came under some attack, [on the grounds] that they were done without a great deal of thought and without a great deal of legislative approval. . . . What I'm saying is that every Sanford program did not always fare that well in later years, and there is no point in us getting into whether that was right or wrong, but a lot of them were done fairly rapidly." Terry Sanford's only regret upon leaving office was that he hadn't done things even more rapidly. In an interview near the end of his administration, Sanford told a reporter that he had at first underestimated the power of the Governor's Office, through influence, to get things done. If he had realized the extent of this power sooner, he could have done much more. As it was, he approached the end of his term feeling much like the state's reigning beauty queen when she told the press: " 'I don't see what you want to select another Miss North Carolina for, anyhow.' " [11]

Terry Sanford's adventurous spirit enabled him to attract iconoclasts, radicals, and dreamers to the service of the state: "The mundane to Terry Sanford is a bore," his former state budget officer has remarked, "He hasn't time to fool around with what he's already heard." Hugh Cannon concurs: "With a lot of other governors, nobody would have had even the slightest idea of proposing the school of the arts in North Carolina. Terry Sanford would try any good idea. I mean, he had the audacity, and he had the people to get things like that through." Perhaps the most significant of those people whose ideas on education excited Terry Sanford's audacity was John Ehle. "If I were to write a guidebook for new governors," Sanford mused in 1966, "one of my main suggestions would be that he find a novelist and put him on his staff." [12]

The value of this unusual advice was demonstrated in a 1964 *Newsweek* profile of Ehle. Calling him, in the jargon of the 1960s, a "one-man Rand," a "brain-truster" for Terry Sanford's "New Frontier-style" administration, the magazine listed as projects either "spawned," nurtured, or organized by Ehle the North Carolina Fund, the Governor's School, the North Carolina Advancement School, the North Carolina Film Board, Shakespeare in the Schools, the Learning Institute of North Carolina, and the North Carolina School of the Arts (NCSA). As "ambassador plenipotentiary to the great foundations," Ehle had been phenomenally successful in funding his ideas; from all sources, both foundation and government, *Newsweek* reported, he secured more than $18 million during his eighteen-month sojourn in Raleigh. Years later, recalling how the school of the arts had begun, Hugh Cannon reflected that among all those people whose contributions had been essential, "John Ehle was . . . the central thread." [13]

A native of western North Carolina, John Ehle was an associate professor in the Communications Center at the University of North Carolina (UNC) at Chapel Hill when he first caught Terry Sanford's attention. A born writer, Ehle was employed by the center even before he had earned his bachelor's degree in radio in 1949; by 1953 he had a master's degree in drama and a steady job teaching playwriting. From 1954 to 1956, Ehle achieved national recognition with his American Adventure Series of radio plays; produced in the studios at the university and broadcast on NBC radio, the series won the Freedom Award. Ehle's first novel, *Move Over, Mountain* (1957), was perhaps the first serious novel about a southern Negro written by a white man and undoubtedly suggested to Ehle's audience the author's unconventional (for the time) imagination and his liberal politics. His second novel, *Kingstree Island* (1959), set in a North Carolina coastal fishing village, met with commercial success both here and abroad and undoubtedly suggested to the author himself the direction of future financial rewards. His third novel, *Lion on the Hearth* (1961), inaugurated a series of now seven books about the North Carolina mountain people, for which he has been winning critical acclaim for more than twenty years.[14] But in 1962 the governor of North Carolina interrupted the flow.

By the time Terry Sanford was elected, John Ehle was on the verge of a break with the University of North Carolina at Chapel Hill, a break born in the luxury of a young man's anger and frustration—"anger at the way universities suffocate young artists," he recalled a generation later. On February 24, 1961, Professor Ehle wrote a highly critical letter to the university administration: "Not in almost a decade have we hired a writer to teach here, or a painter, a sculptor, a composer . . . we haven't even replaced the ones who have left or retired . . . we have no scholarships in the creative arts, no awards or prizes . . . our administration shows little understanding of the differences between the mind of the scholar and the mind of the artist." This letter so impressed Professor Clifford Lyons of the University of North Carolina English Department that he showed it to his friend, poet Robert Frost, who had come to Chapel Hill to give his annual spring lecture and reading at the university. Ehle recalls that on the evening of March 3, he walked from Cameron Avenue, where he had been working in

2. *"If I were to write a guidebook for new governors, one of my main suggestions would be that he find a novelist and put him on his staff."* Governor Sanford's special consultant, novelist John Ehle (photo by Peter Julian).

his vegetable garden, directly to Memorial Hall. There, so as to be as un-
obtrusive as possible in his work clothes, he went up into the balcony, only
to find himself the dusty and astonished hero of Frost's opening remarks:[15]

> I've been thinking this afternoon a little bit about a letter I saw by a
> practicing artist, a writer, in which he worried about this college, this
> university, whether it was a good place for a young practicing artist,
> painter, poet, novelist, short story writer. Now you, most of you,
> don't know [it], but that's a life-long anxiety of mine. . . . You see . . .
> the time for a young artist to begin to be an artist, to have it come
> over him, to have a passionate preference for art come over him, is
> somewhere between fifteen and twenty-five, and that's just the time
> you're around education. . . . Out in the world is a rough, tough place
> where nobody knows what an artist is. The only person that knows
> what an artist is in the world is educated, the educated. . . . It's largely
> a matter of our educated America, many colleges. Now the reproach.

Frost candidly scolded the academics, who he felt were failing in their
responsibility to understand and nurture creative minds: "Our young artists are lost in learning in those ten years between fifteen and twenty-five,
when the great thing comes over them, when, like St. Paul, they see a light
. . . and want to give themselves to something." Some of Frost's friends,
fellow writers at schools like Stanford and Iowa, were striving to devise
programs more suited to the needs of student artists "because they think
there's something lacking in the place." The "something lacking" was perhaps an understanding of the different requirements of the artist and the
scholar: "I have faculty friends that wonder with me, what's the difference
between me and them?" Frost wryly queried. "I have somewhat the same
knowledge they have . . . but it seems come by in a different way." Adjustments had to be made by the universities, both in program and attitude.
"The artist is a problem child in the middle of all this learning," Frost admitted. "And the people who own the institution—see, I grant that right
away, the real owners of it whose property it is, are the scholars, and it's
their patronage the arts ask for." Conceding, too, that he did not know just
what the colleges should do, the aging poet went ahead to formulate a
moving plea that educators put only kindness in the way of the young
artist:

> It's a stern thing. It's one of the sternest things of all. It's sterner than
> learning . . . it's sacrificial. And you mustn't be with people that make
> a slighting, a triviality of it, a mocking way of it. . . . The tenderest

thing you can have as patron of the arts is a sense of that almost unexpressed in the young person between fifteen and twenty-five, his first passionate preference.

Belief . . . comes with this passionate preference, this dream of something to be. You know, you believe yourself into what you're going to be. You don't know yourself into it, you believe yourself into it. At the age of twenty, you can't go before a committee and tell them what you're going to be, not very well. It's going on all the time, but just how crude a thing it is, that's the secret, sacred secret. It's a very, very precious thing.[16]

Encouraged by Frost's words—"a great speech on the place of the artist, the student artist, in our universities, something that I was floundering about with"[17]—Ehle went gloriously public with his concerns. In a wide-ranging critique in the feature section of the *Raleigh News and Observer* Sunday edition (May 14, 1961), he wondered "What's the Matter with Chapel Hill?" and lent urgency to his question by quoting Robert Frost's fear that "our young artists are lost in learning." (Curiously, none of the local papers carried the text of Frost's March 3 speech. Without Ehle's reference to it in his later article, few North Carolinians would have realized that Frost had chosen their state university podium from which to deliver an admonition against university arts education all over the country.)

It is no wonder that John Ehle attracted Terry Sanford's attention. "What's the Matter with Chapel Hill?" demonstrated a maverick philosophy of education, and in its questioning of the policies of the most powerful educational institution in the state, it showed considerable nerve. Ehle began his article with the shortcomings of the program in which he was teaching, creative writing. It seemed to lack the fire of the old days, he observed, when young Thomas Wolfe began mining native material in Frederick Koch's writing class in the folk play, or even the excitement of more recent times when Betty Smith, acclaimed author of *A Tree Grows in Brooklyn,* wrote and acted in student plays in the Forest Theatre. Today, the drama department has only fourteen majors, Ehle sadly noted, and the music department seven, and North Carolina's premier playwright Paul Green writes to him: "Why is it that no composers have come out of the music department?"

Throughout the university Ehle found the creative spirit in woefully short supply: UNC Press was "dull" and UNC television "docile"; most of the teaching was being done by graduate students rather than by the professors who supposedly were there to lead and inspire. Even the editor of the student newspaper, the *Daily Tar Heel,* felt aggrieved about the quality and range of speakers appearing on campus: "Not even three innocent Beatniks can get a podium for their rhythmic readings," Jonathan Yardley told his fellow students.

Ehle literally left no stone unturned in his criticism of the university; even in matters of architecture and land use it reflected no new ideas and showed a lack of foresight and concern for the effect of physical surroundings on the student body. Perhaps Ehle's most damning evidence, however—and the heart of his attack on the state's leading educational establishment—was the poor showing of UNC's humanities departments in the area of research, of developing programs that would "send out creative sparks to influence their students." Of the sum total of grants to the university for research and training in fiscal year 1959–60 (all from foundations and government agencies) "the least amount went to the Humanities. . . . The amount . . . was, as a matter of fact, nothing." Oh, yes, Professor Ehle went on, he did think to inquire about money from past grants still on deposit, and an administrator added them up for him. The total amount for all departments in the humanities was "$60.23 (sixty dollars and twenty-three cents)."

In absolute amazement Ehle unfolded the sad story: the sum total of grant proposals submitted to foundation and government agencies from UNC's humanities departments for 1959–60 was two. Ehle noted further that of the nearly $5 million in grants received by the university in 1959–60, nearly all of the money came from the federal government. In the fiscal year under study, UNC–Chapel Hill received from Carnegie, Rockefeller, and Kellogg nothing; from Ford, it received $17,752. Yet creative proposals in the humanities were flowing outward from other major universities, and from the foundations the dollars were flowing back in to try them out. Here was a great untapped source of funding. Here was money for new ideas in education in the arts and in the humanities, and North Carolina was getting scarcely any of it. Indeed, North Carolina's great university— one of the greatest universities in the South—was not even trying to get any of it.

In 1962, not quite a year after "What's the Matter with Chapel Hill?" appeared, the brash young professor went to work for the lame-duck governor as a special assistant for new projects, "ones that did not need state money, because he didn't have any," Ehle told an audience in Texas some twenty years later.[18] Terry Sanford had wanted to be governor all his life, and his term was already half over. With only one more session of the legislature left to him, and his Quality Education Program fully funded with state revenues, Governor Sanford wanted to do still more for the children of North Carolina. His choice of Ehle was masterful; so successful was the governor's special assistant in seeking outside funding for experiments in education that the Ford Foundation eventually hired Ehle for its public affairs staff—in self-defense, no doubt.

John Ehle's feeling that universities were anathema to the arts was shared by McNeil Lowry of the Ford Foundation, who was offending university administrators in yet another area of the South in 1961. On October 24, Lowry, in the full southern meaning of the term, "spoke to" the Association of Graduate Schools in New Orleans. His credentials for delivering what amounted to an admonishment on the subject of the university and the creative arts were impeccable. As director of Ford's Program in Humanities and the Arts, Lowry had been traveling around the country since 1957, evaluating the situation of the performing arts in America, pursuant to the granting, by the Ford Foundation, of hundreds of millions of dollars to symphonies and theater, ballet, and opera companies. Lowry's extensive fieldwork had given him some uncomfortable insights into the plight of the professional performer in the United States. The good news about the arts in America in 1961 was that a cultural explosion was taking place: the steadily growing number of college-educated Americans provided a larger, more appreciative audience than ever before, and this audience was willing to pay for more performing centers and more education in the arts for their children, so long as a diploma was attached to the program. And herein lay the bad news: numerous lavishly funded university and college programs for training in the arts provided the only reliable economic base for artists and the most attractive and readily available training for students, whose parents were being asked to finance these dubious undertakings. Building auditoriums and attending performances was all well and good, the middle class grumbled, but being asked to sacrifice one's firstborn for the arts was another matter entirely. Hence the gradual, ongoing strangulation of conservatory and private and apprentice training in the arts and the growth of B.F.A. and M.F.A. degree programs at liberal arts institutions. The reasoning was simple and wholesome: if she can't earn her bread dancing (or piping or yodeling), at least she can teach. And so, though the supply of educationally certified arts teachers and the demand for educationally certified arts teachers were keeping pace nicely with each other, serious training and performance opportunities for the wholeheartedly committed artist were, as Lowry expressed it, "woefully inadequate."

Thus from 1957 to 1975, the Ford Foundation concentrated its arts funding on the improvement of professional (as opposed to educational) institutions for training and performance.[19]

Not unmindful that problems existed in graduate education in the creative arts, the Committee on Policies in Graduate Education of the Association of Graduate Schools invited Lowry, as an acknowledged expert on the condition of the arts in America, to address its deans. In analyzing the impact of the universities on the arts, Lowry found for the schools in the areas of aesthetics (meaning history and theory) and enrichment insofar as they provided the opportunity for informal participation in arts activities, important to the development of the well-rounded citizen. In both cases the objectives of a university education were being met. The study of the history and theory of the arts was appropriate to the training of the scholar who, at the graduate level, was expected "to grasp a whole corpus of systematic knowledge and subject it to philosophical analysis." At the undergraduate level, sampling of the arts by way of amateur theatricals and the school orchestra was appropriate to the achievement of a liberal education. But "what," Lowry queried, "is the relevance to either of these objectives, of training in the *techniques* of painting, acting, directing, dancing, instrumentation, musical composition, creative writing, or any other branch of artistic creation?" Can a university, given its primary objectives, offer such training, using professional standards?[20]

Lowry answered with a resounding no; the university, which says its primary function is the liberal education of the individual, acts as though it is also training young people to be professional artists. But it cannot. Artistic discipline requires, at the professional level, a huge, a distorted amount of time and concentration, and the prerequisites for a bachelor's degree do not allow for such distortion of the individual's development, are designed, in fact, to have quite the opposite effect. And so the university's claims to professional training are fraudulent and its achievements spurious. The aspiring young artist, having taken courses in theory from professionals (practicing scholars) and courses in technique from amateurs (nonpracticing artists), goes out to New York or San Francisco and finds he is unemployable as a performing artist because he is not equipped with professional skills. The artist must now seek a professional apprenticeship (if there is time left for him in his particular discipline). If such a place cannot be found, or if the artist is too late, he returns to the university or the college or the public school system or the community, to teach.[21]

Thus Lowry concluded: "The university has largely taken over the functions of professional training in the arts but in the main has sacrificed professional standards in doing so." For those students who wish to pursue their arts careers with the benefit of a safety net, he went on, the university programs are fine. The degree in arts education is appropriate for those who, though they may hunger for art, are not willing to starve for it. As for the rest, Lowry closed with a chilling judgment of university arts training: "Under present conditions the best service you can perform for the potential artist is to throw him out."[22]

John Ehle's impact on education in North Carolina is yet to be fully measured. His latest brainchild, the North Carolina School of Science and Mathematics (NCSSM), in Durham, North Carolina, opened its doors in September 1980,[23] a generation after Terry Sanford recognized in Ehle's anger and dissatisfaction a constructive voice of extraordinary energy and originality. Like NCSSM, which is a residential high school for North Carolina students gifted in the sciences, the first of the Ehle-instigated schools to open was oriented toward the academically gifted. This was the Governor's School, which held its initial session in the summer of 1963 and is still going on every summer on the campuses of Salem College (Winston-Salem, North Carolina) and St. Andrews College (Laurinburg, North Carolina). The second of Ehle's schools, the North Carolina Advancement School, opened in the fall of 1964 and was designed to rescue academic underachievers before they were lost in the shuffle of the public school system.[24] Although the North Carolina School of the Arts was the third of the special schools to open (September 1965), it was the earliest of Ehle's experiments in education to be undertaken by the Governor's Office.

Terry Sanford recalls a general concern in his office for development of the arts in the state. The governor's administrative assistant, Tom Lambeth, particularly remembers great interest on the part of Joel Fleishman, who "had talked from time to time about the possibility of the state creating what in the beginning I assumed was some sort of conservatory because the frequent reference was to Juilliard." Fleishman, a graduate of Yale Law School, was Governor Sanford's legal assistant, but, he says, "I was generally thought of as the person in the office who was interested in the arts." When John Ehle came to work for the governor in the spring of 1962, Fleishman talked with him about this idea of a music school, perhaps something similar to the Yale Music School, a conservatory that would be part of a university. Sanford's idea at the time was of a conservatory "at the advanced graduate level, and that's, of course, because I didn't know what I was talking about."[25]

John Ehle was hired because he had notions of his own to bring to the

Governor's Office. Soon after the 1960 election, Professor Ehle had submitted a proposal to Roy Wilder at the Department of Conservation, for a North Carolina Film Board, and so found himself meeting with Sanford in the Governor's Mansion. During a 1983 interview, Ehle consulted his journal, kept in the early 1960s:

> "I had my first session with Terry Sanford, and he took us upstairs in the mansion where we could have a drink." He didn't serve drinks on the first floor because his servants were prisoners, and it was against tradition in that house. I remember his son and daughter were there. The son kept sliding down the banisters. If you know the mansion, that's a dangerous thing to do—it's a very long sweep, and Terry, Jr., kept sliding down the banister, and the little girl was all over the place, and Margaret Rose came in and she had read *Kingstree Island,* the novel I had written some time before . . . and we had this drink, and somebody mentioned this project every once in a while, and in writing it up in the journal, I spelled Sanford S A N D F O R D, so that's how well I knew him as of January 21, 1961, or it's how well I spelled as of that date.

Ehle went ahead with a series of projects for the film board, at the same time that he was sparring with the university. In March of 1962, he was invited to dinner at the Governor's Mansion. Ehle remembers Joel Fleishman telling him that "it was supposed to be a meeting of Terry's closest advisers, and I was astonished. I said, 'I'm not one of his closest advisers. I'm still misspelling his name.'" Nonetheless, Governor Sanford felt enough of an affinity with John Ehle to ask him (in spite of the presence of his closest advisers) for ideas about what he should do with the rest of his term in office. Ehle recalls that he had no answers for Sanford at that time, but after the second such dinner in the spring of 1962, he wrote in his journal, "I decided on April 15 . . . to accept Terry's offer to work for him. . . . April 24 I mentioned to Terry my model high school, which was to be in the arts, and sciences and math, and languages and the humanities, social studies—but each with its own campus, contiguous to one another."[26]

Ehle went immediately to the great foundations to seek funding for his ideas. As early as May 2, 1962, he met with Margaret Mahoney of the Carnegie Corporation to discuss a residential high school for academically gifted students and a fine arts school. His memorandum reporting on this meeting to Governor Sanford also suggested a fine arts training center that would including painting and sculpture as well as music and drama. In July, Governor Sanford supported John Ehle's efforts for such a school when he signed Ehle's letter to McNeil Lowry, requesting an appointment with Lowry at the Ford Foundation for the governor's special assistant for cultural affairs.[27]

John Ehle had to wait seven weeks to present what Lowry remembers as "a whole smorgasbord of things about the arts in the state." Meanwhile, Terry Sanford was invited to attend a Governor's Weekend in western North Carolina, at James Christian Pfohl's Transylvania Music Camp. On the last weekend in July, Hugh Cannon flew up with Governor Sanford in the state plane. "Governors always like to have handy staff around," Cannon explained in 1981, "and I was one of his righthand men in terms of accompanying him on trips to various places." Although traveling with the governor was a routine duty, repeated on innumerable occasions during the Sanford administration, Hugh Cannon speaks of this particular trip as "one of the most memorable times in my life."[28]

The scent of hot pine needles and the sight of the Appalachians make a summer's day in the Great Smoky Mountains a convincing kind of experience. When cool breezes from the ancient forest rustle the heat, even a governor gets to feeling like he could hunt bear. Certainly Governor Sanford was feisty enough that day in July to borrow a pair of swim trunks from Jim Pfohl's son and dive fearlessly into a lake of cold mountain water. The change from an air-conditioned, claustrophobic July in Raleigh to a front porch picnic lunch at the camp lodge with the Pfohls was undoubtedly invigorating, as was James Christian Pfohl's enthusiasm for his camp and what he was achieving there with his young musicians every summer.[29]

As a high school student in 1929, James Pfohl had won a scholarship on the string bass to the newly opened National Music Camp at Interlochen, Michigan, founded by Joseph Maddy. Maddy himself conducted the All-Southern High School Orchestra in Asheville, in which young Jim Pfohl had won first chair bass and played well enough to win the scholarship. "That summer at Interlochen gave me a complete new outlook on life and on music," Pfohl reminisced in 1981, "and I was determined that some day there would be a school of that type in the mountains of North Carolina." The type of school that opened the world for a child from North Carolina was run by Maddy on the principle that talented and ambitious students deserved every opportunity to develop their gifts at a professional level. The summer music camp that he started in 1928 eventually developed into a four-year residential high school where students divided a ten-hour school day equally between academics and arts training.[30]

Inspired by his early experience at Interlochen, Jim Pfohl opened his first summer music camp only seven years later, on the Davidson Col-

3. *In the Great Smoky Mountains even a governor gets to feeling he could hunt bear. Governor Sanford at Transylvania Music Camp, with James Christian Pfohl (North Carolina Division of Archives and History).*

lege campus in Davidson, North Carolina, where he was director of music. After four years Pfohl wisely moved his camp to Queens College in Charlotte because the girls' school was willing to have boys on its campus in the summer, whereas all-male Davidson would not allow girls on its. But Pfohl still wanted a real camp in the mountains, and during World War II he found it in an abandoned boys' camp at Brevard: "We had gas rationing then, so we . . . walk[ed] . . . about two and a half miles from where we were . . . staying, and I came up over a hill and looked through the two wrought iron gates that were there, and said, 'This is the place.' I said that with the lake being absolutely empty, no life there at all except an old cow munching in the grass." Pfohl borrowed on his life insurance, ran the cow off, and turned a deserted scene from *Boys' Life* into a summer music camp of national reputation, with a professional faculty that featured such visiting luminaries as Jan Peerce and Beverly Sills.[31]

Although the surroundings were a draw ("we believed in bringing the faculty members there with their families and giving them a complete vacation while they were teaching"), Pfohl's commitment to demonstrated excellence as the best teaching method must have been gratifying for the professional musicians who devoted part of their summers to teaching at Transylvania Music Camp:

> I brought in a tremendous faculty, feeling that the best training these young folks could have was playing with fine musicians. The concert master, for instance, would not sit with the first chair student violinist, but would move around during rehearsal. . . . I had a professional on every instrument of the orchestra on the faculty, and I had what I called an orchestra within an orchestra, in that I could stop and say, "Listen to the faculty play this passage, students . . . now let's hear what you can do" . . . there's a rub-off there from the professional to the student that you can't beat any other way.[32]

It isn't hard to imagine with what zeal Jim Pfohl bent the governor's ear at lunch that hot summer's day. Not unmindful of a governor's influence, he wooed Terry Sanford with more than swim trunks and fried chicken; he offered as a persuasive example his extraordinary achievement of an Interlochen in Appalachia. Now why not a Juilliard for North Carolina?

Governor Sanford had long been seeking major action for the arts in North Carolina. Joel Fleishman had talked a lot about a conservatory, and John Ehle was waiting to see McNeil Lowry about funding for his own idea of a professional arts training center. The governor himself had been encouraging development in the arts for East Carolina College in Greenville, at the opposite end of the state from Brevard. Perhaps the best policy at the time seemed to him to be to set as many ideas in motion as possible and see which ones made it to the finish line. "In any event," he says now, "my conversation up there brought to a head my determination to see what we could do."[33] When Hugh Cannon, with the guide Jim Pfohl had arranged for him, joined the others at the lunch table, Governor Sanford pulled Cannon aside: "Hugh, Jim Pfohl has this idea that North Carolina should establish a music conservatory . . . that would be a state-operated institution. . . . Do you think the legislature would go along with setting up an institution like this? We're talking about something from whole cloth—you know, brand new from scratch?"

Cannon was nonplussed. "It never even occurred to me to do anything like that, and I don't know if the legislature would go along with it or not," he told Sanford.

"Well, get your ideas together, and we'll get back together at dinner time"—and Sanford left his aide to ruminate in the company of his camp guide.

Hugh Cannon's guide happened to be an outgoing, attractive young woman who played the harp professionally. Worrying that he didn't "have the foggiest idea about a music conservatory," Cannon began to think out loud with his companion about this unexpected assignment the governor had handed him, "wondering how these things work." Whatever Hugh Cannon may have lacked in musical knowledge he made up for with instinctive resourcefulness. His guide obligingly took the hint and came to his rescue—spectacularly, as it turned out: "My husband Vittorio is very much interested in a conservatory; in fact, he's [a teacher] at Juilliard." She was Joan Adler, Giannini's second wife, from whom he was divorced the following year. Hugh Cannon had never heard of Vittorio Giannini—it was "an absolutely strange name" to him, he remembers—but the governor had suggested Hugh come up with something and Vittorio Giannini was what he had come up with, so off they went, Hugh and the harpist and a highway patrolman, to drive into Brevard, where Vittorio Giannini was hospitalized, recovering from a heart attack. Hugh Cannon vividly recalls what happened next:

We walked into the room, and Vittorio was lying straight back. . . . His wife walked over very gently to the bed . . . and she says, "Vittorio, this is Hugh Cannon. He is on the staff of Governor Sanford, and Governor Sanford and Hugh and some of his people are interested in starting a state music conservatory in North Carolina, and he wants to ask your advice."

[When] he acknowledged that I was there . . . I said, "Dr. Giannini, let me ask you: do you think the state of North Carolina should have a conservatory of music?"

At that point he had been lying straight back in his bed, and when I asked this . . . Vittorio rose straight up in his bed, his eyes were just shining, and he was completely alive. He had been so docile until that point. He came completely alive, and he then gave what was perhaps the most beautifully stated position for the arts in America as a government responsibility that I've ever heard. It was succinct and was not more than four minutes long. It started off by laying the ground work as to what government does do: government provides highways, public health, and of course, back in the sixties we were talking about going to the moon, and he went into the space program, and he said, "Government does these things, but what about the soul of man?"

I cannot start to repeat what he said, but it was an absolutely poetic experience. . . . "The answer to your question, Mr. Cannon," he said, "is yes. The state of North Carolina not only should set up a music conservatory; it has the absolute obligation to the people to do this."

Well, at that point, I realized I had only one other question. . . . "Dr. Giannini, will you help Governor Sanford do this in North Carolina?"

And he said, "Yes." He says, "How can I help you?" . . . I said, "Would you be willing to come to Raleigh and meet with the legislature and appear in committee meetings and request them to consider this? Would you meet with Governor Sanford and his staff people, and would you give of your time?"

And he says, "I will absolutely help, and that is my commitment." He made a flat-out commitment to me from that bed within ten minutes from the time I walked in the door, that he would help us, and the reason that he indicated he would help [was] his own statement of why the state should do it. I gave no argument as to why he should do it, and he was very enthusiastic, his eyes were fiery. . . . The nurse came in, and she said, "I think that this is probably as long as the visit should last," and I said, "Dr. Giannini, you don't know how much I appreciate this. It will make all the difference in the world."

That evening we were in a car, I in the front seat and Governor Terry Sanford was in the back seat . . . and Terry says, "Well, Hugh, what do you think about the conservatory? I need to let these people know what to do." And I said, "Well, Terry, I have no problem with it, in that I think we can get it through the legislature." And he asked what made me think that?

I said "I've got Vittorio Giannini's commitment that he'll help us."
He asked, "Who is Vittorio Giannini?"
And I said that I actually did not know, "But God, isn't that the greatest name in the world? With the name Vittorio Giannini, we can't lose in the legislature!"[34]

John Ehle has described Vittorio Giannini as a short, dumpy man, who wore a tam and smoked dark cigars. Upon first meeting Giannini at the Sir Walter Hotel in Raleigh, to discuss the work of the recently appointed North Carolina Conservatory Committee (NCCC), Ehle remembers that his "mind's image of a distinguished music professor went tottering. [Vittorio] smiled. He had a toothy smile, totally disarming. . . . He reminded me of a panda bear."[35] A first-generation Italian-American from a Philadelphia family well known in music circles, Vittorio Giannini had chosen to convalesce in a hospital in a small town in western North Carolina because of his friendship with James Christian Pfohl and his delight in Transylvania Music Camp. For ten years Giannini had come every summer to Brevard, where, Pfohl remembers, he was not so much a faculty member as a resident composer. Giannini's presence gave the students an opportunity to premiere the works of a professional, and Giannini apparently found his relationship with the students and faculty refreshing:

Vittorio was just part of Brevard. Always happy, always cheerful, always counseling with students and faculty for their every need. . . . His sincerity was one of the things that always impressed me, and his interest in detail, and in doing works that were very unusual . . . and he was also one who had many hobbies . . . we used to talk about his racing cars and he used to see how fast he could go . . . one night I remember, [he] sat down to entertain the students by playing the way he used to play in the moving picture houses in New York. He was a pianist, and he would sit and improvise as the picture went on . . . giving the mood which went along with the picture. . . . It was an art that very many people have now forgotten, but he made his first living by playing piano for the silent movies in the old days.[36]

His friends remember Vittorio as a warm and vital man of great charm and intensity, who lived with the flair and temperament of the true artist. He

4. *"With the name Vittorio Giannini, we can't lose in the legislature!"* (Archives of the North Carolina School of the Arts.)

was a romantic—"there has never been an ugly woman in Vittorio's eyes," John Ehle remarks—and an eccentric, preoccupied with his art: "He was frequently noticed composing, and as so many did, he composed in his head; he would just take out a pad and jot down the music . . . he was always listening to music in his head, but he didn't like to listen to it in restaurants and car radios and so forth; he thought that was an intrusion." In "A Letter about Vittorio Giannini," John Ehle's tribute to his friend, the author recounts an anecdote that reflects the distracted but responsive nature of Giannini's personality: "He was attending a concert in New York years ago, and at intermission as he walked up the aisle, he noticed an attractive woman and she smiled at him. In the lobby he kept wondering who she was; he had met her somewhere. He was walking back to his seat when it struck him. 'I believe that's my first wife.'"[37]

Vittorio Giannini, born in 1903 in Philadelphia, was the son of an Italian immigrant, Ferruccio Giannini of Lucca, Tuscany, who had come to America in 1885, at the age of seventeen, to join his father, a poet and architect then working in Detroit. Ferruccio attended the Detroit Conservatory, where he met and then married a young violinist, Antonietta Briglia. In 1893 they settled in Philadelphia, where they contributed not only their own considerable talents to the development of the city's musical life but the gifts of their four extraordinary children as well: Eufemia, Dusolina, Vittorio, and Francesco. One critic has described the Gianninis as a "prodigious musical family," in the tradition of the Scarlattis, the Garcías, and the Pattis. Ferruccio himself was a tenor of amazing entrepreneurial energies. In addition to making a series of phonograph records for Emile Berliner, possibly the first tenor arias to be recorded on flat disks (1896–99), Ferruccio brought sixty musicians from Italy to form the Royal Marine Band of Italy. Though neither royal nor marine, the band was decidedly Italian. With Ferruccio as vocal soloist, the group toured the United States, Canada, and Cuba for three years, after which many of the players joined the newly formed Philadelphia Orchestra. Ferruccio then rebuilt the old Verdi Hall in Philadelphia, where he produced commedia dell'arte plays and thirty-five operas, regularly starring the teenaged Eufemia as prima donna, with her father as tenor hero. Eufemia went on to study in Milan (accompanied by her indefatigable mother and two younger brothers) and later became a teacher at the Curtis Institute, using her married name, Mme Gregory.[38]

Although musically trained by both parents, as were his brother and two sisters, Francesco chose not to pursue his cello studies professionally. He became a psychiatrist, but his and Vittorio's sister, the soprano Dusolina

Giannini, achieved a notable career as a "free-lance prima donna." She con-
certized successfully all over Europe and appeared with the Metropolitan
Opera from 1936 to 1941, where her first Santuzza received a "prolonged
ovation." Max de Schauensee rates Dusolina as an "extremely fine concert
singer," "a true dramatic soprano, backed by strong temperament and impeccable musicianship." In the family tradition of professional liaison, Dusolina played Hester in the premier of Vittorio's opera *The Scarlet Letter*
(Hamburg, 1938).[39]

As a child, Vittorio Giannini studied violin with his mother until he
won a scholarship to the Verdi Conservatory in Milan, at the age of nine.
In America, he attended Juilliard (1925–30) and afterward won the Grand
Prix de Rome in composition (1932), which awarded him four years' study
at the American Academy there. Beginning in the 1930s, Giannini won recognition on both sides of the Atlantic primarily as a composer of operas,
though he was prolific in chamber, choral, and orchestral music as well.[40]
Thomas Marracco, evaluating Giannini's music for *The New Grove Dictionary of Music and Musicians* (1980), has described the composer's work as
neo-Romantic, though "in texture and form, which he handled with mas-
tery, he drew on Baroque models."[41] Vittorio Giannini characteristically
wrote in the tradition of eighteenth- and nineteenth-century Italian opera,
perhaps because he brought to his music a remarkable sense of the me-
lodic. Tracing Giannini's career for his comprehensive volume *American
Composers,* David Ewen writes that in two operas commissioned by CBS
radio in the late 1930s—*Beauty and the Beast* and *Blennerhasset*—Giannini
showed "a strong gift for mobile Italian lyricism," a gift that reached its
finest level of development in the composer's opera *The Taming of the Shrew*
(1950). Although NBC television had commissioned Giannini's variations
on Shakespeare's comedy (libretto shared with Dorothy Fee, certain of the
sonnets, and *Romeo and Juliet*), the opera was premiered by the Cincinnati
Music Drama Guild and the Cincinnati Symphony on January 31, 1953
(Thor Johnson conducting). The following March, NBC Opera Theater
produced Giannini's distinctively Italian *Taming,* which won the 1954 Music Critics Circle Award. As Ewen describes it, Giannini wrote a score that
is "ebullient, witty, insouciant . . . skillful in its contrasts and climaxes and
spilling over with gay or poignant Italianate melodies, sprightly ensemble
numbers in the tradition of opera buffa and Verdi's *Falstaff,* and sensitive in
its balance between voices and orchestra." Ewen notes that among Giannini's many works the composer wrote several by "invitation" or commission, ranging from *In Memoriam Theodore Roosevelt* (1935), for the Trustees
of the New York State Theodore Roosevelt Memorial, and the *IBM Sym-*

phony (1939), to *Canticle of the Martyrs* (1957), for the Moravian church, and Symphony no. 3 (1959), for the Duke University Band.[42] Giannini's commissions are striking in their variety and number and testify that although for most of his professional life he was a teacher, concurrently at Juilliard and Manhattan, Curtis (from 1955), and Transylvania Music Camp (summers), Vittorio Giannini was always a working artist.

In 1958 Giannini began to write band music, gaining "recognition and respect for music considered to be old-fashioned when it was still new." Four of his five band pieces—all of which critic M. L. Mark says are "excellent"—have become part of the standard band repertoire at high schools and colleges throughout the United States.[43] It is a touching reminder of Vittorio Giannini's youth that in the last years of his life he would turn to the composing of band music, a genre in which he had been so flamboyantly preceded by his pioneering father.

Remembering Giannini during this time, his nieces Maura, Evadne, and Christina recall that "Uncle Victor was dreaming": "It was a dream that he had, and . . . he tried to get a lot of different places to buy this dream. New York said, 'Oh we don't want it, we already have a school.' They had limited vision, unfortunately; but North Carolina's a funny kind of a place. . . . They use their money in kind of a selfless way." At least as early as 1958, Vittorio Giannini began shopping for a location in which to realize his dream of a different kind of education for aspiring artists. Influenced by his conservatory training in Italy, Giannini felt it was wrong to force children to do their schoolwork in the morning, leaving only afternoon and evenings for them to practice their art: "His theory—and he isn't wrong on this one—is that you don't find dumb artists; they're usually bright people. So, it's not going to be that they're hardly able to get through school . . . they'll sail through school . . . but give them a chance. Let them go to ballet at 8 : 45, or composition, or go practice at 6 : 00 in the morning. But don't bind them down with endless courses and driver's ed and strange things, and then finally at 4 : 30 get a ballet class. That's brutal." In what Maura Giannini believes was a reaction against old-style European conservatory training, however, he believed strongly in a good academic background for arts students: "I think he really had about the equivalent of an eighth grade education, but he was a very learned man . . . so he felt that the academics were very important . . . that you have to have a knowledge of history . . . and literature to correctly assess . . . whatever it is you're doing."[44]

When McNeil Lowry began exploring the condition of the arts in America in 1957, Vittorio Giannini was one of the professional artists he came to know well and with whom he talked about what was most needed in the country. By the summer of 1962, Lowry had succeeded in turning the Ford Foundation's interest strongly toward support for independent conservatories and schools of art and away from the already well-funded academically oriented arts programs at colleges and universities. In addition, Lowry had focused Ford's interest on the Southeast, where a talent drain was carrying the region's young artists away to seek professional training in the Northeast and Midwest. "At the very moment that Sanford and Ehle began to talk to Giannini," Lowry says, "I and my staff, who had been doing all kinds of field work around the United States, were considering between Atlanta and North Carolina as the two rivals for the most likely place for professional involvement in the arts." The choice of Atlanta might have seemed obvious because of its large metropolitan population and active Atlanta Arts Alliance. But what impressed Lowry about North Carolina was its "way of beginning in a state-wide context . . . [for example] you could have the North Carolina Symphony. You didn't have the Georgia Symphony, you had the Atlanta Symphony." More important, in North Carolina music and drama had long been vigorously pursued at the "grass-roots level" by such outstanding professionals as Paul Green and James Christian Pfohl, who believed in staying at home and working with young people in the arts right where they were. That his friend Vittorio Giannini had spent ten summers at Transylvania Music Camp was a reinforcing factor for Lowry—indeed a reassuring one, for he and Giannini had talked for years about the "concepts and principles" that should underlie the Ford Foundation's efforts in the performing arts. Thus when Vittorio Giannini suddenly rose up from his sickbed in Brevard, North Carolina, to make an impassioned speech, the place and the time only seemed unlikely—not, after all, a "funny kind of a place" in which to find a working artist, nor even a funny kind of a time for a man with an endangered heart to pledge his last energies to a stranger. And it was an especially fortunate time as well, for what McNeil Lowry says he "couldn't tell Governor Sanford or Mr. Ehle or even Vittorio, who was pretty close to the foundation, was that I had already succeeded in getting an appropriation for a special program in professional training in the arts of ten million dollars added to my program."[45]

On the drive back from Brevard, Governor Sanford wrote a memo to Joel Fleishman on a yellow legal pad, instructing him to begin putting together a committee to "look into the possibilities of a music conservatory in North Carolina which would be organized to serve this entire region."[46] Governor Sanford's determination to see the school established before he left office perhaps explains the speed with which the project moved forward. On August 1, 1962, only a few days after his visit to Transylvania Music Camp, Governor Sanford wrote letters of appointment to the first group of possible committee members:

> Because of your interest and leadership in the musical and cultural life of North Carolina, I would like you to serve as a member of the North Carolina Conservatory Committee. I know that I do not need to impress on you the vital role which such a conservatory might have in the musical life of the entire state. For this reason alone, the work of this committee will be of greatest importance to the cultural life of North Carolina and the Southeast. More than that, however, this conservatory ought to take a place of importance equal to the other great schools of music in this country and abroad, and, consequently, we will bring North Carolina in still another way more firmly into the mainstream of American life.[47]

The North Carolina Conservatory Committee was not geographically representative of the state. Only one member of the governor's commission lived in the coastal plains of North Carolina and none in the mountains (although Ehle is a native of Asheville); all were residents of a still predominantly rural state's relatively urban areas (Charlotte, Raleigh, Winston-Salem, Greensboro, Chapel Hill, Greenville, and Southern Pines). One member, North Carolinian Henry Hall Wilson, remained in Washington, D.C., as an assistant to President John F. Kennedy, throughout the committee's deliberations, and another, Vittorio Giannini, was not even a citizen. Fortunately, his faithful summer residences in Brevard gave New Yorker Giannini credibility, as one who did not just rush about in a tourist frame of mind littering southern states with small, irresponsible musical empires. Against the press of time, the men and women appointed to the conservatory committee were those whose names were readily available to Governor Sanford and his staff—two artist-instigators and thirteen prominent citizens and political supporters who had demonstrated or expressed an interest in development of the arts in the state.[48]

Martha Dulin Muilenburg of Charlotte, who chaired the North Carolina Conservatory Committee, had studied under Lee Strasberg at the Actor's Studio in New York City and later worked in radio and television in Charlotte. For many years she was actively involved with the Charlotte Little Theatre, Arts Council, Choral Society, Arts Fund, Symphony, and Opera Guild. Katherine Castellet Bell, also of Charlotte, was active in a variety of North Carolina arts organizations but ascribed her appointment primarily to her husband's prominent position in North Carolina politics. J. Spencer Bell was a judge on the Fourth Circuit Court of Appeals and had vigorously supported both Kennedy and Sanford at the 1960 Democratic Convention. Katherine King Bahnson, of Winston-Salem, was president of the Winston-Salem Arts and Crafts Association and helped to found the Winston-Salem Arts Council, Inc., the first such council in America. She belonged to the Winston-Salem Symphony Association, the Winston-Salem Gallery of Fine Arts, and the North Carolina State Art Society.

Gordon Hanes, of Winston-Salem, was president of Hanes Hosiery Mills and state senator-elect from Forsyth County. In addition to his involvement in business and civic affairs, Hanes had served as first president of Winston-Salem's Arts and Crafts Association, as a member of the executive committee of the Winston-Salem Arts Council, Inc., and as vice-president of the city's Civic Music Association. Robert Lee Humber, of Greenville, was, like Hanes, both a state senator and a phenomenally active contributor to his state's cultural life, serving on the North Carolina Art Commission, the Board of Trustees of the North Carolina Museum of Art, as a trustee of the North Carolina Symphony, and as president of the North Carolina Art Society. Fred Weaver, secretary of the University of North Carolina, represented the cultural interests of the university community, which proved, in general, to be loudly critical of the proposed school, although Weaver himself was not.

Two members brought to the committee the obvious power of the fourth estate. C. A. "Pete" McKnight (another of James Christian Pfohl's ubiquitous music students) was editor of the *Charlotte Observer* and an effective supporter of the Charlotte Symphony and the city's United Arts Fund. Sam Ragan, executive editor of the *Raleigh News and Observer,* was well known in the state as a writer and poet and as author of the widely read column, "Southern Accent." In addition to holding prominent posts in several professional news organizations, Ragan had served as chairman of the North Carolina Writers Conference, moderator of the North Carolina Literary Forum, and president of the Raleigh Little Theatre. As both a staunch Democrat and a well-known North Carolina voice in public affairs, Ragan was a high-profile choice for commission membership.

Following his initial appointments on August 1, Governor Sanford selected four additional members. On September 4 he invited Pearl Taylor Moore, of Raleigh, to join the commission. Pearl Moore was author of *North Carolina Musicians* (University of North Carolina Library Extension Department, 1956), an active member of numerous city, state, and national music associations, and a fundraiser for the Transylvania Summer Music Camp Library. Elizabeth Mendenhall Younts, appointed on September 27, was music and program director for radio station WEEB in Southern Pines and had previously worked as a professional musician in New York. Interestingly, she had been a student at Juilliard when both Vittorio Giannini and Robert Ward were teaching there. To represent Greensboro, Governor Sanford had originally appointed Martha Eskridge Love; because of the sudden death of her husband, Burlington Industries executive J. Spencer Love, however, she declined membership. On the advice of John Ehle, the governor appointed Sydney M. Cone, Jr., president of Cone Mills Corporation of Greensboro and a founder and charter president of the Greensboro Arts Council. Ehle's suggestion came as the result of a phone call in late September from William Snider, editor of the *Greensboro Daily News,* who was anxious that Greensboro be represented on the committee and recommended Cone because of his long-standing interest in the arts and his friendship with Joseph M. McDaniel of the Ford Foundation. Letters appointing Cone and Louise Ashworth Durham, of Chapel Hill, were sent early in October. Louise Durham was the enthusiastic choice of James Christian Pfohl; she had served on the Board of Trustees of Transylvania Music Camp and accompanied Governor Sanford on his recent visit to the camp at Brevard. At one time the head of the voice department at Atlantic Christian College, Mrs. Durham had demonstrated her qualifications as a grass-roots supporter of music training for North Carolina's young people during her term as president of the North Carolina Federation of Music Clubs. Her membership was additionally valuable because her husband, Carl T. Durham, had long been the Democratic congressman for the Chapel Hill district.[49]

Obviously, the members of the North Carolina Conservatory Committee were chosen with care. For the most part politically loyal to Sanford, they could be relied on to support the governor's vision. Although theoretically Sanford appointed them as a "special commission to determine the feasibility" of establishing a conservatory to serve the state's children, Governor Sanford had already decided that such a school would be created, as Hugh Cannon points out: "You always have to have a study, and the study always has to find that there is a need, and then there is a plan . . . as a practical matter, though, the commitment was made then that it would be done. . . . I myself . . . had no idea of what was involved in a conservatory. At that stage there was never any mention of dollars or budget. It was just a commitment that that was something we needed to do."[50] Thus the role of the conservatory committee was never actually to determine whether a school should be started, a point later interpreted in a hostile fashion by the press in Greensboro, where opposition to the conservatory idea proved to be strongest. On May 12, 1963, the *Greensboro Daily News* editorialized on the committee's failure to visit the Woman's College to evaluate its program for training performing artists. The editor charged that for that reason "the commission's report inescapably gives the impression not of thorough and impartial investigation, but of enshrining someone's prefabricated conclusions, in which case no study was needed." On May 14, the column "Tar Heel Talk" recapped John Ehle's criticisms of the education of young artists at Chapel Hill, as voiced more than two years before, concluding that, given Ehle's well-known "bias," "it is no mystery that the Governor's Conservatory Commission, under Mr. Ehle's inspiration and tutelage (not to say domination), came down on the side of an independent performing arts school which would be more or less insulated from the presumably soul-searing disciplines of academia."[51]

If its criticism was vehement, the *Greensboro Daily News* was nonetheless on the right track. The North Carolina Conservatory Committee was created to bring to reality another aspect of the commitment Sanford had made before his election and had renewed by asking John Ehle to work for him. But the men and women on the conservatory committee were crucial to the second step in establishing the school. Their range of practical experience and their ready-made network of knowledgeable arts supporters in business, politics, and civic organizations gave them the resources they needed to justify the school to the public and to collect the budget information that would support an argument in the state legislature. And, too, with this group of respected citizens to represent the people and keep things down to earth, Sanford was able to balance the presence on the committee of artists John Ehle and Vittorio Giannini—the former controversial, the latter exotic. Although Giannini brought to North Carolina the persuasive emotionalism and cachet of an artist in the European tradition, his charm might conceivably be viewed askance by some Tar Heels, as Governor Sanford fully realized at his first meeting with Giannini, in the bar at the Pierre Hotel in New York City: "I remember he had on his beret, and I couldn't help but wonder how that would go over in Winston-Salem."[52]

The wisdom of the governor's way of proceeding escaped Ehle at the time: "I was very disappointed to get that letter from Terry appointing a Conservatory Committee. I thought, well, here, my gosh, he does no more than hire me to work on these projects, and the next thing I know he has appointed a commission without even mentioning it." Ehle was in New York at the time, writing a novel, but on August 23, 1962, he met with

McNeil Lowry at the Ford Foundation to present the ideas he and Sanford had earlier agreed on—creation of a residential high school for academically gifted students, a fine arts center that would offer professional training in the performing arts, and a state-supported repertory theater—as well as the newly proposed music conservatory. Lowry recalls discussing several arts proposals with Ehle and being struck that

> Ehle—and therefore Sanford, if Ehle actually spoke for Sanford—was very much concerned with the resources of the state overall, not just piece-by-piece in the arts, but that there [had been] little effort as yet to make a distinction in the state between professional, educational, and general amateur activities in the arts. And, of course, in my view—and I knew it would be the same in Giannini's, and it became clear to me that it was also the same in Ehle's and Sanford's view—the conservatory would be an effort more and more to professionalize the state's interest in at least the performing arts.[53]

It was this issue of professionalism in the performing arts which lay at the heart of later controversy and won for the North Carolina plan Lowry's reluctantly given encomium, "innovative":

> This was a very daring, refreshing exploit on Terry Sanford's part. The idea that a state could go in between the high school and college age to make a conservatory that would have professional standards in the performing arts, and that the legislature could be made to support it, along with private support, in a state like North Carolina, in a region like the Southeast, was very, very daring. This idea was almost meriting a word which Ehle and a lot of people in the Ford Foundation were using at the time, but which I forbade. . . . The word was "innovative." . . . Nothing wrong with the word—I just don't like the way it's used as a rubber stamp all the time. . . . Anyway, it was, if I ever could use the word, it was innovative.[54]

Four major elements informed the context of Lowry's excitement and his willingness to invest in North Carolina. First, there was not at that time—nor is there now—a state-supported residential high school and college, existing solely for the purpose of offering professional training in the performing arts. Thus at the most obvious level, the North Carolina conservatory was indeed a new concept.

Second, nationwide attitudes toward the arts were practical in the extreme. Reviewing twenty years of growth in the performing arts for the 1977 meeting of the American Assembly, Lowry pointed out that supporters of the arts in the 1950s advanced arguments that accepted the arts as "a means to some other end," such as providing "purposeful occupation" for young people and improving America's image abroad. Furthermore, "Many of the proponents of these claims were busy translating their interest in the arts into buildings, a rash of cultural centers across the country. The so-called 'cultural explosion' of the fifties and sixties was in great part promotional."[55] This bricks-and-mortar interpretation of an arts awakening was comfortable for Americans and therefore lavishly embraced. By 1969 the *Wall Street Journal* was lamenting the "boom that has left a number of shiny new cultural centers dotting the American landscape but, not infrequently, with little to put in them or too few people to attend."[56] The widespread popular acceptance of the building committee as the place to begin any artistic enterprise explains Lowry's contention that the cultural explosion of the 1950s and 1960s was "in great part promotional." Support for the arts in America had crystallized as a flashy marriage of convenience between things of the spirit and adequate parking, based on the illogical notion that the ineffable will flutter down and take hold just as soon as we have provided the something utilitarian on which it can perch.

A third factor, the philosophical component of the building committee approach, further points up the originality of the North Carolina proposals. John Ehle and Terry Sanford were telling McNeil Lowry that they meant to begin with professional artists and thereby go against the strong tide of amateurism abroad in the land. The arts as enrichment and recreation had many friends in the Southeast, where Lowry had focused Ford's interest. But John Ehle's uncluttered commitment to professionalism stood in relief against the encroachment of the university liberal arts tradition, which had gradually moved from its appropriate role of educating audiences in art appreciation, to claiming a legitimate place in the preparation of the creators and performers of that art. The attempt to meld in one seemingly efficient locus two opposing though vitally interrelated traditions had resulted in a confused hostility, as was noted in the 1965 Rockefeller Panel Report on the future of the performing arts in America:

> Amateur antipathy toward the professional is frequently and regrettably inculcated on the university campus by educators whose principal interest seems to be in directing their students away from professional work and into educational and community work. While this is in part dictated by a realistic appraisal of the limited professional employment possibilities, it is frequently a reflection of the teacher's own bias against professionalism. . . .

So long as neither professional nor amateur confuses the two areas of expression and both retain a perspective toward excellence, the relationship between them can be lively and constructive.[57]

Unfortunately, although professionalism was in no way acting as an enemy of the amateur spirit—it is, indeed, the best of encouragers—the amateur spirit was ferociously strangling professionalism by siphoning off funds and fostering a skeptical attitude toward the mission and status of the artist.

A certain bias against elitism and a distrust of government intervention in matters of the mind and spirit are inherent to the democratic process. When Governor Terry Sanford proposed marshaling his state's legislature in support of the creation of a professional artistic elite, he presented McNeil Lowry with a fourth uncommon factor—a duly elected official championing an idea historically antipathetic to American republicanism. In Europe, patronage of the arts is traditionally a responsibility of governments, which are charged with preserving the cultural heritage of their individual civilizations. In the United States, however, such patronage has remained for the most part in private hands, with the result that direct government funding of the arts is frequently viewed with suspicion by the populace and its representatives. Lincoln Kirstein, founder, with George Balanchine, of the School of American Ballet, reminds us that Franklin D. Roosevelt's Works Progress Administration (WPA), "the greatest arts patronage this country ever enjoyed," was dismantled by Congress "mindlessly" because it was perceived to be a boondoggle. This skepticism, which questions the validity of a nation's supporting full-time artists, goes back to the historical basis of the country, as Kirstein succinctly points out: "The universal mechanic"—he who could both fiddle and notch logs—"was a cheerful ideal when the country was still to be conquered in its physical boundlessness."[58] But it is an ideal that is no longer useful. Nonetheless, in the absence of a centuries-old tradition of government-supported excellence in the arts, many Americans have continued to apply the principles of egalitarianism to the matter of artistic standards in a perverse reflection of our nation's political ideals.

In his caustic description of a citizenry's worst moments vis-à-vis the arts, Kirstein ridicules the "beefy innocence" of such popular democratic statements as "I don't know much about art, but I know what I like," and "This [painting or tone-poem] doesn't do a thing to [or for] me":

Condemnation of the complex, multilayered, or unfamiliar is a proud assertion of the ordinary citizen's right to be simplistic and ordinary. It follows that everyone else should be equally and democratically passive and mindless. . . . Art, the broad and deep practiced play of imagination, therefore requires no prior preparation, attention, or sympathy. We cannot trust our artists as we trust any banker or surgeon. And, as for the problem of elitism, the elite as possessing a discrete place or attitude (unlike blind prejudice or apathy), is clearly [an idea that is] supercilious, superior, undemocratic.

The bitterness of Kirstein's attack on those "whose self-centered criteria arrange the subsidies from which we starve,"[59] points up the urgency of Lowry's mission to pour massive amounts of money into professional arts training in the late 1960s and early 1970s. Kirstein's attitude lends additional insight as well into the hard edge which Ehle turned against the liberal arts tradition of the university, which he believed interfered with the training of a professional artistic elite.

In the 1960s, pride in amateurism was as strong in North Carolina as anywhere in the country. "The most important thing to know about the arts in North Carolina at that time," John Ehle points out, "[is] that they were non-professional." In Winston-Salem especially, the Moravian tradition was strong:

It was, the businessman plays the trombone in the band . . . a person was a musician and also was a cobbler. In fact, when the Moravians were coming to America, they [cast] their group of settlers/immigrants . . . according to trade and musical talent, in order to have an orchestra . . . and so if they had a choice of two blacksmiths, and one played the fiddle and one didn't, it depended upon whether they needed another fiddle player, and of course they did, because everybody always needs another fiddle player.

Ehle recalled that long before negotiations for the North Carolina conservatory began, McNeil Lowry had made a speech in Winston-Salem, in which he suggested that some of the city's many amateur efforts in the arts should become professional, and "there was a real uproar about that—just the suggestion, and he was criticized in an editorial in the Winston-Salem newspaper for suggesting such a thing."[60] It was, however, this strong amateur spirit that had nurtured a broad appreciation of the performing arts and later came strongly and unambivalently to the support of the new conservatory.

There were others in state government besides Terry Sanford who went on record in the early 1960s as supporting development of the arts in North Carolina, but the key difference between their efforts and those of the governor and Ehle was the issue of professionalism. On March 29, 1961, Dr. Rachel Davis of the North Carolina House of Representatives had held a planning meeting for her committee, Cultural Advancement for North Carolina, "to Discuss the Idea of Establishing in North Carolina a Cultural and Recreational Center." Among those present in addition to members of the North Carolina legislature were Ralph Andrews of the state Recreation Commission, Tom Morse of the Department of Conservation and Development, Dr. Jacob Koomer of the state Health Department, Edwin Gill, state treasurer, Bob Cox of the Youth Fitness Commission, Vivian Whitfield of the U.S. Forestry Service, and Charles Carroll, state superintendent of public instruction; professors from Meredith College, from East Carolina, North Carolina State, and Duke universities; and businessmen including James Newbold of Carolina Power and Light, and George Watts Hill, Sr.[61] This partial listing suggests the broad constituency for the arts which Ehle and Sanford could tap in support of the new conservatory, provided their argument for professionalism was accepted. It would seem, however, that the very idea of art taking precedence over recreation was not to be taken for granted. As is clear from the planning meeting minutes, committee members were agreed that the proposed cultural center should serve the state and its youth and that a number of cultural activities should be housed in it, or at least coordinated by it. This consensus fit in generally with Ehle's idea that a reservoir for training in the performing arts should be established to serve the state, but the committee's plans were indissolubly linked with the concept of a state recreation center. Thus facilities for music, drama, and opera were also to include crafts and hobbies, and possibly even a technical or industrial museum, along with an emphasis on youth fitness. Vivian Whitfield of the U.S. Forestry Service came closest to discerning the problems awaiting the committee in this tangle of purposes when he observed that the new center should put culture first and physical fitness second.[62] The essential point—that art and recreation are not the same thing—had yet to emerge, not just in North Carolina but all across the country. On January 4, 1963, Siebolt Frieswyk, consultant on the performing arts to the National Recreation Association, advised Ralph Andrews, director of the North Carolina Recreational Commission, that "a State Center rendering recreational services to all cultural segments of North Carolina's communities would be much more appropriate and important than one limited to a specific and limited function."[63] Fortunately, Andrews's vision was broader; in that same month, he wrote to Governor Sanford, expressing the Recreation Commission's interest in the per-

forming arts and his willingness to suspend its work toward a cultural center for North Carolina until the conservatory committee had completed its
study. Andrews enclosed the minutes of the first meeting of Dr. Davis's
committee and a few days later wrote to Ehle that Rachel Davis unself-
ishly "wish[ed] that we set her plan aside and join in with . . . Governor
Sanford's."[64]

MANY DANGEROUS

HORSES

*J*OHN EHLE remembers McNeil Lowry as "a very difficult fellow," who "asked quite intelligent questions about North Carolina . . . as I was leaving he told me he liked what I had told him, and he liked me, and he thought maybe he could be of some help with a so-called conservatory and a repertory theater." Lowry agreed to talk with Governor Sanford later, and Ehle left Raleigh, feeling "very far along." [1]

At the state capitol Ehle was given the office of the lieutenant governor (who had died shortly after the election) from which to conduct his operation, which was "to encourage projects that could be supported by private money. It was never any more restricted than that. It never had anything to do with cultural things or the arts or education or poverty or civil rights or whatever. And in fact, we developed projects in all of those fields. Most everything that was started in that office succeeded . . . except the repertory theater. We never launched it. . . . We had no actors." Ehle's official title was special consultant to the governor, but he always signed his mail "Special Assistant" because it seemed to him that "a consultant really didn't have any authority. The fact that I didn't have any authority I didn't want to announce to my own mother." Later Ehle was told that "special consultant" was a higher title than "special assistant," "so I had deprived myself of that honor." [2]

The entrance of an artist into the governor's inner sanctum, with or without authority, drew mixed reactions. Sanford's administrative assistant Tom Lambeth was frankly dismayed:

> My first reaction to John Ehle's involvement in the governor's office was . . . I wish he would go away. . . . John . . . did not fit comfortably into the routine of an office . . . [he] was prone to slip in the back door . . . and at the last minute want Terry to call up somebody that he thought could be helpful to some project, or he wanted to tell you

that he had the chance to bring somebody down, like Jan Peerce who was going to be in Raleigh at a concert . . . and the governor just ought to give him an hour, and [I'd] tell him, well, that there were already five hours less than we needed, and I just remember my first reaction being gosh, this fellow is just completely disrupting everything here. In time, obviously, I came to appreciate his great value, but it does show you that it is good that you should never let the routine organizers control a governor, because I think a lot of good ideas we get would be abandoned. . . . Fortunately, Joel was there, because Joel had pretty good perspective both on the necessities for organization and routine and getting the nitty-gritty done, and also for the time that ought to be spent in dreaming.[3]

Ehle himself wryly explained his understanding of the division of labor between the governor's secretaries: "Tom was the appointment secretary to the governor; Joel was the legal secretary for the governor. One had the front door and one had the back door to his office. If you had an appointment, you went through Tom's door; if you didn't have an appointment, you went through Joel's."[4]

One of Ehle's first actions as special consultant to the governor was in effect to request control of the conservatory committee: "I remember I had written the governor a little note, you know, there in the office, to ask if I might serve as secretary of this commission because I was so scared it was going to say something or do something I didn't like, and secretaries can draw up the minutes, you know, and just eliminate this, and they do that, and they say we decided this, and unless it's changed at the next meeting, it's all set. So he wrote back and said yes."[5] In the committee file, Ehle had found a telegram to Governor Sanford from Vittorio Giannini, asking to present his plan for a conservatory at the first meeting. On the morning of September 27, 1962, Ehle met for the first time with the chair of the conservatory committee, Martha Muilenburg, and the two of them went to lunch with Vittorio Giannini and his wife—whom neither had met before—at the Sir Walter Raleigh Hotel. The meeting went well, in spite of Ehle's initial misgivings: "I had experienced only disappointing meetings with music educators. I had also experienced many disappointing meetings with committees . . . I had not trusted an arts educator or a committee in my life." Nevertheless, the three committee members—at least one of whom was extremely wary—managed to agree over lunch that the new conservatory would be both a high school and a college and that it would include the three performing arts. That afternoon, the governor's conservatory committee held its first meeting, and Ehle's fears subsided: "I got to know all the members of the commission, and it was a very good group indeed."[6]

In preparation for this meeting, Ehle had written Mrs. Muilenburg on September 19, explaining that the governor had asked him to assist her with the committee's work and outlining an agenda. Vittorio Giannini was to present his plan for a conservatory, and the governor would discuss the possibilities for foundation support. Ehle pointed out that subcommittees did not yet need to be named because much of the research to support their proposal would be done by the state library, the Department of Public Instruction, and the Boards of Education and Higher Education. The governor wanted the committee to set the report deadline date. Ehle also wrote to McNeil Lowry on September 22 to inform him of the NCCC's first meeting, at which Giannini was to present his plan. Ehle requested a meeting with Lowry on the twenty-eighth, obviously anticipating that he would be able to report favorably and forcefully to Lowry the outcome of the conservatory committee's first deliberations.[7]

Because the North Carolina Conservatory Committee members had received their letters of appointment to a commission that was to look into the establishment of a school for professional training in music, some if not all of them must have been taken completely unawares by the sudden enlargement of the governor's proposal. Whatever the case may have been, the group proved to be receptive to Giannini's presentation. They had, of course, been prepared somewhat, not by the expected appearance of the governor but by Joel Fleishman, who arrived in his place. John Ehle remembers being anxious—"We had these plans, and we were ready to present them to this unknown group"—and he was counting on the governor to smooth the way for the revelation that the committee was no longer solely concerned with a music conservatory. But "the time came to start— where was Terry? Where was he? It's his commission. At least he can come up and say . . . I agree that it should be in the three arts—you know, I'd talked to him about some of these things. One word or two like that, you know, and it's all over, there's no battle. But where was he?" Joel Fleishman recalls that he attended the first meeting of the NCCC and was authorized to say that "the proposal that was submitted had the full support of the Governor." Fleishman's appearance, Ehle has written, "was fortuitous, because we certainly needed all the assurance we could get."[8] With the governor's mandate in mind, the committee members could proceed without discussion or squabble about their newly defined mission.

Undoubtedly, Vittorio Giannini's personal magnetism was a factor in gaining the members' immediate confidence. Ehle's minutes report that Giannini gave an animated presentation of the concept of an arts school for the South, which underlined the governor's appeal to the committee members' chauvinistic and competitive instincts when they had gathered in his office earlier to receive their commissions. "There is no conservatory in the South," Governor Sanford had told them, "and the most important thing is that there be one and that it be located somewhere in North Carolina."[9] Not surprisingly, given Giannini's many years of acquaintance with McNeil Lowry and his budding friendship with John Ehle, the plan Giannini unfolded was precisely what Ehle and Lowry, separately, had envisioned.

At this new school, which would be unique in the country, Giannini told the committee, students on the college, high school, and even elementary level would be trained as professional artists in music, drama, and ballet, while receiving their academic education as well. Giannini offered the example of the New York High School of Performing Arts to show that these students would not suffer academically by being allowed to devote half their time to the pursuit of their art. Students at the New York High School of Performing Arts—familiarly referred to as "PA"—ranked third in the city in academic achievement, as measured by college entrance tests, yet the school's students were admitted solely on the criterion of talent. Franklin J. Keller, PA's founder, had already been contacted for advice, as had Marjorie Dycke, the head of PA's drama department.

Giannini explained that performance was the key difference between the new school and the training programs that already existed in the state, which were oriented toward art appreciation and teacher education. Not only did southern students have to transfer to conservatories in the North to get professional training, but they frequently were inadequately trained, having lost the early years when their talent should have been developed to higher levels. These years were irrevocably lost to the young artists. Giannini also pointed out that performing artists must be part of a group in order to perform and to be trained to perform and that these groups must be made up of similarly gifted young artists if the students were to develop through competition with and exposure to excellence. Obviously, outside New York City, such a need could not be met in one limited geographic area or school district. The Southeast sorely needed a residential performing arts school if the artistic gifts of its children were not to be wasted.

Giannini spoke to practical as well as idealistic concerns. The staffing and equipping of a combined performing arts school would cost little more than for a conservatory of music alone, and, the composer assured the committee, students would be available. He had come armed with the statistic (undoubtedly provided by Ehle) that eleven hundred students competed each year in music contests in North Carolina alone. With the exception of the academic division, the school would be directed and staffed by professional artists. These men and women could further broaden the advantages the school offered to the state by educating the community at large to the appreciation of art, through performances by the faculty and by the young professional artists-in-training.[10]

The nine committee members present readily agreed to proceed along the lines of Giannini's proposal, with the possibility held open that painting and sculpture might be added to the school later.[11] The group also agreed that an architectural firm should be asked for estimates on the construction of a new school, designed to accommodate five hundred students, but that members should also be on the lookout for usable buildings. The subject of financing was broached but discussed only in generalities. At this point the group was still somewhat more idealistic than practical in its approach; several members felt that the location of the school should be selected on its merits as a center for professional training only, rather than on any inducements (such as contributions of buildings and land) which the individual cities might offer. The next meeting was set for a month or so later, and members were asked to acquaint themselves with the existing arts training programs in their own regions in the meantime.[12]

The following day John Ehle wrote to McNeil Lowry that the North Carolina Conservatory Committee had agreed enthusiastically to consider all the performing arts, and, of equal importance, "there seemed to be wide understanding of the dangers of putting the school in a liberal arts college, which pleased me." The next step would be determining costs. Gordon Hanes said that he would engage "an architectural firm to make an estimate on a new campus without cost to the Committee." The figure of $14 million was mentioned as an endowment for the school; "Nobody seemed to flinch . . . although I assure you . . . I did inwardly." Apparently Lowry had been planning to visit North Carolina in December, for Ehle urged him to come sooner, "before the Governor has committed in terms of his own thinking the large surplus of funds."[13] These last words must have been pure bluff, given the evidence of Sanford's commitment to the school before the committee members were appointed. More than likely, Ehle wanted another opportunity to influence Lowry's thinking on the disposition of Ford Foundation funds.

John Ehle's papers in the North Carolina Division of Archives and History indicate that his office quickly became the clearinghouse for every sort of information, problem, or prospect relating to the work of the North Carolina Conservatory Committee. The impression these papers convey is of a staggering multitude of details, which accumulated for some months at a breakneck pace. Ehle appears to have handled it all with alacrity, tact, and imagination. Indeed, it may have been above all his irrepressible good humor and charm that ultimately kept the project on track: Ehle proved to be not only a good organizer but a shrewd assessor of both people and situations.

Even a light sampling of Ehle's October 1962 correspondence in the Division of Archives and History reveals a diverse traffic: an October 2 memo from Joel Fleishman to Ehle advised him of land in the Southern Pines area that might be available for the conservatory (probably the home of author James Boyd, which Louise Durham visited later in the month [14]); an October 3 memo from Ehle to Fleishman suggested that Sydney Cone of Greensboro be added to the conservatory committee; on October 9 Ehle wrote to Henry Hall Wilson to keep him posted on the work of the committee because Wilson was working for President Kennedy in Washington and could not attend the meetings. McNeil Lowry responded to Ehle's letter of September 28, saying he would see Governor Sanford in New York on November 14 and planned to come to North Carolina on December 5 for a two-day visit. On October 22, Ehle had his secretary, Frances Wrape, send the minutes of the NCCC's first meeting and a copy of Vittorio Giannini's proposal to new member Sydney Cone, along with notification that the second meeting would be held November 2 at 2:00 P.M. in the Senate Chamber of the Capitol. On October 25, Cone responded that he would be unable to attend the NCCC meeting but that he had arranged an informal meeting in New York with Joseph M. McDaniel, secretary of the Ford Foundation, to "clarify the Ford Foundation plan as it relates to a possible Conservatory in North Carolina." He said he was undertaking this conversation with McDaniel on his "own responsibility and without prejudice to the Committee's activities." Ehle, obviously concerned that an untried force was entering the delicately balanced negotiations with Ford officials, replied quickly to Cone, urging him to be cautious and noting that the governor's work with the Ford Foundation went back several months and that meetings with Lowry and Henry Heald, president of Ford, had already been arranged. [15]

In addition to putting out brush fires, Ehle continued with his task of constructing an argument for the establishment of a performing arts conservatory in North Carolina. Among the material he collected was a 1960 newspaper article on the New York High School of Music and Art, organized in 1936 with the help of Mayor Fiorello LaGuardia. Mayor LaGuardia called it "the most hopeful accomplishment" of his administration; 90 percent of its graduates went on to college.[16] On October 22 Ehle sent statistical data to committee members on degrees conferred in the fine arts and music and art education in North Carolina in 1958–59.

Leaving aside degrees conferred in music and art education (the new school was to teach the performing of the art, not the teaching of it), the numbers showed that there was more than enough room in North Carolina for a conservatory. For the academic year 1958–59, no fine arts degrees were conferred on the undergraduate or the graduate level, either in North Carolina or anywhere else in the six other southern states Ehle scrutinized (Virginia, Tennessee, South Carolina, Georgia, Florida, and Texas), in dance. In drama, music, and art, North Carolina's showing was somewhat better, but not by much, as shown in Table 2.1.

In drama, among the southern states under review, North Carolina not only tied with Georgia in giving the least number of degrees, but gave the lowest percentage of its bachelor's degrees in that art among the states. And even if Texas were disregarded, North Carolina's numbers still lagged far behind those of perhaps more comparable states such as Florida and Tennessee. In music, North Carolina awarded a little less than half the number of degrees given by Florida. But again, North Carolina gave the lowest percentage of its undergraduate degrees in music, as compared to the other states. And finally, in art North Carolina ranked fourth among the seven states in number of degrees given and fifth in the percentage of its degrees awarded to students with an art major.

National figures showed that in 1958–59, 385,151 undergraduate degrees were awarded, with 9,699 going to students in the fine arts. By comparison, North Carolina granted 9,424 undergraduate degrees, of which only 95 were in the fine arts. Thus, although North Carolina gave 2.4 percent of the country's undergraduate degrees, it gave less than 1 percent of its fine arts degrees. The state's annual commitment to the training of young artists appeared to be small; in fact, at 0.98 percent, it might be called trifling. Within a few weeks, critics of the proposed school began to argue that an additional college-level program in the arts would dry up existing arts departments. Such opponents viewed these statistics as sufficient evidence that the pool of potential arts students was quite small and therefore could not support another training program. Looking at the figures for institutions that were frequently named as among the endangered does reveal that the pool could hardly have gotten any drier: in 1958–59,

TABLE 2.1. *Fine Arts Degrees Conferred in Seven Southern States, 1958–59*

	Number	Percent of all under-graduate degrees
Drama		
Texas	246	1.23
Florida	65	1.00
Tennessee	53	.70
Virginia	28	.45
South Carolina	23	.53
Georgia	17	.27
North Carolina	17	.18
Music		
Texas	199	1.00
Florida	99	1.53
North Carolina	45	.48
Tennessee	43	.56
Georgia	39	.62
Virginia	38	.61
South Carolina	31	.72
Art		
Texas	170	.85
Florida	67	1.04
Virginia	60	.96
North Carolina	33	.35
Georgia	28	.45
Tennessee	22	.29
South Carolina	13	.30

Source: Earned Degrees Conferred, 1958–1959 (Washington, D.C.: U.S. Department of Health, Education and Welfare, 1961).

Salem College gave 2 undergraduate degrees in music, 2 in art, and none in drama; the University of North Carolina at Chapel Hill gave 3 in music, 8 in art, and 5 in drama; the University of North Carolina Woman's College at Greensboro, whence came the most vociferous bleats of despair, gave an impressive total of 10 in music, none in art, and 3 in drama; and East Carolina, whose head of the dramatic arts department vigorously attacked the idea of a special school offering professional training in theater, gave 2 in music, 1 in art, and none in drama. East Carolina did, however, award 21 degrees in music education and 7 in art education, which pointed up the real question: might not the smallness of the performance programs at these and other North Carolina colleges be the result not of the size of the pool of artistically gifted southerners but, rather, of the focus of liberal arts institutions on educational rather than professional training?

John Ehle informed the NCCC not only about these statistics but about the role of the Ford Foundation in arts funding and, more specifically, W. McNeil Lowry's agenda for the Ford grants, as outlined in Arthur Gelb's October 5, 1962, *New York Times* article, "Ford Fund Plans Wider Aid to Art." Gelb pointed out that Lowry was responsible for Ford's grass-roots approach to the arts. After interviewing thousands of artists and visiting some fifty communities across the country, Lowry had decided that Ford's new program would support artistic growth outside New York City. The significance of Lowry's choice lay in the fact that in 1962, the Ford Foundation was the major single source of funding for the arts in the nation. Gelb's article clarified the one financial point which Ehle knew the committee members would have to be able to articulate clearly to the new school's detractors and possible supporters: for North Carolina to get a share of the Ford money, the state would have to meet McNeil Lowry's dicta on the granting of funds. First, no money was to go for construction; planners of cultural centers had failed to realize that "both the core and the promise of success for any artistic enterprise is the individual artist or the artistic director. The development of these people is what the Foundation is chiefly interested in because that is what the arts are all about." And second, in the area of art education, Ford would assist only independent conservatories because they were needed to provide a vitally important alternative for young artists unsuited for liberal arts institutions.

If the North Carolina Conservatory Committee members did not know it before, they surely knew it now: John Ehle's strategy for establishing a performing arts school in North Carolina was to keep W. McNeil Lowry persuaded of the state's serious intentions to comply with the Ford plan. Without Ford Foundation seed money to attract major contributors and to reassure the state legislature that the entire burden of the toe-dancing would not fall on the taxpayers alone, all the human resources and logical arguments in the kingdom would not be able to put the school together. Thus Ehle kept Lowry informed every step of the way, pressuring him constantly, as Lowry candidly recalls: "Ehle's pressures . . . were always much stronger than anybody's, and I understood that this was one of his roles. He kept the pressure on all the time. He was quite aggressive about it, much more so than Sanford, but I knew, of course, that Sanford could be the way he was by virtue of having Ehle to be the way he was. This is politics." In this way, Ehle was able to tap, for the benefit of North Carolina, McNeil Lowry's personal zeal for the establishment of a state-supported conservatory; it promised to be a prototype, the representative of years of Lowry's effort at Ford: "Could it be a model? I was very skeptical of that. But damn it, it was worth trying. And now I'm talking about worth it to the Ford Foundation, not to North Carolina or these proponents. Because it wouldn't be North Carolina that would have either the opportunity or the responsibility if we took it for trying to use it as a pilot somewhere else in the country; it would be us. It was worth trying."[17]

The North Carolina Conservatory Committee came together for the second time on November 2, 1962; in his notes Ehle described the members as even more enthusiastic than before. The importance of the school's serving the Southeast was clarified as the committee considered sources of financial support. In later years, the argument for excellence would be used in the state legislature to justify maintaining a student body with a high percentage of out-of-state students. Now, however, the NCCC was realistically concerned as to whether, after the school was built, it would be able to continue. Certainly attaining the broadest possible base for financial support would be crucial. Gordon Hanes reported the estimate of $7,260,000 for building a basic physical plant, which included classrooms, dormitories for five hundred, and the necessary performing arts studios and auditoriums. Another $2 million would be needed, he said, for equipment, furnishings, scholarships, and miscellaneous needs. A subcommittee made up of Hanes, Sydney Cone, Katherine Bahnson, and Sam Ragan was named to continue the inquiry into sources of funding for the school.

Gordon Hanes also reported the first disturbing signs of what would become a heated controversy. He had met that morning with officials at the Woman's College of the University of North Carolina and the branch of the university that had made music its special concern. Lee Rigsby, dean of the Music Department at the Woman's College, had told Hanes that he was "wholly unsympathetic" to the idea of the new conservatory. He said that such conservatories were dying out, their functions taken over by out-standing public universities such as Indiana and Florida. If additional money were to be spent on music education in North Carolina, it should go to the existing institutions in the state. Finally, Rigsby charged that a conservatory such as the committee proposed would destroy the music departments at the Woman's College, East Carolina, UNC-Chapel Hill, and Salem College.

Both Gordon Hanes and Pete McKnight, though committed to the concept of the new conservatory, were measured in their response to this criticism. McKnight pointed out that the proposal for a conservatory was in no way an attack on the liberal arts schools, "who are already doing more for music than should be expected." General college courses must be open to the public, and under such conditions, first-class professional training could hardly be provided. Hanes said that he had told Dean Rigsby that the new school was meant to be supported by private funding sources. Hanes observed that "we owe these schools" for their continuing efforts in arts training in the state and expressed his interest in getting additional money to help support the programs at Woman's College.

In its very first meeting, the NCCC had clearly defined the difference between the training to be offered at the proposed conservatory and the training already being offered at liberal arts institutions in the state. Discussion of Rigsby's opposition led quickly to reiteration of the members' understanding that professional training in the arts at the highest possible level was to be the mission of the new school. There was no conflict with the state's liberal arts institutions, for the new North Carolina conservatory was meant to serve only the relatively few students in the Southeast who had the dedication and the genius to make their lives as performing artists.

Surprisingly, the *Greensboro Daily News* did not report Rigsby's opposition in its November 3 story on the meeting; both it and the *Raleigh News and Observer* led their reports with Sam Ragan's motion that the committee endorse "wholeheartedly" the proposal for a conservatory of performing arts and urge that "its feasibility be explored to the fullest." The motion was reported both in the papers and in Ehle's minutes as unanimously approved, which drew a letter dated November 9 from Sydney Cone to John Ehle. Cone had been unable to attend the meeting but wished to respond to Lee Rigsby's comments, as reported by Ehle, and with which he agreed, and "that makes me a dissenter from Mr. Ragan's motion of November 2." Cone enclosed a copy of a letter dated October 21, 1962, from Professor Edward Cone of the Princeton University Music Department.

Professor Cone expressed the opinion that conservatory training had become outmoded and suggested the Yale Music School, attached to Yale University, as a model for any new North Carolina school of music. Sydney Cone also expressed his concern that the need for a dense population to provide an audience for the artists in training should be discussed, and he promised to attend the December 6 meeting.

Of the state's leading newspapers, only the *Charlotte Observer* reported that opposition had appeared on the campus of a branch of the politically powerful University of North Carolina. The *Observer* reporter shrewdly led his story as well with the promise of additional uproar: the North Carolina Conservatory Committee invited "the state's leading musicians, dramatists, and other artists" to its December 6 meeting in Raleigh, along with the directors of the arts programs at the state's various colleges and McNeil Lowry of the Ford Foundation—all to discuss the idea of a regional performing arts conservatory. "Don't know how we'll see all these people in one day," Martha Muilenburg wrote plaintively to John Ehle. "Ordinarily," she went on to understate, "[they] have strong opinions— and rarely see eye to eye."[18]

At this point it was unclear who in the state supported the new school. Even the *Winston-Salem Journal,* which soon became a staunch ally of the conservatory, editorialized on the controversial nature of the proposal. On November 6, the paper urged caution in the face of a statement by Dale H. Gramley at a meeting of the Council of Church-Related Colleges in Raleigh. Gramley termed the state-supported conservatory "a serious threat" to church-related colleges in North Carolina. The *Journal*'s desire to consider his fears is understandable, given the musical and educational heritage of the Moravian church, whose presence in Winston-Salem had enriched the community for some two hundred years. The paper balanced its discussion, however, by quoting Vittorio Giannini's opinion that the new school would not conflict with existing programs in the state because of its commitment to "top-flight professional training." Opponents of the school soon came to resent the implications of this argument, taking it as a slur on the quality of teaching in their music departments. They charged that the conservatory committee had not adequately surveyed the resources of the state, that, in fact, the school was not needed and the committee was ignorant of the condition of arts training in North Carolina's colleges and universities. Yet as far back as May of 1961, Ehle himself had pointed out that at UNC–Chapel Hill, the Dramatic Arts Department had only fourteen undergraduate majors and the Music Department a mere seven. Archival material shows that Ehle immediately began an intensive survey of postsecondary education in the arts in the state. From Gene Strassler of East Carolina University he received a qualitative assessment. As of September 23, 1962, there was little music training in North Carolina of conservatory quality. Although Duke, UNC, and East Carolina University were all developing performance degrees, their programs were still weak because of a lack of funds for scholarships, faculty, and equipment. Also from East Carolina, Dean Earl E. Beach of the School of Music pointed out that there were only six string instruction programs in the state and that 70 per cent of North Carolina schools had "no contact with professionally trained music teachers of any kind." And from State Supervisor of Music Arnold E. Hoffman came a letter reporting on the musical activity being pursued in North Carolina's high schools and colleges. The city public school systems offered chorus, glee club, and band, with many larger schools supporting orchestras. But because music teachers were paid out of supplementary local taxes, only 30 percent of the county schools had full-time music teachers. Few of the state's high school graduates went on to major in music in college, and most of those who did went into teaching. For example, "At the University at Chapel Hill the main emphasis in the School of Music is on Musicology and consequently, most of the students major in that field." [19]

But the committee did not embrace the conservatory model for training without conducting its own investigation. Pete McKnight remembers that the one question on all their minds was whether children could receive an excellent academic and performance education in such a school. At the November 2 meeting a program committee was named, consisting of Giannini, McKnight, Weaver, and Durham, who were to visit the best known of the northeastern schools and report back. On the afternoon of November 27, the group of three visited Juilliard (Weaver had been unable to go); on the afternoon of the twenty-eighth, the New York High School of Performing Arts (which McKnight recalls as having the greatest impact on him); and on the following morning, the Manhattan School of Performing Arts. At all three schools, committee members asked about financing, quality and backgrounds of faculty, academic standing of the students, and the nature of the physical plant. At each school they were impressed with the enthusiasm of the students and their high level of achievement and activity. They collected figures on costs and financing (for example, Juilliard received 50 percent of its annual operating revenue from endowments and gifts, whereas Manhattan depended on tuition for 80 percent of its operating budget) and sought advice from faculty members. All those consulted agreed that the major obstacles facing the new school would be adequate financing, luring professional faculty to North Carolina, the dearth of performance outlets in the state, and the difficulties of recruiting and identifying talented students. On November 30, Giannini and Durham talked with Louis K. Wechsler of New York's High School of Music and Art (of which PA was the vocational branch), who characterized his students as academically prepared to enter any college and highly dedicated to the pursuit of their art. He said there were no discipline problems at the school.[20]

As the storm of criticism gathered before the important public meeting on December 6, so, too, did expressions of support. On November 30, 1962, the president of the Winston-Salem Arts Council, Mrs. T. Winfield Blackwell, wrote to Martha Muilenburg to say that the council had passed a resolution on the twenty-eighth expressing its interest in having the proposed conservatory in Winston-Salem "if it would complement the existing cultural organizations in Winston-Salem and cooperate with them."

From Allegra Snyder, daughter of Buckminster Fuller, came an intense, dedicated eight-page letter, expressing to John Ehle her support for the concept of a combined performing arts school, along with a thumbnail education in the dance, which at that time had few adherents in North Carolina. Snyder provided Ehle with the names of important American dance professionals and articulated superbly the philosophy of arts education which Ehle, Giannini, and the other members of the NCCC were trying to express to the citizens of North Carolina. Snyder felt that by bringing all the arts together, the proposed conservatory could "instigate a new creative awareness" that would benefit both the performing artists and the creating artists (the composers, dramatists, and choreographers, whose art cannot be realized without the aid of highly trained performers). She pointed out that having the arts in one institution would be a return to the earliest beginnings of art, when the art forms were all part of one another. Perhaps most significantly, Snyder expressed her belief in the importance of education for artists, not only in their own but in the other arts as well, and in the liberal arts.[21] It is interesting to note that one of the strongest arguments advanced against the proposed conservatory was that the education it would provide would be too narrow; yet none of the proposers and early supporters of the school wanted a narrow, old-style conservatory. Rather, they wanted to shift the emphasis so as to create a new school, one that could train performers professionally, while giving them a good basic general education.

As invitations to the December 6 meeting went out to eighteen of the state's most prominent arts authorities and educators,[22] John Ehle called McNeil Lowry to ask if he and Vittorio Giannini could join Lowry and Governor Sanford for lunch on November 14. The four met at the Berkshire Hotel in New York City, where they talked about the proposed conservatory "in extensive terms," Lowry making clear what he calls his "provisos of interest"—that any Ford funds that were granted would require matching; that such funds could not be spent for capital construction or development; and that no commitment could be made in advance. "But even the amount that Sanford was talking about was not impossible, if all these other considerations and his winning support in the legislature, others in the state getting a site—if all that succeeded." Hugh Cannon has described the situation with the Ford Foundation as "a chicken and egg problem": the legislators would not be inclined to appropriate money for the conservatory unless they knew that a major foundation intended to fund it, and the Ford Foundation was unwilling to make a grant until the legislature had created the institution to receive it. "Frankly," Cannon says, "what we decided to do was, to indicate to each one that the other had already made the commitment":

John Ehle took me to New York to indicate to the Ford Foundation that we had every possibility kind of more or less lined up, that the legislature was going to appropriate x dollars . . . and that all the Ford Foundation had to do was come in . . . with what was called "matching money." Back in the sixties, everything was called matching money. So I went up with John, and John said, "Hugh" (of course I knew nothing about what I was doing), "just get on the plane with me, and when we go in, don't say anything except just indicate that everything is okay." And we went in and talked with Mr. Lowry. John would say to me, "Well, Hugh, how do you apprise the situation?" and I'd say, "Well, at this point I think everything is all set, and the legislature is going to appropriate the million dollars, and the leadership is all behind this." Then, of course, I believe that was the extent of that meeting, and we had lunch with McNeil Lowry, and the project was all very "healthy." . . . There was not any substance as far as the legislature knowing the actual fact. The legislature hadn't met, there had been no legislative committee, and I was expressing a hope in more concrete terms than perhaps should have been done in a judicious way. McNeil Lowry later said we "conned" him, and I would deny that, because we don't con anybody, but we did perhaps state it in very sanguine terms, and if we had been pessimists—which we never were in those days—we would have not expressed it in quite those terms.[23]

The necessity of securing public and legislative support required Ehle to use Lowry's presence in North Carolina to whatever advantage he could at the time of the crucial December 6 meeting, when knowledgeable critics would express their complaints against the school with full press coverage. Lowry arrived in Raleigh on December 4 for a dinner with the governor and a number of arts leaders, who had been instructed not to inquire directly about a grant. But such coyness did not suit conservatory committee member and state senator Robert Lee Humber, who, after "a few casual comments about the weather . . . put his face up close to Lowry's, as was his manner, and said, 'Are you going to give us the money?'" John Ehle relates that Lowry's reply was a "non-commital groan."[24] Lowry was groaning because of the extreme delicacy of his position; although he represented the serious interests of the Ford Foundation and could validly encourage the North Carolina project, he had no authority to promise Ford funds. Indeed, the $10 million which he had just gotten appropriated for his program to support professional training in the arts could not be turned into a grant until 1965. As a responsible staff person, Lowry could not speak for the president or the Board of Trustees of the Ford Foundation,

in advance of the kind of formal action that is required, and a great deal of discussion. . . . We used to have a saying in the Ford Foundation that anybody can say no; it takes everybody to say yes. That's true, all the way through the board. . . . If they don't, you're in trouble, because you might say yes, and find out you've led somebody down the garden path, because the board could say no, right? . . . Well, if you are conscientious about this as a staff person, and you understand it, then you're also conscientious about making people outside understand it. And you have to do it in ways that are quite literal and objective, so that after a while they understand that if you're going on talking to them over and over again, you're traveling back and forth yourself to North Carolina, as well as their traveling to New York, you have to be interested in it. Why would you be doing it otherwise? Just to amuse yourself?

But . . . they press you: "I can't understand why you're not willing to give us more commitment. We could use it with the legislature, we could use it with a certain community that we might want a site from, probably could use it with other private donors." I'd say, "Yes, and the other way around, too. You get that done, you could use that with us, right?"

They think, in a way, you're dealing with them. You're negotiating. You're playing poker, right? And sometimes they think so innocently, and sometimes they think not so innocently.[25]

Innocently or not so innocently, a reporter was waiting the morning of December 5, when McNeil Lowry hoped to meet privately with the North Carolina Conservatory Committee in the House Chamber of the Capitol. John Ehle told an audience in Texas in 1981 that Lowry instructed him to lock the doors to keep the reporter out:

> I didn't know how to lock the doors; I didn't know whether there were any locks on the doors.
>
> But Mac said he wasn't going to speak in public.
>
> Well, it was courageous of him to be there at all, that's true. Later I worked for the Ford Foundation and came to realize how courageous it was for Mac Lowry to have been there, because the Ford Foundation at that time did not like to have its name connected in the paper with controversial matters.
>
> So, I locked the door, but the reporter and his photographer crept into the balcony. There we were, a little conservatory committee, huddled in the front of one of the legislative chambers of the old Capitol, trying to listen to this whispering Ford Foundation executive tell us to go forward, just as we were.[26]

The disgruntled reporter went back to his paper and wrote somewhat waspishly that a "closed-door" session of the North Carolina Conservatory Committee had been held in the Hall of the House and that John Ehle had asked the *Times* correspondent to leave because the "speaker" did not want coverage.[27]

Today, Lowry admits that the issue of press coverage caused "a little bit of a problem" between him and Ehle:

> I did want to keep the subject of the North Carolina School of the Arts out of any discussions with the press until we made a grant. I said I had nothing to talk about. That was not always appreciated. You see, I don't blame John. John was a political staff person. He was working for something, and he could use both press and other leverage with the legislature, with other people. I had a key to some of that if I

wanted to give it to him, he thought, right? But I was very careful not to . . . I was aware that the presence of a Ford Foundation officer, in that meeting, as far as the press was concerned in North Carolina, was a little bit more meaningful than the presence of some of the other people there. . . . I was also aware that there would be some further advantage in the evolution of this project which an astute person like Ehle could make of it, if the Ford Foundation were present, and its presence were known, and some statement of interest and support for the idea were made. I knew that would be of value to him, but that's exactly why I couldn't do it. And also, and I would say this to John— we've always been able to be very frank with one another—if it had been somebody else, I could have managed it more easily than I could with John, because John was very good at that kind of thing, he was very adept at it. . . .

When I, therefore, demurred from having [press coverage], instead of just saying, okay, Mac, and so forth, we'll have a press conference without you, [Ehle] said, "We are going to say you were here," which I didn't object to. John pushed back so hard, that that by itself threatened to become a story—you know, it was said, "Lowry is here, and he wants a secret meeting with these people," you know, and so on. That I much regretted; and that, I'm sorry, I did blame a little bit on Ehle. But it didn't change me about opening up to the press. And in my position I couldn't have. . . .

Let me just say, I hope you don't think that with any of this, which has all been in good humor, I have any problems with John Ehle. I have a great admiration for John Ehle, for what he's done in that state. Forgetting about his being a novelist and things he's done other places, the thing he tried to do about science and math did work. And a lot of other things down there—all very, very valuable . . . the end of Sanford's term did not end John's usefulness . . . even now in North Carolina to many of the university programs there and lots of other affairs. He has a very admirable character.[28]

John Ehle was apprehensive about the December 6 open meeting, primarily because of the dearth of professional artists in the state who could be counted on to come forward and speak in favor of the school:

We needed professional groups. We needed actors and performers who were professional people on the stage somehow. I was conscious of that because I tried to find some to come down here and talk . . . but you just try to find anybody in North Carolina to come to a meeting by the conservatory committee. We called it a hearing at least once. We wanted people to come in there and speak to us and tell us what we ought to do—the public, you know, the public. We're now ready to listen to everybody, anybody who wanted to come.

And naturally, I tried to stack the deck because I was one of the dealers. I called up various people: Jim Pfohl, founder of the Transylvania Music Camp at Brevard, and the head of the North Carolina Symphony, Ben Swalin, and Paul Green, playwright in Chapel Hill. And you kind of come to the end of the road. It's amazing. Everybody else in the state, [his] professional credentials seemed to be that he *taught* in those fields—never done it. Except he had done it through his own department, or whatever it was on his campus.

Well, we rested a lot, often, on Paul Green, Ben Swalin, and Jim Pfohl, now, I'll just tell you.[29]

Ehle's fears proved to be justified. After brief presentations by Vittorio Giannini, Pete McKnight (who reported on the subcommittee's visits in November to Juilliard, the Manhattan School of Music, the High School of Performing Arts, and the High School of Music and Art, all in New York City), and Marjorie Dycke (president of the American Educational Theatre Association and head of the drama department at PA [30]), a series of North Carolina arts educators rose to blast the school. The scheduling of speakers indicates that Ehle and his committee had done what they could to balance the opposition with strong supporters. Ben Swalin, founder of the North Carolina Symphony, spoke first for the school, followed by another predictable supporter, John Lehman, artistic director of the North Carolina Ballet Company. Then came Lee Rigsby, dean of music at the Woman's College of the University of North Carolina, Greensboro, and undoubtedly the proposed school's most persistent and outspoken enemy. Rigsby warned that the conservatory would drain the state's existing music programs of their finest students, a fear that other music educators echoed as the day wore on. Rigsby favored putting emphasis on creating conditions in ongoing programs such that the talented could fully develop their talent, rather than pouring sorely needed funds into a school to train professionals.

Rigsby's speech was followed by another negative opinion, that of Henry Janiec, director of the Charlotte Symphony. John Ehle recalls that Janiec "spoke fluently and well in opposition"; he may have been the unnamed symphony director whom the *Greensboro Daily News* quoted as saying that after graduating from a famous European conservatory of the old style, he had had to go back to college for two years to get the broader education he needed.

Around noon Paul Green rose to speak eloquently and effectively of the great challenge and opportunity inherent in recognizing that "our present system has failed." He termed the idea of the new state-supported performing arts conservatory "bigger than the educators grappling with it. . . . The people already have seen beyond our educators." Before the lunch break Ed Loessin, the director of drama at East Carolina College, and Harry Davis, director of the famous Carolina Playmakers at UNC, proved Green right. Both wanted funds to go to existing university departments rather than to the creation of a new, more professionally oriented conservatory.

After the lunch break, John T. Caldwell, chancellor of North Carolina State, made what Ehle has characterized as "one of the most welcome speeches of the day," at least from the point of view of the conservatory committee. Caldwell said that he would welcome a separate institution such as had been proposed and suggested it be located in Research Triangle, near his own school. His attitude reflected "a love of the arts," Ehle wrote, "and a genuine affection for the hope that the State would seek out ways to train artists." Among the educators who spoke that day, however, Caldwell was an exception. In her December 7 column in the *Charlotte Observer*, Harriet Doar described the division among those who attended the hearing: "Roughly, they split along professional lines. Educators favored expanding existing facilities, preferably the ones they were connected with, while the directors of musical and other organizations were more concerned with establishing a separate school or center." Doar reported that all present agreed that the Southeast was "an arts wasteland"; the argument lay in determining what should be done about it.[31]

In all fairness to those who opposed or at best doubted the new school, it must be pointed out that the fine arts departments of most colleges and universities are traditionally underfunded, standing in line not only behind the humanities (which had created the universities in the first place) and the sciences (which had won World Wars I and II and kept on going) but the football and basketball teams as well (everybody's favorites). To those who had devoted their lives to the struggle of the arts in academia, the proposal to pour hundreds of thousands of already inadequately apportioned state dollars into a new arts school—one for which its proponents claimed an unlikely if not impossible level of achievement—must have seemed a bitter draft indeed. Ben Swalin still remembers that opposition was so intense shortly after the December 6 meeting that he was accosted at a Christmas cocktail party by a university faculty member who angrily told him that he

> should have been interested in seeing that other people who were in the arts . . . had the funds for [development], and I recall I told him, "Well, you won't get the funds. This is being generated for a separate institution . . . such as we have not had here." . . . There were only a few people . . . who really stood up for it . . . most of the people had the attitude, as I recall it, [of] "Why don't you give us the money for this thing, and we can deliver a bigger institution." [32]

Another attendant at the meeting who was impressed by the level of hostility evinced by the proposal for a state-supported conservatory was Vera B. Lawrence of Charlotte, president of the North Carolina Council of Women's Organizations: "All statements were very challenging and distressing," she wrote to John Ehle. "It is very difficult to realize that there is so much opposition to giving opportunities to children in North Carolina." For their part, the conservatory committee members, too, were distressed. John Ehle has recalled that Martha Muilenburg became increasingly upset by the "negative attitudes" expressed as the afternoon wore on and that it was during the December 6 meeting that for the first time he realized how ill Vittorio Giannini was. As the stress of the meeting began to tell, his wife "held his hand [while] he listened to one person after another testify against the school." When Giannini rose to speak at the close of the meeting, the composer called for everyone to set aside extraneous concerns and ask himself only, what is best for the young artists? [33]

The attack on the school, Ehle says, "made some of the members of the commission rather mad, angry. They felt that the opposition simply hadn't given us credit for any mind at all, and I don't know of anything that brought the commission members closer together in union to support the school, than that meeting where the opposition was allowed to speak to them. That's the finest thing they ever did, as a group." In his follow-up letter to Lowry, Ehle reported (without apparent rancor) that at the December 6 meeting, "professionals favored a professional school. The academics were disappointed that their current programs are not thought adequate." Ehle enclosed articles from the *Raleigh Times* and the *News and Observer* and informed Lowry that the next step should be to bring in "8 or 10 top professional people in the performing arts, people of national stand-

ing, who will, I suspect, tell us that there is a need for a professional training center in the South. We can with that meeting generate much interest
on the part of the press and hope to gather some of the impetus we need to
move to the actual start of active work." [34]

Both opposition and support continued to brew after the December 6
meeting. On December 14, Mrs. Blackwell (president of the Winston-
Salem Arts Council) wrote again to Martha Muilenburg, only two weeks
after her first letter expressing the arts council's interest in the proposed
conservatory. This time, however, she pressed Winston-Salem's case without reservation. Whereas the first letter had expressed interest in the school
if it would cooperate with and complement the city's "existing cultural organizations," Mrs. Blackwell now wrote that the trustees of the arts council
wanted the arts school placed in Winston-Salem. She cited such organizations as the symphony, the civic ballet, the Moravian Music Foundation,
and others as evidence of strong local audience interest and as attractive
facilities—along with seven nearby colleges—that could prove helpful to
the new school. Apparently the more familiar the idea of the school became, and the more it was discussed, the more appealing and feasible it
seemed to be, at least in some quarters. Sydney Cone, the committee representative from Greensboro, where the school most needed support to
counter political opposition from the Woman's College, remained uncon-
vinced. Although he had been unable to attend the December 6 meeting,
Cone had apparently conveyed his continuing doubts to the governor, who
asked him to stay with the commission and "work with it and try to come
up with a unified proposal which will give our State the best possible professional training in the arts." Sanford went on to urge that a minority
view not be given "until the majority view has been more clearly determined." He also pointed out that the committee was likely to recommend
strengthening existing arts programs in addition to establishing a separate
school and closed with the hope that "segmenting the Commission into
various parts . . . won't be necessary." Cone responded in a reply to Martha
Muilenburg, asking if he should prepare "an alternate to improve on the
Juilliard proposal, a proposal that I have not been persuaded to accept?"
He also regretted that he would be unable to attend the committee's January 25 meeting. [35]

Both John Ehle and Governor Sanford labored to win support from the
Greensboro forces by pointing out that the North Carolina Conservatory
Committee was not hostile either to the Woman's College or to the state's
other arts institutions. To Dean Mereb Mossman of the Woman's College,
Governor Sanford wrote:

I believe you have every right to be concerned about the decision the Conservatory Committee might make, for they are, as is true of most Commissions, walking on important ground.

I have followed the meetings, have gone over the many letters which have come into the office from all over the State, and I have talked with arts leaders, including Lee Rigsby, here in my office. I believe there is a severe difference of opinion about the value of our existing arts programs; the difference is determined by whether one is talking with an educator in the arts or with a professional artist. I have not found many artists who like our arts teaching methods, and I have not found many educators who don't.

Maybe this is a problem we cannot very well negotiate, but I think artists have a right to an opinion in the arts, and I believe our educators, regardless of the findings of the Commission, ought to turn more of their attention to the artists. If they are not our best authorities on the arts, I do not know what our arts are all about. We need more artists, and better ones.

I hope that you at Woman's College will continue your work, and that your program will take on the stature and strength which you want it to, and which I know Dean Rigsby wants it to. I offered to support some of the ideas . . . he brought to my office several weeks ago and will still do so if he likes. Our State needs to achieve more, to rise far higher than it has in the arts. In the Commission we are seeking a way to go. I hope the Commission's report, when it is ready, will show us a good one and set us on it. Please give them all the advice and help you can.[36]

To Mrs. George C. Eichhorn of Greensboro, who had written to Governor Sanford expressing her doubts and concerns about the conservatory, John Ehle clarified the issue of the availability of funding, which had apparently remained obscure to many of the school's critics who spoke out at the December meeting and afterward:

The question is not really whether or not we can afford to put money in such a school rather than in existing programs. Resources which are available for such a center—the Ford Foundation, for one source, has indicated an interest in the matter—are not transferable. They are to be engaged in the forming of a conservatory for the South, either in our State or in Atlanta. These are the two most likely spots at the moment.

To build such a school does not mean that we should not support what we have; we should. We absolutely must do so. As you suggest, we ought to do far more for the N.C. Symphony and for the N.C. Ballet Company. But these two organizations, Mrs. Eichhorn, are most enthusiastically working for the proposed conservatory, for they see it as their best hope.

The question is most involved, I know, and I don't claim to have any pat solution.[37]

The impression that the conditions on the Ford money remained unclear, in spite of newspaper accounts of Lowry's reported interest, is further reinforced by a note to Ehle from Hargrove Bowles, Jr., of Greensboro, a politically active Democrat (Bowles later ran for governor against James Holshouser in 1972), to whom Ehle had sent a copy of his letter to Mrs. Eichhorn: "Your letter . . . gave me a piece of information I hadn't had before. I didn't realize that the Ford Foundation was going to be footing the bill for this. If that is the case, and if they are not interested in putting the money in an existing program, I agree with you that we have no choice but to go ahead and do our best to get the funds for a conservatory."[38] Once having accepted the seriousness of Lowry's and Ford's intent, it seemed obvious that the state should establish the school, for otherwise North Carolina's most artistically gifted children would continue to go out of state for intensive training in the arts, at greater financial sacrifice than if a state-supported school existed. In addition, the economic benefits and the glory of a successful southern conservatory would all go to Atlanta— when North Carolina could have had it. To those, like Bowles, who were ambitious for the state, once the circumstances were clarified, there was "no choice."

On January 25 the North Carolina Conservatory Committee met for the fourth time and agreed to recommend to the governor the creation of a new school. John Ehle drafted the motion, which Martha Muilenburg included in her letter of February 4, reporting to the governor:

The Committee agrees that the chairman and secretary be authorized to represent to the Governor that the Committee sees the desirability and feasibility of forming a State supported and sponsored public school of the performing arts, and that the chairman and secretary discuss the fiscal and administrative possibilities for such a school with the Chairman of the Board of Education and the Superintendent of Public Instruction. Consideration of other matters before the Committee is continuing.

"I'm sure John Ehle has kept you in touch with the activities of our Committee," Martha Muilenburg added. "The proposal . . . comes after a long look at those needs which prompted your assignment to us. To cultivate and sharpen creative abilities at the level indicated here seems the best 'beginning' toward excellence in these fields."[39]

Sydney Cone had been unable to attend the January 25 meeting of the committee, but John Ehle forwarded a copy of the minutes, which Cone appreciated: "Your minutes are full of interesting material, and they furnish plenty of subject matter for thought and study. My compliments to you on this achievement." After some thought, however, Cone continued to feel troubled that the NCCC was proposing to establish yet another publicly supported school:

> We have performing arts in 19 North Carolina colleges now, counting 722 music majors. Mr. Giannini is quoted that these music departments need not fear competition from a 20th. Incidentally, Mr. Giannini is not well acquainted with these 19 college courses, or their faculties. But neither are we. The Conservatory Committee is qualified to pass on the practical aspects of a Conservatory rather than its technical aspects; unless we do in fact accept Mr. Giannini as a qualified expert on how our needs are being met.
>
> You are busy with many things, so I will cut this short. I suggest that our Committee needs a *subcommittee of education experts to state the shortcomings of our current system, and to agree on a program of improvement.*[41]

Whether Cone fully realized the limitations on the alleged Ford grant, or that such a grant would almost certainly go to Atlanta if North Carolina did not act, is not clear. It is evident, however, that he felt uncomfortable leaving the evaluation of arts training to the artists and that he discounted the negative evidence in favor of trying a new approach. In 1963, North Carolina was not known among the cognoscenti of San Francisco, Los Angeles, Chicago, Philadelphia, Boston, New York City, and the major European capitals as a place where young artists were being trained to standards of international excellence in performance and in theater design and production, as is the case today.

It was Ehle's audacious willingness to entertain such grand thoughts that set him apart from the school's more cautious critics. He prophesied that the school would be of "national import" and was relentless in planning for it. On February 14 Ehle notified Governor Sanford that Lowry had phoned and gave the governor a rundown on their conversation. Ehle had told Lowry that the state could pay the teachers' basic salaries and administrative costs and that he hoped to use state money for a campus. Endowments would be needed for teacher supplements and scholarships. North Carolina wanted not only a high school–level conservatory but a professional college as well, which the North Carolina Board of Education might authorize as part of the state's community college system.

Lowry had reiterated his position that he would support North Carolina's school only if both its programs and faculty were excellent, and he questioned whether dance and drama could be taught at the school because of the lack of competent teachers in the area. "I said to Sanford, Ehle, and Cannon," Lowry recalls, "that part of the Ford Foundation's commitment will depend on the professional criteria of the people who head these departments and are on the faculty. We will not have anything to do with imposing them, but we'll know how to get consultants to evaluate them." To strengthen North Carolina's position with Ford, Ehle had talked with Winfred Godwin of the Southern Regional Education Board and believed the board could "help make it a truly regional school in terms of students and private financial support." Godwin agreed that Ehle could "represent this SREB interest to the Ford Foundation and others."[42] (Interestingly, however, Winfred Godwin remembers that when the conservatory came up for discussion in SREB's Executive Committee, the general reaction was one of reserved disinterest. Committee members thought such a school would be "great to have," but there appeared to be no demand for such a service from any particular group, especially from students outside the state of North Carolina. And, too, some questioned whether the proposed school would really be a collegiate-level institution; education beyond the high school was actually SREB's focus.[43])

Ehle suggested to the governor that creating a state repertory theater would strengthen the proposed school's drama department, especially because "Lowry would doubtless support it," and he asked Sanford to call Lowry to discuss the ideas outlined in the memo: "You can later use that contact to advantage: if he approves our going ahead and working toward such a program in cooperation with the SREB, he ought to support what comes out of it." John Ehle proved to be a skillful and adroit negotiator; a month later, on March 12, he successfully juggled Ford officials in New York—Education at 9:00, Arts at 11:00, and Public Affairs at lunch. "All three divisions are ready to invest in projects of immense significance to our people," Governor Sanford wrote in an invitation to Charles H. Babcock to dine at the mansion with Buckminster Fuller. The "arts man" whom Governor Sanford discreetly avoided identifying in his letter was, of course, McNeil Lowry. On March 18 in his cover letter forwarding the NCCC's final report, Ehle thanked Lowry for the "encouragement in our meeting Tuesday." Ehle's sketchy notes for the meeting, apparently prepared beforehand, suggest that he anticipated discussing music faculty and cost estimates.[44]

While John Ehle continued his assault on the Ford Foundation, the NCCC dealt with other of the necessary details pursuant to making its final report to the governor. Martha Muilenburg suggested Sam Ragan and Pete McKnight as the best choices to "beard" the Board of Education and the superintendent of public instruction, and Elizabeth Younts met with Franklin J. Keller, founding principal of the New York High School of Performing Arts. She's "much impressed and has some notes," Martha Muilenburg wrote in a memo to Ehle, who recalls that Marjorie Dycke had recommended talking to Keller. Ehle hired him as a consultant, and Keller moved to Raleigh, where he lived during the time the school was being started. Ehle recalls:

> He was a delightful elderly gentleman, and in fact, he moved in over at the same house on East Jones Street where I had a room . . . and we often met and talked endlessly about high schools and art, drama and so forth. . . . He was in on . . . the early meetings about the budget of the school, and I know he was horrified at how much we wanted, not how little. I remember distinctly him sitting there listening to Vittorio go over what he thought the teachers ought to make. Of course, Vittorio thought the music teachers ought to make more than the drama teachers or the dance teachers . . . he said, "But I can't hire the best music teachers for that amount, you know, for the lower figure." And I said, "Well, you can't hire the best drama teachers, either, can you?" . . . Dr. Keller and I would talk to him about it a little bit, but Dr. Keller mostly didn't say anything in the meetings. It was after the meetings that he would come around and tell me what he thought. He was a dear man.[45]

The North Carolina Conservatory Committee met for the fifth and last time on March 15, 1963, at 2:30 in the governor's office (the governor was away). Sydney Cone, Henry Hall Wilson, and Pete McKnight were all out of the state and absent. Gordon Hanes was ill. Vittorio Giannini had been out of state but arrived on the overnight train from New York City. Senator Humber asked early in the meeting that the draft of the proposed report, which members had read individually, be approved without change. The motion was seconded and unanimously approved, and the committee requested that special thanks be placed in the minutes for the work of Mrs. Muilenburg, Giannini, and the secretary. Before adjourning, the North Carolina Conservatory Committee inaugurated the work of siting the school by hearing a presentation by a committee from Southern Pines and officially recognizing letters of interest from Charlotte, Raleigh, and Winston-Salem.[46]

John Ehle reported to the governor on behalf of the North Carolina Conservatory Committee on March 21, 1963. "We have served the task with considerable pleasure," he wrote, "and make this report less formal than most documents, for the arts deserve some sort of pleasure and composure."[47] If Ehle's report was informal by state documentary standards, it was no less cannily prepared for being so. Buried in the middle of the second paragraph is the committee's final—and irrefutable—rebuttal to critics such as Sydney Cone and Lee Rigsby, who had charged that the NCCC had not adequately surveyed the resources for training in the arts already available in North Carolina. "It was never our assignment to investigate the existing music programs of the State," Ehle flatly remarked. This statement was, in fact, quite true. Anyone looking back at the original letters of appointment to Sanford's nominees for the conservatory committee can see that the governor considered that he had already taken that step:

> For some time I have been very much concerned about the lack of adequate facilities for thorough and advanced training in instrumental music in North Carolina. Most serious students of music have regrettably found it necessary to pursue their studies at schools outside the state. Although a very few institutions of higher learning have begun intensive programs in instrumental music, there seems to be no question about the fact that these programs do not represent the cultural fulfillment of the state's obligations to those of its citizens who desire to study music.

Ehle went on to note in the committee's report, however, that leaders of existing arts programs and organizations had been invited to speak to the committee at an open hearing, and he responded directly to their opposition in his argument for a college-level conservatory program a few pages later:

> There has been a level of dissatisfaction from several existing music departments concerning the possibility of this new school operating on the undergraduate college level. Certainly there is no question but that in the past forty years the trend has been away from professional

training centers, and toward liberal arts universities. There is no question about the importance of the liberal arts programs and their suitability for most students; however, we have turned our attention to the predicament of the southern region, in which the trend away from professional centers has completely eliminated them, so that the type of professional training which Juilliard offers is not available in the South, and the talented student who does want such training is obliged to leave the region, often at great expense and often at a loss of his further attention to arts developments in the South.

The relative modesty of the committee's opinion that one alternative should be available was further buttressed by the recommendation that it should be small and that it should be designated as serving the entire southern region.

The proposal for a high school program had been less controversial, partly because of the excellent example of New York's High School of Performing Arts and partly because it did not step on collegiate toes. Ehle was able to report that after meetings with board of education and public instruction officials, "the inclination of the education leaders who discussed the matter was enthusiastically in favor of such a [high] school," a reaction diametrically opposite to that of educators who had spoken against the new college on December 6. Certainly there was not even the appearance of a duplication of services in the training of younger students in the state:

> The high school program is, in the mind of this Committee, severely needed. While it is possible to get into many of the public schools of the State excellent instruction in languages, sciences, social studies and other areas, it is all too difficult to find in many places large enough groups of exceptionally talented musicians, actors or dancers to compose a competent learning situation with professional artist-teachers in residence. The situation, particularly in rural places, requires new solutions. . . . [The school we propose], serving the region, would perform a most worthwhile service, provided it accepted into enrollment only the most gifted applicants, only students who on the basis of talent should indeed devote the major portion of their attention to the development of that talent.
>
> [Such a school] would be the first of its type in the South, and, if it does gain State support, it would be the first State supported high school of performing arts in the country.

Both components of the school were to take their mission seriously, in recognition that "the talent is available in the South for a great professional arts school" because the committee had been told by authorities at such schools as Juilliard and Manhattan that "a disproportionate share of the most talented students" was from the South. Accordingly, standards of acceptance should be the highest, not only for the students but for the faculty as well, for "it would be far better not to have a school than to have one which chooses to bring economy about through the selection of its faculty." The distinct nature of the curriculum would make the school neither a liberal arts institution nor an old-fashioned conservatory, for it was to teach "the doing of the art itself" without sacrificing "the academic material" necessary to educate students in "basic aspects of thought and knowledge."

Although the North Carolina Conservatory Committee recommended that the governor select a smaller site committee, one "better qualified in terms of judging the artistic temperament of communities," it did specify that the chosen city must be able to supply an adequate audience for performances by both the students and the artists instructing them—indeed, the city "should obligate itself to support the school." In return, the school must "serve in the community as an arts center," and, in light of the interest of national foundations in establishing a training center in the South and the positive response of the director of the Southern Regional Education Board, Winfred Godwin, "the school might very well help its city earn the right to be called the culture capital of the South."[48] Although Ehle most feared the school's being subsumed by liberal arts administration if placed within or near an existing college, he conceded in the report that sharing facilities might be beneficial. But he sought to safeguard the new institution by stating that it should retain "control of its own facilities and full control of its future, its curriculum, its staff, its faculty, its purpose, and its future location, should it decide to move."

The summary of the committee's recommendations that followed had been drafted by Pete McKnight in a memo to Martha Muilenburg, dated March 14, 1963. In 1979, McKnight recollected that Ehle had called and asked him to write the core of recommendations, based on the total experience of the committee, probably because as an editor he was used to producing concise, accurate reports. McKnight "got it down" at one sitting and was later surprised to find that Ehle had incorporated his list into the report virtually without change. Undoubtedly Ehle, a fast and prolific writer himself, wanted an immediate written check on his own interpretation of the committee's findings and confirmation of absent member McKnight's opinions. He was quick as well in getting written endorsement from two of the three other absent members. To Henry Hall Wilson he enclosed a note with the report, remarking that they were "getting a fast start" on the school and that four North Carolina cities (Charlotte, Raleigh, Winston-Salem, and Southern Pines) already had "nominated themselves," on the understanding that they would have to provide land and some buildings. To Gordon Hanes he commented, "Our decisions give the Governor freedom to work out the school along realistic lines as support develops." The three basic problems now facing the school were pinning down foundation support so as to get off to a good start; finding a suitable campus that could be donated by the host community; and developing a workable plan for providing continued support once the initial foundation funds had been exhausted. "The Governor intends to go into all three areas and try to work out a practical and certain scheme, which might very well give to one of our cities an inheritance of true value and state and regional significance," Ehle closed.[49]

The governor's practical scheme—and one that is never certain—was to win the approval of the state legislature. The report Sanford endorsed fully and released to the press on March 27, 1963, was therefore both an inspirational and a practical document designed to win support from a heterogeneous body of state representatives, while preparing the way for conciliation of the school's opponents, many of whom could be expected to attempt to influence that body. Ehle accordingly called for the governor's attention to the state's other arts organizations—including the North Carolina Symphony, the North Carolina State Ballet, and the hoped-for North Carolina State Repertory Theatre—and concluded with a statement of generous spirit and intent:

> Let us plead for the increased support for existing teaching programs and schools, which have laid the groundwork for even more successful teaching of music and drama in our state. We do not see the proposed school as competition to them. Surely it cannot be a threat to them; it is relatively small, particularly when one considers it as a regional institution. Support which the Committee feels might possibly be available for a regional professional arts training center cannot be transferred to other types of institutions or liberal arts programs, but we believe that the programs of existing institutions are basic ones, essential to the healthy development of our society, and needs for assistance which some of these schools have expressed to the Committee seem to us to be most worthy ones indeed.[50]

The press release from the Governor's Office, dated March 28, placed the committee's plea for "increased support for existing teaching programs" early in the story, and it was accordingly reported in newspapers across the state. The governor and Ehle provided additional undergirding by contacting individual editors and asking for advice.[51] Governor Sanford wrote also to Sydney Cone, who was in Europe (as Ehle was scrupulous in noting at the end of the conservatory committee's report[52]), saying that he was sorry that the "need for speed" had required that the report be completed while Cone was away. Sanford suggested that "it would be a good idea . . . [to] sit down and talk about the report once you get back," recognizing that Cone might very well not support the college level of the new conservatory and hoping to head off further public opposition. John Ehle tried to win over Lee Rigsby for the governor, enclosing a copy of the report and reminding Rigsby that he had promised to support the NCCC's recommendations: "What we are doing . . . ought not to interfere with what you are doing and might serve to help you immensely, and if you would like to talk about that, we would certainly be happy to meet with you here or in Greensboro." Rigsby replied cordially, thanking Ehle for his "nice note," inviting him to visit the Woman's College campus soon, and signing himself, "Lee."[53]

During this time, John Ehle held a complicated and uniquely uncomfortable position in the governor's service. In addition to doing "a million dollars worth of projects a month"—involving arts, antipoverty, racial unrest, and education—he served as the link between the artists and the politicians, the vision and the economic reality. And all concerned, he recalls, had "their own ideas," which could be a problem, as when musical comedy writer Richard Adler phoned:

> Dick was a college roommate of Terry's, and Terry must have told Dick about this school . . . and he called me and . . . told me just what it ought to be and where it ought to be—ought to be in the mountains, he said. I said, "Dick, we don't have any legislative support up in the mountains, and we don't have any monetary support in the mountains. I've been trying to awaken some interest up there in Asheville and Junaluska, but as yet we haven't gotten anywhere." It was a big disappointment to Dick that I was thinking that way, you know, in these mundane terms. Dick saw it coming out of the sky. . . . His idea about the school was that it should be a whole lot more musical comedy than Vittorio would have thought. Although Vittorio rather liked musical comedies, too.[54]

In April of 1963, as Governor Sanford prepared to go to the state legislature with his hopes for a state-supported conservatory of the arts, John Ehle pondered in his journal the frail and chancy structure on which those hopes were built:

> We are riding many dangerous horses, of course. We have Vittorio who has heart trouble, he being the best leader of the dream that I know. We have Paul Green, who keeps trying to bolt the traces and get the thing over into the university, that being the way he has been for decades. We have Adler trying to zap the whole thing over into a more dramatic and perhaps more popular role in the arts. We have the Ford Foundation's interest, and McNeil Lowry knows what he wants at all times. We have the governor, who is a friend of Adler and who must, by reason of his office, consider other men of influence as well. . . . We have the interests of Charlotte and Raleigh both burning bright, and a somewhat less bright interest in Winston-Salem and Southern Pines. We have the possible interest of three other foundations [other than Ford], Babcock, Reynolds, and Carnegie. And so far as I know, I'm the only one who knows where all the strings are at this point, and I have not set up a conservatory in my life. But then, who has? [55]

FOR THE

PROMOTION OF

MATTERS OF THE

HUMAN SPIRIT

THE FIRST of Governor Sanford's political strategies for passage of Senate Bill 396 (House Bill 791) was to delay the choice of a site for the new school. He hoped in this way to retain the support of representatives from the state's major cities through the legislature's voting, as they calculated the economic advantages of such a school to their own districts.

His second strategy was to win national publicity and support for the proposed school. At John Ehle's suggestion, on April 10, 1963, the governor sent a copy of the conservatory committee's report to a number of well-known artists and critics, along with a simply phrased and earnest cover letter:

> There is something in the air today in the South which makes us want to try to span the distance which has for so long separated us from the mainstream of America. This is so in many fields; it is so in the arts.
>
> In the enclosed paper, on which a North Carolina commission recently has labored, is an idea for a school, a different, special type of arts school. This school, I am told, is badly needed in the South, where today no school offers professional training in music, drama, or dance.
>
> I am sending you a copy of this report in hopes that you will have time to read it and to write me concerning it, advising me as to whether or not it contains a valuable idea in terms of the needs of today. If such a school is needed, I will try to have it built.

From José Limon, then at Juilliard, came a moving handwritten response in support of the school: "That a Commission has been appointed and has labored and has presented such a report, and that you, the Chief Magis-

5. *The Honorable Terry Sanford, Governor of North Carolina, 1961–65 (photo by Fabian Bachrach, courtesy of Duke University Archives).*

trate of your state should favor it, is to me no less than a triumph for the forces which create culture and civilization and nurture and elevate the human spirit, and by which and through which a city, state, region, or nation is known, understood and remembered." John Gassner of the Yale School of Drama wrote that the project filled him with "jubilation." And critic Walter Kerr, "eager always to see the performing arts sheltered," expressed his one reservation,

> that the school should be clearly known as a professional school, and not offered as a substitute for regular liberal arts education, or presented as a mixture of the two . . . I do not feel that it is wise to introduce such programs on a large scale into existing universities. I think it only compromises the work of the student at the university without compensating sufficiently by giving him a full training in his craft.

George Grizzard also provided specific advice:

> I would put special emphasis on the opportunity given students to perform under professional conditions. There is no substitute for this experience. I hope the existing music and drama departments of the local colleges and universities will not . . . look upon the Conservatory as a competing body. Its job will be . . . to turn out performers—not teachers. The college music and drama departments from what little I have seen of them do not place their major emphasis on performing . . . indeed it is an extraordinary student who is able to leave such a college and find work as a performer.

Elia Kazan's response expressed fervent enthusiasm:

> We are far behind Europe in this kind of thing [where cities] have theatres, have training groups, have dance groups. There's no reason in the world why we the wealthiest and freest country in the world shouldn't have the same. Furthermore, an organization like the one you are considering will be a great source of pleasure. In fact a blessing to the people in your State. It would be wonderful if specifically there could be dramatizations of the stories and legends of your own State. And this would help to reinforce in your people the sense of their own identity and special history. And as I say I am enthusiastic and stretch out a hand to you. And anything I can do to help, feel no hesitation in asking.

And from favorite son Paul Green came pithy words from one who had a right to speak:

I believe that the principles and creations of beauty actually are the fire and fervor of a people's life and where they are weak and of little or no interest the people tend to perish spiritually and too often take defense in a fierce and dehydrating folk-god orthodoxy—as has long been the fact and practice in North Carolina. I have heard it said that a good North Carolina Democrat is one who chews tobacco and owns a book, the Bible. . . . I think the idea of creating a center for the arts in this state is a tremendous thing. . . . In the words of our former orators . . . it will prove "a beacon light for the wandering ship of state." Do it, do it, and count on me to help in any way I can, blazing or menial.[1]

Favorable replies came from all to whom Governor Sanford wrote: Sidney Blackmer, Norman Cordon, Louis Persinger, Efrem Zimbalist, Sir Tyrone Guthrie, Peter Mennin, Ben Swalin, Mark Schubart, Martha Hill, and Brooks Atkinson, who helped further by featuring the proposed school in his *New York Times* column, "Critic at Large." Atkinson wished the project well—"anyone concerned with the arts naturally hopes that Governor Sanford and the state of North Carolina succeed"—and used the occasion to articulate the sacred mission of even a nascent conservatory that hoped to protect and encourage artists:

The surge of interest in the arts today is a criticism of American society. They compensate for something people are losing in their private lives. For the life the nation is living tends to submerge individuals. Their economic and social life is increasingly administered by oligarchies of power—government, industry, unions—that are either anonymous or remote.

The arts are not substitutes for the powerful organizations that dominate the nation. We need the products and services they provide. But the arts extend the range of our lives by deepening the human spirit and identifying points of view. Since they are concerned with the meaning of life, it is difficult to know where the arts leave off and religion begins.[2]

After the artists' letters were released to the press, they were collected conveniently in booklets along with the conservatory committee's report and, eventually, supporting newspaper articles and a copy of the arts school bill. These booklets, titled *A Statement Concerning the Proposed Performing Arts School in North Carolina,* were "duplicated and bound by prison labor in Raleigh," John Ehle recalls. "Whenever we exhausted the supply of copies or came upon more material, my secretary, Lois Haswell, sent it all back over there, and the prisoners did a new edition."[3] Having mobilized the inmates for art, Sanford thought to prod Hugh Cannon; on April 30 he sent his administrative director a packet of information on the proposed school, a copy of a memo by Ehle on the subject, and his own message to Cannon about the proposed legislation: "Don't let the grass grow." On May 1, Cannon responded: "The grass is not growing." The bill was being prepared by the attorney general's staff. Cannon remembers sitting down with Ehle to talk about what the bill should contain, and apparently they agreed to divide the labor:

> We had to come up with a piece of legislation that would actually establish the institution. . . . I got in O. B. Brown, who was my chief budget analyst . . . and we outlined the institution. Now, obviously what we did was, we took the format of the later-formed institutions such as the University of North Carolina at Charlotte, Wilmington, and Asheville, and we said, Okay, let's just set up a parallel of that format . . . we did all this in the course of about forty-eight hours. O. B. Brown came back to me, and he said, "Okay, here's your school of the arts"—I'm not sure we had named it then, but "here's your institution and here's your enabling legislation." . . . At this point there was a standardized format for a state institution of higher education. This one, of course, had the unusual concept that it also included high school, and for that reason, O. B. Brown had had to put in the Department of Public Education participation.
>
> The statute was written in such a way that it would accommodate almost anything. The statute is expansive rather than restrictive. . . . O. B. Brown was . . . very, very thorough and very dependable, and what he came up with was an all-purpose vehicle, and that is what we told him to do.
>
> Now, we had a little predicatory language in there concerning the arts, but I think in the original enabling legislation, we could have almost put an agricultural station in that school.[4]

The "predicatory language" was the "Whereas" statements, which Ehle first drafted and sent to Cannon on May 2 and further revised on May 3 and 4. In them Ehle stated, with his characteristic combination of grace, practicality, and wiliness, the reasons for creating the new school. Citing North Carolina's tradition of "leadership in support and development of the arts," as evidenced by the state's firsts in the arts—the first state-supported symphony orchestra, art museum, and outdoor drama—he appealed to native pride: "It is fitting that North Carolina should maintain her position of leadership in providing for the promotion of matters of the human spirit." Ehle went on to emphasize the need of the children of the region for the proposed school:

> W H E R E A S, there is no school in the South which offers professional training to high school musicians or other performing artists, and no conservatory . . . for college students; and
>
> W H E R E A S, many of the rural children of the South are deprived of the opportunity to receive intensive training . . . for which they are preeminently qualified; and
>
> W H E R E A S, the cultural heritage of our Nation has been greatly enhanced through the training given talented artists . . . and the lack of . . . training facilities in the South is depriving many of our most talented young people of . . . opportunity . . . at the age when it would be most effective to create interest and proficiency in the performing arts; and
>
> W H E R E A S, there exist foundations which will support the first regional performing arts training school to be established in the South . . . and. . . .
>
> W H E R E A S, it is in the public interest of the people of our State that a regional training school of about 400 to 600 students be established to provide North Carolina and other states of the South with professional training for musicians and others gifted in the performing arts; N O W T H E R E F O R E, The General Assembly of North Carolina do enact. . . .

On May 3 and 4 Ehle also worked on changes in the first draft of the bill itself, which had been sent over by Andrew Jones of the attorney general's office. Ehle's handwritten alterations on this version were incorporated into the final bill. He honed the instrument to a statement of clear purpose, lest either the bill or the school go astray. For example, to part 116–64, "Establishment of school," he added the word "professional" to the phrase, "for the *professional* training of students having exceptional talent in the performing arts," and he narrowed the definition of the school's intended student body, who were to come from "North Carolina and other states, *particularly other states of the South*." Ehle saw to it that the school's mission was repeatedly clarified in the bill: under part 116–65 [116–66; bracketed figures refer to section numbers in the final bill], "Enumerated powers of board," he added to item (4) [5], the board's authorization to employ teachers, that the chief criteria for employment were to be the candidates' "excellence in the performing arts and their professional standing . . . rather than academic degrees and training." To item (8) [9], the board's instruction to require entrance examinations for prospective students, he added the grounds, "so that the professional training shall be made available only to those students who possess exceptional talent in the performing arts." He added item (14) in its entirety, which instructs the board to confer with the SREB and other such organizations "to establish the school as the center in the South for the professional training and performance of artists." Under part 116–67 [116–69], "Purpose of (school) program," Ehle added that instruction at the school was to place emphasis upon "performance, on the actual presentation of the arts and not on academic studies of the arts." (The final wording reads "performance of the arts, and not upon academic studies of the arts.") Even the title of the bill showed Ehle's meticulous attention to detail. On the initial version, "A BILL TO BE ENTITLED AN ACT TO ESTABLISH THE NORTH CAROLINA SCHOOL OF PERFORMING ARTS," Ehle erased NORTH CAROLINA, changing the name to THE SOUTHERN SCHOOL OF PERFORMING ARTS. This he changed to A CENTER FOR THE PERFORMING ARTS. Then, in apparent frustration, he wrote in *title* and went off to think some more. Finally, he settled on IN NORTH CAROLINA A SCHOOL FOR PROFESSIONAL TRAINING IN MUSIC AND OTHER PERFORMING ARTS FOR THE SOUTHERN REGION.[5]

Ehle's final choice accurately reflects his three major concerns in drawing up the bill: to keep the school regional, to keep it professional, and to keep the word "dance" out of it:

> In North Carolina at that time, music was accepted, it was even used in churches. Drama was accepted, particularly if it took place out of doors. Dance was unacceptable; it was sinful and it was of the devil. Even in my first letters to Governor Sanford, I never referred to dance. I recall after I had first talked to Margaret Mahoney, this was the summer of 1962, I wrote him about my hopes for a professional training center in the arts, and I referred to music, acting—I think I've got the letter here—"to offer professional training in music, painting, sculpture, acting, stage design and perhaps other areas." *Perhaps other areas* was political language for the dance. I didn't know Terry very well then or I wouldn't have had to be evasive.[6]

The delicate political overtones in the concept of "dance" best explain Ehle's omission of "choreographer" from his addition to the bill urging the school's Board of Trustees to employ for the school a chief administrative

officer "who shall be preferably a noted composer or dramatist." Certainly
he already knew and liked Agnes de Mille for her good taste in wanting to
create a dance based on his novel *The Land Breakers*. It was not a prejudice
against the corps de ballet that seemingly omitted the danseur or danseuse
from explicit consideration in heading the school but political prudence.
Nonetheless, a broad commitment to choosing a creative artist to lead the
school dictated Ehle's statement. To his mind then and now, something
had to be said on the subject:

> I think the artists should run the arts schools. I notice the head of the
> Bowman Gray School of Medicine is a doctor. That doesn't surprise
> anybody. I notice the vice-president of medical affairs at Duke is a
> doctor. You say the arts school should have a head who is an artist,
> and they all look at you rather askance. Well, damn it, would you want
> an artist running the medical center, or a doctor running the arts cen-
> ter? They do, seemingly. I don't understand it. It seems to me obvious
> that the artists have to be responsible for the arts. And if they aren't,
> then nobody is really responsible for the artists.

Vittorio Giannini also believed that artists should run arts schools, and he,
too, specified the creative artist over the performing artist for such a role.
"As you very well know," he wrote to John Ehle less than two months before Ehle began work on the bill,

> performing artist[s] are different than creative artists. The performing
> artist is usually of short vision, seeing the arts only in relation to his
> participation as a performer in it, therefore unconsciously using any
> artistic activity as a platform for his performance. This is one of the
> elements in the make up of a performing artist that propels him for-
> ward. The creative artist instead works within himself and alone and is
> prepared to wait for an evaluation of his work which is set down for all
> time. This tends to widen his vision if he has any and [to make him]
> think in larger spans of time than the performing artist who has only a
> few years in which to make his mark, if any. This also explains the
> many conflicts among performers; they are many and the opportuni-
> ties for them are few, and they cannot wait. A creative artist can wait
> for centuries, he may not like it, but he recognizes that it may be nec-
> essary, knowing that if he has something to say, the years will not
> lessen his power, on the contrary enforce it and make it more felt and
> understood. Beethoven means more today than he could have ever

meant in his lifetime, even if he had been recognized then as a great artist. But whoever was the great singer, actor, conductor of his time is forgotten today except by a few who enjoy knowing such things. This is why the great art schools of the world have a long tradition of having creative artists as heads.[7]

On Saturday, May 4, Hugh Cannon showed the bill to Governor Sanford, who looked it over and approved it. On Monday evening, May 6, it was introduced simultaneously in both houses of the North Carolina General Assembly—in the Senate by Democrats Tom White, Robert Lee Humber, and Ray Walton, and in the House by Democrats Rachel Davis, Grace T. Rodenbaugh, and Gordon Greenwood. The bill was immediately referred to the Higher Education Committee of each body. On Tuesday the bill won the approval of the Senate committee and was referred to the Appropriations Committee, but it was not until Friday, May 10, that the House Higher Education Committee passed it on through with approval. On its way to the Joint Appropriations Subcommittee, the bill had run into trouble in the House. Ben Roney, at that time director of secondary roads, remembers that the first time he ever heard of the North Carolina school of performing arts was at one of Governor Sanford's famous breakfasts (according to John Ehle, a cornerstone of Terry Sanford's political tactics: broken down into their component parts, those tactics were 1. country ham 2. grits 3. red-eye gravy 4. good biscuits 5. scrambled eggs 6. strong coffee):

Governor Sanford had his lobbying crew, I reckon you would call it, over to the mansion for breakfast . . . to outline what they were going to do that week in the legislature. . . . They were talking about different things, and . . . the legislation I had was all through, and I just wasn't interested in the conversation much at all.

But then [Governor Sanford] asked somebody in the group about the school of the arts, and they said that they understood that that had been killed in the House. And he says, "Roney, I want you to go down there and get that bill out of committee, and see if you can't get it passed."

I said, "What bill are you talking about?" (I had never heard of the school of the arts.)

So he said, "You go see John Ehle, and he can tell you about it." . . . So I went to see Ehle . . . when I found out what it was, I asked [him], "You mean, this is what all that crowd of long-haired folks over at the university has been sittin' around the Appropriations Committee for days, waitin' to go in there and get heard?"

He said, "Yes, that's what it is." . . . He told me that he didn't know *where* [the bill] was down there.

It turned out that it had been killed in the Calendar Committee. Hugh Johnson was chairman of the Calendar Committee that year, so I went to see Hugh to find out if that was true.

And he said, "Yes, we killed it yesterday or the day before yesterday."

And I said, "Well, what's the chance of getting it out?"

He said, "Well, hell, Ben, it's killed!"

I said, "I know that, but you can bring it out."

He said, "Well, what's the use of bringing it out? You can't do anything with it anyway."

I said, "Well, the only reason I can tell you is, the Governor told me to come down here and get it out if I could."

And he said, "Well, you know it doesn't have an appropriation."

I said, "I understand that."

So he said, "If you think you can do anything with it, you talk to"— I forget who was there—so-and-so, "and if he agrees, we'll see if we can't get it out."

Well, I went up to the Governor's Office, and I told him, I said, "Terry, I found out about your bill. It's dead." I said, "The thing is killed. The fact is that money is tight down there, and . . . that's the reason, I'm sure, that they killed it." . . .

And he said, "Can you get it out?"

I said, "Well, I've talked to Hugh Johnson, and he said that he would bring it out."

Well, he got it out.[8]

John Ehle had been summoned to speak for the bill at both the Senate and House committee meetings and afterward expressed guarded optimism in his journal:

I believe we have a better than 50-50 chance of getting this school. This past week I appeared before the Senate Higher Education Committee, which unanimously approved the bill. On Friday morning, I appeared before the House Higher Education Committee, which approved it also. There was a motion by a representative who said he had some letters he had left in his office—a motion that it be defeated. His motion was quite handsomely defeated. Then a man moved that since there had been very little time to deliberate on the motion, that it be sent on to the Appropriations Committee without prejudice. This made a good deal of sense, of course, for indeed there had been almost no time to discuss the bill, I admit. But that was defeated also by a close vote. The motion to approve the bill was then taken up and passed handsomely.

Later Hugh Cannon told me how he had grabbed the arm of the legislator next to him, who stood at the wrong time; this was on the nonprejudice motion. Hugh pulled him back down.

"No, you don't want to stand now," he said.

"I don't? Why not?"

"Well, sit here and I'll tell you," Hugh said. "Now stand up," he said, and the man did and was counted, and by a vote of sixteen to fifteen we defeated the motion to send it down without prejudice.[9]

The letters in the representative's office were undoubtedly from the Greensboro opposition, which had briskly resurfaced, despite Lee Rigsby's note of April 1, replying cordially to Ehle's reminder that Rigsby had agreed to support the conservatory committee's findings. One of the strongest and most immediate responses to the introduction of the arts school bill in the legislature came from Harold Luce, director of special services at the University of North Carolina Woman's College. Luce fired off a letter to Hugh Cannon in high dudgeon, reacting to Cannon's remarks in that day's issue of the *Greensboro Record*. The *Record*, reporting that the bill had "won quick approval" from the Senate Higher Education Committee, quoted Hugh Cannon as saying that "there is no school for professional training of performing artists in the Southern region." Luce wrote that he had read Cannon's statement "with shock and dismay" and that the Woman's College was "a first class institution for the training of professional musicians." He charged that the school's program had been "ignored" by the governor, the NCCC, and Ehle, none of whom had visited the campus: "Our invitations have not even been accorded the courtesy of an answer . . . the report . . . is a most incomplete report and a totally inadequate basis for major legislation." Ehle was alarmed by the vehemence of the attack and worried that it would gather strength. "I don't like the letter just in from the staff member of the music school of Womans College," he wrote in a May 8 memo to Sanford:

I phoned Lee Rigsby to see how he was getting on, and he was quite upset about the proposed Conservatory. He intends to organize a drive against it, so far as I can tell, and I hope you will use your influence to head him off. . . . My position with him was that moving

Juilliard Conservatory to N.C. would not hurt music in N.C. or this region; it would help music everywhere in this section. He agrees, I believe, but what he fears is that it will hurt the Womans College. He is looking at the thing from that spot, of course, and he is going to fight as long as he can or dares. I do hope you will cut him off at the pass.

In his reply to Luce, Governor Sanford pointed out that a significant number of nationally respected artists had expressed their support for the proposed conservatory. He quoted Peter Mennin's comment: "It is obvious that your Committee has labored long and intelligently concerning the need for such a school," and his closing left no doubt where the governor felt Luce's duty lay: "The school will almost certainly be started, and opposition of an unreasoning sort can only damage it; it cannot kill it, but it can damage it. I urge upon you proper consideration lest your action be more destructive than constructive." [10]

On May 10, Cannon was scolded by yet another member of the Woman's College faculty, a violin instructor, who charged that in ignoring the Woman's College School of Music, the NCCC showed a "lack of information (or stupidity, 'play' of politics)." On May 16, Governor Sanford replied to a number of students at the Woman's College who had written protesting the new conservatory, "all pretty much alike in zeal and substance":

Why the proposed school is more of an issue in Greensboro than elsewhere, I don't know, but I do welcome opinion and believe a discussion is always helpful.

The new school is likely to be put in the southern region. Whether it is put in North Carolina or nearby is one issue you will want to consider.

I think too that you will want to consider the advantage this school offers those young people of high school age who have rare talent but who have in their areas less than adequate professional training or cultural atmosphere. Many children in the South are of this type.

In the proposed school, the emphasis will and ought to be on the high school level, as I see it. We will have, however, a college program and must have one in order to have the advanced students that are needed and in order to get the top faculty members that are needed.

That is a brief review of a reason or two in favor of the proposed new school. Of course, it might be part of an old school. We don't know as yet where it is to be put but it is to be a new start at offering training in several arts to young people of different ages from this and other states, and the resources which I believe are available for its support are not on the whole, or even in any substantial part, transferable to an existing program.

I urge you to develop as friendly an attitude toward this undertaking as you can. We already share respect for the arts and appreciation of the needs of young artists. The more we do of quality, the better our competition, the greater is likely to be support generally for the arts, and for us all, and for all our institutions.[11]

By this time, Hugh Cannon had begun to get a little testy. "Hugh has been assaulted by letters from the girls at Woman's College," John Ehle confided to his journal, "since at that first hearing he was quoted in the paper as saying professional music training doesn't exist in the South":

Hugh has got quite angry. When I told him earlier last week that Rigsby was going to launch an attack and said we could write him, [Hugh] said we could write him out of the state if we wanted to. I told him no such attempt would be made. Hugh evidently phoned Bill Friday, angry as fire. We come to a problem here involving academic freedom, but also involving political maneuvers. Bill is supporting this bill, and in return, so far as my limited knowledge goes, there might have been many concessions made to U.N.C. Very well. That might have made sense to the University. Now the political apple cart is turned upside down by Lee Rigsby, and the issue becomes a political one.[12]

Certainly the issue was no longer purely one of education, as reports in the state's press indicated. Sanford's May 8 reply to Harold Luce's criticisms, sent to Otis A. Singletary,[13] chancellor of the Woman's College, must have contributed to the public encouragement expressed by the chancellor the following week, when he wired two members of the General Assembly to express his support for the new arts school. By May 19, the *Raleigh News and Observer* was reporting that the other chief officers of the Consolidated University of North Carolina had closed ranks behind the governor. A joint statement of support had been issued by President William C. Friday and Chancellors John T. Caldwell of North Carolina State and William B. Aycock of the university at Chapel Hill.[14] At this point, Dean Rigsby's mission to oppose the school began to take on something of a kamikaze air. Over lunch, he told John Ehle that he would reverse his position and support the school, if Ehle would locate the school at the Woman's College. Ehle replied, of course, that they couldn't do that, and "he threw everything at it. And he told me . . . that he thought he was doing maybe not the right thing in terms of the needs of the state, but he was serving the Woman's College, where he worked." [15]

Lee Rigsby's opposition may have been zealous, single-minded, and shortsighted, but it made good press in Greensboro, and the city's *Daily News* was one of the four major newspapers in the state. The state's legislators would undoubtedly read it, and Ehle was worried—"I did worry about it. I worried a lot about it." The paper planned a major spread on the conservatory controversy on May 12—a Sunday issue—and Ehle phoned one of the *Daily News* editors, Bill Snider, to suggest that the articles might profit from "a broader view" than those represented by Lee Rigsby and Sydney Cone. Executive Editor Miles Wolff responded by offering Ehle the opportunity to write a rebuttal for the following Sunday's issue (May 19) because there was no more space available for text on the school in the May 12 feature section, and the rebuttal would have more importance when Ehle's response could "have the stage to itself." [16]

John Ehle still shudders at the remembrance of the May 12 broadside:

Now out came this issue of the Greensboro Daily News at a ticklish time for this school indeed, and there was Sydney Cone writing an article describing the conservatory committee's work as he knew it. Ostensibly, he was favorably impressed with us, and you've never read an article that was more damning in your life. Then there was an editorial blasting the school, saying that we had not had time to think about it, and all that sort of thing. There were four articles about the school in that one issue . . . and it was devastating, really. [17]

The *Daily News* feature included a straight news report by David L. Owens reviewing the facts of the story (and beginning by erroneously reporting the date of the appointment of the conservatory committee as October 9, 1962 rather than August 1) and then Sydney Cone's article "Committee Work Told." Though not overtly hostile to the school, Cone's laconic comment on his own opening summary of the NCCC's work—a dense listing of the matters the committee had had to review—must have left a question in some readers' minds as to whether the committee's work did, indeed, have Cone's full confidence: "It will occur to the careful reader that these five sessions of the committee must have been considerably concentrated and lengthy to cover even in a cursory fashion such a wide and substantial range of subject matter. Such was, in fact, the case." Cone went on to emphasize the not-so-veiled criticisms expressed by arts educators toward the idea of a college-level conservatory—that arts graduates must teach to live and therefore college programs had developed the necessary focus on teacher certification (not to be a goal or even an option at the new school); that the state's college arts programs were already suffering in the competition for highly talented students because of the inadequacy of scholarship money; that conservatory education is too narrow and specialized to provide the broader-based studies which today's performing artists need; and that the total of nineteen degree-granting music programs in North Carolina argued that the performing arts were already developing rapidly in the state. Cone closed by stating that a high school program was much needed and pointing out the fair imperative of locating the school in a heavily populated area such as the Research Triangle or Greensboro to provide adequate audiences.

The third article, "School of Performing Arts Opposed," reported the arguments against the school advanced by the faculty at Woman's College. After repeating the now familiar warnings that a state conservatory would "dry up" existing college programs by draining them of the best students and subsequently the best teachers and that the national trend was away from professional schools in the arts, the paper quoted Lee Rigsby's defense of the Woman's College program. His school, Rigsby maintained, "has what the Governor is after, except we can't make him see it." Rigsby characterized the Woman's College program as similar to that offered by Juilliard and said that with sufficient time and money the school could offer the same caliber of training as well, just as was the case at Florida State University. The Woman's College's high standards included admitting only 10 percent of those who applied to become music majors and requiring that each student take an end-of-term jury examination before the faculty. Rigsby said that the emphasis at Woman's College was on "doing the art," just as the NCCC had recommended. Because the committee had recommended that the new school be located near an existing institution so as to share facilities, why not locate it at the Woman's College, where a planned annex would soon be available to house some four hundred music majors?

The interview with Rigsby was followed by one with Herman Middleton, head of drama and speech, who essentially echoed Rigsby's statements and strongly opposed professional acting school training in drama, on the principle that students need a broad liberal arts background first before concentrating on professionalism (indeed, Middleton actually charged that professional schools harm students by depriving them of the opportunity to acquire this base). He suggested that existing drama programs in North

Carolina be given additional money and that a professional acting company be established at the University of North Carolina.

Middleton contended that the NCCC's investigation had been superficial, a point strongly echoed by Harold Luce, whom the *Daily News* reporter had also interviewed. Luce's sentiments were similar to those which he had expressed more privately to Hugh Cannon (who, at the end of the article, was once again lambasted), with additional warnings about the dire consequences of establishing the new conservatory, which, in the clear light of newsprint, took on a somewhat jeremianic tone—the conservatory "would end public performances of college groups" because they would be left with the weakest talent; the state would lose the public recitals and concerts of "talented faculty" because they would have left in pursuit of good students to teach; and the end result would be that the "primary source of cultural life in many communities" would "dry up."

Ehle's distress is understandable for the criticisms of the school offered in such huge gulps in the feature section appeared plausible, voiced as they were by educators at one of the state's outstanding schools and not in the least gainsaid by a member of the original conservatory committee. The *Daily News* completed the ensemble attack with an editorial sympathetic to the "amply justified" "dismay" of the Woman's College faculty when confronted with what they and the paper perceived as a "pell-mell rush" to create a new school for the performing arts and a gratuitous slam from the mouth of the bloodied but unbowed Hugh Cannon:

> When the Governor's Office, a few weeks ago, canvassed views on the commission's report, there was a feeling, if we are not mistaken, that the report marked a good beginning but, in its sketchiness, required more extensive study.
>
> Imagine the surprise with which those actively concerned with schooling performing artists in North Carolina—at Woman's College and elsewhere—awoke to find that bills embodying the yet-sketchy proposals of the conservatory commission were already in legislative channels. Imagine, too, the shock with which the fine arts faculty at Woman's College beheld in the press a statement from state director of administration Hugh Cannon that "there is no school for professional training of performing artists in the Southern region."
>
> With a self-advertisement more than pardonable, the fine arts faculty at Woman's College protests that there is such a school in the Southern region (and others besides) and it is at Woman's College it-

self—whose offerings in dance, drama and music enjoy not only regional but national standing. . . . Apparently, the premature speeding of the "school for performing arts" to the legislative stage is fueled by the prospect of foundation funds if North Carolina demonstrates "it means business," in Mr. Cannon's words.

The editorial commentator closed with a warning against the lure of foundation funds which would merely duplicate existing programs, and thereby weaken them, rather than offering an opportunity to expand from competence into excellence (a comment at odds, it would seem, with the claim that Woman's College enjoyed "national standing" in the performing arts).

Ehle was unable to use the proffered space for rebuttal: "I appreciate your invitation to write a piece this week for the Greensboro paper about the proposed school," he wrote Miles Wolff on May 14. "I can't take advantage of it, for I'm supposed to leave fairly early tomorrow morning for a meeting, to which a foundation has kindly invited me, in Oakland, California."[18] Privately, however, Gene Strassler of East Carolina University in Greenville, North Carolina, took the time to make notes for a reply to the Greensboro arguments and forwarded them to Ehle: "That there is a 'trend . . . away from conservatories' may be true . . . but that is not to say there is no place for them." Certainly Juilliard, Curtis, and Eastman were not lacking for students. Clearly, talented, career-oriented students needed a "far more objective, intense and critical type of teaching" than they could get in an academic community. They also needed the competition offered by equally gifted fellow students. Strassler noted that teacher training within a liberal arts program is important, but it is different from professional training, which requires "sacrifice, dedication, discipline." A state conservatory would not drain other state institutions of the best talent because the new school would not be drawing from the same pool. Rather, those students who were now going north for professional conservatory training could find it in the South, stay home, and provide stimulus in the arts that would make North Carolina a cultural leader. The further point that Ford funds were not available to programs at existing educational institutions had suggested to the *Daily News* editorial writer that the arts school's proponents were guilty of "tailoring projects to fit the bountiful purses now entrancing scholars," with the result that the state would merely duplicate programs already being offered. Many of the school's opponents seem to have missed the point that Ford Foundation experts—most notably McNeil Lowry—had been surveying the state of the arts in

America since 1957 and had concluded that a new professional training center in the arts was badly needed in the South. After so much fieldwork preparatory to pouring hundreds of millions of dollars into the performing arts, the Ford Foundation had made a more than credible effort to be well informed and was hardly likely to "throw away money on a duplication," as Strassler noted. He then summed up the six major points in the debate, beginning with the issue of the infamous Hugh Cannon "insult":

1. Supposed "insult" lies in interpretation of function.
2. Faculty selection is the key difference—specialization all through the curriculum artist-teachers—versus "window dressing" names or "credentials." . . .
3. Academic respectability anathema to objectivity in results of curriculum and level of teaching—self-justification—lack of competition.
4. Professional musicians require concentrated studies on technical proficiency to meet the fiercely compet[i]tive demands of making a living with music.
5. The trend away from conservatories to college schools of music is not healt[h]y. If students need job insurance to back up their ability, they don't belong in a conservatory in the first place. Besides, training for teachers and professional musicians are two separate approaches. Teaching and performing are both noble professions—they should not be antagonistic.
6. Finally, I cannot agree that Florida State is on a par with Juilliard. Proof is the quality of graduates and the success they achieve. . . .
(Dubious value except to infuriate)[19]

Another strong reaction to the May 12 article came, unexpectedly, in a letter from the wife of a former faculty member in the Woman's College music department, whose husband had left at the end of the 1961–62 academic year because of "the *standard of excellence which he expected* of his students":

The *standards* of this School of Music are at an all time *low*, in spite of the way it may look on *paper*. For example: students seeking admittance to the School of Music have *Never* auditioned before the full faculty, as was stated in today's paper. In fact, last fall the piano faculty heard auditions of students and recommended that some of them *not* be accepted as piano majors because they were not qualified. A few days later they were, in fact, admitted as piano majors. . . .
    North Carolina *does* need a professional training school of the per-

forming arts, but Woman's College is *not* the place for it now under the *present administration* of the School of Music. . . .

You will receive many letters supporting Rigsby's stand, because I know for a fact that he has asked the students, and some of the faculty to write to you. I know most of the music students at WC, and tried today to count the number of students now enrolled, who might be in a conservatory type school if it were now in existence. I counted 5! I think Rigsby's cry of "we would dry up" is completely without foundation. Woman's College does not, as a rule, get the "cream of the crop" that a conservatory would, and *should,* get. Woman's College actually has nothing to lose by the establishment of this school.

Governor Sanford replied with appreciation: "One can never have too much support for a piece of legislation, and certainly the arts are less predictable than most areas." He remarked that he found the attacks on the school "more emotional than objective . . . all of them sharing the same enthusiasm for fragmented facts and views." Sanford promised to use the letter "with discretion"; that a blind copy of his reply went to UNC's William Friday suggests that the president of the Consolidated University may have been sent a copy or perhaps a summary of the original letter's contents.[20]

The *Greensboro Daily News* followed up its Sunday morning repudiation of the conservatory idea with an attack specifically directed at John Ehle two days later. The column "Tar Heel Talk" gave a hostile nod to Ehle for influencing the decision of the conservatory committee:

Some two years ago, Mr. Ehle, having canvassed his notions with friends, set out on a one-man crusade to do something about the decline of arts education in the state generally, and at Chapel Hill in particular. He circulated a brief of figures and observations that documented with apparent conclusiveness the decline of the arts as a part of formal college study in North Carolina. . . . Mr. Ehle coupled his careful statistics with several general observations about the place of young artists in the academic milieu. "The atmosphere of the humanities," he wrote, "is heavy hung with old notions and old studies. Even our arts departments and creative courses are dominated often by the atmosphere, methodology, and attitudes of the scholar, not the artist. . . . I cannot imagine a young artist surviving the General College in Chapel Hill without severe damage. It is not without reason that an artist rarely comes out of it. . . ."

At any rate, Mr. Ehle's bias is detectable in his earlier pronouncement on the relationship between formal study and the arts. Given that bias, which may indeed be wholly appropriate, it is no mystery that the Governor's Conservatory Commission, under Mr. Ehle's inspiration and tutelage (not to say domination), came down on the side of an independent performing arts school which would be more or less insulated from the presumably soul-searing disciplines of academia. . . . [However] Mr. Ehle and his friends have gratuitously slammed (by implication anyway) teachers who are far from hostile to the creative. The W[oman's] C[ollege] people are angry that the Governor's cultural attachés, proceeding from postulates gained in the more formal academic routine of Chapel Hill–Raleigh, have presumed to noise it about that North Carolina has no adequate centers for training in the "performing arts." Of the arts there can be no surplus; the world may be big enough for Mr. Ehle and the Woman's College arts faculty. But it must be wryly noted that after two years of buzzing feathers down the well, Mr. Ehle has now, and surely not to his surprise, heard a loud splash.[21]

Three points should be noted about the columnist's attack on Ehle, at least two of which were persistent misunderstandings in the Greensboro press: the perception that workers in the vineyard of the arts at the Woman's College had been the object of deliberate insult because the NCCC had given more credence to their record for producing teachers of the arts than to their aspirations to produce performers; and the failure to mention the Ford Foundation survey, preferring instead to focus on the issue of "bias" and the NCCC's failure to conduct on-campus surveys in North Carolina. On the third point, however, the column showed an understanding unique in the state's press, for no other report or editorial comment gave so much credit to John Ehle's determination and influence in the founding of the North Carolina School of the Arts. It is ironic to realize that at the time, the author's guiding role received full public recognition only in the mocking negativism of "Mr. Ehle's Feather."

Not surprisingly, the Greensboro position was echoed in the *Chapel Hill Weekly*, in, if anything, even stronger language. "Gut-Shot Aimed at the University" suggested that a disaster was about to be brought about by the foolish proponents of a "dazzling," outdated, and romantic idea:

The Center bids fair to gut the fine arts programs of the Consolidated University—a particularly fine one at Woman's College and a promising one here. . . . It is fatuous to believe that by the establishment of a new institution, with new buildings and faculty with the announced aim of producing artists, the end result will be anything other than just one more institution—which in itself is particularly odious to the truly creative temperament—or that its effect on higher education and the arts will be anything other than a needless dilution of resources.

Three days later, in a waspish mood, the paper snapped—more than a little unfairly—that "need, of course, should be the determining factor, and not Ehle's plaint of culture for appearance's sake."[22]

Fortunately, the Greensboro papers and the *Chapel Hill Weekly* were exceptions in the state's press. Other newspapers gave generous support in the days before final legislative approval was sought. The *Twin City Sentinel* in Winston-Salem admitted to having changed its mind about the school, which, as a conservatory of music alone, had at first seemed to be overlapping educational programs already offered in the state. "Five significant developments" had eased the paper's reservations: the inclusion of drama and dance, two areas in which opportunities for talented North Carolinians were limited; offering high school and elementary grades, thereby filling another gap in training in the state; the regional nature of the school (validated by SREB backing); the offer of foundation matching funds, which would ease some of the financial burden of establishing the school; and the requirement that a local community provide the site and physical plant, further reducing the state's initial outlay. On Sunday, May 19, both the *Raleigh News and Observer* and the *Charlotte Observer* ran full spreads on the school in their feature sections, replete with pictures and quotes from its most famous supporters. Although they had been released to the press on May 11, the artists' replies to Governor Sanford's April letter asking advice and guidance in creating a state conservatory were given an effective—and full—review at this time in the Charlotte paper. Both stories were highly favorable, lengthy, and thorough, but neither reported the Ford survey, which had definitely established the need for such a school in the southern region, and both reported that over a million dollars in start-up funds had been promised by a major, unnamed foundation—an inaccuracy that the Sanford administration let ride, for obvious reasons. John Ehle remembers being called before the legislature's Joint Appropriations Subcommittee "to explain this Foundation grant that we had in prospect. Of course, that was funny, because we never knew we actually had a grant, and we never could even name the Foundation."[23]

The open hearing at which Ehle spoke was held by the twenty-five-member legislative Joint Appropriations Subcommittee on Thursday, May 23. The agenda of speakers whom Sanford's aides had lined up to report on the school suggests that a breathtaking impact had been planned, perhaps intended to overwhelm by the very speed of supportive onslaught:

Mrs. Paul L. Muilenburg, Chairman, the North Carolina Conservatory Committee.
to give background of Committee, general review of studies made, meetings, and final report. (3 min.)

Mr. Sam Ragan, Committee Member, Executive Editor of Raleigh *News and Observer.*
to affirm thoroughness of Committee's work, and to indicate genuine interest of citizens of Raleigh. (1 min.)

Mrs. Carl Durham, Committee Member.
to indicate visits to other Conservatories in making thorough study for need and for kind of program. (1 min.)

Mr. Gordon Hanes, Committee Member, Senator.
to affirm committee's work, and to indicate interest of citizens of Winston-Salem. (1 min.)

Mr. John Ehle, Secretary to Committee, Governor's Staff
to explain survey of South East by Ford Foundation which established need, and to indicate the interest of Ford and other Foundations. (2 min.)

[no one named]
to indicate approval of program and genuine interest of citizens of Charlotte. (1 min.)

Bill Herring
to indicate approval of program and genuine interest of citizens of Winston-Salem. (1 min.)

Mr. William Friday, President of the Consolidated University.
to indicate position of University and its desire to cooperate in Program. (2 min.)

Mr. John Caldwell, Chancellor, North Carolina State.
to indicate need for program in South East and to affirm interest of University officials and Raleigh citizens. (1 min.)

Mr. Leo Jenkins, President of East Carolina.
to explain how School would compliment [sic] Music Program at East Carolina, and to indicate interest and cooperation. (1 min.)

Final Summary by Mrs. Muilenburg (1 min.)

Total presentation: 15 min.

Speedy or not, however, "nobody was able to speak," according to John Ehle, "because the Conservatory Committee's Chairman, Martha Muilenburg, excited and dedicated, talked the whole allotted time, all except one minute at the end that I was given."[24]

A month remained in which to gain legislative support for the bill establishing a school for performing arts. Letter after letter went out from Governor Sanford's office. To those who had written expressing their support for the proposed school, he replied with thanks, urging them to write letters to their representatives and newspapers in favor of the measure and reinforcing their enthusiasm with his own statements of commitment—"I am convinced of the importance of this School." "[Our young people] deserve to have the best training possible." To the continung opposition expressed in letters from Greensboro, Sanford took pains to reply at length, reiterating the arguments for the school (sometimes enclosing a copy of the NCCC's report), emphasizing the dearth of training available in the state for high school age students, and seeking the reasonable and most rewarding stance for all concerned:

> We will need to approach the situation creatively and see [the school] as a companionable institution to those now in existence, not as an enemy at the gate and not as a duplicate of something we already have.
>
> . . . you are opposing a School which you might want to support.
> I find much misunderstanding in Greensboro about this matter. I judge from the many letters I have received that the misunderstandings are widespread and are uniform, and I judge also from the mail that there is no such set of misunderstandings in any other city or town in the State. Please read the enclosed material . . . and then let me know if the School is really a duplicate of any now in existence and if it is, indeed, not needed by our people, particularly its high school aspects.
>
> I don't know that either one of us can see in any truly comprehensive way the needs of the whole State and region, but we must try to do so. I respectfully submit to you that competition does not depress the arts and it does not destroy healthy situations; it causes the whole situation to grow stronger.
> Certainly the high school aspects of the program—and I am one of

the many people who believe that the high school aspect should be the larger part of it—will not hurt you; it ought to help you. The college program will be divided among three or more art forms and will not be large in any one, and when one thinks in terms not only of the whole State but of the whole region, the competitive situation doesn't strike me as being desperate.

You are a teacher and I respect that. Let us work to do what is best for the State and region, and most of all for the students, and with every intention of assisting, not harming, existing institutions. . . .

A storm has arisen in Greensboro which clouds everything. There is a great deal of animosity, and it might be too late for the Greensboro people to want to work with us. As for myself, I lean toward cooperation and I assure you that no commitments have as of this time been made concerning the site for the high school and college center which has been proposed.[25]

Working vigorously behind the scenes, John Ehle left the Greensboro fracas in the soothing hands of the governor—"your judgment is going to be far better than my own." As Ehle passed along another letter from the opposition, he grumbled, "I never know what to do with a group as unpredictable as the Greensboro one." On other fronts, however, Ehle proceeded without hesitation. He saw that a copy of Harriet Doar's May 19 article on the school in the *Charlotte Observer* was sent to each legislator with a note from the governor. He kept a weather eye on possible contenders for Ford's arts funding in other areas of the South—"On night before last [May 13]," he informed the governor, "600 citizens of Huntsville, Alabama agreed to raise $6,000,000 to build a cultural center . . . gives us immediate sharp competition." He sent persuasive ammunition and suggestions to Hugh Cannon. "The point . . . to make with the Republican leadership is that an arts project ought not to be a political issue at all . . . if [the Republicans] will get behind this project . . . they will serve the arts in our State well for now and later." To help Cannon provide convincing statistical evidence of the "smallness of existing programs," Ehle sent along the latest edition of *Earned Degrees Conferred*, with a memo referencing the page numbers of the North Carolina tabulations and a summary comment on the state's national standing: "In all these, we rank very low by any comparison. If our music and drama programs were doubled, we would still rank below the national average. In terms of our population, we rank behind neighboring states and far behind some southern states such as

Florida and Texas in the percentage of our college degrees which go to music and drama."[26]

While Hugh Cannon and Governor Sanford concentrated on the political battle in North Carolina, John Ehle was fighting for the school on two fronts, at home and in New York, with the "unnamed Foundation." Recognizing that the press in both places was their strongest ally, Ehle worked for national publicity, even as he stayed in close communication with the state's major newspapers. At least as early as April 26, the May 19 feature articles in the *Charlotte Observer* had been planned, with the able connivance of editor and conservatory committee member Pete McKnight. Also in late April, Ehle was able to offer a thirty-five-hundred-word story on the school by a Raleigh writer to the executive news editor of the *Winston-Salem Journal-Sentinel*. Keeping a good press for the school seems never to have left his thoughts; on May 17 calling from California to dictate a letter to his secretary Lois Haswell, Ehle thought to leave a reassuring message for the governor about the Sunday editions in Charlotte and Raleigh: "We will get a good deal of support from these papers and their articles doubtless will be used in some of the other papers as well."[27] Ehle took every opportunity to promote the new performing arts school with the fourth estate. In April he had lunch with Arthur Gelb of the *New York Times* and talked about the arts in North Carolina and "what we were trying to do in the Governor's office." In June he met with a reporter from *Arts Management,* a New York news service for people involved in financing and managing the arts. Through Paul Green, he was able to approach Richard Coe of the *Washington Post* with a long letter explaining that the North Carolina approach would avoid ending up with an excess of artist-hungry cultural centers: "Unless the world decides to turn upside down [this bill] ought to go on through. . . . It was the Commission's feeling, and it is Governor Sanford's, that a professional training school is the best place for us to start putting down footings for the cultural development of this area."[28] Ehle's letter was printed in Coe's June 13 column, "One on the Aisle—N.C. Voting on Arts Aid."

On June 10, the *Raleigh News and Observer* carried a brief item, noting that the Joint Appropriations Subcommittee, working under "new secrecy rules," had approved $325,000 for a school of the performing arts. The subcommittee had met in executive session. "We didn't have any problems with sunshine laws and all that," Hugh Cannon recalls, "and we carved the melon pretty much the way we wanted it, and Tom [White] got it through that committee," along with Judge David Britt:

BRITT: After the bill was resurrected from the House—the Calen-
           dar Committee—it then went to the Appropriations Sub-
           committee. I was chairman of the House Committee on
           Appropriations, and, of course, co-chairman of the sub-
           committee, and Tom White from Kinston was my counter-
           part in the Senate. So we convened the subcommittee . . .
           and had very little trouble with [the bill]. . . . When it was
           found out that the governor was very much for it, and
           wanted it so badly, and we *did* have a little money, we
           voted it out of there. . . . There's a little preface that needs
           to be made here about this whole thing, which shows how
           badly that Governor Sanford wanted this proposition. . . .
                The practice over in the legislature at that time was—
           and as far as I know it still is—that no what we call "spe-
           cial" appropriations bills would be considered until after
           general appropriations bills had been passed by the House
           and by the Senate. That was necessary, to pass those which
           dealt with the total operation of the state government, as
           well as funding capital improvements projects and all that
           sort of thing. It was just necessary to get those, what we
           call the "big" bills, out before you would know if there
           was going to be any money left to use on these "special"
           appropriations bills.
                All right. The governor had the foresight to fight off a
           number of things that would come under the head of gen-
           eral appropriations, and I remember very definitely, sala-
           ries, for instance. State employees, they got very little that
           year, in 1963. And the money was a little bit tight, because
           we were having to continue the big surge in education
           spending that the governor had brought about during
           1961—and rightfully so. That year, of course, we voted the
           food tax, so to speak, sales tax on food, and got a lot
           more money . . . money for public education just got a
           big shot in the arm as a result of it.
                Of course, in '63 we didn't have any new money coming
           in, that is, new sources of revenue, so we had to really
           watch the general appropriations bills in order to have
           anything left for these special bills.
                But I think that needs to be said, because [Governor

Sanford] had to incur the wrath of a lot of people in order
to keep the money from being spent for general appropriations—in order to save it to the end so that there would
be some for these special projects that he was so interested
in. . . . He laid the groundwork when he tried to hold
back some of the expenditures in general appropriations.
That was the roughest day's work I ever did in my life,
and Ben [Roney] was right there when he had the general
appropriations bill, and the state employees were doing
their best to get an amendment to it, you know, to get
more money.

RONEY: Well, nobody thought *this* bill could be passed.

BRITT: The state employees—that was the reason this bill wasn't
even mentioned, because, I mean, the school of performing arts? But the governor had it in the back of his mind,
holding back, to hold back some money, and then he was
going to come forward with these special projects he was
asking for.

True to his election promises of 1960, Governor Sanford held back money
from general appropriations in 1963 so as to fund his special education
projects: for the establishment of "Statewide educational television,"
$1,500,000; for a "More Diversified and Comprehensive Program of In-
struction in Industrial Education" in the public school system, $1,500,000;
for a "Program to Deal with the Problem of Mental Retardation in This
State," $1,822,652; for the purpose of "Establishing and Equipping Com-
munity Colleges," state matching funds up to $2,500,000; for a perform-
ing arts school in North Carolina, $325,000.

RONEY: All I know is, nobody knew anything about it.

BRITT: I didn't, until maybe the bill was introduced, or about the
time it was introduced, or until after you had resurrected it
out of the Calendar Committee, and it got over there. He
either called a bunch of us that were on the subcommittee
over to the mansion, or to the Capitol, or he came down
there—I don't remember which it was—but he really made
a forceful plea for it, and we went along with it.

ZINN: Was there agreement pretty much on keeping money for
these special bills?

BRITT: Well, so many folks had their pet projects, legislators . . .

for instance, the representatives from Chowan County.
There are a couple of houses down there that they've been
trying to restore for thirty years, you know, and every session of the legislature they want ten or fifteen thousand
more dollars to go into it.

RONEY: Small appropriations.

BRITT: That's right. And then, the Roan Mountain Festival up in
Mitchell County. We had a Democrat in the House that
year, from Mitchell County, the first one since the Civil
War, and there hadn't been one since.

RONEY: Had to give him something.

BRITT: Oh, yeah . . . Ernest Poteat, his last name was Poteat. I
believe his given name was Ernest. And there are just a
bunch of those little things. And Wilmington down there,
they were trying to get money that year for the Battleship
North Carolina, and for the sound and light feature for the
battleship. And for a number of these—like Old Brunswick
Town. Odel Williamson was trying, wanted to restore Old
Brunswick Town.

RONEY: Oh, he's always after it.

BRITT: And more money for Fort Fisher, and—you know—you
have ten or twelve or fifteen or maybe more of those special
appropriations bills. Well, that's what we argued to the legislature. Well, we got to hold back some money for these
other bills.

ZINN: That must have been a drop in the bucket, compared to
general appropriations.

RONEY: Oh, hell, it was. General appropriations, the state, the
whole budget that year was well in excess of a billion dollars . . . so it wasn't a big deal, you know. But still, passions
could get pretty high sometimes over small things.[29]

The approved appropriation for the new school of performing arts was
small enough—$75,000 for fiscal year 1963–64 and $250,000 for 1964–65—
and guarded. The bill had been amended to read that the state funds were
contingent on "receipt of a firm commitment for the gift of matching
funds from other sources." The *Raleigh Times* reported that the announcement of such a grant was "expected shortly," a reflection of the determinedly optimistic stance adopted by Sanford, Ehle, Cannon, and others

of the governor's staff, rather than any change in the facts.[30] Although the impression given in the news throughout this time was that a grant from the Ford Foundation was expected, John Ehle was scrupulous in his own presenting of the situation, as his letter to Senator Wilbur Jolly, written before the debate in the Senate, reveals:

Hugh Cannon left word on Friday that you would like to have information about foundation interest in the proposed performing arts school. . . .

[Governor Sanford] has talked with officials of [a national] foundation on four different occasions about this project. It is his impression that the foundation will support the proposed school. *We have no definite commitment and won't have any until the location, name and other features of the school are decided upon.*

We have competition from other places in the South for the support of this particular foundation, which expects to be able to support only one such training center in the South. Atlanta is most anxious to win the support. . . . The competition is heavy, but it is our opinion that we are going to win, provided this bill passes. If it doesn't pass, we will not be able to get our part of the money. . . .

To cover ourselves, in case we fail with this particular foundation, we have approached two others to see if they would consider the matter, and both have indicated interest. None will help us, however, unless we participate ourselves.

Of the three foundations contacted in all, one has made a five-year study of the arts in America, and all three are familiar with conditions existing in the South. All three feel that the proposed professional training school is needed in the South, and all three of them are pleased with the high school—college plan recommended by the North Carolina Conservatory Committee. By congregating a portion of the top talent of the region, they agree that we can attract a portion of the top faculty members of the country, and begin in the South a school of excellence that will attract national standing quite soon. . . .

If you need any further information, please phone me. I will be happy to meet with you today, if you like. In the opinion of many people high up in the arts, this is the most important arts bill before any Legislature in the country—now or in recent years.[31]

On Monday night, June 17, the 113th legislative day of the 1963 General Assembly, Senator Tom White introduced Senate Bill 396. As expected, the bill passed easily—"Most of our bills," Judge Britt explains, "we wound through the Senate first, because Tom White, if he was for a bill, there was no problem in the Senate." John Ehle remembers Hugh Cannon that night,

> standing in the doorway, leaning halfway in and halfway out. He wasn't supposed to be in, you know, not on the floor. He could be in the committee meetings, I think, but not on the floor. And he was damn near in . . . I don't think Clarence Stone [Speaker of the Senate because the lieutenant governor had died in office] was for the art school, but he was that night for it. "We've got a lot more to do tonight, let's move along, we call for the vote"—and he just banged it on through.[32]

Ehle and Giannini had watched the Senate debate from the crowded gallery, Giannini wearing "his immutable expression" and his tam. Senators White and Humber spoke in favor of the bill, but Senator Clyde Propst of Cabarrus County sounded an ominous note when he rose to blast the school in a floor speech which the outraged *Charlotte Observer* described as the kind of talk that would get North Carolina "branded as a state of clods, as a modern day survival of Tobacco Road, and as the ignorant doormat of the nation." Senator Propst said that if one of his boys came to him, "and said to me, 'Daddy, I want to learn the ballet but there is no institution for me in North Carolina,' I'd say, yes there is—it's right out there at Dix Hill [the state mental institution]." Propst argued that to spend money on the arts in the face of mental patients' needs was "sick, sadistic, barbaric." Senator Jolly defended the bill, pointing out that the state had "provided adequately" for retarded children and now "owed it to talented people to establish this school for them." The next day Vittorio Giannini wired McNeil Lowry: "I was in Raleigh last night and witnessed the Senate pass the performing arts bill."[33]

Judge Britt has described the character of the legislature that year as "reactionary." The 1963 General Assembly, for example, passed the infamous Speaker Ban Law, which prohibited known communists from speaking on the campus of a state-supported school.[34] And the most conservative members were concentrated in the House. Knowing the dangers the school was likely to face, Governor Sanford had called on Sam Ragan—unofficially— and on Ben Roney, his director of secondary roads, to ensure the passage of the bill: "So I said to him, meaning a pun, and not intentionally a very clever one, 'Ben, I want you to pave the way for this school.'" Hugh Cannon explains what Sanford meant: "Ben was the czar of secondary roads.

The governor actually had the ability to give out secondary roads wherever he wanted to, but as a practical matter, Ben decided where they went, and Ben could give out more goodies just about, than anybody else in the legislature."[35]

Joe Doster has remarked that nobody would have believed that Ben Roney would support an arts school, and Roney concurs: "Well, you can imagine how amazed I was when Terry put me on *that* thing. Of course, I found out why he did, because I was the only one had anything left to trade. . . . I can tell you my reaction when he told me about it. I just said, "Are you kidding?" . . . I wasn't even in favor of it. I mean, it was all right with me—the man said to go down and do it, and he was my boss but hell, it sounded kind of silly to me." Roney and Ragan sat down together and divided up the work: "Ben and I started almost immediately going over names of every legislator. Ben knew all of them, and I knew a few, and I talked to the ones that I knew best. And I called their friends back home who knew them better, and they also did some talking. And I called the wives of several legislators, and enlisted their support. And each day Ben and I would check off the list." With Sam Ragan working persuasively in the background, Ben Roney held back the roads in Raleigh until he figured he couldn't get there any other way. Gordon Hanes recalls that Roney "went around to all the country representatives. And he said, 'Now you know highway 67 runs through your area, and you promised you would get that paved if they reelected you and they did, and you want to run again. Let me tell you, I am going to be sitting in the gallery and we are going to call for the ayes and noes, and I promise you, if you don't vote for this school, route 67 won't get paved until the year 2000.' And he meant it too; he wasn't kidding." One legislator stubbornly opposed the school on the grounds that it would be racially integrated. Roney reportedly replied, "Well, that's damn unfortunate. We might just have to build a by-pass around your little town." And he got the vote. "All kinds of little North Carolina communities have got secondary roads today because of the school of the arts," Terry Sanford admits. By the end of the first day of vigorous lobbying, members of the General Assembly were undoubtedly pleased with themselves for having dubbed the unlikely lobbyist "Maestro Roney." He "talked about it in terms of raw politics," says Joe Doster. "The silent truth is that he loved what was being done, and felt a deep pride in it. . . . He will argue that he would have made the same effort for a fertilizer plant, but that's simply not true. In his own way, Ben Roney, too, was a visionary."[36]

On June 20, the night before the vote was to come up in the House, Ben Roney called Sam Ragan. "We've got it," he said. But the governor wasn't sure:

> I remember so well. I wasn't at all sure the night before. I never was sure the night before that anything was going to pass. It was always a risk. And for something like this, a special risk because it was so vulnerable to ridicule. It was very easy to see how this just might be laughed out of the legislative halls.
>
> No other state was supporting such a school. Some advisers thought that the legislators would feel that it was not a worthy project, and surely not a necessary one. It was certain that if we went to the legislature and failed we would eliminate all hope of foundation support. The plan would be dead.
>
> I decided to take the chance. I remember a response John Motley Morehead had made to critics who, when he gave the University of North Carolina a multimillion-dollar planetarium, complained that he should have provided instead for some of the more essential building needs. "Let the legislature mend the University's pants," he told them. "I am going to buy it a new top hat." I had a hunch that when the legislators had finished mending the state's pants they would be willing to buy a top hat. We went to the legislature.[37]

On the motion of Representative David Britt of Robeson County, House Bill 791 had been placed on the calendar for the full House that Thursday, June 20. The next day, it reached the floor of the House, where opponents led off the debate, "as many smiled, others talked and some read newspapers," the *Charlotte Observer* reported. One representative, I. C. Crawford of Buncombe County, "entered a door next to where the newsmen sat and struck a ballet pose with his hand daintily on his head." Judge Britt and Ben Roney recall that Phil Godwin from Gates County "started off as the leader of the opposition," calling it the "toe-dancin'" bill, a term of derision that had lately come into general use around the legislature. Hugh Cannon thinks that the term originated, ironically, with one of the performing arts school's supporters, Senator Tom White, "when John Jordan, about two sessions earlier, had introduced a bill for a school of ballet or a North Carolina Ballet Company, or something like that, and John Jordan on the floor of the Senate had defended his bill, and Tom White had risen to ask if the Senator would yield . . . and Tom said, 'Senator Jordan, do boys do that—that toe dancing?' . . . and that came back to haunt us in 1963." The opposition immediately brought up issues that had been raised by officials at the Woman's College. Scotland Representative Roger Kiser read letters against the school written by faculty members at Greensboro and at St. Andrews College. Representative George Uzzell of Rowan County read a letter from Catawba College, arguing that the conservatory concept was obsolete. Robert Calder of New Hanover charged that the new school would "dry up cultural development all over North Carolina," that the education to be offered would be too narrow, and that the idea was "expensive, experimental, untried and unknown." "It is a bad bill," he said, and to complete its damnation, observed that the bill was one in which "the executive branch of this government has been extremely interested."[38]

"The thing could have gone either way," Judge Britt remembers:

BRITT: Ben and Hugh Cannon and other members of the governor's staff had really worked hard the night before.

RONEY: No, Hugh wasn't even in town. ["I was at that point in the National Guard," Cannon says, in Charlottesville.]

BRITT: He wasn't?

ZINN: Joel Fleishman, maybe?

BRITT: It's possible.

RONEY: Well, Joel, Joel was considered in the hippy group.

BRITT: Well, anyhow, Ben and somebody else [Sam Ragan] . . . they had really worked on it. They had covered the waterfront talkin' to the House members and trying to line up support. But even then, it was touch and go . . . and I knew that one of the most conservative members of the House—and probably as reactionary a member of the House as there was—was Representative John Kerr from over in Warren County. And he had served as Speaker of the House in 1943, and had been back and served quite a bit since that time.

RONEY: Incidentally—interrupt you a minute—he also was the man who put that bill through for the art museum.

BRITT: And he had been the father of the legislation making appropriations for the art museum back in the '50s some time [1949] and had gotten a lot of favorable acclaim for that. So the night before, or maybe the morning before, the morning that it was coming up, I talked to John about this thing, and I didn't get much satisfaction out of him.

He didn't promise me he would or he wouldn't. But the line of my talking, my efforts, were that, "John, you made history for yourself when you became the father, in effect, of the North Carolina Museum of Art, which placed North Carolina out to itself as a leader among the states in the Southeast." And I said, "You have a further chance now to help do the same thing, and I want to know if I can count on you."

He said, "Well, I'll have to think about it." He didn't give me any satisfaction.

RONEY: . . . and I went to see him, with his wife sitting there with him, and told him if he would make the speech on the floor of the House—I said, "John, you haven't had your picture in the *News and Observer* this whole session. If you'd make this speech, and go along with David, and support this thing, and you make a powerful speech, I guarantee that that picture will be on the front page on the left hand column of the *News and Observer* the next morning." . . . But before I made that commitment, I called Sam Ragan, and Sam was managing editor of the *News and Observer,* and Sam is an arts man, you know, he was interested in it, too, and told Sam if I could get John to agree to make that speech, would he put the picture up there? And he said that he would. And you know, I went back and told you that John had agreed to do it!

BRITT: Then, when the debate started, he kept hanging back, he kept hanging back. And a bunch of folks started wanting to be recognized, either on one side or the other. And I remember Representative Dan Simpson from Burke County, Republican, he got up and made one of the most sarcastic speeches against it that you could possibly hear. I'm quite sure it was—it was Dan.[39]

Simpson, chairman of the Joint Republican Caucus in the legislature, had complained that he was "against all this spending. I just don't think we ought to spend money to learn people to pick banjers and toe-dance, and sing in foreign languages. . . . If we have money to spend, we should make it possible for everyone to get a low-cost college education. I don't think we should use it to turn out people like Liz Taylor and Richard Burton."[40]

Supporters countered by emphasizing the importance of culture, which had manifestations perhaps more significant than the stars of *Cleopatra*. Representative Alden Baker of Pasquotank pointed out that "this could make our state not only the educational and scientific center of the Southeast, but the cultural center as well." Representative David Britt said that the school would help North Carolina shed its label of "a vale of humility" and that it offered "a unique opportunity" to the state to establish the first such school in the Southeast, "at comparatively little cost."[41] As the debate continued, Representative Britt "eased around" to John Kerr:

BRITT: I eased up there to John. He was sitting down there about five seats ahead of me . . . and I said, "John, we need your help, and we need it now! I sure hope you'll help us."

He says, "Well, you reckon the Speaker would recognize me?" 'cause four or five would jump up every time anybody would sit down, wanting recognition. I says, "He'll recognize you."

So I eased right on up there to Cliff Blue, he was favorable to it. I told Cliff, "When John Kerr rises, please recognize him above everybody else." And I walked on back to my seat. And that old John lumbered up, and, uh— "Mr. Speaker!" And by God, he got recognition!

RONEY: I said, "Thank God!"

BRITT: Well, sir, we have speakers' microphones over there on the desk, that you're supposed to talk into, and the rules of the House provide that the members shall stay at their seats when they're addressing the House. But John wouldn't use that microphone. He had a voice that you could hear all over the place in there. And then, he had to get up and walk the aisles.

Well, some of these folks that spoke against it were way on the other side of the House, toward the back. And he actually got out of his seat when he got warmed up, and got in the middle aisle of the House. He just—he started going up there, and he got within almost touching Dan Simpson, as I recall. And he says, "MR. SIMPSON! You referred to it as a toe-dancin' bill." He said, "I don't know of anybody that's done more toe-dancin' around here in this legislature than *you* have." And he took off on several things, positions that Dan had taken that were a little bit inconsistent, you know, and it was—it was awful.

And then he turned around and headed toward Phil
Godwin. Phil had made the speech, and old Phil was
turnin' his back on him. He didn't want to face him.

RONEY: *Phil* was a toe-dancin' man. I mean, he was the one that
was giving us hell.

BRITT: Oh, he was the first one to speak out. Well, sir, John was
going so strong, and the members of the House were eatin'
it up, especially these boys from the small counties. Well,
Representative Rachel Davis, a medical doctor from Kinston—fine lady, she was so interested in this thing—and she
had been trying to get recognition. Well, we knew that
that would hurt . . . if she spoke [because] the thing had
its best chance after John Kerr got through. So, I don't
know whether I went around to see her, or whether I sent
somebody. But I told her to please not speak, that we
thought that we were ready for a vote when John Kerr
had finished.[42]

John Kerr was coming to the end with a flourish, in the tradition of the
great stem-winding orators of the Old South. "Man cannot live by bread
alone," he cried in ringing tones. "We brag about our industry, our great
industrial structure, but we are after all human beings and in the breasts of
all of us beats the same kind of heart. . . . Now, some of you have ridiculed
this legislation as a toe-dancin' bill," he said, surveying the assemblage, a
threat to swoop down on any inattentive legislator in his stunned audience. Then, striking a pose, he concluded in a mighty voice—"Well, if
there's going to be toe-dancin', I want to be there"[43]—and the moment
was immortalized, as promised, on the front page of the *Raleigh News and
Observer,* in the left-hand column, John Kerr, captured in midflight, his
right arm flung up and outward, his index finger pointing to the heavens,
his "gesture for culture," as the picture was captioned, virtually jumping
off the page in all its stentorian splendor.

RONEY: The minute he sat down, you called for previous question.

BRITT: I think—I think we called for previous question, and—

RONEY: That means cutting off debate.

BRITT: —the motion was carried, and we took the vote, and it
passed by a very comfortable majority. But it was one of
the most dramatic moments that I ever spent in the
legislature.

RONEY: No question.

ZINN: What was the feeling right after Kerr sat down? Was there any cheering or anything?

RONEY: No—it was done!

ZINN: You could hear a pin drop?

BRITT: The opposition was completely floored . . . old Phil Godwin was just sittin' there shakin' his head like that, as much to say, "Well, how in the heck are we going to fight anything like this, when the most conservative member of the House has taken the position he has, and put such feeling into it?"

ZINN: Besides saying a "toe-dancin'" school, what were their objections?

RONEY: Well, you see, they had it the "toe-dancin'" school, and I told them it wasn't just "toe-dancin'," it's "toe-dancin'" and "flute-tootin'." You can't toe-dance without having music, boys. In other words, we kind of laughed it through, didn't we?

BRITT: We presented the positive side, and that was that you just have any number of high school students in the tenth and eleventh grade that are just absolutely not interested in the academics, but they have great talent in some form of music. . . . Well, I had a little reservation about it right at first, but after the governor explained the reasoning behind it, and I'd seen—I'd seen kids down in Robeson County with, you know, just outstanding talent, and no way in the world to develop it. And then when I found out how much private money was going into it—the state was just putting in a comparatively small amount—I had no trouble with it.

RONEY: I've got a granddaughter that's a junior now in that school, so it finally got around to where I'm benefitting from it.

BRITT: In the long term.

ZINN: It seems to me that there were a lot of in-between people, that it didn't really concern them either way. . . .

RONEY: They didn't understand it, that was the main thing. You had to explain it to them.

The bill passed the House 80 to 18.[45] The vote was reported erroneously the next day in the *Greensboro Daily News* as having been 70 to 36. "I suppose they feel that numbers don't really matter," John Ehle wrote to Pete McKnight. "*The Chapel Hill Weekly* reported . . . that the appropriation somehow got through and was for a *study*. Any ideas about what we ought to study, Pete?"[46]

4

A LOCAL

HABITATION AND

A NAME

And as imagination bodies forth
The forms of things unknown, the poet's pen
Turns them to shapes, and gives to airy nothing
A local habitation and a name.
A Midsummer-Night's Dream

Y THE time the summer of 1963 was drawing to a close, John Ehle had begun to feel a bit like the Light Brigade. "Sometime when we both have fewer things to do," he wrote McNeil Lowry, "I will tell you how it feels to have a Governor on one side, 3 Mayor's Committees at my rear, artists on all sides, and way off—the Ford Foundation." In his inimitable fashion, Lowry was holding firm, a staunch ally of the school—and cold comfort:

> You seem to believe that the first thing is to get a campus in order to meet the North Carolina situation. You will have to go ahead to do that without any commitment from us. . . . In fact, our potential assistance to a conservatory in the Southeast may not involve any assistance whatsoever to a campus or capital construction. And since we do not know whether we are interested in one in North Carolina or elsewhere in the Southeast until we see what kind of artistic personnel and program can be promised, our interest in location within a given Southeastern state is academic and unimportant. I am always available to [Giannini] or to you if we're talking about the core of the school and its professional potential. I believe you will have to develop the financial and matching details and all those other things without us, at least until after December.[1]

In other words, no but yes.

This frustrating colloquy with the Ford Foundation had begun only two weeks after the conservatory bill had passed the state legislature. On July 4, Henry Heald, president of the Ford Foundation, and three of his officers (Paul Ylvisaker, Henry Saltzman, and Lester Nelson) arrived in Raleigh to meet with Governor Sanford, who at that time had three proposals before the foundation. John Ehle picked the visitors up at the airport and took them to the Downtowner Motor Inn, the only integrated hotel in Raleigh at that time. "In the suite we began at once talking business," Ehle recalls. Although Heald was in somewhat of a "grumpy" humor, according to Pete McKnight, he told Ehle that "he had not come all the way down to Raleigh to say no," that two of the governor's projects would be funded. "Well, that's wonderful," Ehle replied. "What about the arts school?"

> "No, no," he said, "Not this time round, maybe later."
>
> I said, "We have to match this $325,000 from the state or we can't spend it, and we must somehow or other get this school started. We have a lot of problems and need the money."
>
> He said, "Well, maybe in a year—when you get the school going."
>
> I said, "We—you know, we made a public statement about this school. Now, we didn't mean to put your name in it, but that sneaked in. It's a known school. The Tippy-Toe School is known from one end of this state to the other. The Governor is standing out there in public, expecting to see this school open."
>
> Mr. Heald said he was sorry.
>
> I took a chance—a dangerous thing to do with Mr. Heald, whom I scarcely knew, but I reasoned leaving the matter right there was going to be a disaster for us. So I said, "Mr. Heald, I told the Governor the other day that the Ford Foundation might not give us the money and asked him what we were going to do if Ford didn't. And the Governor at once looked up from his desk and said, "If they don't give us the money, don't invite them to the opening."

Heald laughed till he cried, McKnight remembers, and asked to hear more about the arts school. John Ehle's quick reaction had changed the mood of the meeting.[2]

Anxiety was mounting in the Governor's Office. In a letter of warm appreciation to Martha Muilenburg for her "fine contribution" as chair of the North Carolina Conservatory Committee, Sanford expressed his own commitment and hopes and an undercurrent of worry: "I hold for this new venture every confidence. Perhaps at this point we have less reason for confidence than for concern, but I think in the heart of this new School there has been planted real strength, maybe greatness. It will not fail us, and we will not, and I know you will not, fail it." Realistically, there was pressing need to arrange for the school's opening before Governor Sanford left office. Otherwise, the project would "lose the considerable advantage which the personal interest of a Governor gives a State project," Ehle pointed out to Lowry after talking with Henry Heald. They had discussed the governor's "hopes [that the school's] design and needs could be arranged for expeditiously—here, and at the Ford Foundation, and in the city which is selected to provide the campus. . . . It would be very much to the School's advantage if we could make progress on all three fronts, and if the three fronts could move along more or less together." Ehle felt acutely the weakness of their position in asking North Carolina's cities "to mount a drive for a campus and buildings, or even to arrange temporary quarters for the School" until it was clear how "money [is to be] obtained for its operation." A month later, in a lengthy communication detailing the history of the project and its current status, Governor Sanford pleaded urgency to Lowry in a letter he did not send: "Delay will endanger our budget and authorization. Allow me to help from the Governor's office. This is my last chance. . . . Please help and advise." He sent instead a shorter letter promising to forward more information on curriculum development and faculty and requesting a meeting in New York on October 16, to include Vittorio Giannini.[3]

Meanwhile, Ehle and Giannini were forced to juggle the problems of funding and finding a campus, selecting a faculty, working out a curriculum and budget, and choosing a Board of Trustees and an Advisory Board of Artists—all without assurance that Ford Foundation money would, indeed, be provided. Dovetailing these matters drew an uncharacteristically glum and laconic response from Ehle, who supposedly was sending good news to an American Fulbright scholar at the University of Cologne. The bill for a conservatory had passed, he wrote, but "now we are busy trying to figure out how to implement the plan, and that is, of course, where the cart begins to creak at every seam."[4]

The two artists divided the work of developing the school. They might have seemed an unlikely pair—one, a canny mountain man of southern Appalachia, a bred-in-the-bone horsetrader and shrewd judge of people; the other, an Italian from Philadelphia, with an uncanny ability to inspire and lead. Together they made a remarkably effective and complementary team. Ehle's primary task was to drum up interest all over North Carolina in providing a home for the school, and he emphasized its concrete needs—

buildings, land, and money—which, Ehle told the *Charlotte Observer,* would be sought by the governor's site committee. Described as "young, pipe-smoking, and practical," Ehle was a contrast to Vittorio Giannini, whose reply to the same question—what do you seek in a city?—was irresistibly quotable: "A faith in our youth and the talent of our youth. A realization of the place art has in our civilization."[5] These were Ehle's sentiments exactly, but wisely left to Vittorio:

> He seemed to like North Carolina, and North Carolina people well enough. He liked people, period. He had just worked on a study done by HEW on music in our public schools, and he had been absolutely horrified at what had been found . . . he thought it was a disaster. He wanted to do somthing for our children, and tears would literally come to everybody's eyes as they listened to Vittorio talk about our children. And then he would take out a big cigar and light it and sit there puffing on it. And he didn't even know our children.

During the development of the school, Giannini traveled back and forth, residing variously and seasonally in Brevard, Raleigh, and New York, but he and Ehle stayed in close touch:

> He was in the state during the summers, but the rest of the time he was in New York, and he found it difficult to get down here because he couldn't fly. There was an overnight train ride—in each direction, an overnight train. So he would come on that. . . . And I saw him sometimes in New York. We would go to dinner at the Stockholm, which was one of my favorite restaurants up there. We always, Vittorio and I, always went to the Stockholm. And back then, for a modest amount of money one could eat all the lobster he wanted, or all the shrimp, because they had a Swedish smorgasbord table and big piles of lobster and shrimp. So you'd just go right on up there and get what you wanted, and Vittorio loved to eat. He was a master at it. We would talk about the art school.

Looking back on the speed with which so many new projects came out of Sanford's office in the incredibly short period of eighteen months, Ehle pinpointed as a key element the philosophy behind his partnership with Giannini:

> One reason we were able to succeed so well—. . . I always gave everybody the distinct impression that I was not going to have anything to do with running these projects. That was true of the Film Board, that

was true of the Governor's School, it was true of the school of the arts, it was true of the North Carolina Fund, it was true of the Learning Institute of North Carolina, it was true of the Advancement School . . . I didn't want to run them, didn't want to be on the board, didn't want to be anything . . . always we were able to represent them without anybody feeling, he's trying to set up something for himself. . . . And we were also able to find the best person in the United States to do these things. And I don't happen to think I'm the best person in the United States to run a film board, or whatever.

So we were able to use Vittorio, to push him forward and say, Vittorio is the one who can run this . . . you asked me what I thought of Vittorio. I always thought he was the best thing we had going for us, because he was an artist, and we didn't have any other one . . . [when] Terry proceeded to have Vittorio nominated in his presence . . . [it was] about the only time I ever knew Vittorio to cry. He was good at making *other* people cry. . . . Vittorio was exceptional.[6]

The earliest reference on record to tapping Giannini as president of the new school occurs in the draft of a letter from Governor Sanford to McNeil Lowry, dated August 12, 1963. In a list of six points for Lowry's information in presenting the North Carolina request to Ford's trustees, item 4 states, "Giannini will . . . be a top administrator. . . . He seems to be willing." On September 27, Sanford officially brought the matter before Giannini, in a letter asking him to select nationally prominent artists to head the music and drama departments and to nominate, but not commit to, a "top ballet person":

I hope you realize how much I personally want you to be part of the School. You ought to be the chief designer and leader of it. Whether that means you want to be President (or Director) of the School, or Dean of the Faculty, I don't know. We can talk about this, too, and about the duties that will fall to each official. . . . Will you join us in this important enterprise? Rather, I should ask if you will continue to be with us as we go ahead. . . . We need you and want to work with you.[7]

Giannini needed no encouragement to labor mightily and wholeheartedly in the North Carolina cause; he was very much a part of the drive to open the school by September 1964. Already, in a July 4 letter to Lowry, Ehle had reported that a tentative curriculum for the music school had been worked out by Giannini.[8] Ehle had also asked the composer to evaluate the music program at the Governor's School. Giannini's reply is a pertinent articulation of the twin philosophy of training, which he would bring to the new school of performing arts:

> The young people brought together come from various communities, some of which without doubt have no concept of a high standard of achievement. That these youngsters be made aware of what high degree of excellence is necessary to achieve some standing in our society is perhaps one of the most valuable services the school performs. . . .
>
> It seems to me that certain fundamental knowledge is lacking. There is one answer: Supply it. There is no point in adding more advanced learning if basic knowledge is not there, or if present, inadequate. It is like adding more stories to a building whose foundations are weak or non existing. Sooner or later the whole structure will collapse and result in confusion.
>
> I suggest that they should not be concerned only in giving courses that look good on paper, but courses in which the youngster who needs it can be drilled in basic skills. In music courses such as: Sight-reading, sight-singing, ear training. Insist on these until the student develops a good ear and a facility in the reading of music. These skills are absolutely necessary; for an instrumentalist, a singer, conductor or composer must make use of these skills constantly. . . .
>
> Everywhere this lack is recognized but seldom is anything really constructive done about it. Mainly because they are not "glamour courses" or if given, not thorough enough and taught without imagination and thereby distasteful. . . . That Juilliard, a college level school, should find it necessary to give such basic elementary courses in music and also remedial English, for high school graduates and even for students who transfer from other colleges is an indictment of some of our schools and pro[ves] the need for such fundamental learning.[9]

Although curriculum and faculty development were Giannini's chief responsibilities, Ehle's office remained the central clearinghouse for all matters related to the development of the school, including staffing. Correspondence in the archives reveals as well that Giannini and John Ehle worked together on securing a faculty. The numerous letters which Governor Sanford received from applicants seeking a position at the new school were routed directly to John Ehle. His correspondence with most was noncommittal; he thanked them for their interest, promised to keep their applications on file for Giannini to review, and explained that hiring had not yet begun, although they hoped the school would open in the fall of 1964.

In actuality, the search for professional artists to fill the major positions at the school was going on in earnest. On October 4, Giannini wrote that he had talked with McNeil Lowry, who "was cheerful on the phone. No hitch so far. He said if we get stuck in the ballet end he'll give us several good teachers . . . he seemed glad we're keeping him informed." Throughout this period both Giannini and Ehle stayed in close touch with Lowry, especially on the matter of faculty selection, as Lowry had suggested (albeit obliquely) in his letter of August 8. He was apparently more explicit in a September conversation with Giannini, whose report on a recent visit with Lowry was "optimistic . . . Mac is ready to help gain the attention of key prospective faculty." This does not mean, however, that Lowry's candidates were uncritically accepted, nor is there any reason to believe that Lowry expected that they would be. At least one applicant was rejected outright by Ehle because his background was too academic—"he doesn't seem to me to ring true as a professional performer or director. I'm a bit baffled by this, as Lowry recommended him so highly," Ehle reported to Giannini.[10]

Letters between the two men indicate that they were in frequent congress about possible faculty members and that they acted as equal partners in seeking and selecting. Of an applicant in drama, Giannini commented, "He may be just the man we need . . . if you agree we both can talk to him." In October, Giannini wrote that he had contacted Leon Fleisher at Peabody and Ruggiero Ricci, both of whom seemed interested in the new school. Balanchine was out of the country, but Giannini expected to be able to talk to Lincoln Kirstein soon. For his part, Ehle had heard that "Agnes de Mille might be interested in making a change. . . . Wouldn't she be just the one for dance?" And over in Chapel Hill, he had made a point of meeting with British director Eric Salmon (of Theatre Outlook of England), who was then in residence at the university's Department of Radio, Television, and Motion Pictures. "Make use of me in any way that seems appropriate," Salmon responded. Together Ehle and Giannini met with Ruth R. Mayleas of the American National Theatre and Academy, who offered four ANTA services to help in starting the new school: a New York office for interviewing and auditioning, an artist and speaker program, a placement service, and a publications service.[11]

Meanwhile, the less glamorous task of contriving a budget had also to be attended to. On the fly to New Orleans, Ehle dropped a note to Vittorio, warning him that compared with other state schools the conservatory's tuition rate was too high. Alternatives were to charge a higher rate for out-of-state students, to charge a separate private-lesson fee, or to cut the budget. Otherwise, "we might run into stiff legislative opposition . . .

we want the [high] standard maintained. . . . Can this be done? . . . I'll smoke a cigar for you." Giannini responded the following week with a new budget that would allow the school to give scholarships to 40 percent of the students. This plan rested on the concept of endowed chairs for the major areas of study—"The Babcock Chair in Violin or the Duke Chair in voice . . . a permanent testimonial to the generosity of the donor. . . . Hope you enjoyed New Orleans, and the cigar." Cigars notwithstanding, Ehle and Giannini went on tossing budgets back and forth, incessantly, and for many months, insolubly. Too many factors had to be figured in; for example, there was the issue of the student body mix:

> We don't yet know what percentage of the students will be high school and what percentage college. We have been saying here in the office that most of the children would be pre-college. This made sense to us, because of the fact that the school will need to build on its own foundations, and because there is no other high school for residential students in these fields, except the one in Michigan, up in the woods [Interlochen]. . . . The number of students in each art form is something that has to be decided by the Board of Trustees. I would think the percentages you've outlined will do very well, but this isn't known securely enough for us to budget definite sums. The North Carolina high school students have to be admitted free. We don't know quite what it means in terms of room and board, but we know that no tuition can be charged North Carolina high school students. So that throws the thing off, too. I would say, therefore, we still have a severe money problem, and that the solution might be beyond us for now. . . . My hunch is we can't do much more than we've done until we find out where the school is to go and what relations it can work out with existing arts institutions.[12]

Efficient budgeting seemed to require siting the school as quickly and advantageously as possible, and siting the school advantageously quickly came down to a game of round robin. The legislature had made state funds dependent on the receipt of matching money from foundation sources; the chief foundation source was Ford, which, according to McNeil Lowry, almost certainly would not assist "whatsoever . . . a campus or capital construction." Therefore, the North Carolina city in which the school was located would have to provide land and buildings and proof that it could raise the money for any necessary renovations and additions. To do this, each city that wanted to be considered would have to embroil itself in complicated negotiations with city and county government, local school boards, local donors, and industry to prepare a proposal that could not be evaluated until the Board of Trustees and Advisory Board of Artists had been selected. But the governor was delaying the appointment of the Board of Trustees because, according to a mid-November report in the *Raleigh News and Observer,* "matching money" from a foundation source was not yet "in hand." As a result, "no firm offers" had yet come in from any North Carolina city as of December 30 because no Board of Trustees "to consider such offers" had been appointed. Truly, this was the house that Jack built—and no housing was too outlandish, unlikely, or notional for Jack to consider. Because at one point, "I was getting desperate, fellas," Ehle recalls. "I didn't have any place to put that school."[13]

In all fairness, it wasn't for want of anticipating the problem. One of Ehle's earliest memories of the genesis of the arts school idea goes back to the early spring of 1962, when it was associated in his mind with the Biltmore House in Asheville:

It was [after] the second dinner, when I was one of [Governor Sanford's] advisers . . . he asked me one more time to come to work for him, basing this on something that I still do not understand, because I'd been at two of his meetings and had not contributed anything. But I think he kind of likes that. . . . I said, "Well, Terry"—I mean Governor—"I don't have any idea at all except if we could get the Vanderbilt house in Asheville we could make one hell of an arts school out of it."

He says, "I'm going up there Friday, and you get on the plane."

I said, "You're going up where?"

He said, "I'm going to Asheville." So I got on the plane. . . .

So he went up there, and talked to Mr. Cecil, George Cecil about it—I think it was George; it could have been his brother—. . . We cornered him, got him out to the airport—Terry didn't have much time—we were going to found this damn school on the run. He got him back there in Arden, in the airport, in a little corner in the dining room, and asked him for the Vanderbilt house.

George wouldn't give it to him. I thought it was very narrow-minded of him. I sat there and listened to them. . . .

Cecil said . . . "Where would the students sleep?"

And we said, "The bedrooms." Terry turned to me and asked me where they'd sleep, and I said they'd sleep in the bedrooms.

George said, "Well, they leak, and the beds are old."

And I said, "Well, we'd get some new beds."

He said, "The kitchen doesn't function. Where would you cook?"

I said, "We'd fix the kitchen somehow or another. There's bound to
be a place for a kitchen in that thing."

Well, this was the first effort to start what was called an arts school.[14]

Neither George Cecil nor (possibly) his brother succeeded in curing
John Ehle of his desire to house the new conservatory at a private estate.
Such quarters offered too many appealing quirks: "I asked Charlie Babcock . . . if we could have Reynolda for the conservatory. A glint of interest
came in his eye. 'It's got one of the finest organs in the world already in it,'
he said. . . . The house has an olympic-size swimming pool indoors. . . . It
also has a bowling alley, greenhouse, shooting gallery. . . . We would have
the only conservatory with a shooting gallery."[15] The shooting gallery may
have suggested new directions. Ehle recalls talking about the arts school
with the head of the North Carolina prison department. The state at that
time was closing prisons, and Ehle, as always, was prepared to seize the
day. No suitable prisons were available, however, in a population center that could supply audiences. But ever undeterred in the face of overwhelming opportunity, John Ehle remained alert, to improve the shining
hour at the 1964 New York World's Fair. Sometime during the peak of the
activity surrounding the effort to find a location for the school (November
1963–April 1964), John Ehle persuaded Governor Sanford to acquire an
option for the state on the fair's cubistic Tower of Light. The idea had been
to house the new performing arts school in the building, but that, not surprisingly proved "impractical"; according to *Newsweek*, the price for moving
it would be $500,000. "Sometimes," the magazine quoted Ehle as saying,
"you get a bird and you look around to find him a birdhouse. We've got a
birdhouse, but we don't know where the damn bird is."[16]

John Ehle's flexibility on the issue of housing a school for the arts was as
broad as it was high, ranging from religious retreats in the western part of
the state to a military installation on the coast. Anticipating that one of the
competing cities might not be able to provide a permanent site for the
school by September of 1964, Ehle began looking into the possibility of
temporary housing for a preliminary two-year period. Ridgecrest Baptist
Assembly, in the mountains near Asheville, was not winterized, he learned,
but the Methodist camp at Lake Junaluska farther west seemed likely, especially because Giannini had visited and found it "quite adequate." James
Fowler, superintendent of the assembly, the trustees, and staff all thought
the "plan for the School . . . is a wonderful one," as Fowler wrote in a
warm response to Ehle's suggestion. The buildings, however, were a cooler
proposition. They had no heat, as winterizing had proven too expensive to

pursue. From the opposite end of the state came another creative suggestion: the town of Edenton had been deeded a military installation in the Albemarle Sound area. The list of facilities surely must have piqued Ehle's flagrant imagination, for intact on the site were a chapel, gym, pool, barracks, and an airport; North Carolina would have the only conservatory with its own airport.[17]

But the new school needed more than buildings, land, a shooting gallery, and an airport. The conservatory needed money, as Ehle had succinctly pointed out in Charlotte, and the students needed audiences before whom they could perform frequently. Gradually it became evident that only four North Carolina cities were in a position—and of a mind—to give both tangible and intangible support. Surprisingly, Durham was not among them. In fact, it scarcely entered the lists. In January of 1964, Mary D. B. T. Semans wrote to John Ehle, asking him to meet with the Long-Range Planning Committee of the Durham Chamber of Commerce: "They are fully aware of Durham's dilatory behavior in the past, but they want to make sure of whether or not anything further can be done." Ehle met with the committee on February 12, and chairman E. J. Evans promised to set up a committee to present Durham's case at the March 17 meeting. Although the *Durham Morning Herald* supported the idea of bidding for the school, the paper carelessly reported that Durham was the only major city that had not made an official bid (Asheville, for example, had never even formed a committee) and listed as among the competitors Southern Pines, which had essentially dropped out by November of 1963. (Southern Pines had expressed an early interest in providing a home for the school and had sent a small committee to make a presentation at the last meeting of the North Carolina Conservatory Committee, on March 15, 1963.)[18] Durham never bid for the conservatory, however, although the city could provide a broad audience, with Duke University in town and nearby, the University of North Carolina at Chapel Hill, and the state capital and another major branch of the university at Raleigh. Durham offered only a plan to locate the school in the Research Triangle Park, but the Advisory Board of Artists felt that the school might be "smothered" under "too much chemistry over there" (as Sidney Blackmer expressed it).[19] More significantly, the city offered no buildings and no money.[20]

Undoubtedly the most aesthetically appealing plan was presented by the town of Hillsborough, which quixotically remained in the bidding for the school to the very end, though it was never able to raise the necessary financial support. The 1963 General Assembly, which had approved the bill creating a state-supported conservatory, had also established the Historic

Hillsborough Commission, to direct the restoration of the once important colonial village. Predictably, John Ehle was struck by the possibilities, and in October of 1963, on the way to view a possible site in Winston-Salem with a professor of architecture from North Carolina State University, Ehle suggested a tour of Hillsborough. Professor Harris was impressed, even excited, and agreed to have his class in design undertake the project of planning a campus for the new school. With a population of 1,349, the town was small enough that it could be completely identified with the conservatory. And as the *News of Orange County* pointed out, the school would make an ideal industry for the beautiful old town. Hillsborough's historic courthouse could become the school's theater; two hundred students or more could be housed and fed in private homes; and a large tract of private property was for sale just east of the town, where three classroom buildings could be constructed, looking out over woods and fields to the hills on the other side of the Eno River. Audiences could be drawn from Durham, Chapel Hill, Raleigh, and even Greensboro, less than an hour away, making Hillsborough's rural location less of a drawback than it might seem. The local newspaper supported the plan, and civic leaders were enthusiastic. The chairman of the Historic Hillsborough Committee, Robert Murphy, also chaired the Hillsborough Site Committee. The architecture students designed what Sidney Blackmer later described as a "wonderful" plan, with "a nice hillside and warm friendly people in the town that would just take everybody right to their hearts. And they had paths for the citizens to walk and a place to park . . . they had everything but a nickel." The "somebody" with a "big bankroll" who might have solved "an interesting problem in the development of the arts" (as the *Greensboro Daily News* described the situation)[21] never appeared, and the Historic Hillsborough plan went the way of the Biltmore House, the Tower of Light, the prison system, the shooting gallery, the fort, and the Protestant missionary movement into southern Appalachia.

At the time that he appointed the North Carolina Conservatory Committee, Governor Sanford had assumed that the school would go to Charlotte, the state's largest city. Accordingly, he had chosen three members from there—Martha Muilenburg, Katherine Bell, and Pete McKnight, editor of the *Charlotte Observer*. Sanford recalls:

There were two or three buildings in Charlotte that struck me as being very suitable for a conservatory. . . . Furthermore, Charlotte had been very supportive of good projects that we'd tried to run out of the Governor's Office, and the relationship with Charlotte to the rest of the state and to the Governor's Office and to the political structure was better than it has ever been before or since. Why, I'm not sure, but it was great, and I thought we could do about anything we wanted to do and get the support for about any kind of a project if we looked at the Charlotte community. . . . And so I suppose, if you look at that first committee, I stacked it slightly in favor of Charlotte, with the idea that that would probably be our best bet.[22]

John Ehle agreed. In April of 1963, Ehle noted in his journal, "I was told by Pete McKnight that he could get two million dollars for the campus in Charlotte. I was told that twice by Pete."[23] Two months later, just after the conservatory bill was passed, Ehle still believed that Charlotte would get the school. He and Giannini had gone site visiting in Giannini's Fiat, first to Winston-Salem and then to Charlotte, where they viewed several possible sites, including a hotel and a warehouse. In an informal meeting the following morning with Pete McKnight, the vice-president of Duke Power, John Paul Lucas, Bob Lassiter, and an architect, they concluded that campus needs for the school—"dormitories, classrooms, studios, practice rooms, offices, dining hall, recreation areas, library, an auditorium seating 750 to 1,000, a small theater for 250 people"—could be met "for something under $3½ million, so the Charlotte leaders decided to try to get that much."[24] In a memo to Governor Sanford written immediately after the Charlotte conference, Ehle summed up the situation in each of the three strongest cities, noting their current site offerings but speculating most interestingly on the intangible properties of each. Raleigh offered close identification with state government and with such other state-supported cultural "firsts" as the art museum and the North Carolina Symphony (based in Chapel Hill until its move to Raleigh in 1973), which would be appealing to most legislators. Because of its identification with state government, however, the city had no tradition of "supporting its own things with its own money" and seemed to lack a "flourishing cultural climate." In addition, Ehle felt that if the school were located in the state capital, it might be "harder to build" as a regional institution. Winston-Salem offered "sophistication . . . wealth . . . public spirited, artistically inclined people," and a "tradition of culture." But Ehle worried about the town's "tradition of amateurism [in the arts], which it cherishes and won't part with willingly," as well as its "desire to control whatever it finds itself responsible for." Of the advantages in Charlotte, Ehle listed the city's "wide-open feeling" and its status as a regional center with a growing population. And the community seemed to have a "sense of professionalism in the arts which is quite healthy." The city's size might be a detraction, though, because "money is scattered about and will take time to gather," and the school "won't have the impact on Charlotte itself which it might have in either of the other cities." The final disadvantage Ehle saw as offering exciting possibilities:

> In Charlotte, things happen without controls; they explode into action . . . this school in Charlotte will not be controlled and in turn will not control other things. It will not, therefore, have the impact on Charlotte that it would have on Raleigh or Winston-Salem. . . . It will set off in Charlotte a series of cultural explosions [resulting in the creation of the] arts capital of the region. The school, therefore, will be safer in Raleigh or Winston-Salem, but the potential is greater in Charlotte; so are the chances.[25]

Like Charlotte, Raleigh and Winston-Salem had sent letters of interest to the last meeting of the NCCC. Interest in Raleigh seemed to be substantial ("The Raleigh Chamber of Commerce is pumping hard for Raleigh as a site for a proposed Performing Arts Center," the *Times* reported), and those in the Governor's Office were soon encouraging renovation of a downtown site. In May, Sam Ragan and Hugh Cannon speculated that a building then in use for state offices but soon to be abandoned might do. A local firm of architects reported that the site was safe and pleasant, with good off-street parking, and Ragan wrote to Cannon that the Raleigh Chamber of Commerce, Junior Chamber, and other city organizations would find housing in apartments nearby, to provide a good temporary site. John Ehle ruminated—and suggested that the students could use the Senate and House Chambers of the old capitol for their concerts and the Highway Department auditorium for plays.[26]

The earliest organized community interest in the arts school had come from Winston-Salem, in November of 1962, when the North Carolina Conservatory Committee had met only twice. Mrs. T. Winfield Blackwell wrote to Martha Muilenburg that the Executive Committee of the Winston-Salem Arts Council had passed a resolution of interest in having a state-supported conservatory in Winston-Salem. In December, shortly after the NCCC's tempestuous public meeting, Mrs. Blackwell wrote again, saying that the trustees of the arts council wanted the school placed in Winston-Salem. And before the end of February 1963, more than two weeks before the conservatory committee's final report went to Terry Sanford, the persistent and bumptious voice of Philip Hanes was heard in the Governor's Office. And heard and heard and heard. McNeil Lowry once remarked good-humoredly that when Phil Hanes wanted something he was "all over you like a tent all the time, you know."[27] Aside from the members of the North Carolina Conservatory Committee and the governor and his staff, no signature appears more frequently on Archive correspondence about the arts school than that of Philip Hanes.

Until 1977 the president and chief executive officer of Hanes Dye and Finishing Company in Winston-Salem, Philip Hanes recalls that he took up the arts at Yale because he "thought maybe they would be crip courses," and he took up the arts in Winston-Salem after he graduated from Yale because Katie Bahnson (later a member of the NCCC), got to him first:

> She said, we've got this little arts council we've just started, [the first in the country] and we have got to have some businessmen involved, and one day your dad's going to let you be president of the company, and we want you . . . as a board member. I said, God, Katie, I don't know anything about the arts. And she said, well, I know you'll work for some organization. If a hospital came to you, would you go to work for them? I said, probably. And she said, what do you know about cancer and tuberculosis? And I said, even less. She said, so come work for us.
>
> In those days [1949], around here to work for the arts you had to be light on your heels. You really did. The whole works. And so the more I got involved in the thing, the more people thought that was sort of strange. And that made me madder and madder and madder . . . and the madder I got, the more involved I got.

Fortunately, Philip Hanes has a long fuse; judging from the intensity of his subsequent involvement with the arts, he was still pretty mad in 1963. "In a strictly unofficial capacity I would like to go on record with you concerning the North Carolina School of the Performing Arts," he wrote vigorously to John Ehle on February 27:

> I think we could round up enough funds and interest to get it going here in Winston-Salem. . . .
>
> We not only have the oldest Arts Council in America but are considered to have the finest arts management in this country. . . .

Winston-Salem . . . has the largest cultural program by far of any city in the state. . . .

Winston-Salem . . . can provide larger audiences for amateur performances than any other city in our state. . . .

Winston-Salem has the finest fundraising record of any city in the state in everything from the United Fund through its art programs. I will say that if our community as a whole decided that they want the high school program, we will pay to get it and (most important) having gotten it, support it with all the facilities we have available.

Philip Hanes hit the ground arguing. He does not remember the date of his first meeting with John Ehle, but he does recall feeling that he "didn't have anything in common with [Ehle] . . . but that wasn't the point. The point was that I wanted that damn school, and in a working situation I can work with anybody to get a job done. . . . And John had the ball, and so I had to work with John. And it took me a long time before he became my best friend."[28]

By the spring, Philip Hanes and the Winston-Salem Arts Council had gone to work in earnest, with full coverage and backing from the *Journal and Sentinel,* whose executive editor had twice been president of the arts council. On May 16, 1963, Hanes sent Governor Sanford a *Twin City Sentinel* editorial, urging Winston-Salem to decide immediately whether it wanted the school: "Some sort of steering committee should be set up," the paper urged, so that when legislation for the school was passed, Winston-Salem would be "armed and ready." The town—or at least the arts council—heeded the call to battle. On May 21, Mayor M. C. Benton appointed a committee to get the arts school for Winston-Salem, with Philip Hanes as chairman.[29] He immediately wrote to John Ehle, protesting his innocence—"I had no idea I would be appointed head of the Winston-Salem Committee. I thought it would be the mayor"—and deploring lost opportunities: "If there were as much information on the Conservatory as there was on the Governor's School . . . we would have known how to proceed and could have made some sort of testimonial for you before the Legislators." Philip did write to his cousin, state senator Gordon Hanes, expressing his concern that Atlanta might succeed in getting foundation support for a conservatory: "If a large city [such] as Atlanta should get it, there is no question who would have the head start in cultural development in the [South]. For the future of our state we must think of the fine arts and their encouragement of ideas and imagination so vital to industry and business." Competition from Atlanta was a burning issue for Philip Hanes; when the

June 1963 issue of *Show* magazine featured the Georgia capital in two articles, calling it the "pace- and taste-setting capital of the entire Southeast," he fired off a blistering rebuttal to editor Marvin Barrett. "Frankly, I am disillusioned [with your magazine]," he wrote, and proceeded to list Winston-Salem's considerable accomplishments in the arts, from classical radio and community theater to art exhibitions and a home for the symphony; from the vitality of the Winston-Salem Arts Council to the matter-of-fact mixing of the races. "All of our arts groups have been integrated for many years. . . . When we integrated our arts we felt no need for plain-clothesmen to be present," he remarked, skewering the Atlanta Arts Institute, which in January 1963 had desegregated quietly, with the help of plainclothes police and the substitution of a nude man for the studio art life classes. "If you want an article that will dumbfound people, send us a writer and we can show how Winston-Salem, for its size, has done more for the arts in America . . . than any city of less than 300,000 in the United States. . . . [Write] an article on the city that helped Atlanta," Hanes closed.[30] Not surprisingly, a copy of the letter of protest found its way to the Governor's Office.

It might seem that the energy and pizazz of Philip Hanes would be enough to build and support an empire of arts schools, but full community support was essential, not only for the major financial commitment that would be necessary but for the active audience support the students would need as well. In June of 1963, the major donors in Winston-Salem were cautious about supporting the school, and John Ehle was still fearful that the amateur arts tradition in the town might prove inimical to professional training. "We have a fairly complicated situation," Ehle cautioned Governor Sanford, "and I do hope no immediate decision in favor of any one city will be made. It is perfectly apparent . . . that Winston-Salem is not ready to go at this point, or is not ready to say it is ready to go." But Philip Hanes was more than ready to say he was ready to go, with or without money. On August 16 he sent the first formal site proposal received at the Governor's Office, a carefully organized fourteen-page summary with photographs and a map, which presented Winston-Salem's advantages as the home of an arts school and the offer of City Memorial Hospital (for dormitory space) and Central Elementary School (for academic space), near the campus of Salem College. Mayor Benton's committee suggested that the new school could use Salem College facilities temporarily, including the School of Music, the library, the science laboratories, and the new dance floor at the gymnasium. The proposal carried the endorsement of Franklin J. Keller, who had been working that summer as consultant for the performing arts and faculty member at the Governor's School, in session at Salem College. The ongoing search for a home for the new "Regional School of Performing Arts," he wrote,

> has reminded me sharply of my hunt for quarters in New York City back in 1945 when, as principal of Metropolitan Vocational High School, I proposed a division to be known as the High School of Performing Arts. (Incidentally, we actually coined the term "Performing Arts," which has since come into general use for music, drama, and dance.) We finally found an old abandoned elementary school, virtually in the middle of Times Square, the heart of the performing arts area. It is now 73 years old, has been twice rehabilitated by the Board of Education, and is functioning most effectively.
>
> The point of all this is that the Central Elementary School, along with facilities apparently available in Salem College, the old Moravian Church, the Little Theatre at the Community Center, and the Reynolds High School auditorium—these combined resources would provide markedly larger, more modern, and more adaptable quarters than we have ever had in New York. I have compared the two plants, item by item, and have concluded that, insofar as structure and space are concerned, you would be in a much more favorable position than we can ever hope for until the proposed new building is erected at the Lincoln Center for the Performing Arts.
>
> Experimenting in remodeled buildings originally built for other purposes will present certain advantages and disadvantages. In organizing a new kind of school you are bound to make many mistakes, as we did in New York. Making these mistakes in temporary quarters, you will learn what you will actually require in the new building or buildings which you hope to erect.[31]

Keller well knew that the spirit of the students could make almost any place acceptable.

In Winston-Salem, temporary housing seemed to be in hand, but the money was still in the bush: "If the Board of the new school were to select Winston-Salem as the site, the . . . committee . . . would at the proper time proceed to solicit funds. . . . We cannot, because of other scheduled fund raising campaigns, assure the Board of the new School of the Performing Arts that the necessary funds for a complete campus can be raised in the immediate future in our community."[32]

The other scheduled fundraising campaign was for the Bowman Gray School of Medicine, about which Philip Hanes had warned John Ehle earlier in the month and which he cited again at the end of August to lend urgency to the Winston-Salem proposal: "I understand you are having a little bit of trouble with foundation support. I know you are in as much of a rush as anyone else, but the later we wait, the harder it will be to shake loose facilities and get the necessary capital for improvements. This is especially true with the monstrous fund drive to be held by the Bowman Gray School of Medicine." Ehle replied the following week, perhaps a bit stung by Hanes's obvious knowledge of the Henry Heald episode and Ford's refusal to make any commitments:

> We are not having trouble with the foundations, but we are forced to move at a speed much slower than we would like, and slower than the best interest of the project dictates. This is a complicated matter of scheduling and that's about all it is, but it is a serious handicap. I know how this can affect to the detriment the plans you and your committee have made, and I hope that we will have some further word later on this month and some further word still next month. Your committee's proposal is in an honored place on my desk. We are anxious soon to move on to the evaluation stage. Thank you for all your work and for your confidence in this new school.[33]

On September 23, only three months after John Ehle had told Governor Sanford that Charlotte seemed the most likely to provide a good home for the school, he had to report that "Charlotte's best plan for the school fell through . . . because of fire laws. Cannon and I think the Raleigh plan doesn't have much substance yet. It is to our advantage to encourage Winston-Salem actively and begin to work out the details." This decision came, however, after virtually dismantling the August 8 Winston-Salem proposal:

> Winston-Salem leads in their enthusiasm for having the school. Their initial proposal is to house the children in the soon-to-be-abandoned City Hospital and teach them in a soon-to-be-abandoned public school building in Old Salem. This doesn't have much of a ring to it, even though both are good buildings.
> I went to Winston-Salem this weekend and got with Phil Hanes and Charlie Babcock on Sunday morning at Charlie's house. I explained the plans for the remedial (or advancement) school, and told them you would like to see it put in the hospital. This, of course, left Philip's Conservatory Committee without half of its proposal to us; I mentioned to Charlie that you would look with favor on his Reynolda

property as the residential part of the school. The children could live there in the village built by R. J. Reynolds, near the small lake . . . on the 19 acres which are still available (these 19 acres being in the center of a larger park). . . .

Phil Hanes and his committee will come along with this new arrangement, even though they will need to build several new dormitories, clean out the lake, build a concert hall. . . . This will cost them, by my estimates, over $1,000,000. . . . I will, if this is . . . your wish, push Winston-Salem fast ahead.[34]

This proposal had the John Ehle ring to it; North Carolina would have the only conservatory committee that cleaned out a lake.

But the Reynolda plan fell through quickly, for by the middle of October Philip Hanes was preparing Ehle for less glamorous offerings:

It is all well and good to say the Ford Foundation wants such a school in highly imaginative buildings, but Dr. Keller said it was better to start with existing structures and build after a year or two to fit the pattern the school takes. Down to the finish line much of our offer is to be based on proof of past support of what we undertake. I'm sure you can get the buildings you need anywhere in the state, but I don't think you could find the basic foundation necessary to continue and foster the school in the method you'd like. Bear this in mind the next few months. We'll do all in our power to make an attractive bid.

More and more the problem of siting the school was coming down *not* to an attractive location or suitable buildings, but to whether or not the community could raise the money to adapt whatever site was available:

I enclose herewith the kick-off notices for the new medical center . . . when you see that $6,000,000 for this will be raised . . . right here in the community, you can see why I am tremendously concerned about the possibility of raising too much money for a School of the Performing Arts within the next 18 months. . . . Needless to say, we will of course make the old college try, but I do want you to know that if we get a school for the performing arts we will put every bit of energy behind making it the finest in the entire country. . . . This town is something incredible when it comes to doing things for itself but there has to be some kind of limit and we can't do every single thing at once.[35]

For Winston-Salem and the arts school, the Bowman Gray fund drive was beginning to look like a disastrous coincidence.

Anxious for the school to open before the end of Governor Sanford's term in office, John Ehle worked on through the drear and unhappy winter of 1963. "I'm going to *try* to get to Charlotte and Winston-Salem next week and stir up interest," he wrote Vittorio in New York City. "I talked yesterday with the Raleigh chairman, and he said the situation in Raleigh is not hopeful. But we have faith."[36] Ehle learned from a letter written by George Hall to Raleigh committee chairman Bill Joslin that the Southern Regional Education Board in Atlanta was surreptitiously dangling a tempting morsel on the side of a Raleigh location for the arts school. Reportedly planning a "multi-million dollar ETV [educational television] research and production facility somewhere in the southeastern states," the SREB had let it be known that "one of the requisites for the selection of the Research Triangle site would be the location of that proposed Conservatory here in Raleigh, since it would enable the production people to call on performing artists with relative ease. Indeed, we have been led to believe by SREB that if the Conservatory were to be located elsewhere in the state, then North Carolina would be passed over altogether." Hall went on to make a strong statement for locating the school in Raleigh:

Personally I think the Conservatory ought to be here anyway. It seems to me, North Carolina cannot afford to disperse and diffuse its few cultural resources. They need to come together for a cosmopolitan and mutual nourishment. What is a more logical place than the capital, a city already the home of several resources without peer in the state and in the southeast: the Museum of Art, the three major University campuses in the close neighborhood, the several smaller colleges, the Hall of History, the Little Theatre, Friends of the College, the State Library, etc. Then, too, there is in this area the intellectual and artistic climate in which such a seed as the Conservatory idea could grow to a wonderfully blooming plant indeed. The more industrial centers of the state which are seeking the Conservatory may be more bustling, more populous, more aggressive, but it is certainly not inevitable that art can take root in places so busily committed to the merely material. Indeed, I should think it likely that artists would find living in such places sterile and disheartening. But here in Raleigh surely could they find a spirit compatible with the rhythm of their own thought and lives. . . . The ETV facility . . . would strengthen

Raleigh's case and, God knows!, we must make the strongest effort not to lose the Conservatory.

John Ehle's idea about placing it in that area around the Governor's mansion, using some of those wonderful old houses, would in itself not only cosmopolize the downtown area but would resuscitate that still genteel but sadly fading heart of our city.[37]

But the year was drawing to a close, and the Raleigh committee had not raised any local money, nor had the Charlotte committee. And Philip Hanes had fallen silent. And then things got worse. "At this time," John Ehle recalls,

the Chancellor of the University's campus in Greensboro asked me to come see what he would propose. Chancellor Singletary's office was located across the street from a large, beautiful building, and he said to me, that could be the Arts School, the home of the School, that was available. He said his University was running an elementary school there in order that the education students could teach students, gain practical experience, but they could do that elsewhere. He said that's all right, you can have it. We have auditoriums, we have theatres. He asked if I realized that, while his Dean of Music and the Greensboro legislators were opposing the Arts School in the Legislature, the Legislature was passing a three and a half million dollar appropriation for a new music building for his University.

I said, Yes, I knew it.

He said, We have that money for a new building. We can work the plans out with the Arts School. We have dormitory space. You can start in September.

I went out of there as sad as I've ever been in my life. Here I had worked with burning anger to help start a new voice in arts education, a non-university voice in the South, and we were down to this university offer. We had nothing else.[38]

Thinking perhaps to surprise the opposition on its own ground, Ehle went to Miles Wolff of the *Greensboro Daily News,* and they discussed using the O. Henry Hotel and the Woodsdale Building in downtown Greensboro as a possible location for the arts school. "I'll see what can be done," Wolff wrote Ehle:

You may recall you jotted down some figures about what would be spent by such a school. . . . Could you give me these and any additional ones you might have on what the school would mean to a community in a material way? I need this information to beard the city fathers in their city hall den. As I told you, the city owns the Woodsdale building and long range plans call for its demolition.

I have been snooping around trying to get information about the O. Henry property. It is owned by the Alsonnett Hotel chain. They have put it up for sale and are asking a mere $1,800,000. They won't get that much.

Even at a lesser price I don't see how we could buy it but I do see some hope from the fact that it has been a losing venture. Since this is the case, the owners just might be willing to donate it for school use and charge it off as a tax loss. It's a long shot but one worth trying.

The only question is: Who will put the bite on Alsonnett? I have a suggestion. The best person would be our governor. Do you think we could get him to try?

"I don't know what Governor Sanford will say when you ask him about the Alsonnett idea," Ehle replied. "I've not discussed any of this with him. He probably would want you to make advance contact. Could you find out if Alsonnett would like to talk with Governor Sanford about the proposed use of the facility on a gift basis to the state?" Ehle provided Wolff with specific budget information and pointed out the advantages the school would give Greensboro in industry-hunting and in keeping the downtown healthy.[39] Then he left the newly reformulated Greensboro faction to its own devices and tried again to raise the promised money in Charlotte. On December 30, 1963, he and Giannini went to Charlotte on what the *Charlotte Observer* called a "window-shopping trip." Reports of the visit in the *Observer,* and in the Raleigh paper, gave the impression that Winston-Salem and Charlotte were competing strongly and that Ehle and Giannini were there to evaluate the possible offerings of an eager contender. But it was the governor's representatives who were doing the courting, not the other way around, and the luncheon that afternoon with eight Charlotte civic leaders yielded nothing more substantial than pie-in-the-sky—although Ehle made it clear that the city had only to meet the school's minimal needs. "Both men would be pleased if Charlotte were selected," Charlotte committee chairman J. A. Stenhouse later reported to the mayor: "They have no objection to the school being downtown. . . . Little campus area is needed. If Charlotte is unable to raise money for a new campus now, they will be quite satisfied to use renovated buildings for five or ten years. They are not seeking plush quarters, and are willing to operate with the bare essentials. A 1,000 seat auditorium is not necessary at this time." To the

Charlotte committee's estimated cost of $2,400,000 for preparing general facilities for the school had been added a second budget for a "Limited campus for 5 years if funds short"—$1,510,000. Even at that, the Charlotte committee's January 22, 1964 report offered no funds although the committee realized that "money available for site and capital improvements is probably the major factor in site selection. The Committee has ignored this since it is an unknown factor and has expressed a preference for a new campus. . . . The Committee thinks it unwise to do more than make casual inquiry until there is some indication funds are available. The Committee decided not to make any detailed site studies until selection was narrowed." Pete McKnight sent a copy of the Charlotte report to John Ehle and phoned to say that the Charlotte committee would "wait on us to supply tangible evidence of interest in Charlotte from the Governor's Office."[40] Site selection across the state had, therefore, been narrowed to zero, and interest in the Governor's Office was about as tangible as blood, toil, tears, and sweat could make it. John Ehle faced the prospect of a disappointment to a governor's program that might very well result in national embarrassment.

Luckily, Smith Bagley called.

John Ehle remembers that one evening during these parlous times he had gone to dinner at the home of Philip and Joan Hanes:

> Phil said he had come to a brick wall in fund-raising. He invited to dinner Smith Bagley, one of the Reynolds family heirs. Phil had been trying to persuade Smith to become chairman of the local Committee. Smith confided in me that evening that he thought the Arts School ought to go to Raleigh. I told him we had no hope of getting local money in Raleigh, so we talked about Winston-Salem and its hope, really Phil Hanes's hope, that the city would become an arts capital of the country.

Philip Hanes credits Ruth Julian—an ardent arts-lover of Winston-Salem—with thinking of Smith Bagley, "and I questioned that [suggestion], and she said, if he gets involved, he has got very good ideas, he's very bright, and he doesn't—he has not been around Winston-Salem so long that he thinks along the same tracks as everybody else, and we need a new mind in this thing."[41]

On January 22 Smith Bagley, who had agreed to accept the chairmanship, phoned John Ehle to arrange for a briefing. "Philip says he has given up [and] wants to help Smith now," Ehle noted in a telephone memorandum. "Phil wants a new committee and a new start . . . Smith says there are few ideas up there now . . . I phoned Phil Hanes. All of this is according to his wishes, so I'm to have dinner with him and Smith tomorrow night and with James Gray if he can break his other appointment." If Phil Hanes was discouraged, it took exactly one night for him to bounce back. The morning after what had promised to be a rather subdued little dinner party, he was once again pelting the Governor's Office with press clippings, updates, and his usual energetic reminders of activity in Winston-Salem:

> Enclosed is an article from the morning paper. Thought you'd be interested. Fun having you and Paul [Green] with us last night. . . . Our little organization is underway on a new task. We're getting a list of various foundations which give to brick and mortar. Smith is checking properties . . . I'll keep you posted. I'd appreciate it if you would advise us if another community has the school in the bag. We are spending much time . . . at a busy time of year.[42]

After Paul Green and John Ehle had left the party, James Gray, Philip Hanes, and Smith Bagley agreed to seek Graylyn for the school. Graylyn was John Ehle's sort of thing, and he went after it, though he "felt like a thief in the manger." The Gray family estate had been promised already to Bowman Gray School of Medicine, but Anne Forsyth offered to give a million dollars to the medical school if Bowman Gray would give Graylyn and its land to the new school of performing arts:

> I wanted Graylyn a whole lot, and I remember getting hold of Vittorio and asking him on his next trip to North Carolina whenever that was, and I took him up to Graylyn and walked him through it, and went to it myself, and we got the plans. I still, I think, have the plans for Graylyn. I may have the only plans for Graylyn. We could have housed, I think, forty or fifty students only in Graylyn, but what beautiful grounds and facilities, and indeed we wouldn't have had to house any students there. We could use the big building for offices or whatever, and have a swimming pool, indoor and out. The important thing is, we had what must be forty acres, fifty acres of beautiful landscaped ground.
>
> The Grays turned that down.[43]

Although John Ehle was telling McNeil Lowry by the first week of February 1964 that "we are ready to go here," he had given up any hopes that the conservatory would open during Governor Sanford's administration. He wrote two applicants for positions at the new school on January 31 that "the probable date for the School to begin instructions is the Fall of 1965." This is the earliest mention on record of the revised opening date; even the idea of opening only the conservatory's music school in temporary quarters—discussed from time to time in correspondence between Ehle and Giannini—had been scrapped. Near the end of February Ehle admitted to Hugh Cannon that siting the school in Raleigh "seems to me to be unlikely." Greensboro had not yet made a formal proposal. Charlotte had nothing to add to its disappointing report of January 22. Smith Bagley and his committee had nothing new to report, but so long as Philip Hanes drew breath and had access to a pair of scissors, Winston-Salem would be heard from regularly:

> Enclosed herewith article from the *National Observer* which might interest you . . . this may give us some good ideas.

> John—Attached hereto is more of your publicity. Who in this world is your agent? . . . Enclosed herewith are a couple of copies of the March issue of *Show Magazine* . . . a story of Winston-Salem as seen by Al Toffler. . . . Hopeful we are still in the running for the School of the Performing Arts . . . Smith is doing a simply marvelous job. . . . Want to send one of these to McNeil Lowry? [44]

Another shift in thinking had occurred in the Governor's Office in response to the delay in getting a firm commitment from any North Carolina city interested in providing a home for the school. According to the bill which the legislature had passed on June 21, 1963, the Board of Trustees of the new school was "to meet, as soon as practicable after appointment, to consider sites which may be offered as a location for the school. From all sites offered, the board of trustees shall recommend to the Governor that site considered most suitable as the location for the said school, and shall, upon the Governor's approval of that site, or of some subsequently recommended site, and pursuant to the authority herein granted to it, establish the school at that approved site." Private correspondence in the North Carolina Division of Archives and History indicates that as late as December 9, 1963, John Ehle expected that the school's first Board of Trustees would select the site for the school, as originally intended. "It might be a good idea to appoint the Board of Trustees of the Performing Arts School, or at least get the list ready, so that when you get word from Ford, you can make quicker progress," Ehle advised. "The Winston-Salem newspaper just phoned. They persist in their attitude that we ought to make a move. I told their reporter that the delay had been caused by our not yet getting the foundation money, that this was a time matter and that soon the Board of Trustees very likely would be appointed." Ehle listed the names of seven-

teen prominent North Carolinians, and for chairman, Dr. James H. Semans of Durham. Seemingly as an afterthought, he added a list of "ten
artists of national reputation . . . to advise the Board of Trustees": Vittorio
Giannini, Paul Green, Richard Adler, James Christian Pfohl, José Limon,
Elia Kazan, Sidney Blackmer, Tyrone Guthrie, and Andy Griffith.[45]

John Ehle had hoped Governor Sanford would appoint the board as
soon as possible after the passage of the bill, undoubtedly to assure the
school's opening before Sanford left office. By moving quickly, they could
take advantage of the high level of public interest in the wake of legislative
furor and the governor's not inconsiderable personal influence. And, too,
an early decision, Ehle pointed out, would "give one of these cities [Raleigh,
Winston-Salem, and Charlotte] time to try to get its money gathered." Obviously, a commitment to one city would give local fundraising efforts considerable help. By July 2, 1963, Ehle had ready a list of suggestions for the
Board of Trustees, including the fifteen members of the North Carolina
Conservatory Committee, five state senators, seven state representatives,
six citizens, and nineteen artist consultants from whom to choose the Advisory Board of Artists—"people who will make it the independent, high-
quality School we insist it must be, and who will hold its feet to the fire,"
he wrote Lowry, less than felicitously. Yet Governor Sanford delayed,
though—predictably—pressures mounted to make the appointments. "I
hope fairly soon to appoint a Board of Trustees to evaluate each community's plans," he wrote Philip Hanes in September, sidestepping a request
for comment on the Winston-Salem proposal. Later in the month he al-
layed Vittorio Giannini's nudges: "I will not appoint a Board of Trustees
just yet, but I agree that we must go ahead with the work of selecting a few
key people—four or five [for the faculty]." By November Ehle was promising Giannini that he would "urge the Governor to start thinking about the
Board of Trustees. Perhaps they ought to be ready to come into Raleigh for
a meeting the first week in January, and the cities by then ought to have
offers ready." Indeed, by now the governor's delay in appointing the board
had become news. "What Has Happened to the Arts School?" the Winston-
Salem press wanted to know:

> Word out of Raleigh about [the school] has been noticeably miss-
> ing lately. It has been almost five months now since the Legislature
> authorized the establishment of a school for the performing arts. . . .
> The Governor was to appoint a board of trustees who in turn were to
> select a site for the school. It has been almost three months now since
> Winston-Salem submitted its formal bid for the school. But if this

and other bids are being considered, there has been no public announcement of it. Indeed, the trustees have not yet been announced. . . . The proposal moved so fast in its early stages (there was even talk of opening the school in the fall of 1964) that this seemingly screeching halt has attracted attention—if not some concern. A progress report from the Governor would be in order right now.[46]

The *Raleigh News and Observer* reported that "Governor Sanford has delayed appointing a board of trustees for the proposed school of Performing Arts because matching money from private sources is not yet in hand," meaning money from the Ford Foundation, which remained nameless in the press. "John Ehle, the Governor's cultural aide, said it would be unwise to take any step toward setting up the school until money for a five-year budget is received." John Ehle, of course, thought no such thing. For months he had been trying to get Governor Sanford to appoint the trustees and move ahead with setting up the school, ramshackle budget or no. And both of them had been working without a net for too long either to expect or require assurances from Ford before proceeding with the school. In fact, the expected assurances from McNeil Lowry, which were to come as soon as the Ford Foundation's board held its final meeting of 1963, never officially arrived. Through private sources at Ford, John Ehle learned that the board had met the first week in December; that the North Carolina plan had received the enthusiastic recommendation of McNeil Lowry; and that the appropriation from which funds for the school would come had been put under Lowry's control. On December 13, as they drove from Raleigh to Durham to attend a meeting, Ehle told Governor Sanford the sub rosa news from Ford. It was then that Governor Sanford—who had kept his own counsel about the matter for months while Ehle and Giannini worked to patch together the school with little more than a legislative act hedged by private funding requirements and mirrors—told Ehle that he did not want to appoint a Board of Trustees until he knew where the school was to be located.[47]

This, of course, was a reversal of the bill's instruction, which clearly intended the trustees to take an active role in choosing the site. The wording of the bill may have been an oversight. Governor Sanford had wisely delayed site selection before the legislature voted on establishing the school for practical and politically expedient reasons. And it was just as logical that the first Board of Trustees, whose role was vitally important in starting the school literally from bricks and boards—that this first board should include hometown representatives of proven commitment and ability. Hugh

Cannon, Ben Roney, and other wise men, however, would hardly want to confront an antsy legislature with a bill that said the governor could choose a site for the school on his own recognizance—an uncomfortable and unfamiliar position for a governor to find himself in.

John Ehle recalls that he had wanted the Advisory Board of Artists to govern the school but had been told that this would never be approved by the General Assembly[48]—to have designated that an Advisory Board of Artists was to be in charge, was to come to North Carolina and actually choose a site for the new school, in the dangerous waters of a conservative legislature would probably have washed out even Ben Roney's roads.

Perhaps everyone at first assumed that before a Board of Trustees was appointed, one North Carolina city would make the best offer, and everything would fall into place. But the issue of siting the school became instead one of nerve-wracking delay. Mid-December of 1963 was far later than anyone had expected the uncertainty to continue, and so Governor Sanford decided at last that rather than toss an innocent but potentially unruly Board of Trustees into this witches' brew of toil and trouble, he would permutate the mixture.

Governor Sanford told John Ehle to bring on the artists.

Was it legal?

Between the lines, yes, such a move could be made. The bill provided that the choice of a site waited "upon the Governor's approval of that site" and also that the trustees were to be "advised and assisted" in the exercise of their authority "by the State Board of Education and the State Board of Higher Education . . . and by the advisory board of the school." But the governor told Ehle to be careful how he worded the announcements that the Advisory Board of Artists rather than the Board of Trustees would tour the sites and make a recommendation to the governor.[49] No voices were raised in consternation, however. Certainly no one in the Governor's Office mentioned that an elision had occurred, and no citizens, in the glamour of the moment, objected to the substitution.

Was it reasonable?

Actually, this was the more logical way to proceed, for the point of the advisory board was to provide professional expertise to guide the trustees, who could scarcely be expected to keep track of all the finer points of a dancer's preferences in floorboards, for example—at least, not at first. In addition, because most of the artists came from outside North Carolina, their choice would be less vulnerable to attacks on the question of fair-mindedness.

Was it fun?

It was more than fun—it was flashy, it was smart, and it was rare, for seldom do our government officials ever see in art and artists a solution to anything. More's the pity.

In January of 1964 John Ehle talked to Vittorio Giannini about choosing the artists. Giannini, then in New York, made inquiries and came up with a list of suggestions that met the North Carolina criteria: artists who were

> interested in young people and from whom we may expect coopera-
> tion and worthwhile advice because of their experience and knowl-
> edge . . . this list seems to have a number that are known to people
> in general and a number that are highly esteemed by the profession-
> als . . . it would be smart to submit to [Lowry] the final list before any
> action on it is taken. We need his money now and in the future, and
> also he has a wide knowledge of who is on the ball in the Arts. Who
> really is interested and who prefer the honor and will do little work.
> They have had on Committees so many people and have seen how
> they work and . . . advice from him would be of great help. People
> like Rudel, Ouroussow, De Mille, Rea are possible employers for our
> students that have outstanding Talent. This is also to be thought of.
> At any rate, mull these lists over. You may come up with a better
> combination.[50]

McNeil Lowry, looking back through his files in 1982, noted that on February 11, 1964, he went to Raleigh "just for the purpose of meeting Sanford
and a group of people."[51] They must have talked about the artist candidates, for only a week later Governor Sanford drafted a letter to Lowry,
asking for his comments "about the proposed Advisory Board." Lowry
remembers,

> When they went into an advisory board, they wanted me to com-
> ment. Now, it wasn't only Giannini that wanted me to comment on
> personnel—it was Sanford in general terms, and Ehle in specific
> terms, and I had to be very careful, because the Ford Foundation was
> so important potentially to this whole project, that talking to Ehle, I
> might find myself naming the advisory board, and I didn't want to—I
> didn't think that was correct. . . . Vittorio . . . knew what I meant
> when I said, "Look, you talk to these people. If they're helpful to you,
> you like their advice, okay. If you don't, forget it. Do just as I would
> do if I came to ask you about somebody I was considering giving a
> grant to, who was running a conservatory or writing opera."[52]

On March 2 Governor Sanford sent official letters of invitation to Sidney Blackmer, Julius Rudel, Vittorio Giannini, Leontyne Price, James Christian Pfohl, Zelda Fichandler, Richard Adler, Paul Green, Eugenie Ouroussow, José Limon, Agnes de Mille, and Frederick Franklin. After giving a brief history of the school's inception, Sanford explained that the role of the advisory board would be to

> hold the School true to its stated purpose, and make of it the best, most fitting, worthwhile place for young people to attend if they have the talent and desire to be artists in the performing arts. . . . [The board] is a group of a dozen artists who agree to guide this School to a proper course, men and women of excellent ability who are willing to attend meetings to see how things are going, and to lend advice. . . . This is the first State supported school in the performing arts in our country. The School will become part of the fabric of the arts, and your occupying the post will obligate you to a deep responsibility. It is because I know you will recognize this that I am writing you.[53]

Julius Rudel, director of the New York City Opera, replied on March 10 that the planned arts school seemed to him "a much needed pioneering step of almost visionary character, and although my time is extremely limited, I feel this project has such importance that I cannot refuse to serve." Blackmer and Pfohl sent in their official acceptances promptly. Ouroussow, director of the School of American Ballet, declined on the grounds that she was not an artist, merely the administrator of a serious ballet school. A few months later, after the smoke of the site selection had cleared, Governor Sanford wrote her again, saying that both he and Giannini believed that her experience would be "most valuable" to the new school. Ouroussow accepted a term on the advisory board ending June 20, 1969.[54]

Leontyne Price also declined, and Zelda Fichandler, producing director of the Arena Stage in Washington, responded with the suggestion of an alternates system, the appointment to be shared with her husband. Governor Sanford wrote back that he felt wary of an alternates system because he "wasn't sure how [such a] system would work out for us here" and feared it "might encourage other members of the Board to do the same."[55] Agnes de Mille remembers that she replied to her invitation on the telephone:

> Well, it was a phone call one morning about eleven o'clock, a very North Carolinian voice, it was John Ehle's, and he said, "I'm speaking on behalf of the Governor of North Carolina, and he wants to speak

to you." I thought that was a joke, and I almost said I'm the Governor of South Carolina and I'm busy—but I didn't say it. The next voice on the phone was Terry Sanford's, and he said, "Miss de Mille, this is the Governor of North Carolina," and of course, there was no question that it was.[56]

Governor Sanford then invited Peter Mennin and Jan Peerce, from whom he apparently refused to take no for an answer, judging from the telegram he sent Peerce: "We do want you on Board and have announced your name with the others. We will understand about your schedule but we do need your help."[57]

A press release from the Governor's Office announcing the appointment of ten artists to the advisory board went out on March 26. Dates set for the site visits were April 28 and 29; the release went on to say that the governor believed "members from out-of-state ought to compose the site committee" and closed by quoting the legislation on the advisory board and its function.[58] John Ehle enclosed a copy of the release in his report to Mc-Neil Lowry:

> Mr. Franklin is in Mexico; we will have to ask him to be on the Advisory Board when he gets back. Mrs. Fichandler wrote the Governor that she could be on the Board only if she might send her husband to some of the meetings in her place, and Governor Sanford felt the acceptance of an alternate system . . . might sometimes result in our having a secondary Board meeting while the members of the primary Board go about their other duties. Therefore, he has written Mrs. Fichandler that he will consider this and will contact her later.
>
> We asked Peter Mennin to be on the Board and he accepted.
>
> All the members of the Board except for Jan Peerce have agreed to come to North Carolina on April 28th and 29th, to visit Charlotte, Winston-Salem and Raleigh to evaluate the sites being offered the School and to recommend to Governor Sanford at dinner on the 29th the best place to put the School. If you can come to dinner on the 29th, or if you would like to send somebody or have somebody else invited by the Governor, he will be pleased.[59]

Ehle also sent releases to Milton Esterow of the *New York Times* and to Richard Coe, who announced Governor Sanford's appointments in his column in the *Washington Post*.[60] To the chairmen of the site committees for Hillsborough, Charlotte, Winston-Salem, Greensboro, and Raleigh Ehle sent nearly identical letters explaining that the governor had appointed an

Advisory Board of Artists to tour their sites, "as provided in the Performing Arts School law passed by the General Assembly." He went on to give explicit instructions:

> When he announces the Board, we might have a lot of scurrying around, people looking for ways to influence Board members to favor one city over another. I hope not. This could get to be a headache for these people. We are, therefore, requesting that nothing be mailed or sent to members of the Advisory Board about the site selection, until the group is ready to listen as a group. We hope, too, that no elaborate or expensive displays or brochures will be presented.
>
> The committee will be viewing places where the School can go by September of 1965, and will be evaluating realistically the ability of the local group to provide the campus and buildings which compose its offer or offers. They must think realistically about housing 400 students and having adequate studio, rehearsal and performance space for them. We hope no city will take them to more than two sites, though that isn't critical.

The chairman of the Raleigh committee took the hint. "No arm twisting will be used," Bill Joslin pledged.[61]

As he was writing to the site committees, arranging for the artists' tour, John Ehle confided to a young friend that he was having fun but had little "time to keep ahead of catastrophe."[62] Indeed, he and Governor Sanford had plunged recklessly ahead, inviting a group of famous artists to move from place to place at what might yet turn out to be a Mad Hatter's tea party—where the hosts had little or nothing to serve, though the guests, like Alice, were persistently offered more. ("I've had nothing yet," Alice replied in an offended tone, "so I can't take more." "You mean you can't take *less*," said the Hatter, "it's very easy to take more than nothing.") On March 20, John Ehle was notified that at last they had more than nothing. Smith Bagley and his committee had gotten wind of the Winston-Salem–Forsyth County School Board's plans to make a bakery out of James A. Gray High School—or a vocational school, or maybe both. Certainly the possibilities seemed broad enough to encompass music, drama, dance, and dinner. "I think we're in," Bagley scrawled across a carbon of his letter to Synergetics, Inc., a Raleigh firm that was to evaluate the architectural plans of Gray High School.[63] Built during the Depression, Gray High School was far from perfect, but it sat on a twenty-two-acre site, and in addition to its main building included a gymnasium, athletic field, baseball diamond, and tennis courts. With thirty-four classrooms and an enrollment of 976

6. *Renovations to the old James A. Gray High School could not begin until June of 1965 (Archives of the North Carolina School of the Arts).*

students, the school was operating at capacity and had no way to grow without eliminating parking space. School officials had been thinking of consolidating Gray and Griffith high schools and using Gray as a central cafeteria for seventeen schools as well as the bakery for the entire system. On upper floors, they thought they might house vocational courses because the school system had to take its students out of Forsyth Technical Institute by June. But none of these ideas had been officially discussed at the school board meetings until the mayor of Winston-Salem, M. C. Benton, acting for Bagley's committee, wrote two letters to the school board, requesting release of Gray for the arts school. On April 3 the *Winston-Salem Journal* reported that the city-county school board had voted 8 to 2 to offer Gray for the arts school, on a seven- to ten-year lease to the state. With little more than three weeks left before the advisory board would arrive, the Winston-Salem committee went to work to find out how much it would cost to transform the old school on Waughtown Street.[64] One thing was sure: Gray High School was no Tower of Light. It was not even a prison. But the governor of North Carolina, as the Mad Hatter pointed out, could scarcely take less.

If John Ehle had ever been so fond as to think that Greensboro might come up with a downtown location for the arts school separate from the UNC-Greensboro campus, those hopes were dashed on April Fool's Day 1964. "Performing Arts School in U.N.C. Framework," the *Greensboro Daily News* (whose editor was chairman of the Greensboro committee) expounded once again, raising the ghosts of complainants past:

> Such a school [as the one proposed] should not be shunted off to some old structure or structures, with renovation costs running high, surroundings not what they should be and atmosphere of the whole undertaking anything but inspiring. What could be more inspiring than a university atmosphere?
>
> We have thought all along that the [North Carolina Conservatory Committee] should have devoted major attention, rather than a closed mind, to fitting the school into the framework of North Carolina's existing educational pattern and program. Six of the seven recommendations which the committee makes point squarely to the University of North Carolina in Greensboro.

On April 7 the Executive Committee of the Greensboro Chamber of Commerce met and decided that the governor's advisory board would be told that the new arts school should be an integral part of UNC-Greensboro:

> Although such a recommendation would be opposite to the position taken by the Governor's adviser on cultural affairs, John Ely [sic], [it] offers a plausible approach in the matter of locating the proposed school. . . .
>
> The local presentation will cover advantages of making the school a part of UNC-G and a possible offer of land for it. . . . Ely [sic] has repeatedly insisted that the performing arts school for talented students be established independently of other institutions.
>
> It is proposed that the school accept students below college levels. Miles H. Wolff, chairman of the chamber's committee on the school, said that Curry School, operated by the education department of Woman's College and offering work for the first grade through high school, would offer "a tremendous advantage" for such students.
>
> Dr. Otis A. Singletary, UNC chancellor, said he would not want the performing arts as an adjunct or adjacent to the local UNC unit. He is strongly in favor, he said, of making it an integral part of UNC-G.

Just before the legislation establishing the arts school was passed, John Ehle had reminded Governor Sanford that the Ford Foundation was "not likely to care which one of the three cities" got the school. But Ford would care "if the school turns out to be another music department of a college or university . . . they feel there are enough of those. . . . The school must be independent in a real sense." Now, as he set up the itinerary for the advisory board's visits, Ehle asked, with an almost audible sigh, whether the governor wanted the committee taken to Greensboro—"I see no practical advantage in it in terms of the School itself." Governor Sanford, more patient in the face of misunderstanding and obstinacy than his aide, returned the memo with a succinct "yes."[65]

From Charlotte there was no news. In Raleigh, the *News and Observer* spoke of "no education in isolation," citing the advantages to the new school of being located in the state's capital, where it would be in both the educational and cultural mainstream of North Carolina. And in addition to drawing on the support and services of nearby institutions such as North Carolina State, UNC, Duke, and East Carolina, "businessmen and civic organizations" had pledged their support, the paper said. But tangible realization of that support remained moot. On April 6, Bill Joslin phoned John Ehle to tell him that the manager of the Carolina Hotel in Raleigh would show it to Ehle and the Raleigh committee. The Carolina, a 250-room hotel with a cafeteria and some space for expansion in the rear, was owned by Joseph M. Bryan, board chairman of Pilot Life Insurance Company in Greensboro. When Joslin approached Bryan about the hotel, he was told that it was not for sale, but, Bryan added, "If the site selection committee likes the hotel, then come and see me." And so, on these less than satisfactory grounds, the Carolina Hotel became the core of the Raleigh offer—the Carolina Hotel, owned by Joseph M. Bryan, whose wife, according to the *Greensboro Record,* had just been tapped by the president of the Greensboro Chamber of Commerce to join an exclusive seven-member committee to aid in making "a renewed and stronger effort" to get the arts school for Greensboro.[66]

Thus, at the end of the first week in April, the score was Charlotte, nothing; Greensboro, worse than nothing; Raleigh, at the mercy of a member of the Greensboro committee; and Winston-Salem, one old high school without soundproofing or dormitories, and no money.

Governor Sanford and John Ehle moved on, just a if there were actually going to be a house party on the twenty-eighth and twenty-ninth, with sites to tour and dinner guests. They had invited McNeil Lowry to the dinner, but he couldn't come (budget meetings). Jan Peerce couldn't come;

Peter Mennin couldn't come; Sidney Blackmer thought he was going to be late. They thought of inviting the chairmen of the local site committees to the dinner (perhaps to fill out the table) but at the last minute decided against it, and it was fortunate they did. In the first place, it was getting hard to determine just who, at any given time, the chairmen actually were. Smith Bagley was the chairman of the Winston-Salem committee, but he let Philip Hanes write all the letters. Carbons of correspondence between the Governor's Office and the Charlotte and Raleigh chairmen frequently went to Pete McKnight and Sam Ragan, respectively. E. J. "Mutt" Evans, former mayor of Durham, had been the head of a committee in February interested in getting the arts school, but then Charles Norton of Triangle Theatre called in April and said that he was now in charge of the Durham committee, if it was not too late. Miles Wolff had to go out of town, so he turned the Greensboro committee over to George Eichhorn, who wrote Ehle that UNC-Greensboro chancellor Otis Singletary would help to present Greensboro's case. Then the Hillsborough committee was piqued because John Ehle refused its invitation to have the advisory board come to tea, and that, of course, might have made subsequent introductions at a dinner party in Raleigh somewhat awkward. Then, becoming anxious because the advisory board actually had no power to contract for buildings and receive bids for renovations, John Ehle urged Governor Sanford on April 24 to hurry up and appoint a Board of Trustees and invite them to the dinner on the twenty-ninth, a suggestion the governor wisely ignored. Perhaps by this time he had consulted Mrs. Sanford. John Ehle had managed in all the confusion to invite Mrs. Sanford ("Dear Margaret Rose, I do hope you'll decide to attend the dinner at your house on the 29th").[67]

Meanwhile, in Winston-Salem, Smith Bagley had come up with an idea for raising money that made John Ehle's dinner party look easy. The architect had concluded that it would take $900,000 to make Gray High usable as an arts school. Phil Hanes remembers, "We had been trying to figure out how we could raise the money . . . I think the other cities largely said—I believe this is true to the last one—that if you give [the school] to us, we will raise the money. Our way is to find out if we've got the money before we ask."[68] Back in January, Philip Hanes had stepped aside as chairman of the Winston-Salem committee because, in the face of the massive Bowman Gray School of Medicine fund drive, he had been unable to get commitments from the city's major philanthropic sources. Now, with only a couple of weeks left before the advisory board would choose a site for the school, the new chairman came up with the crazy notion of trying to raise the money on the telephone.

"It's well known among those of us who raise money," Hanes says, "that raising substantial funds on the telephone is pretty tough." Indeed, it was more than tough; as John Ehle recalls, Hanes told him the idea was "absurd." But Smith Bagley had thought it through. "Look," he said to Philip Hanes, "why don't we ask the major industries and foundations if they will back us up if we can prove that the school is wanted?" Bagley thought a telephone solicitation campaign could demonstrate community involvement—thousands of small donations from the people of Winston-Salem might result in large donations from the city's foundations and corporations. However naive such a campaign might have seemed to Philip Hanes, only a few days were left in which to raise nearly a million dollars, and "Smith's idea . . . seemed like the only possible way to do it. . . . Now, he didn't know how to implement it. He hadn't been in town that long, so he needed me, too. We really ended up almost co-chairmen, but he was the chairman. It was his idea, and that's the big thing. Everybody should always remember about Smith Bagley—it was his idea. But it was Ruth [Julian's] idea to get Smith Bagley involved." They went to the Winston-Salem Arts Council, which

> had the lists of the donors of the community, and we'd been breaking the donors in the community down to interest level and financial capability, so that much was pretty well set . . . in those days we didn't have computers, really. We had McBee Keysort. We had little cards there. And we had people all tabulated as to their interests and this, that, and the other thing, and as to their donating capabilities, and so forth . . . I helped design those things. So what we did, the first thing we did, we knew that these were all art supporters—we went in at those people, as I remember. The real big donations in those days were $1,000. We went in and pulled out all those that were $1,000. We put them in one stack. We went to $500, then $100, then $25, then to $10—that sort of thing. So we had different stacks. Having run a whole bunch of fund-raising campaigns for the arts council, we knew who the best solicitors were. So we had already put the prime givers and the prime solicitors together. Then we did it just like you would do a United Fund campaign. . . .
>
> But we couldn't figure out how we could do it in two days. You know, a campaign, real hard-hitting campaign that you prepared eight months in advance, takes two weeks, and we'd only been working on this six days, so there was no chance to do that. And the only way that we ever got that thing across, and I can't emphasize that enough—the

only possible way that this thing was done [was through] the radio, the television, and the newspaper. All three . . . every day, every time you looked at the paper: are we going to let Charlotte, Asheville, Raleigh, anybody beat us out of this thing? This is going to be the capstone of Winston-Salem's whole cultural life. We've got to have this school. And then they said, we are going to have this telephone campaign. You've got to be thinking about, *now,* what you can do to get this school for us. . . .

So it was mounted, during that whole period; it was like winning a Duke and Wake Forest football game. . . . By golly, we decided we were gonna win . . . and the paper got the whole thing stirred up. They got that rah rah spirit . . . it was on radio, it was on television, and by golly, we're gonna have that damn school.[69]

The first good news from Winston-Salem reached John Ehle on April 22, only six days before the artists' arrival in North Carolina. He was in New York (probably attending to publication business surrounding his new novel, *The Land Breakers*) at the Hotel Commodore, when Smith Bagley called to tell him that Winston-Salem had $300,000 promised from one source. In a telephone memorandum to himself, Ehle noted that he had "told [Smith] we needed to tell Ed Richards something, for we wanted a place for the school and didn't want him to buy a hotel without knowing exact score."[70] Apparently Richards, a Raleigh businessman and developer, had offered to purchase the Carolina Hotel, if the site committee and Joseph Bryan agreed.

Unfortunately, Smith Bagley's was not the only call Ehle got that day. The chairman of the Charlotte committee also had news: "Jim Stenhouse phoned me here says Charlotte . . . ready to toss in sponge. Talked with Mayor and John Belk. Both say don't know where to get money this size. Jim says he's mad with the Mayor." Stenhouse was bitterly disappointed. "The day will come when Charlotte will regret this," he told the press. "We are passing up an opportunity. It may take 10 to 15 years, but the city that gets this school may well be the cultural center of the Southeast." Angry, Stenhouse went on to scold his fellow citizens: "We don't have time for culture in Charlotte. We're too busy doing other things. People wouldn't turn out as they do at the opera or the symphony if it weren't for business contacts." So distressed were the Charlotte leaders that a representative called the Governor's Mansion during the artists' dinner on the twenty-ninth to request more time. John Ehle took the call and left a message for the governor on a yellow pad: "8:15 P. M. In Charlotte, the Junior Chamber of Commerce and WSOC would like to delay decision for 10 days to give them time. I told her I *wouldn't* tell you this and would take responsibility for it. They said they would not cause any embarrassment. I told her you did not blame Jim Stenhouse for the failure of Charlotte. He is in bed sick because of this." Ehle did, however, tell Sanford that night, and the governor reported the request to the Advisory Board, explaining that he felt it would be unfair to the other cities to delay the decision.[71]

The *Winston-Salem Journal* lost no time in pointing out the moral in the Charlotte story: "It should be noted . . . that the same obstacle which Charlotte does not seem to be able to cross now faces Winston-Salem: the raising of adequate funds . . . the Committee has less than a week to pin down commitments, if not the actual cash. This Charlotte apparently was not able to do. It, too, had possible sites to offer, but lacked sufficient enthusiasm"—something Phil Hanes did not lack. The following day—Friday, April 24—he called John Ehle to let him know that Winston-Salem was "rolling." Smith Bagley now had $400,000 lined up, and he and Phil Hanes had kicked off their campaign that morning at a meeting of the Chamber of Commerce Coffee Club. They told the members that Winston-Salem had four days in which to raise $900,000 to renovate Gray High School, and they passed out checks on Winston-Salem banks, which according to the *Sentinel,* most of the two hundred present signed. The checks were to be returned if the campaign failed to meet the $900,000 goal. "But we're not going to fail," Philip Hanes assured the *Twin City Sentinel,* and called John Ehle to give him the details of the planned two-day telephone fund drive. They expected five to ten thousand donations, to indicate "total community support." They had twenty phones and sixty "girls" to call six thousand people. "Looks like we're going to be all right from a financial viewpt.," Ehle noted; "60 girls," he repeated in a telephone memorandum to himself, bemused. To Governor Sanford, John Ehle reported the Winston-Salem pledge that the money to renovate Gray High School would be available by Tuesday, June 28, when the artists arrived. Of the other contenders, Ehle saw only Raleigh as having a serious bid:

> Charlotte seems to be out of the running.
> Greensboro, which we will visit, seems to have nothing.
> Raleigh has a good proposal, involving the Carolina Hotel and other property.
> Hillsboro wants to have the group come by, but they have nothing.
> I hope that Raleigh doesn't drop out. Winston-Salem needs the

pressure up through Wednesday. We'll get more in Winston-Salem if Raleigh stays in, and it might be that Raleigh will win, after all.

As to his own current condition, Ehle reported that he was "running just ahead of the tidal wave, as usual."[72]

By Monday, April 27, it appeared that Philip Hanes had managed at least to stick his finger in the dike; he called to tell John Ehle that he now had pledges for $785,000 from major sources, "not including R. J. Reynolds, banks." But these promises of financial support, which had not come in earlier, obviously depended on the success of the telephone drive, scheduled to begin at 9:00 A.M. Tuesday and to continue until 10:00 P.M. Wednesday. In a newspaper interview announcing the campaign, Smith Bagley stressed the need to demonstrate that a broad base of community support would undergird generous corporate, foundation, and large-scale private donations. And he pointed up the urgency of the campaign: the money would have to be raised during the two-day deliberations of the Governor's Advisory Board of Artists, whose decision was to be announced Thursday morning. To meet this goal, Smith Bagley and his committee had rustled up not the sixty women previously advertised but two hundred female volunteers to call prospective contributors on twenty-six telephones installed for the purpose in the gallery of the Winston-Salem Arts Council, at the James G. Hanes Community Center. At 6:00 P.M. each of the two days, the women were to be relieved by male volunteers from Hanes Hosiery Mills, Wachovia Bank and Trust, North Carolina National Bank, and R. J. Reynolds Tobacco Company. Six of the telephone lines would be kept free for incoming pledges and the other twenty would be used by the volunteers, each of whom was to sit for two or three hours at his or her own card table with a telephone, a stack of phone numbers, and two sheets of instructions—one a summary of information about the school and the other a seven-point sales talk, with advice and suggestions: "Be positive. 'You'd love to participate in this urgent campaign, wouldn't you?'"[73]

Meanwhile, back at the Governor's Office, Terry Sanford, John Ehle, and Julia Ribet (later Vittorio Giannini's administrative assistant) had been laboring—not without danger of inundation—to bring the artists to North Carolina. On April 7, Governor Sanford wrote to the nine expected to come (Giannini, Adler, Blackmer, de Mille, Green, Limon, Mennin, Pfohl, and Rudel):

The Performing Arts School is quite important to me, both as Governor of the State and personally. I believe at last a State can take a firm hand in offering professional arts training, and that this first state arts school can be the prototype of others, and can help put our country on a firm footing in terms of arts training. Therefore, it is altogether important that we do now what is exactly right.

There are two matters which we need your help with right away. One is the selection of a name for the School. One suggestion thus far received is that it be called the American Arts School in North Carolina. The proponents of that name point out that it does not regionalize the arts and that it leaves the way open for other states to form arts schools themselves, which could be named The American Arts School in Oklahoma, or in New York, or in California. We need to have your ideas on the problem of a name.

Also, right away we need to decide on a site. Four cities for many months have been trying to find a site to offer this School. One is Winston-Salem, a wealthy city of about 120,000 people. Another is Charlotte, the largest city in the two Carolinas, and one of the commercial centers of the South. The third is Raleigh, a city of 100,000, the State Capital. The fourth is Greensboro, a commercial and educational center of about 125,000.

We do not intend to ask you to consider sites that are not pegged down, which are not going to be available if they are selected. We have maintained from the start that the local community ought to supply the campus and buildings on their own. We will, in turn, provide from State and private funds the operating costs of the School.

I suggest that we decide on the 28th and 29th which of these cities has the best offer to make, which will be the best place to put the school. This is a significant task. Each of these cities thinks it ought to be the arts center of the State and region. I believe, however, that one or two of these cities won't be able, in the final analysis, to come up with a facility which by the fall of 1965 can be operable for a school of 400 to 500 resident students. In that case, the selection will not be so difficult, nor will the schedule of site visits be so demanding.

May I suggest that we go about the work at hand in this way, that you meet with the other members of the Committee, and with John Ehle, my special Assistant and one other representative of my office on the morning of the 28th in Winston-Salem. That day you can see the sites which are offered in Winston-Salem and Greensboro, which is only twenty miles away. That night we will fly you to Charlotte. . . .

Next day after seeing the Charlotte site, the Committee will be flown to Raleigh, and will see what Raleigh has to offer. After dinner at the Governor's Mansion that night, we will go into the library and talk about where the School ought to be placed, and will make a decision at that time which I can recommend to the Board of Trustees of the School the following week. We will also discuss the name of the School . . . I know you agree that we are talking about a project which is of immense importance, a new step in the arts in America. People elsewhere are watching what we do with this School. Please give us your best help. I assure you of my personal support of the decisions which [are] reached on the evening of the 29th, and of my continuing support of this school down through the years.

That Governor Sanford needed to reassure the artists he would abide by their decisions is evidenced by Agnes de Mille's skepticism. She asked John Ehle on the way from the airport to Winston-Salem "if this was a publicity gimmick." He told her that it was not, that a decision had yet to be made.[74]

On the morning of April 28, John Ehle, Julia Ribet, Paul Green, Vittorio Giannini, James Christian Pfohl, and Sidney Blackmer gathered at the airport in Greensboro to meet José Limon, Richard Adler, Julius Rudel, and Agnes de Mille. Blackmer, a native of North Carolina, had arrived in Salisbury for a vacation in plenty of time to participate as well in the site tours but was called back to Hollywood on April 23. Blackmer had done a cameo role in *How to Murder Your Wife,* starring Jack Lemmon, that so captivated the film's director that he called Blackmer back to do another scene. Blackmer made it a condition, however, that the shooting which involved him be completed on Monday, April 27, so that he could be back on a plane to North Carolina Monday night. According to the *Salisbury Post,* the actor could not "remember when he's been more excited about anything and nothing—not even work—is going to get in his way as far as the new school is concerned."[75]

Although Sidney Blackmer had anticipated being late, he was on time; it was the plane from New York that was late. The scheduled briefing at the Robert E. Lee Hotel in Winston-Salem was omitted, and the group climbed immediately into state trooper cars, which pleased John Ehle: "I liked that—we didn't use the same car, either; we met at different zone boundaries along the highway, got out of one set of cars and into another. Of course, we didn't usually get to work the sirens, sorry to say." Agnes de Mille rode with John Ehle, "who still had an unbelievable accent . . . I said to him, 'Mr. Ehle, I don't want to seem impertinent, but why does

Winston-Salem *want* this school? It's going to be nothing but an expense. It will grow and the expense will get greater. It will be an awful trouble, a peck of trouble.' He looked at me, opened his great blue eyes, and said 'Miss de Mille, we've waked up.' And that shut me up. It moved me very much."[76]

"So, in we whizzed to Winston-Salem," Agnes de Mille recalls, "and it began." Three hours had been allotted for the tour, which began around 11:30 in the lobby of the Hanes Community Center Theater. Arts council volunteers had covered one wall with brochures, arts council calendars and schedules, and newspaper reports of arts activity in the city. The group examined the theater, looked into the orchestra rehearsal room, and impressed James A. Gray with the seriousness and intentness with which they examined the facilities. He told the *Winston-Salem Journal* that the visitors "obviously had ideas of their own" and reported that Agnes de Mille had asked a number of questions about the stage and that Julius Rudel had inquired about the performances given there. Before leaving the Community Center, the artists were shown the "Dial for Dollars" campaign, which had begun at nine o'clock that morning. Agnes de Mille was struck that the drive was "entirely voluntary," that it required "very careful bookkeeping"—because the money was to be returned if the goal was not met—and that it was a "well-organized, well-planned, concerted effort."[77]

The group then dashed off for a quick look at Wake Forest College and Reynolds Auditorium and then on to Salem College for lunch, where Mayor Benton described the Winston-Salem offer in more detail, and representatives of the city's three colleges spoke. Then the artists toured Gray High School and from there left for Greensboro (where they were expected at 3:15), taking with them a fourteen-page brochure spelling out the Winston-Salem proposal and a copy of the *Winston-Salem Journal* with the front-page headline, "Give Us the School." Agnes de Mille was impressed

> that the entire community—and by that I really mean to include the Hanes, the Reynolds, and the other very rich people in the entire community—they were all absolutely behind it, and fervently and intelligently enthusiastic.
>
> This was a very wonderful thing to see in America, because you find it all the time in Europe where you take it for granted. It's new here, this kind of communal enthusiasm for something that is so important and so absolutely unprofitable, except in the spiritual sense. That these rich, rich people, who obviously dealt in making money in one way or another, were interested now in people's souls, struck me as

novel. . . . I remember Phil Hanes left one meeting and said, "Excuse me, but I've got to get a million dollars." . . . Well, I wasn't used to this kind of talk, because I'd run a little dance company. If I'd said I've got to have fifty bucks, it meant a hard lunch.[78]

In Greensboro, the artists were scheduled to spend three hours on the University of North Carolina campus, including a reception given for them by Chancellor Otis Singletary. If they had wanted to sample community support in the *Greensboro Daily News,* they would have had to turn to page 8, where their decision was described as one of paramount importance to "the scope and purpose of the University of North Carolina": "The project ties in with the new plan and vision for development of the reorganized university. . . . The urge is for balance on the Greensboro campus; and the school for the performing arts fits in snugly with what has already been projected. The offer here consists not of an abandoned, outmoded school building but of a strong program on a properly oriented campus and in an atmosphere which only a university can provide." The *Daily News* editorial writer was not wrong when he observed that a "key policy decision" was about to be made; orientation and atmosphere in the training of artists were precisely the points on which Governor Sanford, John Ehle, and Vittorio Giannini disagreed with the University of North Carolina. But their opposition to placing the school on the Greensboro campus—and thus forfeiting the Ford Foundation grant—was not an influencing factor with the Advisory Board. When asked in 1982 what John Ehle had stressed in his "initial briefing" of the artists in North Carolina, Agnes de Mille indicated that no such briefing had taken place: "Well, it was to be a school of the arts, dedicated to high caliber art. Now, they didn't have to spell out that for the crowd that came down because we were in the business. We were playwrights, actors, and whatnot. They didn't have to tell us why that was important—because we'd given our lives to it." The UNC-Greensboro offer, which included established schools of music and drama, in fact emphasized the presence on campus of a kindergarten through grade twelve school run by the Education Department; property already owned by the university, on which a new dormitory could be built; and university food, laundry, and medical services—all of which meant that the school could begin immediately with "minimum capital outlay." Although these factors were important and necessary, they were not the sorts of things Agnes de Mille had given her life to. The Greensboro bid must have sounded painfully utilitarian compared to the plea from Winston-Salem the advisory board had read that morning:

We want the School for the Performing Arts. We want it so deeply that we shall be glad to invest something more precious than money—our time, our enthusiasm and our affection—to make it flourish . . . we are aware that love of the arts is not so deep and so widespread in our community as we would wish it to be, that Winston-Salem shares with too many other American cities the blemishes of our hasty, impatient and acquisitive way of life.

That is why we are so anxious to have the School come here.

By the time the artists left Greensboro that evening, Winston-Salem's "blitz telephone drive" had raised pledges of $214,729 from 1,680 donors, more than half of the 3,000 who had been called by 5:00 P.M.[79]

The next morning, Wednesday, April 29, the artists heard presentations from Durham and Hillsborough at the Jack Tar Hotel. E. J. Evans and Charles Norton presented Durham's proposal, which included a fifteen-acre site at Research Triangle Park and the suggestion that Durham, Raleigh, Chapel Hill, and the state join in supporting the school there, where it would be centrally located and have access to the resources of all three cities. No local funds, however, had yet been raised.[80]

Three students from the North Carolina State School of Design then presented their Hillsborough plan, for which the advisory board graciously "expressed admiration." They showed drawings of a three-auditorium complex to be built on a fifty-six-acre site for two and a half million dollars, none of which was anywhere in view. The following day, the *News of Orange County* angrily complained that the students' presentation in Durham was a last-minute sop to "assuage their disappointment" at the sudden cancellation of plans to have the artists visit the Hillsborough site. According to the *News,* John Ehle had told Historic Hillsborough Commission President Robert J. Murphy that the artists would spend the night of the twenty-eighth at the Colonial Inn in Hillsborough and hear the town's bid the next morning. Pitifully aggrieved, however, the paper huffed,

> The powers, after months of teasing the historic old site along with hopes for the school's location here, pulled out the rug Tuesday morning [April 28] with a decision not to permit its national advisory board of artists to visit the proposed local site. . . . Detailed plans for the presentation had been arranged by Dr. Murphy when the visit was cancelled with the explanation that only Winston-Salem and Raleigh were being considered. Press reports have since indicated bids were heard from Greensboro and from Durham also.

The Hillsborough plan had been John Ehle's idea, and he had hoped that the town would be able to raise the money to build a campus by approaching sources in Burlington, Greensboro, Chapel Hill, and Durham, all of which were located close enough to Hillsborough to provide a good audience base. When no financial support was forthcoming, Ehle was faced with the decision of whether to take the eight board members all the way to Hillsborough to hear a hopeless proposal.[81]

On their way to Raleigh, where they were to register at the Downtowner Inn by noon and have lunch with the Raleigh committee, the board toured Durham's suggested Research Triangle site with Charles Norton. Then from 2:00 to 3:30 P.M. the group heard Raleigh's proposal and saw the Carolina Hotel. Committee chairman Bill Joslin pledged the support of the business community, and Mayor Jim Reid promised the school would find a "receptive atmosphere" in the Raleigh community. The chancellor of North Carolina State University, John Caldwell, promised that his liberal arts program would "accent and augment" the new school; Raleigh's Little Theater director Richard Snavely described plans for a $60,000 renovation of the theater, which would be made available for arts school productions. The presence of the North Carolina Ballet Company was cited and that the hotel "could easily be expanded in its U-shaped rear." But the most interesting point in Raleigh's favor—and the most savvy—was raised by Sam Ragan, who observed that "when the legislature meets in Raleigh . . . the lawmakers will have an opportunity close at hand to see the school in operation in order to decide whether increased appropriations are necessary." Ragan, executive news editor of the *News and Observer* and the *Raleigh Times* and a member of the North Carolina Conservatory Committee, was most likely responsible for the editorial in that day's paper, "Invitation to the Arts": "Because Raleigh is both the geographic and cultural center of North Carolina it is the logical place for the school. . . . Indeed, when the bill to establish this new venture into the arts . . . was passed by the General Assembly in 1963 it was close to 'legislative intent' in the minds of many who supported the bill that it be located in the capital city of North Carolina."[82]

Whether the editorial was correct or not, Ragan was approaching—albeit in a somewhat gingerly fashion—the sticky issue of the school's political survival after Terry Sanford's term as governor ended. More important than local philanthropy and foundation grants was the budget allotted by the state legislature, and the higher education budgeting process was dominated by the powerful Consolidated University of North Carolina,

7. A canny mountain man of southern Appalachia: John Ehle, with still.

under the leadership of its near-invincible president, William Friday. And although Friday had supported the bill that created the school, he felt that he had to support his chancellor in the bid of the Greensboro campus to get it. Between a less than enthusiastic university and an unpredictable legislature, the school was likely to find itself in deep waters from the very day its doors finally opened. To John Ehle, it was the ultimate frustrating irony that the school's survival was finally ensured in 1971 by making it one of the campuses of the university: "I don't know where I was at the time. I probably would have died at that moment . . . I admit the School had proved to be vulnerable to attacks every time the Legislature met; it had proved that it is dangerous to exist alone. It had had to mount every two years a formidable defense of its life."[83] The university was one solution, and it has insulated the school from political attempts at annihilation thanks to the friendship of William Friday and the security of becoming a property of the oldest state university in the country. Another solution would have been the one Sam Ragan seemed to be approaching: to identify the school with state government, by locating it where it could lobby for itself every day, become a part of capital city tours, and eventually be perceived by the state's legislators as an institution as vital to the state's dignity as its museums, the old capitol, the Governor's Mansion, and the statue of Sir Walter Raleigh.

A thunderstorm was brewing by the time the tour of the Carolina Hotel ended. John Ehle, "nudging in the most subtle and delicious way," Agnes de Mille remembers—"I wish he were in our State Department"—shepherded the artists back to their rooms at the Downtowner, where they were to meet in closed session and make their decision before attending the governor's dinner at 6:00. As the advisory board debated, Winston-Salem's two-day telephone drive was nearing its end. With five hours remaining, Smith Bagley told a reporter that an astounding $569,310 had been pledged by 3,622 people.[84]

That night, John Ehle thought to have recorded on tape the dinner-table meeting of the governor with his board. Even more than the transcript of that conference, the tape reveals the genuine excitement and seriousness which the artists brought to their task. Their voices are filled with energy and concern. Sophisticates from the big city they may have been, but the mission of the new little school seems to have touched them deeply, as did the enthusiasm and commitment of the citizens they had met with, something Richard Adler wistfully expressed:

> For the past twenty-five years I've been, on and off, coming into this state, and one thing particularly I've learned: that I've never yet been in a state . . . where there is as much state pride as North Carolinians feel about North Carolina. And this is to me—coming now from two eastern states, New Jersey and New York, where they are pretty blasé about things like this—something to really feel and be a little bit envious of. . . . I wish we had a little bit more of it where we come from.

Governor Sanford appointed Sidney Blackmer to be chairman of the group and asked him for its report, which Blackmer asked Vittorio Giannini to read: "That this board is of the opinion . . . [indecipherable phrase] that the Winston-Salem site appears to be the most desirable for the school. The motion unanimous with that." Giannini's words are followed by an awkward silence on the tape, finally explained by the governor's laughter-provoking remark, "Well, you didn't elaborate on that a lot; I hardly had time to light a cigar."[85]

Blackmer did go on to elaborate, however, revealing that the Raleigh bid had indeed been perceived as a strong one:

> We had a lengthy and I thought a very able presentation from the city of Raleigh, and we debated it back and forth. . . . Culturally and edu-cationally, based on the advantages in this area, Raleigh was most appealing, but the physical aspect of what they had to offer would pre-vent this project from operating properly. It would be cramped, and permanently so, unless they used the park across the street, and we just almost to a man could not see that . . . they come out with some campus area and the possibility of growth, but you can't crowd this sort of artistic endeavor into tight little two-by-four quarters. You simply couldn't do it. No place to rehearse the ballet. There was no theater. There was nothing. And this was disappointing. . . .
>
> And after kicking this around back and forth with many angles, the presentation from Winston was not only the best as regarding housing for this project, but the money backing was remarkable, and we were chiefly influenced, I think, by the spirit of the citizens. Everyone seemed to respond . . . "This we want!"

Governor Sanford assured the board that he accepted its recommendation and that he would announce it at a press conference at 10:00 the following morning. He then went immediately to the matter of naming a director for the school, a piece of business he had not mentioned in his April 7 letter to the board, assigning its first tasks. He and Ehle had decided that it would be in the school's best interests for Giannini to be appointed officially as soon as possible, and he left it to Ehle to convey his wishes to the board. Governor Sanford called on Richard Adler first for general comments on the matter of the director or anything else, and Adler took the opportunity to nominate Giannini:

> I think it's . . . very important to discuss what is going to be the heart-beat of the school, now that we have decided what we think is the proper site. . . . I think that we're particularly fortunate to have right here, in this room, as a member of the Advisory Committee . . . somebody whose qualifications are so unusual that I don't believe that if we searched with a fine-toothed comb through the 190 million people in this country, that we could come up with a more capable, visionary, educator, artist, musician, scholar, and certainly educational leader, than Vittorio Giannini.

So as not to embarrass Giannini, Governor Sanford asked John Ehle to escort him from the room while the board discussed the nomination. Although Sanford had asked Vittorio months before (September 27, 1963) if he would lead the school, the governor made it clear that he deferred now to his board: "I think we ought to talk this thing out. Be certain that this is what you want to do, and then if it is what you want to do, leave it with me." Sidney Blackmer called on Paul Green, who cited "the vision that he [Giannini] has shown and the energy that he's put into it [the school] . . . I don't see how you could diminish the history of his experience . . . I don't see anybody else that I would recommend more highly." When Blackmer asked if anyone had any objections to Giannini's appointment, James Christian Pfohl, who worked with Giannini for eleven years at his summer music camp in Brevard, stated firmly, "I think this: you've got to be sure he has the help he needs to follow this out. . . . He's going to *have* to have an administrator." The issue Pfohl was raising, albeit obliquely, was Giannini's health. As his friend John Ehle wrote of Giannini years later, "His health was poor, he was nearing retirement age, and he had no administrative experience; he was the last man on earth a search committee would ever even interview, but he had come to embody the spirit of the school."[86]

Agnes de Mille recalls that when Giannini was asked to return, "we realized he'd been weeping. I think he knew that it was very dangerous for him to take this job."[87] Giannini made a brief, emotional speech of acceptance:

> You know that I think this school can be a wonderful thing, not only for North Carolina, for the nation, but especially for the great number of talented young people that we have in our country. And if I can in any way help, in the smallest way, help you all to give these youngsters a chance to gain a professional fame, and an ideal and a vision of what the arts can really mean—if I can help in the smallest way, I feel that my life will not have been spent in vain . . . I accept this, I assure you, in all humility, and very much—I wouldn't say frightened—but realizing what it means. . . .
>
> I know, of course . . . that as true great men and great artists, you will be very generous with your advice, with your help, which I'm sure I'll need every step of the way. So I won't ask, may I call upon you? Knowing your heart and your generosity and Governor Sanford's great vision, I know I'll have that. And I pray that I may come to you very often.
>
> I can't say much more. I'm poor at words. My heart is full.

Breaking the intensity of the moment, Agnes de Mille dryly replied to Giannini's "I'm poor at words," by remarking off-mike, "Terrible!" The group began to laugh, relieved that the moment of emotion had passed. When Governor Sanford commented, his southern accent thicker and more sprawling than at any other time on the tape, "I think he'll do all right with the legislature; I notice that he's already sayin' 'We wont the helpa *you all*,'" they responded uproariously.

Governor Sanford asked that they next take up the question of a name, although "it's not absolutely necessary that we select a name right now." In fact, the Board of Trustees later officially named the school, but as with the selection of a site and a president, the board took the advice of the artists. Sidney Blackmer believed the name should be "simple and to the point, and that it should definitely be North Carolina something,"

<blockquote>
because we are sure, as in the other things that you have initiated—other states have immediately adopted them and proceeded on them . . . they can also call theirs the Oklahoma School of, or the Ohio School of, or whatever. But we will have it on record as the North Carolina School. Now, could we have suggestions . . . Paul?
</blockquote>

PAUL GREEN: Well, Governor, I think that to limit this name . . . to a certain phase and practices of the arts wouldn't be too wise. . . . For instance, in drama. You certainly want to look forward to teaching writing of drama, not only performing, and certainly in music—among the very richest possibilities in music is composition. And then, children, natively, like to model with clay. They like to draw. So to put a title on it that would limit it to three things, that is, to performing plays, to performing music, and to dancing, seems to me deleterious. So I thought—we think—a title like North Carolina School of the Arts.

BLACKMER: That seems to say it.

GREEN: And by the word, the plural use of "Arts," [that] keeps it from having too much relevance to the graphical, pictorial.

Paul Green had named the school, although Agnes de Mille objected, on jealously guarded grounds: "I don't like calling it 'School of the Arts' because I think it just doesn't involve architecture and all the graphic arts, painting and so forth. And it [the name] doesn't particularize this, which is professional, for the practice of the living arts, and also, I hope, for the creation. But I think you start by the performance of them. And I think the word "Performing" [in the title]—it doesn't offend me at all, having been a kind of performer for so long."

A lively discussion followed, with Jim Pfohl lining up alongside Agnes de Mille, and Richard Adler leading the forces against "Performing" in the title. Adler made the point that later prevailed with the Board of Trustees: "Jim, Paul Green had what I thought was a very valid point that later on, perhaps several years distant, we might, or the school might, want to enlarge its scope into using . . . the visual arts as part of its curriculum. . . . Scenic designing or anything like sculpture, in which case . . . the 'Performing' ought to be left out." Adler also raised the important point that the school should not be held rigidly to a rule of 50 percent North Carolina students enrolled, nor to a regional enrollment, but that it should draw from the nation, "for the best possible talent . . . all over the country."

As the thunder rolled and a downpour began, Governor Sanford moved to break up the meeting, assuring those headed for New York that night in his private plane that it had radar. Vittorio Giannini, with the proper sense of an ending and the Continental's open regard for the human heart, proposed a motion: "That we express our admiration and gratitude to Governor Sanford, who has had the vision and the courage to be the first Governor of a state to put all his efforts towards the establishment of the first state school of the arts." Embarrassed by Giannini's warmth and praise, the tough former paratrooper, now chief executive, quickly pulled rank and told the first president of the first state school of the arts that his first motion was "out of order!"

On Thursday, April 30, 1964, two special announcements from the Governor's Office in Raleigh were reported in the state's press. The first was page 1 news and easy to find: the new school of the arts would be located in Winston-Salem, by unanimous vote of the Advisory Board of Artists appointed by Governor Sanford. "Certainly the State is indebted to hundreds of people in many places," the governor said in his expression of appreciation to all those involved in establishing the school. "I hope that all the places [that competed] will now work to make this School an institution for the whole State and for the whole South and for the whole country. The children after all will come from every place, and they are the purpose and substance of what we are about."[88]

8. "He looked at me, opened his great blue eyes, and said, 'Miss de Mille, we've waked up.'" John Ehle, still awake some twenty years later, in Duke Chapel.

The second item of news, apparently judged unrelated to the big education story of that day, appeared on page 10, section B, of the *Greensboro Daily News* and was titled "Author to Quit Job as Aide": "John Ehle, 38, one of Governor Terry Sanford's administrative aides, said today he will resign effective June 1. Ehle, who joined Sanford's staff in 1962 as a special cultural and education assistant, said he planned to move to New York City and complete work on a novel. He is the author of five books. A native of Asheville, Ehle was an instructor at the University of North Carolina when he joined the Governor's staff."[89] The tumult of starting the school had scarcely subsided when Ehle, almost anonymously, bowed out. He remained a frequent unofficial adviser to his friend Vittorio, and after Giannini's untimely death, he continued to be an uncompromising friend to the school of the arts—and to all new ideas about schools.

And so the dream was about to become a reality. W. McNeil Lowry helped because he had opinions about arts education and $280 million to give away, and he saw his chance in North Carolina, and he took it. Governor Sanford helped because he had promised to work aggressively for education, and he meant to educate everybody he could get hold of before he left office. Vittorio Giannini helped because he was a composer, and without new generations of highly trained musicians there would be no one to play what composers composed. But John Ehle is a writer, and writing, unlike philanthropy and politics and music, is a private rather than a public profession. Why he cared about starting this school is therefore harder to explain.

Certainly there was no glory in it—as the *Greensboro Daily News* could have told him. There was no money either. And as Agnes de Mille had pointed out, such enterprises grow and reward their supporters with "awful trouble." Publicly John Ehle has frequently stated that artists need a different kind of education and that it angers him that so few universities acknowledge this fact. But privately, in an unguarded moment, he once offered a deeper and more personal reason for his commitment to new schools. In a letter to a child who had attended Jim Pfohl's music camp at Brevard and who hoped to become the first student at the school of the arts, John Ehle confessed that when he was in the fourth grade he had made F's in deportment. "Make no mistake in thinking I was not a success in Aycock School," he joked. "If one makes an F in deportment, he is a success in Aycock School; he is a leader in Aycock School." But Aycock School was not a joke; it was

> a horror-hole of a school which by accident was named after Charles Aycock. . . . [It] was not a school so much as a place of vengeance . . . I did poor work in every way and was in the same predicament that troubles so many thousand students in the poor-quality schools that we have in many of the poorer neighborhoods of our country. I believe the potential I had for learning and achieving was no less when I was ten years old than when I was eight or twelve, but when I was ten years old, in this Aycock School, I was an F student, and I would be an F person today if I had to stay in that place, in that neighborhood, in that sort of shadowy environment.[90]

At the artists' dinner, Governor Sanford gracefully thanked all who had helped develop the new school, but he ambushed John Ehle (as jumpy under the threat of praise as the governor himself) with sweeping tribute, casually phrased: "John has been a father of so many creative things in this state, that it's hard to tell what kind of a state it would have been, if he hadn't been hanging around over at Chapel Hill."

VITTORIO

WINSTON-SALEM was jubilant. "Leaders Say: 'It's A Great Day'" the *Sentinel*'s headline exulted. "At midmorning the telephone switchboard at the Journal and Sentinel was jammed with calls from persons wanting to know the outcome of the Governor's press conference scheduled at 10:00 A.M." In fact, "Winston-Salem interests"—probably Philip Hanes—had called Raleigh at 9:30 the night before, hoping to get word of the advisory board's decision, but the governor and his staff kept the outcome a secret. "Dial for Dollars" was a success; by the time of the governor's announcement, some 4,500 people had contributed, and money was still coming in, Smith Bagley told reporters. "Local banks have reported . . . big stacks of checks waiting to be picked up," so many that the arts council hired extra help to total the contributions and match checks with pledges. When the final count was made, Bagley reported 5,344 contributions, totaling $850,354.[1]

Leaders of the drive gathered to celebrate at the home of Philip and Joan Hanes. John Ehle was invited but never arrived; he was rumored to have remained in Raleigh "to placate citizens there who were irate because their city had not gotten the school." Still irrepressible and still handling Smith Bagley's correspondence, Philip Hanes stood on a footstool and hushed the elated assembly while he read a letter of thanks to Governor Sanford and all who had helped in the campaign:

> Needless to say, we had strong faith that Winston-Salem was the right place for the School for the Performing Arts and we had as much faith in your vision to put it here. We also had faith in our community— that it would produce the where-with-all [sic]. . . . Nevertheless, it still came as a tremendous jolt to know that we would receive the school. I have never witnessed such joy over receiving anything. I have had one call after another all morning. Everyone is delighted and I feel certain the community will stand behind the school.
>
> As former chairman of the Mayor's Committee . . .I should like to give a little credit where credit is due. The first Mayor's Committee

worked with extreme diligence and laid all of the ground work that made the final campaign possible. However, this committee went as far as it could go and new leadership with new thought had to be sought. We found that leadership in Smith Bagley who not only raised the majority of the money by dint of his own single perseverance but who sparked the entire community with [h]is brilliantly conceived "Dial for Dollars" campaign. This campaign gave the people of Winston-Salem a vote . . . cast in thousands of checks.[2]

In his reply offering congratulations and inspiration, Governor Sanford took the opportunity to make two points about the school which he wished to be remembered: first, that among the "hundreds of people in many places in our state" who had helped bring the North Carolina School of the Arts to life, "most of all, we owe a debt to John Ehle for his vision and persistence"; and second, an implied warning, that to ensure "full and lasting success" for the school, it must be perceived as a state institution: "We need now the help of all our people, and we will have it, I believe, and the School will have the support of us all and be in fact and name a creation of our State and its own property. I know that you in Winston-Salem agree with that wholeheartedly."[3] Nearly two years of experience with starting a conservatory had taught Governor Sanford to guard against jealousy.

In Charlotte, a small cadre of arts supporters grieved while the *Charlotte Observer* flayed the rest of the citizenry with a scathing editorial titled "Winston-Salem Action Puts Charlotte Effort to Shame":

Charlotte's chances of getting the North Carolina School for the Performing Arts have gone glimmering. The moving finger of the site selection committee did not even pause at our location on the state map. There was little here to indicate that Charlotte cared enough to want the very best.

The committee found what it wanted in Winston-Salem. The choice did not come about by accident. Winston-Salem's business and industrial leaders, its public officials and hundreds of its culture conscious residents were willing to invest their money, time, enthusiasm and affection in this school. . . .

It may do the people of Charlotte some good to look at what Winston-Salem did to impress the distinguished committee with its bid for the kind of institution that does not come along every day, every year or, indeed, every generation.

Charlotte bid nothing in the way of site facilities or money as the time for decision arrived. There was a vague promise of community backing and passing reference to the community's recent support of financial campaigns for the arts.

No wishful thinking was engaged in by Winston-Salem. . . .

In Raleigh, where the Carolina Hotel was offered as a school site and where a committee of 100 citizens presented the capital's bid, there was obvious disappointment over the decision. But neither Raleigh, Greensboro nor Durham shared the ignominy of Charlotte's failure to even make a serious bid for the school.

Disappointed and irate citizens or no, the *Raleigh Times* maintained strict neutrality in its report of Winston-Salem's victory, the best stance no doubt from the city that had been the only close runner-up. The *Durham Morning Herald* could afford to be overtly gracious because Durham had been a late and never very strong contender:

> To those who have followed the accounts of Winston-Salem's efforts to secure the projected state school for the performing arts, that city's selection, the unanimous choice of the advisory board, will come as no surprise. The people of Winston-Salem worked to get the school with a vigor and an interest which showed they wanted it. . . .
>
> No community seeking the school should feel slighted that Winston-Salem was chosen. To a greater degree than any other, the Twin City undertook to provide what the board wanted. In so doing, it not only secured a project which can prove a great community asset, but it also showed other localities how to make a more favorable impression than the competition.

One Durham reporter, however, could not resist a potshot: "Winston-Salem, home of Wake Forest College, whose students are taught that dancing is one of modern society's subtlest sins, has been named the site of the new North Carolina School of the Performing Arts. Presumably the performing arts school will allow dancing." Greensboro, consistent to the end, took more than a potshot in an editorial ungraciously titled, "A School That Is Yet to Perform." With the pained smile of an offended dowager, the *Daily News* offered frigid congratulations, even as it clucked out its forecasts of doom:

> We offer our congratulations to Winston-Salem upon its acquisition of the state School for Performing Arts. . . . Now that the site of the school has been determined, we trust that cooperation and support

will be devoted to seeing that it makes the contribution which its pro-
moters envisioned.

Actually there was no competition under the ground rules laid
down by those given the assignment of locating the school.

Winston-Salem was far ahead—almost alone—in the community
effort which it waged. . . .

Greensboro's approach was on a state basis. Civic and U.N.C.
leadership joined in urging that the new school be brought under the
university here, that facilities already in existence be expanded and uti-
lized and that faculty and excellent programs in music, choreography
and drama be taken advantage of. . . .

We still believe that the decision to set up a separate and independent school, made in great haste by a committee largely unfamiliar
with the ramifications of the matter, was unsound policy. Administrative, budgetary and operating problems will become more apparent as
the talk of converting a dream into a reality gets underway.

What criticism we have is not of our Forsyth neighbor and its successful campaign but of the selection committee, in its haste, lack of
deliberation and understanding and charting of a policy which affects
the university and the effort to co-ordinate educational agencies, institutions and programs on all levels during the last few years.

Winston-Salem got the school on the basis of what it offered.
Greensboro simply assured its interest, co-operation and support in
what the state already had to offer. We are sure that the Twin City,
while accepting congratulations, recognizes that the real challenge of
establishing the school and making it become an asset to the state and
to the performing arts may be far more trying than the campaign
which brought its acquisition.[4]

Other apostles of the arts doubted as well. Philip Hanes believes that
McNeil Lowry "took a hell of a chance" when he encouraged the development of the school,

because when we did this thing, I proudly told all of my friends in the
arts and other places how wonderful it was that we were going to have
this marvelous conservatory for the performing arts. And there was
just *no response at all*. I mean, they sometimes dropped their mouths a
little, and I'd say, "Well, what's the matter?" They said, "Well, you
know, we wish you luck, but it'll be just sort of a prep school." I said,
"No, no, no, no. We're out for the big time." And they said, "You can't

do that. Do you realize that every conservatory of any consequence backs right up to a major symphony or major opera or major dance company, where people just walk across the street and give classes? Hell, you're four or five hundred miles from the nearest possible place to get these master teachers. How in the hell are you going to do it? I mean, at Curtis . . . they've got the whole Philadelphia Orchestra to draw from. They can draw every first chair player down to come in and add to their faculty, and all they've got to do is pay them to walk across the street. You can't do it. It's *impossible*."

"Well," said Philip Hanes to the detractors, with sturdy optimism, "we'll do it," even though the identity of "we" was already shifting: John Ehle's daily and official responsibility for the school was at an end, and he was packing to go to New York, where he hoped to be left in peace long enough to complete work on his next book, *The Free Men*. As leader of his party, Governor Sanford had now to turn his attention to the 1964 elections. McNeil Lowry had been promoted to a vice-presidency in the Ford Foundation. As the new head of policy and planning, Lowry was now one of three vice-presidents reporting directly to Ford president Henry Heald. That summer Lowry remarked cryptically to Vittorio Giannini that there would "undoubtedly have to be some changes" in his relationships with his "many friends in the arts." If Lowry would now be a more distant contact, the humanities and arts program was nonetheless still his responsibility, under the direction of Sigmund Koch, professor of psychology at Duke University, a North Carolina connection which all hoped would help the struggling school. And finally, although the responsibility for faculty and student recruitment and curriculum development was now exclusively Vittorio Giannini's, the composer could not settle down to full-time work as the school's president until June 1965. Until then, he would commute to fulfill his commitments in New York.[5] Obviously, if there was going to be toe-dancing, the Board of Trustees would have to be there.

On May 28, 1964, Governor Sanford announced the school's twelve-member board: from Winston-Salem, R. Philip Hanes, Jr., Smith Bagley, and Wallace Carroll; from Raleigh, Sam Ragan, Hugh Cannon, E. N. Richards, and Mrs. Everette Miller; from Asheville, James McClure Clarke; from Louisburg, Mrs. Wilbur Jolly; from Southern Pines, Mrs. James Boyd; from Charlotte, Martha Muilenburg; and from Durham, Dr. James H. Semans.[6] The board members represented the state as a whole and brought to their task experience in business, politics, the professions, journalism, fundraising, and community arts activity. In addition, like Philip

9. *Members of the first Board of Trustees of the North Carolina School of the Arts, appointed May 28, 1964. Back row, left to right: Sam Ragan, Ed Richards, Hugh Cannon, Ben Swalin (ex-officio), Smith Bagley, R. Philip Hanes, Jr. Front row, left to right: Olive Miller, Martha Muilenburg, Sybil Jolly, Dr. James H. Semans, Kathryn Boyd (not pictured: Wallace Carroll, James McClure Clarke).*

Hanes and Alice's White Queen, all were prepared to believe six impossible things before breakfast, if that was what it took to establish an arts school "from scratch," as Governor Sanford had directed at Brevard. The board held its first meeting in Governor Sanford's office on Friday, July 17. Accepting Governor Sanford's recommendation, it elected Vittorio Giannini president and selected as the official name North Carolina School of the Arts, as Paul Green had suggested at the first meeting of the advisory board. Dr. James H. Semans of Durham and Duke University Medical School was named chairman of the board, and Wallace Carroll, publisher of the *Winston-Salem Journal and Sentinel,* was selected vice-chairman. E. N. Richards of Raleigh, who had proven his mettle by standing ready to purchase the Carolina Hotel, was made chairman of the committee to hire an architectural firm that would prepare plans for two dormitories, to be built on the Gray High School football field. As memorandums in the archives indicate, John Ehle had had Dr. Semans in mind for chairman of the board for many months but cannily had not mentioned the idea to him before the meeting. Dr. Semans recalls that he arrived late, and

> was met by John Ehle . . . who greeted me by saying, "Governor Sanford is going to ask you to be chairman of the Board of Trustees of this new school, and I hope you won't say no." This came as a shock, and I thought defensively, well, I will at least have to be courteous and say yes today, and I'll call him up tomorrow and say no. I can't embarrass him before eminent people that I have not even met. Though I felt certain that they were all potentially friendly North Carolinians.
>
> That evening I talked with Mary [Mrs. Semans], and she indicated she was extremely interested in this appointment. So we met with . . . Vittorio Giannini and John Ehle, who were having dinner together in Chapel Hill at the Ranch House. In this meeting, Mary and I realized the careful deliberation that had preceded every decision concerning the school. That knowledge plus Mary's enthusiasm to become a partner in this enterprise was most persuasive. After all, my first obligation would be to medical emergencies, and any pioneer project has many emergencies of its own. Now Mary was making herself available for such calls.

Mary Semans still remembers the persuasiveness of John Ehle that night: "[He] is the most disarming person on this earth, and he talks around a subject and in a subject—he's just so charming and enthusiastic in his own way, that we really just listened to him . . . talk a great deal about what the school meant."[7] Sometime during dinner, John Ehle had made of the reluctant physician and his vital wife two unrelenting friends for the school of the arts.

Getting and spending were the immediate, crucial concerns of the new board—getting as much money together as possible and spending it as prudently as they could, for they had little enough to finance the school's opening. For renovation of Gray High School and the building of two dormitories, they had the "Dial for Dollars" money ($850,354) and a $300,000 grant from the Z. Smith Reynolds Foundation. The bill that created the school had stated that no money was to come from the state for capital improvements, nor could Ford money be used for those purposes (if the Ford money ever was provided). Nothing better illustrates the dedication of this board to seeing the school open in September of 1965 than the determined frugality with which it spent its first, limited funds. In a memo written to justify a drycleaning bill from Zinzendorf Laundry, Giannini's assistant, Julia Ribet, explained to a state budget officer that to provide some protection for herself and Giannini from the stares of people walking by, "looking for the Chamber of Commerce," twenty yards of draperies had been given them by one of the trustees.[8] Evidently not even the president's temporary office at the Hanes Community Center (moved to the Quality Oil Company on Northwest Boulevard on February 15, 1965) was to be adorned out of capital improvement money or the finite state allotment for operating expenses, if the trustees could find a way to do it themselves.

The board's attempt to provide for the building of two dormitories they could afford immediately ran into trouble. At the trustees' second meeting (August 14, 1964), Synergetics, Inc., of Raleigh was officially appointed to prepare sketches for the construction and for the renovations needed at Gray.[9] It is not surprising that Ed Richards and the board would have engaged Synergetics; the firm was well known to John Ehle and other members of the governor's staff in Raleigh and had been called upon for an architectural evaluation of Gray High School by Smith Bagley in March of 1964. The firm, which was "noted for its use of curved structures," according to the *News and Observer,* had created the Tower of Light at the New York World's Fair and was associated with the brilliant but eccentric Buckminster Fuller, inventor of the geodesic dome. On one of his earlier gambols through the state, Fuller had built his first large geodesic dome. For the summer session of 1948 at Black Mountain College in western North Carolina, Fuller joined a guest faculty of notable artists and experimenters, among them John Cage, Merce Cunningham, and Willem de Kooning. Fuller inspired the students at Black Mountain to help him build a geodesic dome out of Venetian blind scrap stock, which he had brought with him in twenty-six-hundred-foot rolls of variegated colors. When the dome, predictably, failed to stand, Fuller christened it his "Supine Dome." In a 1967 interview with historian Martin Duberman, Merce Cunningham recalled that observers at the time got the "sort of feeling it wanted to go up."[10] With hindsight it is easy to see why an architectural firm under the influence of Fuller came up with plans which Dr. Semans remembers as "expensive" and "unrealistic." The Synergetics dormitories—however much they may have wanted to go up—would have cost $3 million to build (more than three times what the board could spend), and in addition, the head of the firm, James W. Fitzgibbon, had decided by November of 1964 that he could not "work under the provisions of state regulations," and of course, any buildings owned by the state would have to be built under the guidelines of the Department of Administration in Raleigh.[11]

As if all this were not enough, the superintendent of the Winston-Salem—

Forsyth County School System, Marvin Ward, had belatedly learned that the school board was restricted by statute from donating the campus of Gray High School to the state. The land was owned by Winston-Salem and Forsyth County, which were required to get the value of the land, whether by sale or lease, and the state was required to own any land and buildings upon which it expended money. Thus a chunk of telethon money would have to be spent on acquiring the Gray High School property, leaving even less money for building the dorms. In this crisis the board was fortunate to be able to turn to R. B. Crawford, chairman of the board of Hanes Hosiery Mills. Philip Hanes believes that it was his father, Ralph, who suggested that Crawford take over:

> Well, R. B. Crawford was Mr. Builder around Winston-Salem for years and years and years. And I could be wrong, but it's my recollection that one day I was talking to Dad and saying, you know, we want to build this school, and we really need somebody to oversee it that knows about buildings in Winston-Salem. I just don't know who in the world is going to be chairman of that building committee. And Dad said, "There is only one man in Winston-Salem, and he just loves buildings and that's R. B. Crawford." And I believe that's where it came from, from my father.

R. B. Crawford had begun his career as a builder in 1926, when he was given the responsibility for constructing a three-story hosiery mill in Winston-Salem; by 1959 he had advanced to the known limits of hosiery mill construction with the 725,000-square-foot Weeks Division plant, up to then the largest of its kind in the world. In 1964, one year from retirement, R. B. Crawford "got all hung up in the arts" because, says Philip Hanes, "he loved building buildings." With dormitory construction scheduled to begin in January 1965, in the hope that the school could open in the fall, it was going to take a lot of love and expertise to scratch up two dormitories by September. Crawford began by flying to Rocky Mount, North Carolina, to visit North Carolina Wesleyan College, whose dormitories had been designed by a firm of Winston-Salem architects. Satisfied that with only slight modifications these plans for two 125-student dorms would do, Crawford recommended at the November meeting that the board move ahead with construction based on this compromise between what it would like and what it could afford. Smith Bagley was understandably disappointed that the dorms that would greet the young artists would be so utilitarian in aspect, with their flat roofs and downspouts on the outside and aluminum window frames. He asked if a private donor could give $100,000 specifically to improve the look of the buildings? Hugh Cannon said yes, but both he and Ralph Hanes emphasized that the school badly needed any more money that could be raised for additional facilities. They couldn't afford decorations, Ralph Hanes said. Indeed, when NCSA opened, Dr. Semans recalls, "the only distinguished room in the entire school" was the president's office, which boasted something of decor only because Anne Forsyth had donated a painting.[12]

With Crawford on the job, construction got under way two weeks ahead of schedule, and the *Twin City Sentinel* reported in January that total costs would be $720,000, $30,000 below Hugh Cannon's barest-bones cost estimate at the November board meeting. To save money, the trustees had leased most of the Gray High School property from the county, and to avoid a crisis with the state, they bought the 3.7 acres on which the dormitories were being built—and found themselves in another crisis when it was discovered that the football field they had purchased was a landfill, and more money had to be found for pylons or the buildings would have sunk into the ground. It may be that for trouble, sinking dormitories had nothing on thirty-eight years of hosiery mills, for "this problem," Dr. Semans gratefully remembers, "was accepted by . . . Mr. R. B. Crawford as one of the facts of life." Crawford brought calm meticulousness to a frantic job. "He paid more attention to a doorknob," says Philip Hanes, "than most paid to a façade, and he was a real nitpicker, and he did not miss a trick." Bruce Stewart, the first dean of students at NCSA, remembers R. B. Crawford as

a wonderful but very tough-minded man who wanted results . . . [he] pressed the builders on that site almost daily. . . . I remember walking around with him and inspecting the two new dormitories with the architects and construction personnel, and they were explaining why this was going to be delayed and why that was going to be delayed, and I remember Crawford looking at them and saying, "I don't want to hear any more reasons why this can't be done. I want to know what it takes to get it done and the day that we can do it." And he pressed very hard so that this school could be opened. . . .

He also had a lot of respect among the conservative business community . . . [they thought] if R. B. Crawford was connected with it, it must be all right. And I think that swayed a lot of people. You would expect the Hanes and the Reynolds families [to have an] interest in the school. . . . But I think R. B. brought in by his presence . . . support [from] the hard-nosed business community.

R. B. Crawford's influence and survival skills were what the school needed during "those early days [when] every penny was spent and more than we could raise," Tom Kenan says. "[R. B.] can be credited, really, with getting the school foundation on firm footing . . . [he was a] very astute, wise gentleman."[13]

R. B. Crawford had bravely taken on the additional responsibility of managing the school's limited funds, when he accepted the presidency of the North Carolina School of the Arts Foundation. Incorporated in Raleigh on October 22, 1964, it was modeled after the Morehead Foundation of North Carolina and was created as a federal and state nonprofit, tax-exempt corporation, to receive and distribute contributions to the school. Because NCSA is a state-supported school, provision had to be made for the acceptance and handling of contributions from nonstate sources. Otherwise, private donations made directly to the school would be co-mingled with state funds and thereby restricted by the State Executive Budget Act, which requires that all funds for operations not spent by the end of the fiscal year be returned to the General Fund of the state.[14]

This problem was neither unusual nor difficult to solve, but other problems soon arose that were directly attributable to the harnessing of two such diverse animals as state government and the arts; the two had trouble understanding one another. The Board of Trustees quickly realized that maintaining political support for the school was just as important as fundraising. Such support *was* fundraising, for without someone to speak for the school with the state legislature, NCSA would be cut out of the budget and cease to exist. "There were a number of attacks made on it for the next two or three sessions," points out Andrew Jones, budget officer under both Governors Sanford and Dan K. Moore. "There were efforts to do away with it." One of the things that immediately struck the General Assembly wrong was the inclusion of out-of-state students. Legislators

felt like, if the taxpayers of North Carolina support this thing, these ought to be North Carolina kids who benefit from it, but the Bill Friday philosophy here permeated a lot of Sanford's and Cannon's thinking, that the more cosmopolitan you are, the wider is going to be the base for this cultural activity, and we don't want to have a country string-band attitude about it. We want this to be a nationally recognized competitive school. . . .

We ran into a good bit of legislative discussion on the funding for tuition and very high per capita cost. But that was due to the fact that this is a specialized school, and at that time we had no experience. We were flying totally blind until the first students were out and in the performing arts area. So we had nothing to point to and say, look what they have done.

Now, of course, we have that experience, and we can, in many, many, many cases, say look, this outstanding artist is a product of our school. And there's no way of putting a dollar figure on that.

Jones remembers that legislators were critical of specific funding requests, "for certain equipment, or providing a stage area, or providing a specialist instructor for a short period of time . . . the legislators simply, in many cases, didn't have an overall understanding of the program, and they were hitting at little areas of it to whittle away."[15]

Philip Dunigan, flutist with the Clarion Wind Quintet and one of the first faculty members hired by Vittorio Giannini, vividly recalls the situation in 1965, the school's first year:

I had a couple of students who were absolutely great . . . one of them came unannounced, down from the mountains. . . . She had a bent flute, I mean, it was just terrible. So I had to get her a good instrument. So I went to Vittorio, and I told him, "We are going to have to buy a couple of good instruments for two of the students who are really outstanding but just don't have instruments."

So he said, "Well, find out how much they cost."

Well, to buy a flute of the kind we wanted would cost more than a new price because of a waiting list. If you wanted to buy a Powell flute in those days, it took five years to get it. We couldn't wait five years; we needed one right away. So you have to pay several thousand dollars.

Well, in those days, it was just a few hundred dollars more than the list price. Now it's a thousand dollars more than the list price. Well, try explaining that to someone from the State of North Carolina Purchasing Department. Not only that, but they had a process of competitive bids, and there was no way you could get an instrument that way. First of all, you couldn't buy an instrument and wait six months to get paid; you've got to have the money first, or you don't get it.

Well, the only way we could make this purchase was to get an exception from the governor's [Advisory Budget Commission], which is the only way for the power to do it. So, Vittorio—well, in those days we weren't part of this North Carolina university system. We were a separate institution. We had to go out and beg for money every year and get humiliated when they'd call us a pretty play school and be treated like that. . . . So Vittorio called up Raleigh, and two people came down from Raleigh from this committee to hear me out and to make the recommendation.

And they took me into Vittorio's room, and I had to explain why I wanted to pay a thousand dollars for a flute, instead of buying one for two hundred and fifty dollars. And I had to explain to them the difference in workmanship and materials and how it would hold up and what the intonation was like and things that good old boys don't really understand very well, and I had to really fight my own department, because one of our purchasing people was sitting there in the room saying, "I don't understand this. You want a thousand dollars for a flute. I just bought a desk for eight hundred dollars and they'll paint it any color I want."

And so, I was getting a little irritated by then, and one of the fellows from Raleigh turned to me and said, "Tell me the truth. What could possibly be the difference? I mean, it's the same number of keys. One costs two hundred and fifty dollars, one costs a thousand dollars. What's the difference?"

And I just sat there, seething. I said, "Well, I played in New York for fifteen, seventeen years. I met people who were professional musicians, artists from all over the country, and I never met one from the state of North Carolina."

And there was this awful silence. And the fellow said, "All right. I'll make the recommendation."

As a postscript, Dunigan adds that "they were very nice about it after that." The famous desk, painted in the color of choice, "died after two years," and the infamous flute, which had belonged to a player with the New York Philharmonic, "is now worth five times what we paid for it, and it will be playable for the next one hundred years."[16]

Dunigan found that, as Ben Roney has pointed out, "They didn't understand it, that was the main thing. You had to explain it to them." It fell to the Board of Trustees and the president to do the explaining, as R. B. Crawford and others struggled literally to bring the school up out of the ground. Dr. Semans's approach was a model of diplomacy, restraint, and rationality:

The minute we heard of any anti-feeling for the school on the floor of the legislature, the person was identified who had expressed this anti-feeling. Some person in whose judgment we had very good faith, was asked to call him, and to apprise him of facts that showed that this was a school that was worthy of his support and not worthy of any destructive criticism. Constructive criticism was not only invited but was paid attention to and frequently followed up with pertinent action. So a great deal of the tactics of maintaining the school's reputation was, quickly telephoning and communicating with any[one who had] anti-feeling, explaining it, excusing it, or correcting it.

Vittorio Giannini, on the other hand, relied on emotional intensity: "His very name," Andrew Jones recalls,

attracted a whole lot of derision in the legislature; people would mispronounce it deliberately until they had met Dr. Giannini, and found out that it made no difference at all to him what they called him, as long as he was provided with a place to teach. His dedication was so completely apparent that everybody who met him certainly had to be impressed by his enthusiasm for it, and his feeling that it was really a criminal act not to do something about it. . . . My first impression of him was that I was very much surprised because of the man's enthusiasm. He was wound up. He meant business, and he let you know right quick that he was an expert in his field, and he intended to see this thing go through to the end.

You didn't have time to say, "But what if, Dr. Giannini—" He wouldn't let you go with a question of this sort. Dr. Giannini would sense that you might be wavering, and he would anticipate what it was that you were probably going to ask, and would lead into something more positive than the area that you wanted to talk about. He was an artist at turning the conversation toward the positive aspects of the program. . . . I don't even remember what Dr. Giannini did . . . I think he was a composer, wasn't he? But we didn't get any impression about his particular talents except as an administrator and a teacher, and his enthusiasm for the children, and certainly he bubbled over about that.[17]

To survive the political loss of Terry Sanford, the school needed not only the support of the legislature but, even more important, that of the new governor, who, at this critical juncture in the school's development, could have killed it. According to former state senator Gordon Hanes, Dan K. Moore was an unknown quantity:

I had never heard of him until we were back at Asheville. The legislature went back to the mountains in a railroad car. Southern Railroad took us, and we went all the way back up to Appalachian, and way back in the mountains. We went along little rails where the bushes were slapping the side of the train and people running out on the porch to look . . . and when we got back to Asheville, they had a big party in Biltmore to meet Dan K. Moore, and everybody said, Dan K. WHO? Nobody had ever heard of him. Well, not many people had; he was not a household word.

The election of Dan Moore came as a "surprise to the so-called liberal people in the center of the state in this area," Mary Semans says, "but many people had told us that it was going to happen." She had backed Richardson Preyer because she knew his family well, "and Mr. George Watts Hill called me one night . . . and he said, 'You'll be sorry that you're doing what you're doing politically.' And I said I really, honestly . . . didn't know what he was talking about. And he said, 'You'll be sorry that you're backing the wrong person for governor.' And I said, but I don't know Dan Moore." Nor did Dr. Semans know him. Mary Semans remembers that he received in the mail "a letter about Dan K. Moore from the mountains, and he showed it to me one day, and he said, 'What's wrong with this man? He looks extremely nice to me. . . . Why don't I send him something?' . . . His inclination was to back this man . . . but I was involved sort of openly with [the other] side of the campaign," as was Governor Sanford, she says:

> Most governors, whether they do it behind the scenes or not, don't come out for the next governor, either side. I'm sure most of them do behind the scenes, and most people know where the former governor stands . . . but Terry Sanford made it rather clear, and he had meetings at the mansion, as I remember, and it got fairly publicly out that he was backing Richardson Preyer, so that the feeling was very sharp. So when the Moores came in, there was a good deal of feeling between the two, and the nicest thing is that today they're all good friends, but for a while it was extremely bad.

As he was leaving office, Governor Sanford warned the Semanses that they would have to gain the support of the new administration if the school of the arts was to survive. "That's one of the things, the admonitions, that he gave us," Mary Semans points out,

> because he said that we have the school, but we don't have any money for it, and he said, once you get the Ford grant—which let's hope you get—then you've got to take that and see that the Moore administration and the legislature put the money through.

And I know that a few times Jim and I went to parties, including one here in Durham, and people were criticizing Mr. Sanford's starting of several things on foundation money, with no hard money back of it. Well, of course, I suppose I could understand the questioning, but they were far too critical, because he turned most everything he did into a success. But I know that many of them felt the school would not last. I think that they felt sort of . . . in their bones, "Well, this is all on soft money and it just won't go." And as we heard these rumors, we realized that what we had to do was just jolly well get in there and pitch with Governor and Mrs. Moore . . . because I remembered very well what Sanford said, and I knew a lot was hinging on the attitude of the new governor and his wife toward anything that Sanford started. And he had warned us, and I don't think most people now realize how bad [the situation] was.

An opportunity came, almost providentially, for Mary Semans to make what had promised to be an awkward approach, without strain:

There is something at the North Carolina Museum of Art called the Gallery for the Blind, which was named for my mother [Mary Duke Biddle] because it was started with a government grant and a grant from her foundation, and it is a hands-on gallery for the blind, and it was the first anywhere. We were very proud of that, and [at] the first . . . opening of that gallery . . . we had a meeting of the Board of Advisers . . . and apparently some officials were invited, and I was there at a reception. And I saw a lady across the room, and I said to somebody, "Isn't that the governor's wife?" . . . and they said yes.

Someone had given me an orchid because this [gallery] was named for my mother, and I just instinctively went over, and I introduced myself, and I said, "We are so grateful that you came, and I want you to have this orchid. It's certainly more appropriate for you to have it." Well, apparently that just got to her because we just hit it off, and she also reminded me a lot of my mother. And I just thought, well now see, that's the problem you get into, now she's just about the nicest person I've ever met. And I thought about it all the way home, and I think I wrote the letter then . . . saying that I'd be very glad to do anything that she wanted—you know, just offering. I said the governor and his wife always meant an awful lot in our family because . . . my mother, when I came down to live with my grandmother, she insisted that I listen to Governor Ehringhaus's speeches . . . and she had a real attitude about the governor of North Carolina. She just kind of

10. Governor Dan K. Moore saved the school of the arts during his administration, "knowing that Terry [Sanford] was going to get credit for [the school]. Now, I think that's a big man. He is a big man." Governor Moore with Dr. James H. Semans in Siena, Italy, 1968 (Archives of the North Carolina School of the Arts).

looked up to every one . . . as they came along. They were very special people, and she imbued all those around her with this feeling . . . and we just all felt very strongly about this. So I said, that's the way I feel, no matter who the governor is, and I'd just like to volunteer my services. . . . And *she* called me and [said] that she'd like for me to come over to the mansion and talk about some things that she wanted to do to the mansion . . . she wanted to upgrade it and have a standing committee that would be appointed by the legislature. . . .

Out of that friendship arose a kind of double situation. I brought Jim into that and then we got to see the governor, and we started talking to them about the school of the arts on an informal basis. . . . Now, one of the things Jim and I decided to do was to make a big day of taking Mrs. Moore to the school . . . they were beginning to do some major work on some of the buildings, and they were [using] these jackhammers and they were shooting nails in the ceilings . . . it was in the days of the shootings . . . after the Kennedy assassination . . . and there we were, right in the middle, with her high heels and mine, and we were going across wet cement and all of a sudden they started—BANG! . . . but she gayly went through the whole thing, and she saw each building and inspected everything, and she really was impressed. . . .

Eventually, Jim asked her if she'd be on the board of the school of the arts, and of course, she said, "I don't think I can be as the governor's wife, but if you can make me some sort of honorary member or something, I could do it," so she was an honorary member from practically the beginning, and she took an active interest, and she's been proud of it, and he [Governor Moore] encouraged her to do it, which was just remarkable. . . . It's just to the eternal credit of the Moores— and Sanford said this publicly about two years ago at the school. He stood up and said, "Without Dan Moore this institution would not be here." And that's true, because what he did was really build a constituency for the school because it really didn't exist. . . .

I think that was the only really scary time [when Governor Moore took office] and I don't think that I would have thought it as scary if I hadn't heard one or two people condemn the underfunding and the soft funds, and Terry's way of having gotten foundation funds and then not having followed up. I heard some severe criticisms [from people who] weren't dedicated either to the arts or education the way he was, and they just thought, well, you know, one more school . . . they didn't realize what a tremendous need this would fill. . . . They just thought, oh, well, this is just one more big idea, one more boon-doggle kind of thing. . . .

Governor Moore is not a typical politician, I need to point out . . . he took the job as an obligation and a duty . . . he is—even by the opposition—he is said to this day to have made some of the finest judicial appointments that any governor has ever made. He was to-tally objective about most things. I'm sure he felt obligations to a point, certainly, but on a lot of major appointments he was astonish-ing. He appointed his press secretary, and called him in, and the man came in to his desk and said, "I'm sorry Governor Moore, I know you've called the wrong person, but I was told to come in here."

[Governor Moore] said, "Why did you say it was the wrong person?"

And he said, "I didn't support you, Sir, you don't want me as head of the press."

Moore said, "My dear man, only one major newspaper in the state supported me. Why can't I pick just anyone that I feel is qualified?"

So he could be very objective when he saw something that was good for the state. A lot of other people wouldn't have succeeded San-ford and been that objective, but it did take a lot of nurturing . . . I don't know if [the school] would have survived without the governor. I doubt it, because the Advancement School failed.

During Governor Moore's term, the Advisory Budget Committee of the state legislature decided to eliminate completely any appropriations for the school of the arts—to which Governor Moore replied "with four historic words," as John Ehle relates it: "Oh, no, you're not!" Looking back on those times, Gordon Hanes has said that "one of the remarkable things about Dan Moore is that he got into the Office, and he fought like a tiger for all of the good things that Terry Sanford had started, knowing that Terry was going to get credit for it. Now, I think that's a big man. He is a big man." [18]

The members of the first Board of Trustees bought land, built buildings, raised money, and stretched it; they hired architects and fired architects; they created a foundation; they inspired a governor and lobbied a legis-lature; they found a temporary office for the new school's president and hung curtains in it; they helped the new president find students for the new school that they were building, buying, hiring, firing, creating, inspir-ing, lobbying and hanging curtains for. The student recruitment commit-tee was chaired by Martha Muilenburg, who reported at the November 1964 board meeting that some six hundred guidance counselors at junior

11. *Dr. Vittorio Giannini, President (Archives of the North Carolina School of the Arts).*

and senior high schools across the state were being contacted. Julia Ribet, Vittorio Giannini, and others had begun filling speaking engagements to promote the school, and the committee had compiled a list of more than fifty people to serve as county representatives, providing "information and enthusiasm in interpreting the school and seeking out potential students." The idea of having regional representatives seems to have been successful, judging from the number of volunteers who attended recruiting luncheons in February and March: 50 from northwestern North Carolina gathered in Winston-Salem to hear reports on the school's progress from Giannini and R. B. Crawford, and 160 eastern North Carolina representatives attended a luncheon in Southern Pines, hosted by board member Mrs. James Boyd. Something of Giannini's manner as he spoke to these groups and others like them can be adduced from a recruiting interview he did for WTOB radio in Winston-Salem in December 1964. Speaking quietly and amiably at first, Giannini in his odd, slightly hard accents (to the southern ear bearing something of New York with an overlay of Italy) explains the pertinent facts about the school, describing the faculty he is seeking and his own experiences in music education when he was a boy. Gradually, Giannini becomes more and more intense as he speaks of the importance of the school and its mission. And although Giannini's voice is always measured and pleasant, the listener can discern an increasing tension and suppressed excitement, manifested by the middle of the interview in the composer's rhythmic, light pounding of the table, inadvertently captured off-mike.[19]

Faculty recruitment had been going on even more intensively than the search for students, because it was on the quality of the faculty that the Ford grant ultimately depended. This was a point on which McNeil Lowry never wavered. As late as November of 1964—almost a year after he had recommended the North Carolina arts school to the Ford Foundation board and received an appropriation from which a grant for the school could be made—McNeil Lowry was as willing as ever to blow a chilly wind southward. In a letter to Hugh Cannon, commenting on a memorandum of the school's proposed capital and operating expenses for two years, Lowry wrote: "It is the professional training, and the standards of that training, that is [sic] the only possible objective of the Ford Foundation, if we find that we can actually assist your project. . . . I would also say that until a firm decision is reached on whether this program is to include drama and dance and, if it is, who is going to direct those two programs and on what criteria, we are unable to answer the question of our potential involvement."[20]

Thus all involved in opening the school went forward without the Ford Foundation matching money—money that had been presumed twice in the text of the bill that was passed by the 1963 General Assembly—and without assurances the money would ever come through. Not until the night of November 21, 1965—almost three months after the school had opened—did Dr. Semans learn at last that the money would be granted. "Vittorio had taken us to dinner together with Sigmund Koch, the administrator of the grant we hoped we would get," Semans recalls. They were in New York to attend the recital at Carnegie Hall of Olegna Fuschi, a member of NCSA's piano faculty: "He waited until the intermission to let me know. . . . 'It's highly irregular for the Ford Foundation to do anything in this manner, but we are going to make the grant to the North Carolina School of the Arts.' And he said, 'Now don't bother doing anything about it until tomorrow,' and I said, 'We must call Winston-Salem immediately.'" On December 27, 1965, Dr. Semans received official notice from Joseph M. McDaniel, Jr., secretary of the Ford Foundation, that a grant of $1,500,000 had been approved, to be awarded over a five-year period, specifically "to strengthen the School's program." The conditions of the Ford challenge grant came as a blow to the Winston-Salem fundraisers, especially Philip Hanes:

> We had a special dinner party for [Sigmund Koch] . . . and it was just the happiest group of people that you ever saw in your life . . . and I said, "I'd like to lift a glass to Dr. Koch and to the Ford Foundation for this marvelous thing that they are doing . . . and I'd like to say parenthetically that God, I'd hate to have to go through raising that million dollars again as the match for this million and a half."
>
> Everybody raised their glasses and drank, and [Koch] rose rather slowly, and he said, "Well, look, you realize this grant has not been announced yet. The Ford Foundation does not cast any matching money until the grant has actually been announced. You've still got a million dollars to raise."
>
> Everybody was sitting there with their mouths open. They said, "My God, you can't mean that!"
>
> He says, "It's absolutely so. It's irrevocable. It's in our by-laws. There's no way that that million dollars is going to count. You've got another million dollars to raise."

The first $500,000 of the Ford money was to be matched dollar for dollar by the North Carolina School of the Arts Foundation, and the remaining

$1,000,000 at a ratio of $2 for each $1 granted by the Ford Foundation.[21] Thus, to receive the Ford challenge grant, the school and its supporters had to raise $500,000 a year for five years, from 1966 through 1970, for a total of $2,500,000.

At the joint Board of Trustees–Advisory Board of Artists meeting in New York on November 14, 1964, the first six faculty appointments were approved (not, however, without having been passed by McNeil Lowry first) and released to the press. The appointees were Ruggiero Ricci, concert violinist, who was to give master classes; Gary Karr, double-bass soloist, who planned to come to Winston-Salem on a weekly basis to teach; and the Claremont Quartet (Marc Gottlieb, first violin; Vladimir Weisman, second violin; Scott Nickrenz, viola; and Irvin Klein, violoncello), who were to be in residence at the school while continuing to concertize. On January 3, 1965, the names of the members of the Clarion Wind Quintet were released, bringing the number of faculty members to eleven plus Giannini. Philip Dunigan, flutist, explains why he and his colleagues left burgeoning careers in New York City to teach for not very high salaries at a school that was as yet nonexistent:

> Well, we were in New York and all five of us had very active careers, with the Clarion Quintet and in our separate positions. . . . I was the flute player, and my permanent job in those days was playing with the New York City Ballet Orchestra and also lots of free-lance. [Robert] Listokin, our clarinet player . . . played at the Radio City Music Hall, which was a wonderful job for him because he was never there. They had a free substitution policy, so he could do an awful lot of free-lance. He did a lot of chamber orchestra and chamber music, worked with the quintet, and he did just about everything you could imagine, except burlesque.
>
> Mark Popkin [our bassoonist] . . . was at that time one of the top free-lance bassoon players in New York, and also had a career as a scientist at the Applied Science Laboratory in the United States Navy. Our oboe player at that time was Henry Schuman. . . . Henry Schuman's mother was, I think, a classmate of Mary Semans. . . . And then, our horn player [French horn] at that time was somebody whose name was Howard Hillyer. And we got a call—Henry Schuman got a call, from Vittorio Giannini.
>
> Now let me tell you what I knew about Giannini at that time. Most of us had been associated with Juilliard in one way or another. Listokin and I and Fred Bergstone, [who plays the French horn and

joined the quintet just before NCSA opened] had been students at Juilliard. . . . [Giannini] gave Henry a call and asked to see the Quintet, and we went over to his apartment. And most of us knew him as a very, very conservative composer who hated all the modern music. . . . We knew him as a highly skilled craftsman and a very good composer in a very conservative kind of way.

Well, he got us in that apartment and started explaining to us how he was going to form a school in North Carolina. Well, there we are in New York, which we consider to be the cultural hub of the universe. We've all worked and scrambled very hard to get ourselves good positions, good niches in New York. And the idea of leaving New York— that is hard to explain, but you get so into it that the idea of leaving is just very hard to even conceive of. But he was a mesmerizing kind of speaker. It's hard to explain if you have never known the man, kind of the glow in his eyes when he was talking.

He explained to us that great cultural things were going to be happening, that we'd only be an hour and a half away from New York, and it really wouldn't be that much work. We'd only have—I think it all figured out that we'd have twelve or fifteen hours of work a week and that we could arrange it any way we wanted, travel back to New York and keep our career going as a quintet and developing. And it just sounded absolutely wonderful to hear him tell it. He told us how he was going to keep his apartment in New York and fly back and forth and it really isn't cutting yourself off. And it's just wonderful down there, and the state of North Carolina is really fine, there's just nothing like it.

And, well, I went home to my wife, my first wife, and I said, "Well, how would you like to go to North Carolina?" and she started laughing, of course.

But . . . we were living—I was playing eight shows a week. I had three children; two were very young and I didn't see them very much, and I was one of the musicians that was really making quite a good living and doing very well in New York. And for the amount of money I was making—you spend that on living arrangements in New York, and you live pretty much like a cockroach lives down here. I was right between the fire house and the police station, and just over the 8th Avenue subway. So there was never a moment's quiet, twenty-four hours a day. We had the building all covered up with steel so that people couldn't break in the windows, shootings going on. We lived in a nice neighborhood, that was one of the nicer neighborhoods. . . .

So we thought it over, and the five of us talked it over, and we thought we would accept. Well, this took place—I think this interview couldn't have been more than eight months before we actually were supposed to start work [probably December of 1964] . . . and they were talking about opening the school in September of '65, so you can imagine how quickly things were getting done. And there wasn't any offer to contract or anything like that. But Vittorio had a way of just absolutely just mesmerizing you to the point that you felt his handshake was the strongest bond of anything in the world. Once you agreed, that was it. I think he offered us a letter, and he said that this is the same thing as tenure for life, and you are all full professors, something like that. And he really believed that. That was his opinion about the way he wanted to put the school together, that he wanted all of his faculty to be equal and to be the equivalent of professors in a European conservatory. He had in mind something closer to a European conservatory than the American conservatory like Juilliard. Although we had very close ties with Juilliard, we had that in mind.

Well, somehow I persuaded my wife, and we all persuaded each other that maybe it would be a good thing to come down. But there were two people in the quintet that, upon reflection, decided that they wanted to pursue their careers. Henry Schuman wanted to become a conductor, and he inquired if there would be any conducting for him down here, and Vittorio, who always gave you a straight answer, said we have a conductor, there was going to be no conducting for him, positively no. So we had to start looking for an oboe player, and then our horn player decided to go and play first horn in the Pittsburgh Symphony . . . we had to go to Vittorio and ask if this was all right, to just add two people, and he said well, if you get people . . . that are the same caliber that you are to replace them, that is all right.

So we went out and engaged Clarendon Van Norman from the Chicago Symphony . . . and he was anxious to come down, but then he had second thoughts because he was afraid of the race issue. He [is] . . . married to a lady who is Sioux Indian, and just about that time he was reading something in the paper about the Ku Klux Klan going after the Lumbee Indians, so he chickened out, he wouldn't come down. And he got the job playing for the Metropolitan Opera House for the first time.

We were looking all over [for a horn player]. People were flying in from all over the place. Apparently the word had gotten out, and so a lot of people wanted to apply for the job. And we auditioned people

from absolutely everywhere, and the best one was Fred Bergstone. As
soon as we heard him, that was it. He beat everybody, he just out-
classed all of the competition. And then we got an oboe player who
didn't last very long, Steve Adelstein, who was an interesting character. . . . I think we have had some very good oboe players in and out
of here, you know, but I think now we've got one who is going to
stick with us for a while.

So Vittorio arranged for us to come down here, and my first experience with the school was to come down in the summer time for some
auditions.[22]

On January 16, NCSA announced Giannini's appointment of Saul Cas-
ton, conductor and music director of the Denver Symphony Orchestra.
Caston would take charge of the high school and college orchestras at the
school and teach trumpet. On January 28, Giannini announced that Robert
Lindgren, formerly of the New York City Ballet and the Ballet Russe de
Monte Carlo, had accepted the position of dean of the School of Dance.
Also engaged to teach at the school was his wife, ballerina Sonja Tyven.
McNeil Lowry recalls that

the selection of the Lindgrens to run the dance thing would never
have been made if Giannini had not been dealing with me, although I
refused to make it. I had bumped into Robert Lindgren and Sonja
Tyven in Phoenix, Arizona. I knew about their earlier history with the
Ballet Russe and with the [New York City Ballet]. . . . I had worked
since '57 visiting every conspicuous, able teacher of ballet in a private
studio or in a company, all around the country. That was a part of my
job. I made the biggest program in training on a local, regional, and
national level in ballet that a foundation ever did.

I remember a very hot day—my God, it was 120 in the shade. The
Lindgrens were making six kids in leotards dance themselves to death
for me to look at them. . . . I said, "I don't want you to do this."
[Lindgren] said, "Well, I want you to see them. You come all this way.
Nobody comes here to see about ballet."

Well, the way it happened was this: I told Vittorio about them, but
more specifically, he asked me for a list of people in these various fields
who might be his advisers, and I gave it to him. Several of the people
were Eugenie Ouroussow (now dead) who was the head of the
School of American Ballet in New York, the Balanchine-Kirstein
School; Barbara Weisberger who had just, with our help, started the
Pennsylvania Ballet in Philadelphia and was a noted teacher herself;

Frederick Franklin in the National Ballet in Washington, who has a little different style of teaching because he was more on the Royal Ballet British side of it. I had supported those three.

They then talked, and finally Vittorio said to Ouroussow, "You think I should ask Lindgren to come east and talk to me?" She said, "Yes." And he asked me, and I said "Yes." But you see, I didn't say, "Vittorio, your ballet department and your dance department person is Robert Lindgren." Right? I didn't. Nor did I even say "You could get two for one because he's got a wife who's also a teacher and a dancer."... Vittorio made his best case with the help of these consultants and my helping him spot them. We just shortened history.[23]

Dean Lindgren also traces his selection by Giannini to McNeil Lowry:

I had a telephone call from a man who identified himself . . . as McNeil Lowry from the [Ford] Foundation who was staying at the Westward Hotel in Phoenix, and could he come out and interview me and talk to me about my school, how I got there, what my background was, and what I was doing in Phoenix, Arizona. . . . He spent three days with me, and he said, gosh, how did you start all this? Was this your money that started this company? How did you get the arts council to be interested in dance? How did you arrange for this festival in the springtime? all of the things which we had done, which had taken us four years to do.

So that summer . . . I had a phone call from [Ford] in New York, saying they were going to have a meeting in New York City for three days, I believe in July, and he would like for me to come and be a consultant. They had selected twenty people from around the United States in dance to come to New York and meet . . . at their Board meeting, to discuss this grant, and one of the things that they asked us individually was our career background, and where we came from, and if we were [Ford] Foundation what would we do with the money? That kind of thing. My point of view was that George Balanchine was the one person who had established something in America by his school, who had changed the look and the technique, the thought, the choreography—he had changed the American dance from being Russian to American, which the Americans had not been able to do. And so I said the money should not be fragmented to a little bit here and a little bit there, but give them $10 million and allow them to set it up as a funded school and funded company. [See Chapter 1, note 62, on the furor which this decision caused.] I guess I was partial because I'd worked with him, but still, I believed he was a genius of the age, and so he was the person who could do it because he had done it, and everything I was doing in Phoenix in a sense was copying what I had learned from them [at the School of American Ballet]. . . .

So . . . when the Ford Foundation gave to the School of American Ballet, they sent Eugenie and Maria Tallchief . . . out to my school, and we were the first recipients. . . . So that was how Eugenie happened to be out in Arizona, and knew about [our school]. . . . So [when] Mac had called Eugenie and said well, what does Mr. Balanchine think about Bobby and Sonja? What do you think of them? . . . then she had also recommended me. . . .

On December 9, 1964, I had a phone call from . . . Vittorio Giannini, and he said that he had just been made president of a performing arts school in Winston-Salem, North Carolina, which was unique in America, and would . . . probably revolutionize how the arts were taught in the United States. He asked me if I would like to be dean of the school of [dance]? My salary would be $15,000 a year; did I receive all the material he had sent me about the school in the mail? I said no, I hadn't received any material and that I didn't think I could be the dean of anything because I'm not even a high school graduate, and I'm very happy in Phoenix, Arizona, and I have no real desire to leave. He said, well, let me explain a little bit more about this school. So he spent about fifteen minutes on the telephone, and said to me, "I will call you back, or you can call me back in four days. We would like to fly you to either Winston-Salem, North Carolina, or, since I am composing a symphony which is going to be played by the Phoenix Symphony, maybe we can talk then."

I said, "Well, Dr. Giannini, who are you, what is your background?"

He said, "Well, I was a teacher of composition at Juilliard School of Music, and we are now working with the Ford Foundation to get a grant for them to start the school, a matching grant, and you were recommended to us. Serving on the board [of advisors] is Eugenie Ouroussow of the School of American Ballet, Agnes de Mille, José Limon." These were the dance people he identified. I said, "Gee, I'll call you back in two days." Okay, fine.

So that night I called Guy Taylor who was the Symphony conductor of the Phoenix Symphony. His wife was the accompanist for our dance school, and I said, "Guy, who is this guy Vittorio Giannini who called me about a new performing arts school?"

He said, "Oh, Bob, that's Papa Giannini! He for years taught music composition at Juilliard, and everybody knows about him. For years he's had this idea about starting a national conservatory in Washington, which would involve music and dance and drama, and making a real national academy, but he apparently has received the funds and the okay from North Carolina to start it in that state, and everybody's got their eyes on it because it's sort of a very noble experiment. We want to see how it's going to turn out."

He said why? and I said, "Well, I was just offered a job as head of the dance department." He said, "Wow! It might be worth considering, Bob." I said, fine.

The next day I called up Eugenie Ouroussow, who was then the chairman who ran the School of American Ballet, and the School of American Ballet is the school that belongs to the New York City Ballet . . . she [had known] us as members of the New York City Ballet. . . . So she said . . . "I know you're doing a marvelous job out in Phoenix, Arizona, but we felt that, they were looking for someone to head a school, and you and Sonja had run your own school, you had gone out there and started with nothing—" We had built the school and had gotten involved with the Phoenix Musical Theater, the arts council, the symphony, and we had created a whole dance scene in Phoenix, Arizona. . . . She said, "I'm on the board, and they asked us, and you might consider it," so I called Vittorio Giannini two days later, and said, "Well, I don't know. I have no plans on leaving here, but I'm rather interested to see what the site is, what the people are who are putting it together."

And so he said, "All right." On the day after Christmas, 1964, I flew to Winston-Salem, North Carolina, and met with Vittorio Giannini at the Howard Johnson's Motor Inn, which had just opened on I-40, and we sat there for about six hours . . . we sat there and had lunch while we talked, and then that afternoon and that evening he took me to have dinner with Philip Hanes and Joan Hanes at their home, and Vittorio gave me the whole aesthetic reason for this, his whole aesthetic reason for establishing the school, he gave me the history of Governor Sanford and of John Ehle, of the legislature and of the tippy-toe school and the pros and cons. He also told me about the Ford Foundation grant. . . .

Well, I expected to see somebody who had that kind of charisma that the people that I used to work with had. I'd worked with Massine and Balanchine and Stravinsky—people who have it, you recognize it immediately. I'd worked with Rodgers and Hammerstein. You know great people, therefore—the moment you're talking to people like that, you know you're talking to people like that. And so, when I was talking to Vittorio—even though he had the cigar and the Philadelphia accent, you know, he was dynamite, and when he was talking to you, it was not just a sales job, it was someone who had the passion backed by the knowledge, and a dream to make it happen. And Sonja and I, when we had gotten out to Arizona we just started from scratch. There was nothing. We ate baked beans and free grapefruit off our own trees, so we struggled. And everything that happened there bloomed, like Phoenix, and just made a whole second career for us, and so we felt that this offer to come [to the school of the arts] was just kind of part of the same message. . . .

And so Sonja and I sat down, and we had, by that time, our two children, we loved Phoenix, Arizona, it's the greatest place in America. We loved the desert, we loved the proximity to Mexico and California, the open spaces—so it was very hard to give that up and come back [east]. . . . I said, "Why North Carolina?" and it was only when I'd met Vittorio that he'd told me he'd been lobbying in America in New York and in Washington for it, and that these people . . . here said that they [would do] it.

So he drove me out to this old Gray High School in this Mercedes Benz roadster that now John Ehle has, and he drove me up here to this old empty high school, and he said, "What do you think? Can we make a school out of this place? Whatever your imagination can tell you, that's what we can do."

So I got right into it. We made plans and we talked, and he said, "Robert, you've got to come." I asked who else he was considering. He said, "No one else." I asked [him], out of all the people in America, I'm the only person you asked? That makes you feel very good . . . and Philip [Hanes] you know, when Philip sells you, he gets you by the lapels, and he's very forceful and very convincing, and Philip in his own way is a dedicated man. He believes in the school, he believed in exactly what he was doing. Therefore, you liked people who had that kind of passion, not just a drive, but a passion with their drive.

So I went back to Phoenix, and Sonja and I talked over the pros and cons of moving again, but we both said, well, we didn't know what picked us up from New York and brought us out here. Obviously the same force is doing something here, so obviously, it's meant to be.[24]

On February 9, 1965, the *New York Times* reported, "Rose Bampton of Met will head voice section at Carolina school." Bampton, for eighteen years a leading soprano with the Metropolitan Opera Company, describes Vittorio Giannini as "a wonderful person, very soft-spoken . . . with a great vision, a great aspiration to establish this as a great school." He had come to her home one evening

and said he wanted to have a little conversation with me. And I hadn't seen him for years, and I couldn't imagine what he was coming to talk about. So he told me about his ideas of the school of the arts. I was excited about it, because it sounded as if it could be a young Curtis, where I went, and which he was connected with. So he talked and talked, and finally he asked if I would come down and do a master class. So I said, "Well, Vittorio, how can I do a master class when you don't even have a class of singers yet? You haven't even opened your school, you haven't had auditions!" "Well," he said, "I was getting around to that. What I really want is for you to come down and be the head of the voice department." So that was his very easy way of broaching it to me to come down and do that.[25]

On March 19, Giannini announced that famed Spanish guitarist Andrés Segovia had accepted a position as consultant and adviser in classical guitar at the school and that he had recommended his student Jesus Silva as resident professor of classical guitar. Silva accepted the appointment. On April 1, Giannini announced three more faculty appointments: to teach cello, George Ricci, a distinguished soloist with such orchestras as the New York Philharmonic and the National Symphony Orchestra; to teach percussion, James Massie Johnson, principal timpanist with the St. Louis Symphony Orchestra; and to teach theory and composition, John Chorbajian, a former student of Giannini at the Manhattan School of Music and the 1961 recipient of a Ford Foundation grant as composer-in-residence at Evanston, Illinois. On April 8, the names of William Ball and William Trotman were announced, as advisory director of drama and associate director in residence, respectively. Ball, identified in the school's press release as a "prize-winning New York director of plays, operas, and television dramas," wanted to continue his fast-moving career in professional theater without being hampered by residence at the school. Not only was he kept busy directing plays at major playhouses and companies all over the country and in London and Canada, but he was also interested in developing a resident theater company of his own, which he did eventually in San Francisco—the American Conservatory Theatre. William Trotman had broad professional credentials as well as a strong North Carolina connection to lead him into more immediate serious involvement with the school, [26] but he recalls that he first met Vittorio Giannini in New York—

possibly the most fascinating man I've ever met, and that still holds true today—one of the most vibrant. I was listening to his third symphony last night, which I'm lucky enough to have a recording of. It was written and commissioned for Duke University, I believe, and his music . . . was the absolute epitome of the man: the excitement, the vitality, the theatricality. [He was] one of the most theatrical people I have *ever* met. And it turned out in the first year of the school, probably one of the wisest that I've ever known . . . [he was sympathetic to the drama department] because he composed operas. He was infinitely theatrical . . . he saw one of Bill Ball's productions, *The Servant of Two Masters* . . . and he immediately went to Ball, and he said, this has got to be my opera. . . . That whole idea of the commedia dell'arte, Giannini adored. That was his training in the theater, completely wild, free-wheeling. . . .

I got the job in the drama department [at NCSA] strictly by default. I don't think [Giannini] could find anybody else. As far as I know, he talked to a number of people . . . but he had no contacts in the dramatic area at all. And since I was already there [in Winston-Salem] . . . it was strictly a filler thing, because he really absolutely couldn't find anybody.[27]

Although his name was not well known, Trotman was more than just a "filler." McNeil Lowry agrees that there was difficulty in finding someone to take on the drama department: "[Vittorio] did talk to a number of theater people. He couldn't find them really interested. And then William Trotman got interested, right? I knew Bill Trotman. He came from Alley Theatre in Houston—no, he came from North Carolina, but he went to the Alley Theatre in Houston. He was doing well as kind of a stage manager, actor, semi-director under Nina Vance, the founder of the Alley Theatre . . . he was a pro, he was a real pro."[28]

Trotman was a professional, but not a "name" professional, and, Trotman says, at the time, Giannini was just absolutely overloading the school with every piece of name faculty that he could find. I'll never forget the story of calling Segovia. They decided to put a guitar department in . . . Philip [Hanes] I think it was, called one day and said, "Why are we going to have a guitar department?" and Giannini puffed on his cigar and said, "Well, why not? Who would you suggest?" and Philip said, "Who's the best?" Giannini said, "Segovia's the best." And Philip said, "Well, call him and ask him if he would do it." Which they proceeded to do, and he said "Sure, I'd be delighted," and he picked Jesus as his personal representative. But it was so overloaded—just to show you, he had Gary Karr the first year and Ruggiero Ricci and these brilliant people, and in drama we had nobody.

And Giannini and I talked about it at great length, and we decided that we had to have some name that we could draw against, because it would be so overbalanced, that the drama department would always be sort of an extra navel hanging off the end of a music school, and that's not at all what we wanted. And he didn't want it. So Bill Ball was enlisted to come in the first year. Bill was a very bright, young director in New York, and he was very much a hustler and was also looking for a place to put his company, because he'd been thrown out of two towns, running the theater, producing theater . . . and he thought well, this would be ideal, I could run down to North Carolina and put this major producing company in here. It was much too early, the first year, that kind of thought. But anyway, Bill was to help provide name faculty. . . .

I think it would have been wrong for us to . . . graft Bill Ball's company on to it [the drama department] as he did in San Francisco, but he formed his own school. It was a company first, and then a school to train. This was a school first. I think his company would have been too high-powered. Certainly it was financially; there was no way we could have afforded it . . . they did investigate that the first year. Giannini saw the figures and we discussed that . . . he was . . . fund-raising . . . for the whole school, and what Ball was asking was three times what our budget was, and we knew that there was not the audience in North Carolina, whereas there was in San Francisco. . . .

The first year, it was Giannini—those were Giannini's years. It still is his school to me . . . my only reason for being here was Giannini. I mean, I could have gone right back to Texas and been perfectly happy, but I wanted to join that man in what he wanted to do, whatever he wanted to do. If it had been a school for orthopedic surgeons, I think I would have gone with him because he had that magnetic a personality.[29]

On April 14, 1965, Giannini announced three faculty appointments in piano and organ. Margaret Sandresky, associate professor of music at Salem College, would head the school's organ department, and Howard Aibel and Olegna Fuschi, concert pianists, were to teach piano. Aibel was on the faculty at Juilliard, where his wife, Olegna, had been a student. She remembers how her involvement with the school of the arts began:

Well, it's really quite a wonderful beginning. I was at a party of the faculty of the Juilliard School at a hotel up here on Broadway and West 90th Street, and Vittorio Giannini was there, and Robert Ward was there, quite a few composers and a lot of the students. I was a graduate at the time; I was touring and performing, and we had a long while to chat that evening. My husband, at that time Howard Aibel, and I were with Mr. Giannini, and he said, "You know, I'm starting this school down in North Carolina. . . . You would be just wonderful," he said, "Would you like to come down?"

And I said, "Well, I'm touring and I'm playing and there's so much going on." He said, "We'll work things out, don't worry. . ." I think that was in April, before the groundbreaking . . . and that was the first inkling that I had of it. And of course, Vittorio did persuade us. I flew down every week for the first year. We did have an apartment there, but we maintained New York quarters, and, of course, I was touring a lot. But it worked out very well . . . [Vittorio] wanted to put it on the same level as the Juilliard School of Music, which is a pretty high level, and there would be no compromise. We would take the best that we could get, and lift them up to what our best was. And I always felt that that was what made it what it was, and what made us all come down there. The incentive. The fact that he had those high ideals and would not compromise. . . .

I think one knew Vittorio Giannini forever the first time you met him. You had the feeling that you knew him when he was a baby, and when he was growing up, and that you would always know him, and I still have that feeling, even though he's no longer with us, that presence is there. Maybe it's something between Italians, I don't know. But he was a very special man.[30]

As the days dwindled down to the school's September opening, Giannini went on assembling major artistic faculty, as well as the academic faculty and support staff, with remarkable speed and results. "He attracted people to come there on the faculty and administrative staff," says Hugh Cannon, "that didn't have the foggiest idea of why they were coming, other than that they were coming to work with Vittorio. Any number of them tell me this." Giannini's niece Maura says that his philosophy was "never be afraid to ask anybody for anything" and that he commanded attention: "My mother always said that when she first was introduced to my father's family, that there would be two people in the room. There would be a crowd of people around my Aunt Dusolina and a crowd of people around my Uncle Victor, and that was it. Either you were on one side of the room or the other. They were both such magnetic people. There was something about him." For dean of the School of Music, Giannini once again raided one of the major eastern conservatories, persuading Louis Mennini, professor of composition and orchestration at the Eastman School of Music, to join the North Carolina experiment (May 23, 1965). Norman Farrow, the renowned baritone who appeared regularly with the nation's leading orchestras, agreed to teach voice (July 4, 1965). And less than a month before the arrival of the first students on the unfinished campus, Giannini announced the appointments of dancer/choreographers Pauline Koner and Duncan Noble (August 8, 1965). Koner recalls that she was in Japan teaching a choreography workshop when she received a telegram from Vittorio Giannini:

> I had been warned by José Limon, who I met earlier in the year, that somebody might be contacting me about an interesting project, but he didn't say what. . . . It was, I understand, he who recommended me. And so I got this cable, and I answered that it sounded interesting, but that I would have to know more about it, and I was returning in August. . . . And then, I arranged to meet with Bobby Lindgren. . . . And we talked, we just basically talked about how it would be, and I could only accept it on a part-time basis because I was functioning on my own, and I did not want to become a teacher on a permanent basis and give up my career. . . .
>
> I did not really meet [Vittorio Giannini] until I came to the school, and I found him a most delightful, delicious person—warm, congenial, a person who would listen with an open mind. . . . Now, whether he knew the difference between modern dance and ballet, or whether it was just dance, d,a,n,c,e—that I don't know. I rather think it was

just that—dance—and that he wasn't aware yet until we got going, that there were variations of style and of concept as far as dance itself goes. But he had an open mind. . . .

[José Limon] was extremely impressed that there would be a school like that in the South, state supported, that would be composed of the three arts *on an equal basis,* not like Juilliard, where, you know, I mean, music is the big thing. Well, there's a dance department, but let's face it, it's not as important as the music department or the drama's not as important. Basically, Juilliard is a school of music. . . . I had no idea a state like North Carolina would be interested in anything as advanced as this. . . . I was surprised, and a little amazed, you know, the thought was a little frightening to have to commute back and forth from New York to North Carolina on a weekly basis. But I thought it was worth a try.[31]

Duncan Noble also thought it would be worth a try to have the opportunity to train performers

in an atmosphere where they could also get an education, so they didn't have to do their arts training on a catch-as-catch-can basis, and that's what interested me in coming here, and I think that's what interested every teacher that has come here . . . because all of us who have worked at the school had to study on that basis of going to school and studying after school, or when you could, or you know, hopefully, every day, or maybe once or twice a week. I know for myself, I quit school in order to continue my studies; I couldn't have done it otherwise. . . . Don't misunderstand me: academia is very important, but it has to be a *part of*—if you're training in the arts, academia has to be a part of it, arts can't be a part of academia.

Noble was brought into the school by Robert Lindgren, with whom he had studied in Canada when both were adolescents. Later they worked together in television and on Broadway and shared an apartment in New York until Lindgren married ballerina Sonja Tyven. In 1965, Noble had just quit his job with the Pittsburgh Playhouse when he got a phone call from Lindgren:

I had just gotten back from New York. I had just done my final New York appearance with Valerie Bettis of the New York State Theater in *As I Lay Dying.* I went back to Pittsburgh the next morning, wrote up my notice, handed it in, and the same week on Saturday Bob called me and told me about the school of the arts . . . we discussed it and decided that I would be the third teacher [of dance at] the school of the arts. . . . Then a fourth teacher joined us, Pauline Koner. . . . I actually came to the school as a teacher of modern dance, and so we had two in ballet, which were Bobby and Sonja, and two in modern, which was me and then Pauline. . . .

I really think I sort of looked at Winston-Salem with dismay, personally, because Fort Worth was the smallest town I had ever worked in . . . most of my life has been lived in New York. . . . [Bobby] said "Winston-Salem," and I really didn't put two and two together, and it never occurred to me that Winston-Salem was Winston cigarettes and Salem cigarettes, and certainly it didn't occur to me it had anything to do with Camel cigarettes, nor did I know that Hanes Underwear was here, so it didn't mean very much of anything. Although, oddly enough, when we were in Ballet Russe de Monte Carlo, we were playing in Greensboro, and we came over to Winston-Salem with some of the smaller ballets and played in Reynolds auditorium . . . and I always remembered going to a very fine home to an after-theater party with marvelous food and everything, and much later I was at the home of Ralph and DeWitt Hanes, and I said to DeWitt, "You know, it's very strange, but I feel that I've been here before." And DeWitt said of course you have, and explained it to me, and it was just very odd . . . you know, you don't remember an awful lot about tours. It's very strange that that particular one stuck in my mind. . .

I'll tell you, I came [to the school] because—this is going to sound strange but—I didn't like what I was doing. I was making a great deal of money—which I liked—but I didn't like the way in which I was making it. I was very tired of it. I was working in the theater and—I liked the theater—I was working as a director, a choreographer, sometimes as a writer, sometimes as a producer, but I was being used . . . I was doing work for which other people were getting credit, and my agent was very frank with me. He said, "I'm able to get you the salary I get you, because you can bolster these people up: their egos aren't flattened and everybody comes off well, and that's why you get paid well"—which I did. And I was tired of that . . . I was drained completely. I began to feel like a hack, despite the fact that I consistently got good reviews both as a director and as a choreographer. No one was feeding *me*. I don't mean in ego; I mean in arts education and arts health. I'm speaking a little bit esoterically, but I needed resuscitation. . . .

When I was still at the Playhouse, and I was commuting to New York for rehearsals . . . appearing in *As I Lay Daying* . . . and I had not appeared in New York since I was in *Can Can,* and I suddenly realized that I really wasn't doing what I wanted to do. And people were coming backstage and saying "What are you doing? Why are you not involved in the theater? Why are you not involved in dance? What are you doing in Pittsburgh?" and all I could say was making a lot of money, you know . . . but I just wasn't doing what I wanted to do, and the school of the arts seemed to be a chance. . . .

I like training people, I like the satisfaction of seeing someone accomplish . . . I think that's the excitement of the school for everyone that's at the school, I really do. The ones that don't find it exciting leave very soon . . . the ones that have stayed, somehow they don't get tired. I mean, they get tired, yes, but there's not an ennui, not ever a lack of interest, however tired. They may be exhausted, but if a student needs them . . . they all seem to be people that will tear themselves inside out to help, because they're all performers first and foremost, always have been, and they know what it's about.[32]

The North Carolina School of the Arts opened its doors to students on September 5, 1965, with an extraordinary faculty of performing artists who assembled there either directly because of their relationship with Vittorio Giannini or because of their belief in the ideals of the school, as articulated by him. It is only a tribute to Giannini and the faculty to observe that salaries were low indeed. At the joint meeting of the Board of Trustees and the Advisory Board of Artists in November of 1964, Richard Adler had been apprehensive that enough distinguished faculty might not be induced to leave New York, at the maximum salaries allowed by the state of North Carolina. All of the advisory board members agreed that salaries must be supplemented from foundation funds as soon as possible. (Robert Lindgren recalls that salaries "were incredibly low" during the first years of the school; "we never got a raise for the first five years—we all worked for exactly the same salary for five years"). At the end of the school's first semester, Giannini reported to the Board of Trustees that the school's salary scale was

much lower than the normal salaries in music departments of colleges and universities in the country. As an instance, on a recent visit from the Provost of Oakland University in Michigan where they are planning a school of performing arts the salary scale will be an average of

$12,500. A professor will receive about $18,000 and the Dean a salary of $25,000 and perhaps more. If you contrast this with our salaries you will see the enormous difference.

In music our average is $7156 (based on 25 members)

Our deans receive $15,000

The salary they offer for their dean is higher than mine as President.[33]

In a radio interview broadcast in October of 1965, Giannini tried to explain why the school had the faculty it did. For himself, Giannini felt that it was his "duty" to start the school:

My experience as a young student abroad and as a teacher at the Juilliard School, the Manhattan School, and Curtis had forcibly made me realize that many of our students possess a great deal of talent, but they would come to these schools, which are more or less on a college level . . . and they lacked the preparation which was necessary. And then they had to crowd in a few years, comparatively, the work of almost twice as many years. So here was an opportunity . . . and I just felt that I had to do it. . . .

I think the reason why we have been able to assemble a faculty of this sort [performing artists] is because the *idea* of the School appeals to them tremendously, the fact that they *choose* their students by auditions, and secondly, that they can start them as soon as they are accepted on what they think is the right road, is a thing that appeals to every artist—to be able to get a young talent and go directly to good hard work rather than get them older and have to spend some time correcting previous faults. And I think this is the thing that excites them.

And don't forget that artists are always very generous with what they know, and they get a tremendous—how would you say?—satisfaction in seeing young people learn, because they were young themselves, you know.[34]

The first auditions were held at Gray High School in Winston-Salem, April 17, 18, and 19 (Saturday, Sunday, and Monday). William Trotman was director of auditions, and it was his responsibility to set up a procedure for auditioning "people who did not know how to audition":

It took forever just to get the kids to know how to choose a selection, since the school had not been started. There was such a diversity of opinions of ways to audition . . . the type of space that was required,

the accompanists, lining up all of the people in Winston to help with
the auditions. It was really a mess that first year because everybody
had a different idea about the way it should be done. And Dr. Giannini, of course, did not superimpose his ideas about drama or dance at
all . . . the adjudicators were all over the world. [I was] trying to get in
touch with them and find out what they wanted, whether they could
meet here on one weekend. . .

I'm sure you've been told about the famous telegram from Mr. Jesus
Silva, have you not? I sent a telegram to him, asking if he could be in
Winston for the auditions on Easter weekend. . . . It came back
through the Western Union station in Winston-Salem. I'm sure the
girl had a cardiac arrest because the message was, "Would be happy to
be with you for Easter weekend." (Signed) "Jesus."

Assisting Trotman with the drama auditions were William Ball, Bentley
Anderson, and Mr. and Mrs. Sidney Blackmer. To help him with the dance
students, Robert Lindgren had brought in Russian ballerina Alexandra
Danilova. Chairman of the Board Dr. James H. Semans, feeling strongly
his responsibilities toward every area of the school's development (as did all
the trustees and foundation board members), around this time had sought
outside instruction in the dance:

Since I knew nothing about ballet and felt that I must thoroughly
understand it, I made a trip to New York on the advice of an English
Fellow at Duke University named Mr. Graddon Rowlands, who said
that his colleague at Cambridge University in England, David Drew,
was one of the dancers in the ascendancy in the Royal Ballet. It was on
tour and performing *Romeo and Juliet* at the Metropolitan Opera
Company. David Drew was good enough to accept my Eastern Air-
lines Travel Card as a calling card, and came to the stage door in full
regalia following a performance. After a brief interview and further
identification, he agreed to leave the touring company, see the new
campus, and tell us about ballet. He arrived in Winston-Salem, having
left the Company in Winnipeg, Canada, for a full day.

Our problem up to this point had been that even the dean of dance,
Robert Lindgren, was so difficult for me to understand, not through
any fault of his, but through my lack of knowledge of ballet. I needed
someone more articulate like this Cambridge graduate, David Drew,
at that stage, to discuss it in my language, to state from outside the
school family possible and probable problems, goals, and the general
conduct of a school of dance. Our own School of Dance, I must

hasten to add, had not yet arrived on the scene, so I was free to seek information anywhere.

If one can accept this in a humorous vein, in which the whole project was conducted—Robert Lindgren, now a friend of fifteen years, could have reacted in various ways upon hearing of David Drew's arrival at the school. When it was known that David Drew was coming from the Royal Ballet to the North Carolina School of the Arts before the dean of dance had arrived with his faculty, I like to think—with a twinkle in my eye—that a special audition date was arranged on the same day, conducted by the dean, Lindgren, and one of the best known dancers of them all, Danilova.

Sensing Dean Lindgren's possible apprehension, I had called him in Arizona, explaining my motives in inviting David Drew. I had arranged to bring David Drew to teach me something of the story of ballet because I had not yet absorbed this in my early meeting with Robert Lindgren. I admire the fact that he was sophisticated but tactful enough to take no chances with this Dr. Semans.[35]

For the music auditions, besides Jesus Silva (classical guitar), other faculty members present were Saul Caston (brass and percussion), Robert Listokin (woodwinds), Margaret Sandresky (organ), Marc Gottlieb (string instruments other than guitar), Rose Bampton (voice), and Howard Aibel and Olegna Fuschi (piano). A reporter for the *Raleigh News and Observer* caught glimpses of the artists during auditions, "in dark glasses, tailored suits, and mink," and of Giannini, "bustling" through the halls of Gray High School, talking continuously about his hopes for the new school, "between puffs on a black cigar." Those who recall the first year's auditions, look back on the experience in a series of vignettes:

OLEGNA FUSCHI
I remember sitting in that auditorium. The sun was streaming through the windows. We heard, oh, so many of them. It was really quite interesting, the quality, the level of the talent. Others really couldn't play the piano. I mean, they were playing, they had learned pieces, but you could sort of see in them . . . that they had the tools with which we could work.

WALLACE CARROLL
I remember, I went into an audition that Olegna Fuschi was holding for piano candidates, and this little girl came in from Hickory [North Carolina], and she sat down to play a Haydn sonata. Well, she played

the notes very nicely but it wasn't Haydn. And Olegna said, "Now dear, that's very nice, but try it this way," and then she hummed a phrase, and then another phrase, and the little girl played it, and at the end of ten minutes, she was playing Haydn. Now, this happened again and again and again.

ROSE BAMPTON
The day when we were having entrance examinations . . . there were many nice voices that were coming in, and suddenly I began listening to the languages that they were singing in, and they were just dreadful. So I said to Vittorio, "I don't know what to do. The voice is not bad . . . but the language!" And he said, "Rose, that's why we have the school. We want to give them this."

DR. JAMES H. SEMANS
I have such great memories . . . Sidney Blackmer at the first auditions, asking two drama applicants from Asheville, "Who wrote that exciting dialogue?" and getting the answer, "Him and me!"

GOVERNOR TERRY SANFORD
From the North Carolina hills and the Tennessee mountains came the guitarists and banjo pickers . . . for pickin' and singin' is a grand art in the mountains. And on the first day of auditions, Jesus Silva, young protégé of the man who revived the guitar as a concert instrument, heard this raw talent and noted dryly on one of the applications, "uses pick . . . needs instruction."

One of the stories that touched me more than most any other was the report that there was a young girl from Lincoln County who was auditioning for the dance. Robert [Lindgren] is supposed to have said that she had just pure talent, just animal grace, when he watched her first few movements. Then it became obvious that she didn't know much about these ballet steps and movements. She finally admitted that she had never had a lesson. What she knew, she had picked up watching television. Bob is supposed to have said to Alexandra Danilova, who was there helping audition, "This is what the School is all about . . . we have to have that girl."[36]

Of the 241 prospective students who auditioned in April, Governor Moore, on May 13, announced the names of 92 who had been chosen. They were from Advance, Angier, and Elkin; from Farmville, Horse Shoe, Mount Olive, and Scotland Neck; from Selma and Tryon and Valdese. Their names were Shook, Cutts, and Klavins; Swett, Weavil, and Bivins;

Buchanan and Peeler; Hanner and Crocker—neither places nor names with which someone like Olegna Fuschi was familiar:

> I think the youngest student was a little girl named Polly Love Crocker. And of course, living in New York, and my name being so European-sounding . . . we said, how is she going to make a career with a name like Polly Love Crocker? So we changed it to "Paulina Rokovska." . . . And the other one was James Butt. Now, how is he going to have a career? We all talked about that. We said, well, we'll just stay with James Butt. And then, of course, there was Joseph Smith. So between the three of them and me, with my name of Olegna Fuschi—"Here is my student, Jimmy Butt, and Joe Smith, and Polly Love Crocker." Those were not the names that we were used to in New York.

On June 7, the school was able to announce the acceptance of 27 additional students chosen from the April auditions. The second round of auditions was held the weekend of June 10–12; Philip Dunigan came down for them:

> Summertime of '65 . . . I didn't like to fly at the time, and they brought me down on a railroad car that was a sleeper that they used to park over here. You know, they bring it in and out at four in the morning and park it, and you sleep and get up. . . . They took us over to the Summit School, and there I listened to a couple of piano players. No, one was a flute player. There was a clarinet player who was Arturo Ciompi, who became later a very distinguished player, and there was Bob Sorton, an oboe player, who now plays in the Detroit Symphony. You know, the *quality* we had there, the first time we auditioned—I think Randall Ellis was there, too, at the time. And he plays—he teaches at the University of New York at Albany and plays the Y concerts in New York. He's a very, very fine player. Well, I heard a couple of good players, and then I met some wonderful people . . . the first people that I met when I got to Summit School were Doug and Bingle Lewis. Well, Bingle Lewis, I thought she was the most beautiful person I had ever seen in my life. And Mrs. Wallace Carroll . . . Wallace Carroll was one of the founding fathers, one of the most distinguished men associated with this institution, a great newsman, a great person, and he has a wonderful wife. She took me home that first day at lunch and gave me my first ham biscuit . . . a remarkable experience.

On June 24, 83 names were announced as a result of the second auditions, and on September 1, 53 more. The first day of classes was September 7, and of the 255 names announced, 252 were expected: from North Carolina 171; from other southern states and the District of Columbia, 48; from all other states, 32; and from Bolivia, 1. The final enrollment figure for September 1965 was 227.[37] The school appeared to be serving—as legislated—the state of North Carolina and the southern region.

Evadne Giannini, who came to the school as a drama student, does not recall where she took her drama audition, but she has never forgotten her first sight of the school, glimpsed through the eyes and dreams of Vittorio Giannini:

> I remember going down [to Winston-Salem] with Uncle Victor, and I was by myself with Uncle Victor, and he had an apartment, and I remember that I was starving, hungry. We opened the refrigerator and—typical—there was a box of cigars in the refrigerator. . . . Boxes of cigars and green spaghetti, that's the only thing that would ever be in there.
>
> And I said, "Uncle Victor, we have to go get something to eat." And he said, "Let me go show you the school." And in the car (he had this beaten-up old Mercedes Benz, I'll never forget it), all the way to the school, we talked about what it was going to look like. We went through this long description of what it was going to look like, and I just sort of got caught up in this wonderful fantasy of what it was going to look like, and . . there was just this field, you know, just this field, and there was this high school . . . and . . . I don't remember . . . ever questioning that it wasn't going to look like what he said, because for twenty-five minutes in the car, he and I just sort of visualized this whole different place.

The campus that greeted the arrivals on September 5, 1965, was still in a state of lumber and noise. Bruce Stewart, the school's first dean of students, recalls that when the students actually arrived not all the dormitory furniture had been delivered. "We had two or three pieces of the beds, the rails that the mattress sat on, the box springs and I think the footboards, but not the headboards. So all the beds, when the students arrived, were slanted toward the floor." Joe Goodman of the *Winston-Salem Journal and Sentinel* visited during the second week of classes and reported "raw red dirt," rather than grass, "furniture and boxes" lying in "heaps," carpet littering the hallways, and the smell of paint, all accompanied, however, by the sounds of an art school "in business": the "mutter" of drama students, the "thump and scratch" of ballet, the "honks and tweets" of musical instruments.[38] Although R. B. Crawford had broken ground for the dormitories on December 9, 1964, renovations to the old Gray High School building had not begun until June of 1965, when the last regular classes ended and the school board could release the building to NCSA. And it wasn't only time that was tight. "We had to figure every screw and nail in the budget," Paul Tremaine, technical director in the drama department, explained to a reporter from the *Twin City Sentinel*. When he and Bill Trotman got down to figuring out how to convert the school's old gymnasium into a theater, they discovered that they did not have enough money. At that point the drama department, in what had become already a school of the arts tradition, realized the theater was going to have to be a do-it-yourself project. With four men hired to help him, Tremaine began the work in July; by the time Trotman had completed his contract at the Governor's School that summer and joined them, the crew had built forty-six platforms (ten of them collapsible), twenty-four 12' x 4' frames (to hold three panels each), and twenty-four rolling jacks. The locker rooms were being converted into two large dressing room/classroom combinations, a costume shop, property rooms, and storage areas. The gym's ceiling and steel beams were painted black, and the side walls, bleachers, and risers, gray. The light and sound equipment, as well as seating and platforming, were all "completely portable," to allow for the greatest possible flexibility in the use of space, which Tremaine spoke of as a "void" in which the students could create any type of theater experience they wanted. Looking on the bright side, Bill Trotman staunchly pointed out the advantage of his black box theater with its minimal equipment: "Since our students will be working [eventually] in imperfect theaters, we want them to experiment in this one."[39] The spirit of do-it-yourself glowed brightly, and makeshift quarters were translated into adventure, as Evadne Giannini and her sister Christina, who was hired as the school's costume designer, remember:

EVADNE: I mean, there was no theater. I can remember walking
               in and there was a black box, and thinking that was
               rather marvelous. Now, you're talking to someone
               who was from New York, and at that time . . . if you,
               as a young person, took a class in theater, most of the
               class spaces are 12 feet by 15. So to walk into a huge
               open gym was the most exciting thing in the world,
               because we are not used to that kind of space. So for

anyone who was sitting in that thing, "Where are the chairs? and where are we going to—?" —to us that didn't matter. I mean, we had a huge space which does not exist in the city. So—

CHRISTINA: My costume shop shifted in the first few years. I was first in what had been the shower room of the black box, i.e., gymnasium—just the shower room, with lots of tiles and disconnected faucets. Then I went to what was the workshop in the back of the old wood-working shop . . . it was a tiny little hole. Then I was moved into what had been the cafeteria kitchen, which I adored. It had great sinks and stoves and whatnot. But it shifted around. In the early, early days we grabbed what we could grab and just used it. It was wonderful.

Like Bill Trotman, Robert Lindgren had to build his dance studios in a gymnasium, the *other* gymnasium, the *older* gymnasium:

There were no facilities designed for dance. When I discussed it with Vittorio Giannini, he said I could have the old girls' gym in Gray High School, which was the original gym. When we came here there was a field house still in existence which was where the School of Drama and the de Mille Theater is now (the field house was converted to this). . . We had forty-five students, so I came and I sent plans and told the architects how to build a dance floor. [They] didn't follow my instructions. I told them how to erect barres and put up mirrors in perspective, and so I sent them all the information. [The gymnasium] made very good dance studios. They had high ceilings. The only thing they did was put down hardwood instead of softwood for dance floors.

Pauline Koner recalls that when she saw where she was to work, she "winced":

But you see, being a modern dancer, all our lives we've had to work in very negative facilities; you never had the posh studios the ballet schools had. We've always had to work in makeshift situations. I had had studios of my own that were, in some ways . . . better than what we were given to work with. . . . But I knew that this was supposedly transitory, and another thing is that I didn't have to pay for the studios to work in them. They were given to me and the student body would be there. And when we first started, we didn't even know the alloca- tion, who was to get what studio, until the curriculum was set. We ended up in what we call the dungeon . . . because the modern dance was very much the stepchild of the Dance Department there. And it's understandable; I can understand it with no malice because Bobby Lindgren knew nothing about Modern Dance when he started that department. He had had no exposure to it . . . and he certainly wasn't interested in it. I mean, to him, ballet was dance, and modern dance was something where people threw their bodies around.

And so the ballet was pushed, naturally, the ballet department was given priority, got the one decent available studio, which was the Stu- dio A, the gym, and we were put down in the basement in something that was put together and was damp and long and narrow, and we called it the dungeon. And for years the modern dance was allocated to that one studio . . . but we only had twelve students that first year enrolling . . . the whole student population that first year, I think, was just two hundred and something, so I liked it, because it was a small family, and you knew everyone. It wasn't a huge organization. It was very *intime* and close, and everybody had the same vision in their eyes—there were stars in the eyes of everybody at that time.[40]

Philip Dunigan also remembers the early facilities less than fondly; he had trouble even finding the school:

I got on the phone and I called up, and the operator answered, "The School of the Arts." And I told her who I was and that I'd like to come over. And I asked her what the address was. And she said that she didn't know. And I asked her, "Well, what part of town is it in?" and she said she didn't know. And I asked her a few more questions, and she started getting upset, practically on the verge of tears, and I finally said, "Well, how did you get there?" and she said, "My husband brought me."

Well, I asked around town a little bit and I found out where the place was, and I came over here, and this is what I found: the old Gray High School, their new gymnasium (which we now call the Agnes de Mille Theater) . . . and two dorms which had just gone up, and an old abandoned high school building. And that was it. And they had done a very hasty job of building studios in the basement of the old building. . . . They [had] cut us out from the light . . . bricked up the windows. Put a baffle of some sort to deflect the sound and pounded unfinished blanket materials on the walls. Now, for the first twelve or fifteen years of the School of the Arts, those were the studios that most of the faculty would teach in.

Rose Bampton, too, found the school "a little bit of a shock," but Olegna Fuschi most remembers Vittorio's endearingly rosy view of the school's less than prepossessing address: "I'll never forget Vittorio saying one thing—'Now,' he said . . . 'Everyone in North Carolina, they wanted to put it in the most gorgeous place. They wanted to put it on a pond with flowers, badminton, tennis courts, and swimming pool. . . . If we give [the students] that, they're not going to want to practice!' So here we were on Waughtown Street." And as usual, Uncle Victor was right:

CHRISTINA: Winston-Salem was wonderful because there was absolutely nothing to do but practice, and then rehearse, and then perform a little, and then practice. Once in a while there's a show to go to, but there's so little diversion, it's good.

MAURA: We just worked.

EVADNE: We just worked, we just worked. . . .

MAURA: We were kids and we wanted to practice a lot. We had to go to school, the way they had it arranged then, from nine in the morning or eight in the morning, whatever it was, until six-thirty at night. . . . There wasn't enough time to practice; it was only four or five hours during the day and we needed more time. So we proposed the idea: we wanted to get up early and go to the practice rooms at five-thirty in the morning. The school said, "That's ridiculous. You can't do a thing like that." So we got together a group of people who would do it, and we went to my Uncle, and we said, "Look, we want to get up early and practice, but they won't let us in. They've been chasing us out. We climbed in through the screens, and they came in and they chased us out." And he said, "Well, that's terrific. You really don't have enough time, do you? You want to practice more? If you'll really do it, I'll get a guard and we'll open up the school." And we did.

CHRISTINA: From that time forward, those practice rooms buzzed at all hours.[41]

For the students, no matter where they had come from, the school in Winston-Salem, North Carolina, offered an opportunity to accelerate their lives as artists in a place where they were wanted:

MAURA: The people of the state were very important.

EVADNE: The people were . . . it's true. I mean, there were problems with the school which sometimes Victor solely could not . . . take care of. I remember times when . . . Dr. Semans would come and talk to the student body. Dr. Semans would come into the [school] assembly and sit up there with my Uncle Victor and the two of them—I mean, Dr. Semans was as much a part of the school. He would come into rehearsals, he'd walk down the halls, and say "How are you? What are you doing? I saw you last week in something." It was tremendously supportive. It always seemed the people of that state are really what made it happen. If they didn't believe in Uncle Victor, and if he didn't have them, forget it.

MAURA: It was a marriage.

EVADNE: It was a marriage. It would not have happened.

CHRISTINA: And when you think of those early concerts—rinky-dinky concerts in that terrible little hall. . . . There were really major artists in there playing, and only because of the backing of the local people was there an audience.

MAURA: I remember the time that Ricci played there. . . . He played a solo recital there. I mean, this man is so busy and sought after. He played a solo recital, and the heat was coming on.

CHRISTINA: BOOM! BOOM!

MAURA: And the radiator pipes were banging.

CHRISTINA: Clanking!

MAURA: And he's trying to play the Hindemith sonata accompanied by the CLANK, CLANK, CLANK! And he says, "Well," in this funny little voice. "It's the first time I have ever played to the accompaniment of steam pipes." He was so good-natured about it.

EVADNE: It wasn't in the same rhythm as the Hindemith, either.

"Night after night," says Philip Dunigan, "we would have fantastic recitals here, and the place would be jam-packed with the people from Winston-Salem. . . . We just were taken into the heart of the community. We were always being asked out . . . [but] we were a shock." For the faculty coming south, in spite of very full days and nights of work, there was often a sense of having slowed down, of needing to make a cultural adjustment to the place and to the school as part of that place:

> We were from a completely different background, and when we came down here, we brought with us the image of the life that we'd been in, in New York. The musicians brought with them a mentality that was based on a very, very high pressure, high performance, very fast result kind of thing: union mentality. We want everything spelled out in dollars, cents, powers. What we got was a contrast. It was a letter, one page, saying that you were employed, signed by Vittorio. Which just shows the power that man had to mesmerize us. Because we were used to union-negotiated contracts which had absolutely everything spelled out.
>
> We also brought with us an image of the conservatories that we'd studied in. . . . We brought Juilliard in our heads. Which is a terrible mistake. And I think that everybody that comes here from somewhere else has to go through kind of a decompression, where they adjust themselves to environment, and the situation here. Which, as far as I am concerned, is in every way superior to any other situation in this country. You know, [in New York] . . . when the light turns green, you hit the accelerator, and when you get to Winston-Salem, the light turns green, and you very slowly put the clutch in, and then you put it in gear, and you let the clutch out, and then you go, very slowly, through the light.
>
> Well, imagine what it is like, coming down from New York, to find something like that. Well, that's the way we thought about everything down here. Everything should have been done yesterday. And everything should be done a certain way. And if we had a faculty meeting: what should we do? Well, at Juilliard we did this; well, at Curtis we did this. But we are in a completely different situation . . . it takes at least a year or two for somebody to just get a handle on what this institution is, because it has a life of its own . . . I had to adjust to that. And everyone else had to adjust to that.

In spite of differences and adjustments, however, there was immediately a "sense of musical community" among the music department faculty because of Giannini's dedication to finding people who shared his philosophy: "He laid the groundwork. First of all, there was his feeling about it, and he had very, very strong feelings. And people who were very serious about music would have the same kind of feeling. And he saw to it that the people he engaged had those same kind of feelings. So it was, from the very beginning, a community of artists, rather than a bunch of separate teachers or players." Dunigan recalls how forcefully Giannini shared that philosophy with his entire school at the first convocation:

> The first convocation was something that nobody will ever forget. . . . The high school started two weeks before the college did, and our orchestra conductor wasn't going to come here until the college started. And since I was the first faculty member to get here, Dr. Giannini promoted me to orchestra conductor, an office which I performed in my entire life only those two weeks . . . Vittorio was the kind of man you didn't say no to when he made a suggestion.
>
> So there I was with a baton, standing up in front of these kids. Well, it turns out that the most talented students were the high school students at that time, both in the strings and the winds, so we could put together a pretty good orchestra. And at the convocation we got Sherwood Shaffer to make an arrangement of "Mighty Fortress Is Our God," a fantastic arrangement with trumpet calls and things like that . . . a good number of people from the community came to that. All the students came . . . and then, Vittorio started an oration, and it was an oration in which he more or less charged everybody with what they were going to do: what the students were going to do, what the faculty were going to do. And he let us know in no uncertain terms that he expected us to work our tails off. To get the absolute best results. And he had a way of doing it that scared the crap out of you.
>
> So we opened the doors and we started teaching. I should say something about the cast of characters in the School of Music, don't you think? . . .
>
> Well, the first year, we had an outstanding faculty, not just in ability but in spirit. Everybody really got into the spirit of this place . . . a faculty of names that should never be forgotten. Olegna Fuschi, you know her. Redheaded lady who played [the piano], a brilliant, brilliant player. And she had a husband whose name was Howard Aibel, who didn't have the reputation that she had, but was a wonderful, wonderful player. We [the Clarion Wind Quintet] used to do a lot of chamber music with them. . . . We had a wonderful string quartet

12. Vittorio meets with his deans, left to right: Robert Kimzey, Bill Trotman, Louis Mennini, Robert Lindgren (Archives of the North Carolina School of the Arts).

here; the Claremont String Quartet was very fine and had a national reputation. And they put together a wonderful sound. . . .

.,Vittorio . . . ran the school, basically, out of his hip pocket. There was no such thing as delegation of authority. Well, we were a very small group at that time. And he wasn't really all that interested in our opinion, either. I'll give you an idea: he had been married to a harpist and apparently, it wasn't a happy marriage. And apparently, it had broken up with a great deal of bitterness. So on the basis of his feeling for his ex-wife—and he told me this—he wasn't going to have a harp in this school. So there was no provision for teaching the harp when he first came here. And there wasn't a harpsichord either, because the word "harp" was in harpsichord. That is the way he felt. And he told me that. So—his little prejudices.

Our orchestra conductor . . . was Saul Caston, who was probably one of the greatest trumpet players that ever lived. . . .

Our dean was Louis Mennini. Have you ever heard of him? Lou Mennini was the older brother of Peter Mennin, who had been my theory teacher at Juilliard and at that time he had just moved into the job as President of Juilliard. And Lou Mennini was one of the most wonderful men I've ever met, very low key, easy going, loved music, tremendous enthusiast, an absolute encyclopedia of knowledge of music and love for everything . . . but on the conservative side.

So he and Vittorio hit it off great. They loved music, they loved beautiful girls, they loved to get together and have a little espresso in the morning and a little brandy, and that's the way they started the day. And during that hour in the morning, about ten o'clock, they'd go back in Vittorio's office, and no disturbing them! They had a little conference . . . absolutely wonderful, and then the day's work would begin.[42]

The school began with three categories of faculty: guest faculty, who visited the campus for varying lengths of time to teach master classes; resident faculty, who lived in Winston-Salem; and commuting faculty, who taught on a regular but part-time basis and maintained a home in another city, usually New York. Among the latter were Rose Bampton, Olegna Fuschi, and Pauline Koner. Bampton's routine was to fly down on Tuesday and teach a master class in the evening, teach a regular class on Wednesday, and fly back to New York on Wednesday night. Olegna Fuschi would put on her makeup and have breakfast on her flight from Newark to Winston-Salem, where she spent three days every week.[43] Neither of them thought the commuting a strain, but Pauline Koner found that it did not suit her at all:

[Bobby Lindgren and I] decided that I would come for—I think it was three days every week . . . teach three days a week of each week of the academic year, which I did, and found utterly impossible. I nearly went crazy. I'd wake up and not know where I was, whether I was in New York or there . . . I think I was there maybe Wednesday, Thursday, Friday, and then went home Friday night, and stayed home Saturday, Sunday, Monday, Tuesday, and then came back Tuesday evening, and taught Wednesday, Thursday, Friday—I think that was the schedule the first year.

And I stayed in one of the dorms; they gave me a room there which was my own, and I sort of used that as a place to stay in. It was pretty hectic, with all of the girls screaming around. Nothing I was used to at my time in life. But the thing was that when I came home, I had to work on my own material, and also while I was there I would be rehearsing, because in between I was busy doing my own concerts and keeping myself in condition, and choreographing for myself. So, it

was a very tough schedule, and I remember using lunch hours . . . to
get a free studio space to work and keep myself in condition, you
know, do my exercises and so forth. . . .

[At that time] I had to perform William Schuman's *Judith* with an
orchestra in Oakland . . . Schuman's ballet *Judith,* which was written
for Martha Graham . . . it's a concerto for a dancer and orchestra,
with the dancer on the stage with the orchestra on the stage . . . it was
written for Martha, and no one [else] had ever done it, and Schuman
had said, if anybody else ever did it, he wouldn't mind if I did it . . .
this was the beginning of September, and the performance, I know,
was sometime in October . . . so every time I would come home, I
would plunge into these rehearsals, most of which I choreographed
myself. . . . And then I zipped out there and did the performance and
had hysterics because they didn't have the stage built out in front of
the orchestra. . . . So . . . [I was] involved with the school . . . I was
performing, choreographing—whatever came along.

[My teaching schedule] wasn't too bad, because with twelve students—and see, Duncan Noble was splitting the modern dance department, so the idea was that the days I was there I would have a
technique class and a choreography class—it was two classes a day. I
was the only one teaching choreography, and there was no curriculum
or anything organized, so I just had to do it off the top of my head.
And it was very fascinating because we had some very interesting
things happening there. And when I was gone, the alternate days,
Duncan would take on those classes. . . . I was very careful; I organized every class . . . I walked in, and I knew exactly what I was going
to do all the time. My big problem was in the choreography classes
where I would have a group . . . who had had one year of choreography and were ready to go on to something more advanced. Then
we had admitted some more college students in that group, and they
were just beginning, and how do you structure a class like that? I was
constantly faced with having to invent ways of structuring curriculum
within the class on my own . . . I couldn't progress on a logical basis
. . . it wasn't what I think was the perfect way to teach that particular
course.

And then I taught another course; I taught elements of performing,
which was very much my own, this was my own course. And that too,
if someone had had one semester and was ready to go on . . . then you
had a whole group of people who hadn't had the initial thing and
didn't know where they were. How did you combine it in one session?

So sometimes I would tear my hair out. It was very difficult, and all the time I was there, I don't think it was ever solved . . . you can divide up your groups and give movements more simple to one group and more advanced to the other as a variation within the same class. But you can't do it in the theoretical class, and that was, I found, very tough going. . . .

And then, in those early years, we slowly developed a very small little company of modern dancers . . . and we went out into the . . . elementary schools and high schools. And I took a company, and we arranged a program of dancers in costumes. It was sort of a semi-lecture/demo, and I would talk about it, and we would do little improvisational studies and some pieces that I had set on the company. I don't know how many we were. We had a bus that took us, and we went into the schools, into schools that had never seen live dancers. And at that time, some of the schools were very segregated. We went into black schools and white schools. And you'd walk in and you'd say, "Now, how am I going to get that audience with me?" . . . people who had never seen a man in a leotard in their lives. Hard-boiled high school guys, you know, from the football team, and so forth—in five minutes, I had them in the palm of my hand. I know just how to approach it, because the word "leotard" came from a costume in a circus, that a trapeze artist had invented so he could walk on the trapeze with no hindrance. And so, a leotard was strictly a man's outfit. It had only become a woman's outfit because it was comfortable with dance and it absorbed perspiration, and you could see the body line. When I said that, there was no hooting and no whistling and no nothing, you see.

And then I would talk between each number and show them how modern dance was closely aligned with our everyday activities, like walking and swimming and playing football and ice skating, and how this movement had evolved. I just told them that dance is movement, and you all move, so you all dance . . . this is just a change, only these people have to work longer and it's more specialized. If you want to be a football player, you train; if you want to be a real dancer, you train. And so that way, when we'd leave, we sometimes had standing ovations.

We had two [shows] a day. One, sometimes at 8:30 or 9:00 in the morning, and one at two o'clock in the afternoon. We'd go out for two weeks. But it was fantastic training for the students, aside from what we were doing for the community and educating those people in the schools. But as far as performing, we never even had a rehearsal on the stage. They put their make-up on in the motel rooms. They came all ready to go. We whipped into the costumes. We carried our own lights with us. The crew were the dancers. They put the lights up and lugged the costumes and stuff in and out, and then they got on stage. They had to case it with their eyes. One day you'd have a postage stamp stage; the next day you'd have a stage as large as a football field. They had to case it, and get used to working on the stage without rehearsing. . . . That was an absolutely marvelous training for the students of the school. And it meant that they were dancing for audiences. That's a different feel. You know, the electricity that happens, the projection, the concentration. I briefed them on all the deportment of a performance.

So those early years, they were tough on me. I was dead when we'd come back. But it was also, I found, very exciting . . . we did it on shoestrings, on nothing, you know, with very poor material and everything, but it looked fabulous. I mean, they came out, and they looked like great dancers. . . . They looked beautiful. And the kids just fell for it. And I got the toughest guys to sit quiet. It was very rare that we had an unruly audience . . . certainly in North Carolina, the modern dance was not a very, very well-known term. If ballet dancing was called "tippy-toe" dancing, imagine what they would have called modern dancing . . . "floor-washing" or something. Yet some of the students we had in the first year have come through now professionally . . . some of those early students have made their way marvelously.[44]

The music department and the dance department of the new school were strong from the very beginning because of the reputations and contacts of Vittorio Giannini and Robert Lindgren. The drama department, however, got off to a wobbly start, because its only "name" faculty member was William Ball, who was not in residence. "William Ball is an extremely competent director of drama," says Dr. Semans,

and was [perceived as such] in the eyes of both Vittorio Giannini and the Ford Foundation. However, he put in no appearance at the school, and had it not been for the loyalty of Mr. William Trotman, the associate dean, we would have had no leadership in the beginning in the School of Drama. Finally, I enticed the gentleman to come from Pittsburgh where he was directing the American Conservatory Theater extremely well, to visit the school, and to meet Mr. Babcock of the Babcock Foundation, to see about getting grants to fund the School of Drama. [Ball] had a Rockefeller Grant already and was in-

terviewed by Giannini. The question of Mr. William Ball's involvement in the School of Drama brings out a very important point in
dealing with artistic personalities, because artists have to be duly inspired and motivated even to a greater degree than I have noticed in
any other profession. . . . Mr. Ball's leanings were to continue in Pittsburgh or some metropolitan area where he had wide choice of thousands of candidates rather than of fifteens, twenties and thirties of candidates. He dutifully came to the school and held some auditions.
Vittorio Giannini sensed that his real heart was elsewhere than at the
school, so, in a very tactful way, he said "Bill, if you bring the Rockefeller Grant down and deposit it in the Wachovia Bank of Winston-
Salem, North Carolina, we very much want you to be the dean of the
School of Drama. If not, I think you'd better give us freedom to look
elsewhere for our dean." This was the clear statement that needed to
be made. Nobody was disappointed more than we were to miss the
lofty talents of William Ball. But he soon thereafter left Pittsburgh
and returned to San Francisco where he has successfully run the
American Conservatory Theater, made excellent video tapes and put
on excellent performances, since that famous dialogue with Vittorio
Giannini. Mr. William Trotman loyally and skillfully attracted excellent students to the School of Drama, but, I think, much over-
modestly stated that he did not have the national prestige worthy of a
school of this sort. He departed, as he said, to "sling paint" in other
settings where drama was produced, namely, Houston, Texas, and
Hawaii, where he pursued his profession, as to be expected, at a thoroughly professional level of excellence.[45]

The drama department had trouble at first finding its way, but not for lack
of caring and striving on the part of its faculty of unknowns. "We had excellent people, I thought," says William Trotman:

They were not name people at all. I brought in people to teach theater history who eventually moved over to the academic part of the
school—Marion Fitz-Simons and Gerd Young, who became very
much involved in the academic area, but they started in the drama faculty. . . . Both of them had theater backgrounds, but even more intensely . . . academic backgrounds. I felt a definite need that those students should have a strong academic background in theater for those
intelligent enough to grasp it. For those who did not, they could take
the certificate program. But I felt it should be offered to them. Bobby
and Lou [Mennini] did not feel the same way because they felt that

when they got their students, they had to spend more time on the arts training. I felt that ours had to be given the larger balance academically. . . .

I felt that since it was an art school, that all of the academic areas should be aimed towards the art student. If it was going to be a physics course, it should be in the dynamics of dance, how the lighting instruments operated—let's use those examples. The same way in an English course: it should be aimed toward the art students, for their grasp, designed for them, and I think that's what all of us agreed on in the first year. . . . We had a speech teacher that Bill [Ball] had picked up from Carnegie, who was only one year out of school himself, but quite an intense young man. And then we had a technical director, and I was teaching acting and design as well . . . the philosophy was to keep a strong basic faculty that would teach the basics of theater in that first year when we were feeling our way, and it would be a strong enough faculty, hopefully, eventually, that we could bring in the disparate elements of the theater. The first year we brought in a man from the Royal Academy in England for four months, a man named Hugh Miller. . . . At the same time, we were bringing in people from the Actors Studio in New York, which to young southern drama students was quite confusing. . . . There were some that we brought in for one day that were strictly performers, and . . . many times in the theater you find people who are performers who are totally inarticulate unless they have something memorized . . . [thus] we felt we must provide a very strong faculty to give the students some frame of reference. . . . We introduced all of the students to a technical course. I had had that in school, and I'd talked to Bill Ball, who believed in that very intensely. Even if they couldn't sort of seem to learn how to use a hammer, at least they had an appreciation for what the technical area of the theater was . . . the big advantage, of course, we were advertising to our students [was] that if you came here, not only could you be trained as a symphony manager, a stage manager, but a ballet lighting person. . . .

The students had a rebellion the first year because they saw the music students and the dance students performing, and they were not ready to perform. Most of them had, say, three months training in their entire lives, and were not quite on the same level as some kid who was twelve years old who had had ten years of dance. This was very difficult for them to understand. We had an ardent revolt upstairs one day when all the students faced me down about the performing business, and Ball and Giannini and I talked it over, and adamantly set that as the limit, until they had been here long enough to learn how to perform, they were not going to perform. That was our biggest problem . . . lack of any background . . . the kids came with no background at all. The ones who had been to the Governor's School had the best background, and that was six weeks training. So it was really stark in the very beginning; they had no concept of what it was about. . . . It was difficult for them to believe that there was as much training necessary as there was for a career in the professional field . . . when they were seeing people their own age that were making $100,000 doing commercials already, so we brought commercial actors in from New York to explain to them exactly what was involved in making a commercial—whether that took any talent or not, what kind of agency contacts. We spent the first year drafting a course called Professional Theater Orientation, which . . . Bill has had in his repertory, in his conservatory, from the very beginning, and it is a course just to familiarize the student with what is involved in getting a job and holding a job, and what the proportions are of opportunities to the number of people who want the job. And particularly in the North Carolina school, we found this to be of great importance. . . .

The first year . . . people were already calling the school and saying, can't you send me some tippy-toe dancers to come out and dance at the Junior League meeting or whatever? and the drama students, we simply did not expose them the first year. There was nothing to expose. In fact, our first performance was invited—it was an invited audience. I don't think we ever did a public performance the first year. I hope the hell we didn't . . . there were short things. There were one-act plays. Hugh Miller, when he came in from London, directed *Everyman*, which was strictly a production he had done in St. Paul's Cathedral, and it was not to be seen by the public except those people who were sympathetic to the school, that knew where we were that first year.[46]

Evadne Giannini, as a student in the drama department during the early days, was able to compare the new school to Performing Arts High School in New York:

> [P.A.] was geared to a competitive ethic from the very beginning, from the minute you walked in. . . . Uncle Victor felt about North Carolina [that] it would create an atmo-

sphere and a place where young artists could work and take
risks which you cannot take later on in your life. You could
take risks. I remember in the acting department, you could
be bad in a class, or you could be real bad if you wanted to,
or you could be real great. You cannot be great unless you
are not afraid to be bad. And you can't do that at Performing Arts High. I mean, I know the school, I have been
there, I have taught there. I've seen students that come out
of there. From the time you're in there, you are already
leashed to running to your first commercial audition. You
are already instilled [with] the fear of making a mistake. If
you're afraid of making a mistake in this business, you won't
get anywhere, you won't get anywhere.

MAURA: [Uncle Victor] wanted the students to have the protection
of a school environment where they could make the mistakes. . . . You have to learn to perform. You don't just become a performer overnight.[47]

Perhaps more than anything else, it was the performance opportunities at
the school of the arts which Arturo Ciompi believes made the greatest difference in his training as a professional musician. Ciompi, at age sixteen,
entered the first class at the school as a junior. As graduation approached,
he thought of going on to college in New York:

I went and auditioned, and I was accepted at these fancy schools in
New York, Manhattan, Juilliard . . . but I decided not to go. I didn't
like what I saw . . . I got to talking with the students there, and there
didn't seem to be as much opportunity to perform and to really get
the experience that you need. . . . So I decided to stay [at NCSA] . . .
I had so much experience . . . I think I played in five orchestras down
here while I was in school—played in Asheville, Winston-Salem,
Charlotte and Greensboro, and all my chamber music experience—
When I got into these freelance orchestras [in New York] . . . I was
very comfortable . . . I found that I was doing a lot better than most
of the Juilliard kids, coming out of school. I just had a lot more experience than they did. I mean, they may have had decent teaching, but
they had no playing experience . . . that's a problem with some of the
big city schools . . . as a student at Juilliard, you can't go out and play
in those so-called community orchestras, because of the freelance jobs
that tens of people are trying to get, to pay their rent. I mean, that's
big business up there. . . .

The school offered to some students a tremendous opportunity. . . . You know, when I got out of school, I was a professional; I really was a professional . . . I think that was borne out when I went to play for people in New York. I went to auditions—of course, it's hard and I had a difficult time at first . . . I waited a long time for some openings, but . . . the city opera, when I went in, everyone loved what I was doing and they needed someone . . . and, you know, I was the right person. I was flexible, and I was able to blend in with the people there because I knew how to play under lots of different circumstances. And you don't get that when you just sit and play for a teacher in your lessons. You need to get out and play in lots of organizations. . . . So I just found that my training [at NCSA] . . . had been great for that.[48]

Paradoxically, one of the points that had been brought forward to discourage the establishment of the school—that it was too far from the major metropolitan centers of professionalism in the arts—turned out to be an advantage for students. As Giannini had hoped, the school from the very beginning gave them the opportunity to work in their art and take risks, to grow into professionalism rather than being unloaded into it as their school years came to an end. Another of Giannini's philosophical ideals that proved to have great value was the importance of combining in one school all of the performing arts. "He felt," says Evadne Giannini, "that artists, to really be artists, had to be influenced by the other disciplines: that dance influenced theater, that theater influenced dance, that music influenced all of them. You had to create a place where a creative person could share both the impulses and the creativity, and then the products, of each of those different areas." Arturo Ciompi found that "exposure to all the arts" resulted in practical and personal gains:

Now, being a conductor and doing a lot of mixed media things, I can't tell you how nice it is to really know a lot about dance and know a lot about drama and about tech—especially [the] technical side when you are doing operas. . . . All those things have been extremely helpful to me, not just from a career point of view, but also because I knew some of those people intimately, and so I got to know some of their problems as well, which of course do relate. All of our artistic problems do relate to a certain extent. The premises are different—what causes our problems in the arts are different. But you know, the bottom lines are often very similar in artistic pursuits.[49]

By the end of the first semester at the North Carolina School of the Arts, it had become clear to the academic department, as reported by Dean Julia Mueller, that "the biggest problem of all at the high school level . . . is that of the balance between the academic and arts study and the exhaustion of the students' time and strength." The students had the benefit of a tremendous amount of individualized academic instruction, owing to their relatively small numbers (139 high school and junior high students) and the staff's unusual willingness to adjust instruction to the children's widely divergent ages and backgrounds. But there simply were not enough hours in the day, and Dean Mueller could suggest no immediate solution to the problem of balancing everyone's desire "to provide . . . a first-class college preparatory program and the necessity of an exhausting preprofessional training in the arts." Former Dean of Students Bruce Stewart observes that the academic faculty members had come to the school "with their eyes open":

> They knew that they were the step-children at the family picnic. There was never any pretense made that this was going to be a key academic community . . . I never thought there was anything like what I would call tensions [between the performing arts faculty and the academic faculty] . . . more characteristic . . . was the real attempt on the part of the academic faculty to be creative . . . for example, in the study of history, instead of emphasizing political history in terms of its military conflicts . . . you saw historians trying to emphasize the role of the creative artist in history. When you looked at the Renaissance, you looked . . . more at the composers and painters and writers. And they were trying to teach students what impact the literature had on the way artists began to think, paint, and the architecture they developed. . . .
>
> There were some cases that were aggravating, where students . . . said, "After all, I'm here to play violin, and it doesn't really matter what I do academically," and they kind of knew instinctively that they were right. If they were good enough with what they did artistically, if they wanted to slump off academically, they could get by with it, and that at some point made a genuine problem. But I would say often, that poor academic students didn't turn out to be very serious artistic students. Most of the good art students were at least satisfactory students, and a number of them were gifted.

At least a first step in solving the problem of student exhaustion had already been taken, thanks to the chairman of the board, who had called in as a consultant J. Winthrop Young, the Englishman who had been responsible for the education of the exiled king of Greece when he was a crown prince. Young ran the Schule Schloss Salem in Baden, Germany, a coeducational boarding school where Dr. and Mrs. Semans had observed and been suitably impressed by the way "boys and girls lived together with order and mutual benefit." Young's report did not address the curriculum balance, but rather, appropriately, the necessity for carefully structured living arrangements to keep the students in the best possible health, given their strenuous goals:

> The first thing to combat is merely physical exhaustion; the day is far too long and the end of it is not a fixed time but a choice left open to all. There should be a fixed time for lights out for the Junior High that should not be later than 9.30. the [sic] Senior High could be an hour later. To compensate the day should start earlier; perhaps with a lesson at 8. o'clock before starting in with artistic work. . . . Preparation would have to be cut to two hours in the evening, but I do not think this would be a great loss as they are at present in no state to work concentratedly for three hours late at night.[50]

Arturo Ciompi recalls that the schedule of instruction at the school was extremely rigorous:

> Especially the way Giannini had set it up, because at the beginning it was extremely structured in a sense, and we were overloaded . . . with things to do. So if you didn't like the artistic side of things—if you didn't like theory, chorus, orchestra, and music history, and all these courses that we had to take, not to mention the academics on the high school side—if you didn't like that, then you would find yourself feeling really very unhappy very quickly. . . .
>
> There was too much. . . . [My French teacher] had an artistic background . . . so she liked the arts and she also understood, somehow, what these kids had to go through in order to survive. And she would lighten up somewhat on homework and long papers and that sort of thing, and find you as much work as possible in class, which you know, was a tremendous help to us. You just couldn't be a normal high school student with a normal kind of academic load of long term papers and nightly assignments and still have, you know, five or six musical academics as well, to have homework for. It just wasn't possible, and unfortunately people didn't realize that.

So the first couple of years were very difficult in that respect. Because, you know, being sixteen years old . . . you think you can do anything, and we really could in a way . . . I more or less worked all the time. I averaged about four hours of sleep a night and just worked. . . . I think it's fair to say Dr. Giannini was very adamant about making these music courses very strong and very meaningful— the theory of the solfege, which doesn't exist any more—but I'm very glad that I had it. All those courses were very well taught, and they also demanded a lot of energy. So it was tough! It was tough, but we didn't really realize it. We were just sort of overwhelmed.[51]

Marion Fitz-Simons, who taught in both the English and drama departments, describes the demanding and sharply focused nature of the school:

When [students] told me they couldn't come to class the next morning because they were in rehearsal, I had to tell them, oh, shucks! because I managed to get through the university here [Chapel Hill] and tour with the Playmakers and also write my term papers. . . . It is possible, but it takes an awful lot of energy. . . . I had arrived at the age when . . . my former students . . . were having college-age [children], and I would get letters from them saying, "I have this . . . daughter who has been dancing with the local ballet, and she also is a fine musician, and she also, I think, is going to be a scientist, but your school sounds like the proper place—" and I would have to write, and say "uh-uh." What your daughter needs is a university with some good art sections, because if she came [to NCSA] as, say, a dance student, there was no time in your day to add extra music courses, and certainly there weren't the courses to give a science major. We didn't have any [academic] majors, and we just tried to give enough science to where they weren't totally illiterate in that area. But no, there could not be that kind of cross-fertilization like you'd get in a university. . . .

[The school] trained them in that pre-professional atmosphere that let them know pretty certainly whether this was a life they really wanted. In fact, one of the most gifted young women who was there in the first few years of the school, so gifted that the music department bought her a flute because she was poor and couldn't afford one of her own . . . decided after a year and a half that this wasn't what she wanted at all. . . . Her own music gifts were extraordinarily high, but [what] she wanted was to give music to young people, so she transferred out to Peabody and got a degree in teaching . . . without spinning wheels for a long time, it's hard for people to find out exactly how they want to use these God-given gifts, and I have felt that this was one of the great purposes that school served.[52]

The school also took responsibility for the students' career decisions, something Bill Trotman remembers as another of Giannini's tenets:

The commitment that Giannini had, that every year they would be reviewed, I thought was one of the wisest things in the world, especially in drama. Because after they had a year of intense work, if they had gotten through that and were still interested, then they should be re-auditioned every year. And the families seemed to appreciate that, too, because they knew we were not trying to lead students into an impossible profession unless they could not do without it.[53]

The school, says Arturo Ciompi, "sort of lets you know what it's all about very quickly": "I actually had not made up my own mind that I was going to be a musician . . . the first few weeks of the school . . . pretty much solidified my own feelings about definitely wanting to go into music . . . I like everything I was doing. I LOVED IT! I loved that kind of lifestyle, and where the priorities seemed to be."[54]

The Giannini sisters already knew what their uncle's priorities for the school would be before they got there, but for Maura and Evadne, who were still in high school, NCSA was nonetheless a revelation:

MAURA: The person who's truly dedicated at a young age has to be given the place to fulfill that dedication because . . . competition is a real factor. If you don't put everything you have into it in your early years, you're out of the running. There's no place for you.

EVADNE: But there's another side to that, too. You do have to funnel your energy. It is a little bit abstract to sit in a practice room with a piece of wood under your chin for six hours a day when you see other friends outside of something like a school of the arts, you know, playing and carrying on. But the other side of it is that unless a kid at a young age realizes that there are other kids just like him in six hours of classes and seven hours of classes—I mean, it was very exciting to go to the school of the arts the first year and find another person who was willing to spend seven-and-a-half, eight hours, ten hours a day practicing a craft. It was weird any place else that you came from. And so suddenly, at that age when friends are important, personal identity, personal values, and all the other things . . . there you are at fourteen or fifteen finding people that you can share these values with. In another circumstance, even if you're given time off from a public school and you have to walk out of that class, and they say, "Oh, where are you going?" "Oh, I get out of school early to go practice." It's weird. Whereas, in the school of the arts—and [Uncle Victor] felt the thing I was trying to say—it's not only the act of doing it, it's psychologically being able to handle it at a young age. We saw when we were in public school a few kids like us who were doing what we were doing. By the time they were eighteen or nineteen, they had totally messed around and had quit, or were in the hands of serious psychiatric help. Because they didn't have the experience of understanding that there is nothing odd about this. I mean, kids today . . . who really know they want to be a doctor, their grades in high school are just as important [to them] as [training is to] a musician who realizes the competition is going to hit him the moment he walks out of high school.

CHRISTINA: I would say, "Thank God for the Olympics," in a funny way. You see little Russian children . . . oh so serious, and oh, they're working so hard. . . . Hey, that's what it's about . . . boy dancers at the school of the arts are nothing weird. And I mean, it's a terrible struggle to this day for an average kid, hiding the ballet shoes, to say, "Well, I'm going to class now." Again, exactly what we've been saying, it's a wonderful atmosphere where you could do what you want to do seriously. No joke, seriously. Kids got booted out for a semester because they weren't serious in dance, or serious in drama. Hey, that's great, clear them out, they're not going to make it—they're never going to be dancers, so why confuse them? Don't let them take post-grad courses—too late—out.

MAURA: I wanted to go to the [school] very much; in fact, I
thought it would be a lifesaver, just the concept of the
school, I thought . . . this is heaven, you couldn't ask
for anything better than that when you'd suffered
through public school as most of us had. . . . I really
think that I was probably like all the other kids. We
were just so excited about going to the place that we
really didn't care if the walls were falling down around
us. . . . The first week, my uncle would come into
these student meetings and he'd say, "Well, now, I'm
sorry about this, or I'm sorry about that." The principal would come in and say, "We're going to get
chairs for your desks very soon. They're coming this
week. Don't worry." You know, and things like that.
And, "the beds will be here." You know, that kind of
thing. "We got beds—no dressers. They'll be here in a
week or two." . . . But everybody was just so excited
that the practice rooms were there; that was what was
important, you know, and they were just so excited
that it really didn't matter; it was kind of an
adventure.[55]

In attempting to generalize about the difference he observed that first
year between students at other schools and students at the school of the
arts, Bruce Stewart pinpoints their "intensity of commitment":

You had this odd thing in the sixties of students all over the country
picketing the administration of their schools and opposing the education system, and here in this little place they were breaking into the
school to spend more time playing the pianos, more time practicing
. . . youngsters twelve, thirteen, fourteen, sneaking out at two or
three in the morning and actually breaking into the practice rooms.
It's hard to get upset at one level with people who care that much
about what they want to do . . . when most of the schools in the
country were concerned about the drop-out rate and how to keep kids
in school, we had kids breaking in . . . not breaking out. . . .

The diet issue was a real question . . . a number of these people
were under tremendous pressure to control their physiques, particularly young dancers—the Balanchine look, the stick figures. I had a lot
of young people who were on very strict diets: no breakfast, they
might eat a lettuce leaf and a raisin or two for lunch and a dish of

yogurt for supper. And one was constantly worried about whether that was sufficient because they were working very hard. Don't forget, they had a half a day of academic classes, a full half-day of arts classes, and in many cases, like dancers, that's three or four hours of rigorous physical activity which is much more competitive than football or basketball programs. When I was in college and high school basketball, I never worked this hard, as these dancers . . . they were driven, many of these kids, they had a passion to get where they wanted to go. . . . Young students already dreaming of careers that would put them in their mid-thirties and forties, a sense of goal orientation, of clarity about life that you just didn't seem to find in other academic communities . . . here you had young people who knew which company they wanted to dance in or what symphony they wanted to [play for] or what conductor they wanted to work under . . . I think students in the school of the arts were forced to make choices, to set priorities. They had only a certain amount of time, and I remember Vittorio Giannini giving me an illustration one time and saying that except for composers and for writers and the like, the time boundaries were an imperative working in the lives of young artists. A dancer's life span is very specific, and so, I think, you had to be concerned about whether you could afford to spend your time in a study of history and literature. . . .

I remember when Segovia came to give his master class [April 12–16 and 18–22, 1966], there were students who had come from around the world, literally, to be there . . . to see the great master, just to have a chance to sit at his feet, and you just couldn't help but be overwhelmed by that tremendous sacrifice, and it made its mark on the students who were permanent members of the community, and they valued what they had there, the training.

Most of them had come from places hostile to them, many young males in North Carolina . . . who certainly didn't get a lot of cultural and social support. Finally, in this community they found great esprit, great reinforcement, and the hope, finally, of creativity. It was very exciting. So I think that even though there were major problems, parents on the whole were willing to look at us because of the great assets we had. And then . . . many of the parents simply couldn't afford to provide for their children what the school was providing—the cost of private lessons, the cost of instruments, the opportunity even if you could afford instruments and the lessons for a youngster who played violin—where would you find a violist and cellist to make the trio to go with it? and here in this community you could find the fellow across the hall or upstairs, and they did. And they developed those kinds of skills and they worked late at night and weekends and parents knew they couldn't replicate that at home, and so they took great joy, and generally they worked with us. . . .

Vittorio, much to his credit, spent hours in the dormitories coming over and holding bull sessions with the students in the lounges, talking to them about what it meant to be an artist and convincing them, I think. I remember him saying that inside each human being, particularly inside an artist, there should be a small temple . . . a reverence, a special sense of responsibility. . . . Anyone who has a talent has a real obligation to develop that, and you could see these young people just enraptured with this man, and Vittorio would tell stories of playing the [jazz violin] in a nightclub in order to earn money to study composition. And then he told about his own birth and his developing here a need for leaving the country and leaving his family in order to get the kind of educational opportunity they couldn't afford, and that couldn't help but be a powerful and stirring experience.[56]

Vittorio Giannini was a presence at his school, both demanding and comforting, "a warm, lovely Italian grandfather," says Marion Fitz-Simons. "His quixotic little dealings with the students . . . were of another generation and of another culture—they were not American, and the kids thought it was old-fashioned, but they adored him. And his ideal for the school was a very high one." In an April 1966 interview, Giannini told a Raleigh reporter that he wanted his students to have ample opportunity to find out if their talent and desire were enough to make of them dedicated artists. If not, they could enter other fields "with a clear heart," not "crying out" for the rest of their lives that they might have been great performers. Giannini believed that his students "will know . . . will have had the choice." Agnes de Mille explains what Giannini's standards meant:

I know one thing that distressed him terribly was meeting a lot of southern mothers who couldn't understand why their children were going to be failed in courses. He was trying to show them, you see. There aren't just a set of questions that you have to learn the answer to in these art courses. There's no answer to a tone of music. It's beautiful or it isn't beautiful. When you play Brahms, or when you play anything, you either play it with understanding, or you play it like a fool. You have an entirely different scale of judgment. You cannot bring in marks and regular set questions. And he was applying the professional

13. Happy birthday, Papa Giannini! (Archives of the North Carolina School of the Arts.)

standards. He knew what these kids were going to face when they got out into the world. . . .

You see, every artist is really alone. One has to apply one's own standards and meet them. That's what being an artist means.

Although he could not take time out to teach, Vittorio Giannini remained a caring and alert sojourner among his students. Evadne Giannini says he

> would just pop into a class, and you weren't afraid. . . . "The president of the school is watching you!" He'd sit in class, or he'd go to a practice room, and he'd sit and watch you in the practice room.
>
> MAURA: More important, more important than that, you were working on a piece, and he'd say, "Bring it up and play it for me. I want to hear you guys play that. Come up to my office." Or he'd sit down at the piano and say, "Play that piece for me, I want to hear how it's coming along." I mean, that doesn't happen; people don't show that kind of concern.

Bill Trotman remembers Giannini's pleasure in the development of the dancers: "He used to watch them, sitting there with that unlit cigar at the door of Bobby's studio, and his eyes would just light up. He was just amazed. He never lost that childlike quality of the ability to be amazed, which made him the absolute perfect person for here, the sign of a man with vision. . . . He had the excitement and a certain naiveté that was very, very charming." Giannini stressed that the faculty members should follow his own policy of staying in contact with the children under their care. At a faculty meeting in the fall of 1966, he reminded his teachers that they had a special responsibility because the school was residential:

> Please see your students as regularly as you can. It might at times be inconvenient, but this must be the case. . . . Respond as quickly as possible to a request from them for an appointment to talk with you. It might seem to you at the moment that the problem is not too great but to the student it is a part of his life, he needs help, and it is terribly important that he gets this help. I try to see every student that comes into my office.
>
> Try to stop by the school at night if you have a chance, visit the students, let them know you are interested in them, not only in their

school work but in their social life. They look up to you and will enjoy having you stop by.

Evadne Giannini remembers that students "could go to him and he would listen." For example, "Dancers wanted cottage cheese. They couldn't get it."

MAURA: We had a real problem when the school first started. They got a caterer in and everything was covered with brown gravy and everything was extremely fattening.

CHRISTINA: In a can.

MAURA: A bunch of us . . . were seriously trying to lose weight at the time. We went to my uncle, and we said, "Listen, Uncle Victor, there's no fresh fruit, there's no cottage cheese, so we're just starving ourselves to death. What should we do?" You know, we just told him, "We're just not eating, now what should we do?"

He said, "Oh, that's ridiculous, we've got to do something about that." And it wasn't . . . "Well, three weeks from now we'll take care of it." He'd get in his crazy car and go downtown and buy twenty things of cottage cheese and say, "Here, put it on the . . . trays, what are you doing?" And then it would be okay . . . he'd go out that day and take care of it. But any kid could go to him.[57]

Regulations under Giannini were very strict. "He was very conservative," says Arturo Ciompi, "very old-fashioned . . . very, very disciplinarian. . . . He wanted to know where you were at all times":

The problem with the school was that because of the age balance— You know, many of the dancers were twelve, I remember some of the musicians were thirteen . . . the rules more or less, at least through high school, applied to everyone. . . . Now, those of us who were a little older didn't appreciate that, but at the same time, it was the case. . . .

So I remember, for example, that one had to sign out of the dormitory whenever one left the dormitory, and you had to say exactly where you were going and when you would be back . . . this would be mostly in the evenings, so they would know where you were, and now that I am older, it almost makes sense! At the time, I hated it . . . there was lights-out time, and it was fairly early, as I recall. We used to turn the lights out and . . . just open the door and just talk to each other from across the hallways. We would just stay up and talk, but the lights-out rule was in effect.

Sometimes Giannini made rules for the students' health and safety, and sometimes he fretted about their appearance and deportment. "At concerts," he told the faculty, "they look very nice but sometimes during the day they look horrible":

> It may be a spirit of rebellion, but whatever . . . I think the teachers can help a great deal. . . . Take it upon yourself to speak to them privately or in class. If a student comes in unkempt, dirty, with jeans or whatever it is that shouldn't be, send them right out. Give them an absence. You must see to it that no one comes before you dressed in such a way as to show a lack of respect to you as a teacher. . . .
>
> There is this fad of long hair. Obviously it would be silly to tell them all to have short cut hair like I have or some of you have, this is not important. It is not the long hair that looks bad, it is the straggly, dirty, unkept hair that looks bad. . . . There is no reason for this. . . . I can't give them an absence, I can't give them a failing mark, you can give them a failing mark, you can give them an absence. You must demand this respect for yourself. . . . You can do a job that all of us in the school cannot do because they look up to you, you have the authority over them, and in a sense, make it rain or shine for them while they are here.

Although Arturo Ciompi describes himself as having been "one of the most adamant" of the students about getting many of the rules changed, he nonetheless "genuinely liked" Giannini, disciplinarian though the composer was: "I mean, I think it was very difficult not to like him . . . there was a sense of mission, there was a sincerity about this project in him that was so easy to detect. . . . I was very politically involved that first year in trying to get some of those rules changed; I thought that they were much too strict. But I still never had any resentment toward him about it. . . . I just thought," Ciompi reflects, conjuring up his wise seventeen-year-old self, "that [Dr. Giannini] was misinformed." Sometimes Giannini called the students together in assembly and castigated them directly when matters went beyond execrable hair or blue jeans:

> CHRISTINA: I remember a meeting very early on, you know, a little problem with drugs, a little problem with this and

14. *Graduation Day, 1966: "For those that will not return I want them to know, that even though they may not be here in school, they are still in my heart" (Archives of the North Carolina School of the Arts).*

that, and he had one hell of a rampage, and he explained very clearly that we are here in Winston-
Salem, the whole world is watching us. . . . You want
to lose everything? Go ahead, make fools of your-
selves, go downtown and be a dope. Ransack, make
trouble, get into problems, but remember, you're
being watched. You want to make the world proud of
you, not hate you.

EVADNE: And the fact that he sat up there—
CHRISTINA: And said it—
EVADNE: In front of the entire student body, and said, look,
it's in your hands now, you want to goof it up? feel
free . . . it wasn't like one particular person calls in six
people that they think are the ones, you know what
I'm saying? He addressed us as a group.
MAURA: It was just his ability to both personally and as a
group address us with a feeling of both dedication
and of responsibility. We respected him for that, and
he gave us that kind of respect.[58]

On June 8, 1966, fifty-five students graduated from high school at the
North Carolina School of the Arts: eight in dance, twelve in drama, and
thirty-five in music. President Vittorio Giannini addressed the graduates of
his school only once. He chose as the central theme of his message to
them, not the importance of art to a civilization, or of their roles as artists
in the world, nor did he speak of the hard work that lay ahead of them and
the glory that they all hoped would follow. He spoke instead of character,
slowly, forcefully, almost vehemently:

You are now prepared to assume a much more responsible role, a
much more serious course of study, and a much more important duty
as citizens and human beings . . . *now you must assume the full responsibility as young artists* for the years that are ahead of you . . . the manner, the measure of how you will fulfill your responsibility, the measure of your achievement in your particular field, *will be determined by
your actions* in the next four years. These are crucial years for you . . .
because these are the years when you will mold yourself as a person . . . the kind of person that has the integrity, the honesty, the intelligence, and the courage to face what will be before you and make a
decision. This is what this day means to you. It's a happy day, but also a
day of great responsibility. . . .

For those that will not return I want them to know, that even though they may not be here in school, they are still in my heart.[59]

On Thanksgiving weekend of 1966, Vittorio Giannini went to New York to arrange for the world premiere of his opera *The Servant of Two Masters*. He did not return to his school. His heart was weak, and his friends—especially John Ehle—had urged him to leave the daily work of the school to others, to take instead an emeritus role of leadership and inspiration. "After each heart attack," says Maura Giannini, "they wanted him to rest, and he said, 'I can't rest.' He said, 'I have so much to do, and I'd just be sitting around at home working anyway. I'd rather be here.' . . . His time was slipping through that hourglass, and he had things to do. He felt, rightly or wrongly, he felt that if he lay in bed and waited for the sand to slip, he wouldn't get those things done, and it was going through anyway. . . . He must have had half a dozen heart attacks . . . I can still remember." Perhaps Vittorio's choice had been, after all, the right one. The applause that followed his stern graduation address in June had grown into an ovation that went on long enough to convey a message of genuine affection from the audience of students to their old-fashioned Papa Giannini. He had brought to them the gift of his own dreams, and he had encouraged theirs, and he had tried to teach important lessons. He had been an artist, and his friends missed him. "I, too, was one of his students," Wallace Carroll confessed in his eulogy. "During the past three years I studied the art of living under Vittorio Giannini. And there was one quality about him which I especially wish I could cultivate in myself . . . this school is a monument to his practical idealism. But the quality I refer to . . . was his serenity, and that is not an American quality. . . . He had a serene face, and it was serene because there was serenity in his soul."[60]

He must have had half a dozen heart attacks . . . I can still remember . . . I was in his office and we were supposed to go to this meeting, and I came to just say hello before the meeting, and . . . Uncle Victor was passed out on the floor popping nitroglycerin. And I said, "Jesus Christ, Uncle Victor!" I said, "I'll tell them you can't make it."

He said, "Can't make it?" The man could barely talk; he says, "No, no, no, I'll be fine, just give me a minute, give me—stay here, give me a minute, give me a minute." And he says, "How are you doing? How are things? Are things okay? Are all the students there?"

I mean, here this man is having a heart attack, asking me if all the students are there, and is he keeping them waiting? And literally two minutes later I pick this man off the floor, I help him by the arm, and I said, "Are you all right?" I said, "We can do this another day."

He said, "No, no, no. They're all waiting, I'm fine. How are things? How are you doing?"

And we walked down the hall, and he walked up on the stage to address the school with a major problem . . . I realized there was no way. And he said, "You didn't see anything, did you?"

I'll never forget this. He walked out of the office, and he said, "You didn't see anything, did you?"

"Uncle Victor, I didn't see a thing."

And we just kept walking.

MOVIMENTATA E

FLUTTUANTE

INTERNATIONAL RELATIONS
AND THE
NORTH CAROLINA SCHOOL
OF THE ARTS

ITTORIO GIANNINI had dreamed big. In the kitchen of his friend John Ehle's apartment, not far from the school, he had talked about his plans for the students. His drama students must study each summer in London, where the great tradition of the British stage went back to Shakespeare. His dancers must go to Russia, nurturer of Pavlova and Nijinsky. And the musicians must go to Italy, the cradle of the Renaissance, where the language of music was created and the very stones recalled Vivaldi.

Well, yes, John Ehle remembers saying, that's just fine, but I don't think Russia is going to work out.

Vittorio waved his cigar and dismissed Russian intransigence. Obstacles would, in time, remove themselves. Dreams would come true. He would begin in Italy, for already his friend and music publisher Franco Colombo had been talking again with compatriot Amintore Fanfani about their plan to influence the orientation of American music students toward a greater emphasis on the study of Italian music. Colombo and Fanfani had first discussed their idea during World War II, when they had been in exile in Switzerland. Now Colombo published music in New York City and Fanfani's role as a progressive leader of his country had grown in rank and power. As foreign minister of Italy (a position equivalent to the U.S. secretary of state), Fanfani could make dreams come true. Why not join with Vittorio? Colombo asked him. Perhaps it helped that both Fanfani and Giannini's father, Ferruccio, were sons of Tuscany, an area ferocious—even for Italy—in its regional loyalties. Perhaps it helped that Fanfani was a man

15. Siena, Italy—almost fabulously antique (Archives of the North Carolina School of the Arts).

of education, a professor and political economist at the University of Rome, and an artist, a painter serious enough in his avocation to have had several one-man shows.[1] But perhaps, after all, the explanation for this extraordinary involvement between the federal government of Italy, the city government of Siena, and the state government of North Carolina is simply that great citizens of every state and nation somehow find the time between budgets and speeches to legislate for the world.

In September of 1966, Minister Fanfani attended the opening of the United Nations sessions in New York, where Colombo had arranged for him to meet Vittorio Giannini. Two days after his return to Italy, on September 26, Fanfani called Giannini to come to Siena the following weekend. The Italians and the Americans would come together there, in the chief town of the province of Tuscany, to arrange for a summertime collaboration of the North Carolina School of the Arts and the Accademia Musicale Chigiana. Giannini wanted with him his friends Franco Colombo and Jim Semans, chairman of the board, whom he summoned from Switzerland, where the doctor was delivering a medical paper and riding sky-lifts in the mountains with his wife, Mary, and their children. "Meet me in Rome," he told a surprised Jim Semans, "and you and I and Franco will drive to Siena together." Accompanying them on October 1 from Rome to Siena, a four- to five-hour drive by the scenic route to the north, was Vieri Traxler of the Italian Foreign Ministry, English-speaking adviser to Fanfani, who spoke no English. Jim Semans has recalled that for some miles he was puzzled by the irrelevance of their conversation to the mission at hand, until it dawned on him that Traxler was present to get to know the United States contingent and thus had begun his duties, in the indirect but graceful Italian manner.[2]

The Siena meeting was held on the second floor of one of Italy's numberless Renaissance palaces, the Palazzo del Capitano. In a room with pink silk walls and frescoed ceilings, as uniformed waiters wearing white gloves served San Pellegrino, a favorite red Italian bitters and *analcolici* (nonalcoholic drinks), Minister Fanfani, aided by Vieri Traxler, directed the negotiating of the agreement between Vittorio Giannini and Dr. Semans, representing North Carolina, and Maestros Fabbri and Fenoni of the Accademia, and Danilo Verzili of the Monte dei Paschi Bank of Siena, which would be joining the Italian government in financing this unconventional and very personal, intercultural venture. That day they banqueted gaily at the Villa Marzocchi, on pink Spanish champagne and *uccellini*, little thumb-sized birds. "Vittorio was magnificent," Jim Semans later wrote to John Ehle.[3]

On October 5 the second meeting was held, this time in Rome at the

Foreign Ministry, where two representatives of the Italian Department of Cultural Affairs joined the discussions, along with Franco Colombo and Maestro Fabbri, from the Accademia Musicale Chigiana in Siena. Luncheon that day was served in honor of the two representatives from the North Carolina School of the Arts, in the state dining room, where Jim Semans noted the liveried waiters in stiff shirt fronts and white ties, the red carpet and crystal chandelier, and the thirty-foot-high walls of pale green marble. But for all the fairy story momentum of their resplendent surroundings, the contract the Italians and the Americans agreed on detailed a fully twentieth-century budget and unglamorous practical arrangements. One of Giannini's first concerns was to procure a "general factotum" from the Accademia to unlock the doors in time for rehearsals. Another matter of such anxiety that it was brought up in the Rome meeting was the need for a dean of girls to be responsible "for the girls' conventional behaviour [sic] during the summer session." The financial contributions for the eight weeks of schooling were spelled out: the total budget of approximately $100,000 would be divided more or less equally between the Italian and the American sides, with the Monte dei Paschi Bank contributing $42,000 and the federal Italian government the remaining $8,000. The Italian portion was earmarked to pay most of the air fare on Alitalia for 120 persons (18,600,000 of the 22,320,000 lire expense) and salaries for 16 Italian instructors, rental of instruments, and the costs of using the premises of the Accademia.[4] In the middle of the night in Rome, Mary Semans listened as her husband called the Governor's Office in Raleigh for permission to sign the charter. Later Vittorio confided that he felt scared.[5] He well understood that the program they were undertaking was daring and vulnerable.

The initial contract seemed perhaps deceptively simple and easy to draw up. Giannini would return during Christmas vacation to work out further details, and throughout the negotiations there had been a sense of happy camaraderie, even personal chemistry working among the participants. Outside the official meetings, over casual cups of espresso and informal meals, or walking together the narrow streets set precariously between pastel medieval walls, the dark-suited Italian men and the North Carolinians had begun tentatively weaving friendships, frequently in the exquisitely effective company of blonde and luminous Mary Semans. But portentous and pleasing as these relationships in the foreground may have been, the most fascinating element in the inception of North Carolina's music program abroad is the intricate and ancient nature of the local organizations that stood behind these negotiations. The centuries-old palazzi in which dates and budget and curriculum were set, their walls literally encrusted with Renaissance art, were both body and symbolic evocation of the Italian history on which this hopeful "Sessione Estiva in Siena della North Carolina School of the Arts" was to perch.

The Accademia Musicale Chigiana, the summer session's academic sponsor in Siena, came to life in 1932, cherished progeny of the music-loving and childless scion of a noble Sienese family. Count Guido Chigi Saracini was creator and sole proprietor of the Accademia, which grew into an internationally known school of master classes in musical performance. From July to September each year save two during World War II, the Accademia has offered a course of postgraduate instruction to young musicians, taught by such artists as Arthur Rubinstein, Andrés Segovia, Ermanno Wolf-Ferrari, and Pablo Casals. Among the eminent Americans who had attended the Accademia by 1966 and earned the medal bearing the Chigi coat of arms (and thus the sobriquet "Chigianisti") were soprano Anna Moffo, pianist Gary Graffman, and jazz and classical guitarist Charlie Byrd. In 1960, the *New Yorker* magazine, in a lengthy profile of Count Chigi, conceded that though Siena was still primarily an agrarian center, relatively isolated from the twentieth century and parochial in its attitudes, the Accademia was truly an international center for music each summer, its faculty, "for sheer fame and glamour . . . unsurpassed by that of any other music school anywhere." That he might live among artists and beautiful women, and always within the sounds of singing, of violins and pianos, of harpsichords, organs, and guitars, the count turned his magnificent eighty-room palace into a school. The students and teachers work in rooms hung from floor to ceiling with Renaissance art. In 1923 the count had built within the palace a music room seating three hundred; after seeing it, Bernard Berenson observed that it looked somewhat like "the view one might get when standing inside a gigantic wedding cake." So old is the building which houses the Accademia that its foundations were laid by the Etruscans; from its tower was reported the Battle of Montaperti, the one and only Sienese victory over the despised Florentines in 1260. The palace was at one time owned by another ancient family of Siena, the Piccolominis. When the Saracinis took it over in 1771, they redecorated, seeing to it that Chigis and Saracinis were properly commemorated with plaques, statues, and frescoes, some of which they thriftily relabeled, reasoning that heroic acts and visitations by the Madonna were just as frequent among the Chigi Saracinis as they had been among the Piccolominis.[6]

The count himself was a figure as important among contemporary Sienese as any of the Saracini or Piccolomini heroes and popes may have been. On city walls, the *New Yorker* reported, alongside such chauvinistic and charmingly dated graffiti as "Viva Montaperti!" and "Viva la Repubblica Senese!" (extant ca. 1500) was frequently chalked "Viva Chigi!" At the age of eighty, the tall, lean, white-haired count resembled somewhat "in his general appearance . . . an El Greco grandee." Slightly stooped— "from bending over to kiss ladies' hands"—the count took an active interest in the agricultural concerns of the peasants farming his tracts of Tuscan land and with equal seriousness his responsibility to Siena as rector of the seventeen contrade (districts). This is an elected post which the count held for life and which made him head of the contrade and arbiter of the Palio, a violently competitive horse race held twice each summer in the narrow streets of Siena. To the Sienese, Count Chigi was a symbol of their city's glorious past. "He exists," Winthrop Sargeant wrote in 1960,

> in a world that is outside time and progress, living as a feudal lord, according to the customs of his ancestors. He can recite Dante by the hour . . . and he thinks of St. Catherine and the Madonna as if they were corporeal figures walking the streets of the town. . . . He has long been in charge of the restoration of Siena's civic architecture, and he has carried out his duties with the utmost regard for tradition. He regards any change in his surroundings as a threat to his medieval stability . . . although he has had politely protesting run-ins with the city's various Communist mayors, his position as Siena's great man remains unassailable—a matter of tradition rather than politics—and even the Communist administration is obliged to treat him with the deepest respect.

This, then, was the man who had created and guided the Accademia to its position of international renown, who dictated its artistic policies and shaped its philosophies, chose its faculty, monitored its classes, and poured more than a million dollars of his personal fortune into developing it. By the time Winthrop Sargeant met him, the count had already faced imminent fiscal disaster. Because his dwindling personal fortune could no longer support his hobby—his passion, really—the count had signed articles of incorporation, which, upon his death, would place the Accademia under the control of the Monte dei Paschi Bank of Siena. Signing the contract that would turn over to the Bank the Accademia (with all its accoutrements, including Franz Liszt's piano), the Chigi Palace (with art), and all the rest of the count's estate (both real and aesthetic) was Danilo Verzili, president of the bank and thereby, after the Count's death, president also of the Accademia.[7] This was the reason for Verzili's presence at the negotia-

16. Co-presidents of the NCSA summer sessions, bank president Danilo Verzili and Dr. James H. Semans; Mary Semans stands to the left and behind Verzili (Archives of the North Carolina School of the Arts).

tions with Fanfani, Vittorio Giannini, and Jim Semans, and it provides the beginnings of a glimmer as to why a bank in Siena would be involved in financing a summer school from North Carolina.

In his own tribute to Count Chigi, Danilo Verzili remarks that the signing of the contract enabled the count "to look with serenity on the future of his Accademia," which would now be supported by the bank. The Monte dei Paschi has been doing business at the same old stand in Siena since 1471, time enough to prove its "medieval stability" to any number of Chigis and Saracinis—not to mention the odd Piccolomini. The original institution had been chartered by the city of Siena as a *monte di pietá*, literally a mountain of compassion, to serve as a sort of municipal pawnbroker for citizens in temporary financial straits. Because the bank was a service of the town rather than a for-profit venture, it could make a loan at a reasonable rate of interest against the deposit of some object of value brought by the distressed citizen. In 1625, after a bloody and economically devastating war, Siena became part of the Grand Duchy of Tuscany. In their efforts to rebuild Siena's economy, the city fathers called on the grand duke, now their overlord, for help. The duke's solution to the town's trouble was, according to Vieri Traxler, "extremely modern and quite brilliant." As part of his conquest of Siena, the duke had confiscated numerous tracts of city-owned grazing lands where cattle owners, for a fee, were accustomed to feed their herds. The grand duke designated a portion of these lands, valued at 200,000 ducats, as collateral pledged to the bank; he gave as well the rental income from these lands, valued at 5 percent of the capital. The bank quickly issued two thousand bonds at 100 ducats each, 5 percent interest, guaranteed by the pastures. Now the city and the bank were back in business, the bank with a new name, Monte dei Paschi—the Mountain of Pastures Bank. Today it has branches all over Italy and remains a public institution, owned by Siena and the state of Tuscany. The Italian government and the city government of Siena appoint its directors, and 50 percent of its profits go for the improvement of the city of Siena. Among the modern projects the bank had financed by 1970 were highways, hospitals, a new street lighting system, and a Department of Banking Sciences for the University of Siena. The bank, of course, had always been in the habit of commissioning works of art; in 1965 it went even further, agreeing to support the Accademia Chigiana, and in 1966, the old Mountain of Pastures granted $42,000 to North Carolina, against the deposit of 120 music students.[8]

Though Vittorio had long wanted to see more American music students study in Italy, it was Fanfani's idea to set their program in Siena, in collaboration with Count Chigi's Accademia. It appears that Fanfani's reasons were complex. In the years since its beginnings as an organ school, taught by Fernando Germani, the great Italian Bach specialist, the Accademia had achieved international prestige. Certainly in an intercultural program with young American artists, the Italians would want to show their best and send the Americans back home talking about the Italians' world center for training artists each summer in Siena. To Fanfani, this was a matter of more than pride: unlike much of the rest of Italy, Siena remained a medieval city, its streets, piazzas, and palaces undisturbed by commercial or industrial development. Obviously, the more people who came to Siena to see its art treasures and museums; do research in its almost fabulously antique archives (the Piccolomini Palace alone houses documents going back to 736); and attend its institutes, academies, and university (one of the oldest in Europe), the more likely would be the continuance of a healthy city economy and an undamaged, preserved Siena.[9]

And then there were the less harsh, more gracious considerations. The students would be young, and Giannini and Fanfani feared that in metropolitan Rome they might be "distracted in their earnest studies." Weather in Rome is notoriously bad, heavy and humid, the clammy breath of the sirocco puffing clouds and mildew toward the city nearly two hundred days out of the year. Siena, on the other hand, is relatively small. Its population in 1965 was 62,215 and its inhabitants hospitable. Students could get around in Siena on their own; from end to end of its farthest points is a mildly vigorous twenty-minute walk (strolling couples should allow more time).[10] Summer weather is typically sunny, breezy, and at night, very cool. The town is accustomed to a large tourist and student population each summer and expects to accommodate them; the Monte dei Paschi owned a hotel, the Albergo-Continentale, that could be turned over to the North Carolina session. The Accademia operates only in the summer, and therefore collaboration with another conservatory might be considered an enlargement of its own accustomed activities rather than the creation of an entirely new program for the Americans.

The most compelling reason for setting the program in Siena, however, was practical—in Vieri Traxler's words, "because there was in Siena this institution, this bank, which had the funds and the ability to use them for the purposes discussed."[11] Count Chigi had died on November 18, 1965. For less than a year the Monte dei Paschi Bank had administered the Accademia; it might defensibly be maintained that now was a time to try new things. For the moment, Fanfani held both the power and the means to do so. As a high-level official in the Italian government, he had influence with the government-appointed directors of the Monte dei Paschi, and the Monte dei Paschi now funded the Accademia. Were the count still living, authority would have rested with him, and Fanfani's role would have been diminished to one of patient suggestion. Negotiations would have been cumbersome, power divided among the federal government, the bank, and the frail aristocrat. Agreement could never have been reached swiftly enough to draw on the expertise and inspiration of Vittorio Giannini. As it was, the timing was perilously close.

The October 1966 accords provided that the "new institution" to be established in Siena would be called Summer Session in Siena of the North Carolina School of the Arts, with the Sponsorship of the Accademia Musicale Chigiana. It was to have two presidents, Dr. James Semans, chairman of the board of the North Carolina School of the Arts, and Danilo Verzili, president of the Accademia and of the Monte dei Paschi Bank. The summer session would have two directors: Maestro Vittorio Giannini, president of the NCSA, and Maestro Mario Fabbri, selected personally by Count Chigi to be artistic director of the Accademia. In November 1966, Giannini wrote at least twice to Fabbri to arrange for them to meet in December, but disaster struck in Florence, almost overwhelming Fabbri and preventing both him and Fanfani from attending ceremonies in Raleigh on December 2, when Governor Moore was to announce the inception of the Siena program.[12] Fortunately, Giannini's charm and embracing humanity already had made a friend of Mario Fabbri, whose goodwill obviously would be essential in gaining the cooperation of the Accademia's faculty for the summer session. Fabbri wrote to him in November 1966:

> Most illustrious and dear Dr. Giannini, I thank you very much for your most recent letter and for the words of strength and comfort which you have directed to me with regard to the misfortune which occurred at Florence on the infamous 4th of November, 1966 (a date which we will never forget). The damages are immense and even I, indirectly, have been hit: The musical library which I direct, that of the L. Cherubini [Fabbri was director of the Luigi Cherubini Conservatory of Music in Florence as well as being Artistic Director of the Accademia each summer], has seen more than 10,000 manuscripts (rare and unique in the world) submerged in water and mud! Since the 6th of November, I have been leading an incredibly exhausting life without heat, water, or light, in the midst of a fortune. (We have worked page by page on the manuscripts and I hope to save 95% of the volumes). . . . I have had the courteous invitation and am happy and honored! I believe it will be impossible to leave my duties in these dior [dire] moments of near emergency. I think I should remain to save a musical [art] of great value, I am saddened but what can I do. I will try my best if possible to come, but if I cannot, it will be because I am occupied here.
>
> Awaiting your answer, I shake your hand. With warmth and friendship.[13]

The death of Vittorio Giannini on November 25, 1966, might very well have ended the Siena program, for diplomacy between North Carolina and Italy was being conducted on a personal level. Foreign Minister Fanfani had accepted the recommendation of his friend Colombo, of Colombo's friend Giannini, in awarding this unusual grant from the federal Italian government and the city of Siena. The North Carolina School of the Arts, after all, had no reputation to speak of; it was still an experiment. It had, as

17. Siena, 1967: He was a Florentine. He was a superb violinist. He was a Chigianisti. Giorgio Ciompi steps in for Vittorio Giannini (left to right: Rose Bampton, her husband, conductor Wilfred Pelletier, and Giorgio Ciompi; in left background, Vieri Traxler) (Archives of the North Carolina School of the Arts).

yet, proved nothing—at least, nothing that Italy should take note of. With Giannini gone, there was every reason to think the Italians would renege. And why not? They had agreed to give money to an Italian-American composer of solid artistic reputation, not to an unknown, untried school and an American M.D. and his wife. Jim and Mary Semans, grieving and determined that Vittorio's last hopes and efforts would not be wasted, reasoned that the immediate substitution of another Italian of high artistic rank—someone with whom Mario Fabbri would be comfortable working and whom Fanfani and Verzili would feel they could trust—might preclude cancellation of the program. Within six hours of the discovery of Giannini's death, they were on the phone to Rome. They had only one candidate, an artist-in-residence at Duke University. That there was any suitable candidate available on such short notice in North Carolina is both a miracle and a characteristic of the state. And the candidate was ideal. He was a Florentine. He was a superb violinist. He was a Chigianisti. And in conversation over dinner with Vieri Traxler and the Semanses one night in Siena, Giannini had commended Giorgio Ciompi on both personal and professional levels when Mary Semans intuitively unearthed the fact of a casual acquaintance between Ciompi and Traxler some years earlier in Cleveland. "Now, you should know," Ciompi began, when asked in 1981 to look back on his role in the Siena program,

> that this project was really the baby of Vittorio Giannini . . . he wanted . . . for the American student in music to go to Italy and have the experience of the warmth, the art, and he was a dreamer, in a way, and really, when things start to really happen, he died. So this was a tremendous blow for the entire project.
>
> Now, at that time, I had move from Cleveland Institute of Music, here [Durham], and I had made many friends, among them were Jim Semans and Mary Semans. So they heard that I was a real Italian, you know, because people, they say they're Italian, they speak Italian, and they—they don't. Not only [that] but Florentine, so I speak Tuscan, which is a little different, the real Italian. So . . . they approached me and said "Giorgio, this is the situation. We think you could be what Giannini would have been because you are known there." You see, I had played before the war a lot in Italy. The violin, concertizing, I start very, very young. I was eleven years old when I start to play. "They know you, and in a way, you could represent something when you speak to them. You seem so involved with the American education."
>
> And, you know, I did it because my wife was with me; I could not do it by myself. Especially this was, for me, something of a new kind of job. I am more a performer. And here, you have to deal with the American staff and the American student. And then, at that time, the Italian staff, because at that time, it was slight difference than today. . . .
>
> The project was to bring the student in Siena to study everything connected with . . . music . . . with Italian teachers. So every oboist would have oboe lesson. And this—can you imagine? to write down the contract with these people? It was incredible, incredible. In Italian, in English, and deal with them, and of course, you have to know the Italian approach when you speak about America after the war, you know—"Money is like water!"

18. "Of course, we had the help of the Italian government, Fanfani . . . he's a personality, very direct." Left to right: Giorgio Ciompi, Danilo Verzili, Minister Amintore Fanfani, Commissioner Padalino, Dr. James H. Semans, and Mario Fabbri (Archives of the North Carolina School of the Arts).

> So. I accepted, and we start to organize . . . to approach the people, and of course, we had the help of the Italian government, Fanfani, personal . . . he's a personality, very direct. For instance, he walk almost running, and his walking pace is—is not normal. So . . . he is this little man, you know.

SEMANS: He calls himself the Tuscan pony!

CIOMPI: So. When he goes—tatatata—you know, you have to follow him! And you see people, you know, that *struggle* . . . maybe he enjoy that a little bit, I don't know! Something psychological! But, he is very optimistic . . . and he's accustomed that what he touch . . . must be a success, you understand? And this is good, because these people, they don't take no for an answer for nothing. I think he was a great help.[14]

On December 2, at the Executive Mansion, Governor Moore made a joint announcement of the Siena program with Sergio Fenoaltea, Italian ambassador to the United States. Giannini's brother Francis was present to hear the governor and Jim Semans declare the special summer session a memorial to Vittorio Giannini. Danilo Verzili came and so did the mayor of Siena, Padalino; only the floods in Florence had kept Mario Fabbri and Amintore Fanfani away from Raleigh.[15] It was an astonishing and generous occasion. And it was what Vittorio had wanted. "He wanted to get this Siena session off the ground," Maura Giannini states emphatically, "and he walked up and down those hills with Fanfani . . . and he shouldn't have done it, but he did. And he came back, and he was so proud, he said, 'I've done it, I've got it set up. You can all go there now.' And that was it. I think he knew when he was going to die. He knew it was going to happen."[16]

Suddenly the game was afoot. The Americans scrambled to get publicity out in time to recruit students from all over the country to audition for the eight-week session in Siena. The Italians, Jim Semans recalls in his memoirs of the Siena experience, were "alarmed" when they realized the amount of work that had to be done. In January he and Giorgio Ciompi traveled to Italy to deal with the concrete particulars of Giannini's dream. For Jim Semans, "the experience of working with eminent foreigners on a minimally controversial basis (music)" was an "exhilarating one." In a letter to a friend during this time, he described the negotiating team:

> The Maestro [Fabbri] is a 36 year old Alpinist who envisions our Summer Session as a successful ascent of Mt. McKinley. . . . My colleague [Ciompi] is a violinist of high repute both in Italy (Florence) and America (Toscanini). He needs [h]is native Italian background, as well as the language, to persuade them pleasantly that we are in a hurry. . . . My formal role is to make a decision only when the two artistic directors find themselves in a dilemma. This rarely occurs; but there are so few of us over here that I am in on most of their decisions.[17]

Arranging details of faculty, lodging, and budget turned out to be a wondrous feat. Everything was either too many, not enough, or there was a rule. Even the airline had a rule. Although the Italians were paying the Americans' fares on Alitalia, the contract had to be signed by the Americans because Alitalia wanted to be paid in dollars. The check for a 10 percent down payment to Alitalia to accompany the contract could not be signed, however, by Jim Semans, the American co-president of the Siena summer session, because he was not an artist. Only the artistic directors could write checks on the session's joint account at the Monte dei Paschi because the money was to be spent for artistic purposes; the co-presidents were only to verify the account. As yet, there were not enough rooms. Students were to stay at the Hotel Continentale, but only one hundred of them could be accommodated. Rooms for the remaining twenty would have to be found elsewhere, as well as lodgings for the Ciompis, Olegna Fuschi, Howard Aibel, and Marc Gottlieb, who were coming from North Carolina to teach. And then there was the problem of too many conductors for the orchestra. Confusion had arisen because of Vittorio's habit of relying on conversations between friends rather than written records and formal contracts. Thus Mario Fabbri had engaged an Italian conductor in Italy and Giannini had engaged an Italo-American conductor in America. This situation was resolved by offering the post of teacher of composition and fugue to Giannini's choice, who eventually decided not to proceed because his involvement with the program had been with Vittorio his friend, rather than with the school of the arts.[18]

Innumerable matters had to be seen to. Should the students read the recently published book *The Italians,* by Luigi Barzini, for background before they came? They should do so only if a session were arranged for them to hear another point of view, their hosts firmly decreed. Courses in Italian were to be taught both in Siena and at the school of the arts; for, as Maestro Ciompi pointed out, the language of Italy had had "a long and continuing influence in the field of music . . . even the German composers communicated with the performing musicians in Italian terminology." Instruments brought on Alitalia by students and the school would have to be accommodated in cabin space with the temperature and pressure specially adjusted to avoid damaging them. Others would be rented in Italy, wherever they could be found. Giannini originally expected to rent the large instruments in Florence, but the floods that had drenched Mario Fabbri's library with mud had also destroyed whole inventories of pianos, double-basses, tympani, and harps. "We will probably need from 12 to 14 [pianos]," Jim Semans found himself writing to Mario Fabbri's "general factotum" one day in the spring.[19] Giorgio Ciompi scrounged the student orchestra's best bass viol from a fellow patron at an Italian barber shop. Most of the instruments, however, were coming from Milan and were expected to arrive in Siena just ahead of the students, to be released to the summer session upon payment of $24,000. William Herring, at that time the administrative director of the school of the arts, recalls that he telexed the money from Winston-Salem to the Monte dei Paschi Bank:

And it didn't come. And it didn't come . . . the money [had] disappeared! And we found, finally, through our tracing through Wachovia's correspondent bank in Milan . . . that in the charming Italian way, the bank there decided just to sit on the money for a week or so and enjoy the float that was created by this small amount of cash before forwarding it to the appropriate bank in Siena . . . which I learned later is regular Italian banking practice. You just sit on somebody else's money and get a few days' interest and that takes care of your handling charges and your overhead. But we were just tearing our hair out. I think R. B. [Crawford] was off on a trip some place, and I thought I was going to wind up in Central Prison because I had taken this $24,000 and sent it to Italy, and it had vanished.

From time to time Jim Semans must have wondered what rabbit hole he had fallen down, but he proved himself a prudent man in all seasons: the Italians, he remarked temperately to a friend, "have much to teach the Americans in imaginative enterprise in their daily life."[20] Ads run in the *New York Times* and word of mouth—teacher to student to teacher—attracted music students from such outstanding conservatories as Manhattan, Juilliard, Eastman, and Curtis, as well as a variety of colleges and universities. Forty of the 120 selected by auditions in Winston-Salem and New York that spring would be coming from the North Carolina School of the Arts. The program, of course, was an unbelievable bargain, even in 1967: for $450 the students got transportation to and from Italy on Alitalia, room, board, sightseeing in Rome for four days, plus visits to Assisi and Perugia on the way to Siena; and, incidentally, instruction for the better part of the summer by world-class artists. It was an unparalleled opportunity for the Americans "to have their talents and personality recognized" in an international setting, Jim Semans explained—"also their willingness to concentrate on their careers seriously in a foreign country where everyone has accepted music in operatic, symphonic and vocational concept for many centuries as a part of responsible society."[21] The 120 American students arrived in Rome at Leonardo da Vinci Airport on July 10, 1967. Foreign Minister Fanfani had insisted on a four-day visit in Rome during which the students were to learn something of Italian history and culture, and it was no Latin class field trip. They attended a party in the palace garden at the residence of the American ambassador; they ate lunch at the Foreign Ministry with Fanfani (an occasion featured in the Italian press and television). They even had for their instructor in Italian custom a marchese, who explained, among other pertinent topics, "the inborn artistic nature of the Italian male."[22] Ceremonies in Siena were no less grand; the North Carolina School of the Arts Summer Session in Siena opened before a crowd of eight hundred people in the great Teatro Communale dei Rinnuovati. The mayor of Siena was there. The Siena Chamber Orchestra was there. All the students were there, from North Carolina and from the Accademia, sitting in theater boxes, one on top of the other on top of the other on top of the other—four tiers of students up the sides of the theater in the town's thirteenth-century city hall. Fanfani gave the opening address, and others followed, and between each speech a cordon of townsmen in medieval costume sounded trumpets.[23] The Americans walked on the stones of the Middle Ages and sat in the Palazzo Publico, like Mark Twain's Yankee in a medieval dream-world, adjusting to the incongruities and wondering, where's the part about the bump on the head? The bump was coming.

The faculty of the Accademia had not been consulted about this collaboration with the North Carolina School of the Arts; they had not been included in the planning and, like any faculty, were sensitive about such an omission. They expressed doubts to their artistic director, Fabbri, about "the advisability of such a large American invasion." And then, during the inauguration of the session, Minister Fanfani, enthusiastic, excited, in his emotive generosity, departed from the prepared speech and invited the American students to come to his native town of Arezzo. Perhaps in the excitement he lost his place, for in none of his speechmaking that day did Fanfani express homage to—or even mention of—Count Chigi. And Count Chigi, Mario Fabbri informed his American colleagues, was "next to God in this place." The gaffe was news in Siena. The local paper reported and discussed it. Within the ancient walls of the Accademia there was, Fabbri said tactfully, "some unpleasantness." A faculty meeting was held. Danilo Verzili attended. Feelings were soothed.[24] And then the American concerts began.

At the end of their first week of rehearsals and classes in Siena, Jim Semans reported to Philip Hanes: "The students . . . were literally hungry for work when they arrived in Siena. . . . They beg for more rehearsal time and have scheduled some practices all the way through to ten-thirty in the evening, eliminating all thought of siesta time . . . the students themselves are greatly moved by the intensity of feeling about music on the part of the Italian musicians and people in general." A few days later, he happily described the students' first concert to Bill Herring (still mopping his brow back in Winston-Salem over the session's financial confusions):

> We had been told that it would be quite difficult to get a crowd at this time of the year but at our opening program, where the Tchaikovsky Concerto for Violin and the Beethoven 7th were played, the theatre

was packed . . . and there was standing room only. The "Bravos" and applause would have made you proud and the leading violinist of the Accademia sent a telegram of congratulations to the Session. . . . I want you particularly to know that I have obtained the services of a qualified accountant.[25]

Ever eager and energetic and, most of all, innocent, the summer session students bustled into the Old World, intent on making the most of their six weeks in Italy. The Italians looked on askance, elegant, sunning grasshoppers whose orderly and gracious lives were being disrupted by a troupe of guileless American ants. The students lived in the heart of Siena and practiced in a nearby palace (palaces are always nearby in Siena). They walked quickly and efficiently to their classes and practice sessions every morning. The orchestra rehearsed three times a week and performed every Friday; every Tuesday and Thursday the students gave recitals. And every day they practiced relentlessly. "The rhythm of the life is completely different over there, you understand?" Giorgio Ciompi explained. "For instance, I forgot, after almost thirty years that I was in United State, that from one to four, that the siesta."

ADRIANA: Everything closes.
GIORGIO: Can you imagine, we had scheduled rehearsal all over. We
            almost got all arrested because people did not want to
            hear—"You cannot sing!" you know, the student open
            window and sang!
ADRIANA: And played.
GIORGIO: We had a place across [from] apensione. Everybody left
            apensione! The woman want to sue the school of the art
            because she had lost business.

The pianos, Fabbri reported, had become "the torment of Siena." And something must be done about the "barrage" of American concerts! The Chigiana faculty felt it "ill-advised to give so many concerts." The Accademia students, they gloomily observed, had taken to attending the American concerts rather than their own classes. But the thorn went deeper than the distractions of novelty and temporary inconvenience. The quality of the orchestra, Fabbri went on, had been "a shock to Siena and to the students and faculty of the Chigiana." At the first concert, Fabbri heard the opinions of Brengola, Ferrara, Giurana, and Gazzelloni. "Their impression was that the Summer Session orchestra was worth more than their own orchestra, some of whose members were paid professional players

19. The first summer session, Siena, 1967: "The students . . . have scheduled some practices all the way through to ten-thirty in the evening, eliminating all thought of siesta time." Playing in the Sala Degli Specchi, left to right: Romuald Tecco, Margaret Tait, Arturo Ciompi, Richard Woodhams, Ransom Wilson, Lauren Goldstein, Russell Plylar, and Dan Ashe.

from other Italian cities." Maura Giannini played the violin in that first student orchestra: "In typical American style . . . we whipped together this orchestra that had never seen each other, and in four rehearsals put on fabulous concerts. But there were too many concerts. . . . The Chigiana said, 'What are you doing? You can't be doing this—this is improper. You haven't had enough time. What do you mean, you just came from all parts? And look at all those women in that orchestra, anyway!'" "In fact," Giorgio Ciompi reflected, "I'll have to tell you something that you don't know":

> When Giannini was dealing with the Italian—the Italian are very personal people in a sense, very proud, you know. The civilization—that's the best. The best musician come from there—this is really nationalistic pride, but pushed to the end, you know.
>
> So when Giannini talk about bringing school, here start a little misunderstanding. He meant school of the

art, of course. But, you have to know that when you say *school* in Italian, you get to elementary school. After the elementary school, the word school is *never* used. Here, you have the school of the art, you have Juilliard School, you have Curtis School of Music, Manhattan. So. Giannini meant school of music the American way. They understood "school."

ADRIANA: Maybe junior high.

GIORGIO: So. This is, I suspect, is one of the reason why they let go this project, say "Yes, you are welcome, you come *here* to get educated." And they were very, very sensitive to that fact, you know, that you would bring hundred or hundred and twenty *school* student.

So here, things went on and we put together an orchestra that was mainly school of the art plus other element of the United State, which was incredibly good . . . and we had an excellent conductor, Bellugi, Piero Bellugi . . . incredibly good, young, and full of talent. So. We went and the first concert come. The concert was a smash, a success. But, on the other hand, the administration of the Siena Accademia Chigiana, was incredibly depressed. "We have been betrayed. This is not a school. This is professional orchestra." They didn't believe it, that these are student. That they were all student . . . you know how they could organize in America. That was the cream, that was the top, and they never, you know, heard such a sound in the Teatro Rinnuovati.

We had trouble. Because, you know, they would not allow that, because the *prestige*. Accademia Chigiana was challenge to hear a group of American people that come as a student and play like no orchestra in Italy would play. And today, they don't play so good as that orchestra.

ZINN: How did you prove to them that this was a student orchestra?

GIORGIO: Oh, it was difficult. . . . In this, Gene [Rizzo] is a master, you know, and because he knows how to handle a situation. I would react a little bit like an Italian, a little more sharp. Especially, I knew the innuendo of certain phrases simply because I understood, and that irritates me a lot. Because I know the sincerity with which we had done everything, without, you know, putting any malice. And the things went smoother, but some of the teacher, they were very offended that, you know, we had face them with such incredible talent, and they didn't expect it. They didn't. They expect a school, remember, what means over there little kids, you know? Can you imagine! I was so happy that you don't know. Because I had chose to finish the rest of my life in the United State, and this was tremendous victory. I enjoy tremendous.[26]

The artistic successes went on and on under a smiling muse. "In this country where everyone is his own music critic, an ovation is difficult to come by," wrote those two indefatigable and intrepid correspondents for the *Durham Morning Herald,* Jim and Mary Semans. "At the end of the North Carolina orchestra's fifth concert, the last note of the Bartok concerto had scarcely died away when the entire crowd sprang to its feet and gave the students and their conductor a standing ovation." All was forgiven. "Had there been any doubts about the real value of this orchestra . . . they would have been completely dispelled by this concert," wrote the critic for *La Nazione*:

Let us say at once that performances like that of the . . . Bartok Concerto for Orchestra, are not heard every day. Indeed, to tell the truth, this seems really to be one of the best we have ever heard. . . . It is common knowledge that this piece . . . makes use of the virtuosity of every section of the orchestra. . . . It is thus possible, among other things, to feel the pulse of each group of instruments, momentarily isolated . . . for a close scrutiny. There was absolutely nothing—or almost—found lacking. The Bartok score had the interpretive raiment it merits: splendor. . . .

We cannot overlook the sunny grandiosity of the brass: no trace of coarseness. Of how many orchestras could the same be said?

Indeed! And the sunny grandiosity of the American students seems to have struck a chord with Piero Bellugi. "It's the only orchestra I have ever conducted," he remarked, "which didn't want to stop rehearsing." He arranged a concert in Assisi, paid for by an organization there. "This was really luck, to have such a wonderful conductor," Ciompi explained,

because the personality—this is a key position . . . Piero Bellugi, Florentine also like me, he was an excellent violinist when he was young, and he started a conservatorio there [Florence], Luigi Cherubini. But somehow, he develop this kind of talent of conducting. And talent for conducting is very complex. You must be very flexible. You must be ready . . . to give to the orchestra when they deserve something, and to be strong. And the orchestra enjoy him very much. . . .

You have to know also that in Siena, in the normal period of the Accademia Chigiana is a great teacher of conducting. And this is Franco Ferrara. This name is not very well known in America, but conductor knows that name very well. In fact, you can mention any of the great conductor in America, sometime in their life they crossed the path with Franco Ferrara. Mehta, for instance, study in Siena with Franco Ferrara. Also he was a Sicilian I think, but live in Florence for many years and I knew him as a violinist. Great conductor . . . come from string players—the greatest. Is a question of timing in the bow arm. Oh, you have exception always, always, but—Toscanini—all these . . . all these, from the bow arm, timing.[27]

Vittorio Giannini had brashly carried his young school into the domain of the ancient Chigi Saracini only some ten months after the death of the count. Maura and Christina Giannini point out that he did so not just because Vittorio knew how much the students needed exposure to the teachings of Europe to get into the "mainstream" of artistic life. It was also, says Maura, because

Americans have a terrible inferiority complex about themselves culturally, and this is something that we needed very much . . . to see, that we really were good. . . . We have some of the best training—my uncle used to always say that—we have some of the best training here, and the best artists, and the best, you know, schools and things. We just have to be aware of it and put it on the platter and be proud of it, and I think that was something very valuable that came out of that Siena experience.

Giannini had shown faith and nerve in planning the program; the Ciompis and Semanses showed nerves of steel in carrying it out. "You have to know," Giorgio went on,

when you have 120 student in a foreign country, different food, different water, wine—they drink a little bit wine—even normally they would feel it because they don't know. So. About ten or fifteen per cent, some, they would be sick, every day. And they should go to the doctor.

ADRIANA: But they didn't speak Italian, so I had to take them.

GIORGIO: So that was her. She bring them to the doctor.

ADRIANA: Every afternoon after lunch I would go with the group of sick people, and stay and translate, you know.

GIORGIO: This was interesting, exciting, and sometime there were nerves, tension. They had to perform maybe in a couple of days, already they could feel the stomach trouble. And then, other sort, you know, we had to watch, of course, the girls going out at night, with whom, because this is a different world . . . the American people *are* very friendly. In fact, the girls should not, could not be so friendly.

ADRIANA: Giorgio was telling them, "Don't be too friendly, don't smile at people in the streets."

GIORGIO: This episode . . . some soldier go after the girls, and the girls were sensitive, you know. They wanted to go up-stairs into the rooms of the girls. I said, "Are you crazy? You *don't pass this, this* line in the lobby! You can't go up."

So. But then it was the episode of the checking of the police . . . you have to know that when you go to Italy, you have to be register, every student should have a reg-ister at the police. Now, you American don't know. You go to the hotel, you give any name you want. There, you have to give the passport, they have to know who you are and where you live, and your address, and why you are there. So here we had 120 student. . . . You have to tell about.

ADRIANA: I was supposed to take them down [to the police], and . . . they didn't understand the form that was written in Italian, write everything, you know, by hand there with every *one* of them, take them in groups, so I decided, you know, this is impossible. So I talk to the chief of police, there, captain of the police. So I said, "Listen, I have an idea. You give me all of the schedules, and every-thing, I bring them to the hotel with me. Then I do a translation of that, and then all the kids will fill it in. I'll come in and bring them all tomorrow for you." In an hour, we did everything, you know, because I told them exactly what it was. Everybody filled it in. I brought down all the passports and everything. So he said, "Ah, you should come here and reorganize the police station for us!" This was so simple. Instead of something that should have taken days to do, with all the waste of time, mine and the kids', you know, the students were in classes. In a few minutes, everything was done. But, you had to be there and be ready to jump in and to improvise, and to help in any way you could.

GIORGIO: Problem would come at night, you know, late . . . we don't mention the names, but one student got very much involved with a girl—very in love—and at three o'clock in the morning . . . he came to the door of my room, which was in the hotel (I was living there), and he said, "Mr. Ciompi, we have to find a rabbi." "Rabbi? What you want for a rabbi?" "Immediately we are going to get married." I say, "Listen, now it's 3 : 00 A.M. First of all," I said, "I bet in Siena you don't find a rabbi . . . second, we have to go to Florence, and then you have to sleep over there. I won't give you any permission." And then, the next day, the things change slightly, and everything calm down. But you see, this is one of the things. . . .

We had really some happy time, I must say. The trips also that we went out from Siena to play. I remember we had a party after a concert [at the Basilica San Lucchese], and they pass with the wine, and they serve *such a* spaghetti, you know!

ADRIANA: It was in an abbey, and all the friars were there, and the friars were bringing in these steaming bowls of spaghetti, and cheese, and wine . . . in these incredible surroundings.

GIORGIO: *After* the concert!

ADRIANA: They had such a good time. It was a whole new experience, very beautiful . . . such a chance to go and to see a new country.

GIORGIO: In Italy, you don't have black people. They don't exist. So, a black person is a curiosity, is interesting, is something. *When* this curiosity is a beautiful girl, Italian lose their heads.

ADRIANA: It's a success incredible.

GIORGIO: Now, we had several beautiful specialty singers, beautiful girls, black. They would come, "Mr. Ciompi." I say, "What?" "I don't want to go back to America." I say "What?" "They treat me so well." You know, they would come with flower after the concert. They would go out for dates with those beautiful guys, Italian. And kiss their hand! And they wouldn't want to come back. They had the happy time.

ADRIANA: Like living in a dream.

GIORGIO: And I would say that many, many of this faculty group [at the Chigiana] that, at first, were a little surprise . . . became great friends. They understood the sincerity and the generosity I must say, because we really spend a lot of money there. . . .

But, it was not easy. Maybe it was more complicate than [Vittorio] thought.

SEMANS: Don't forget, he said "I'm scared!"

GIORGIO: He said that?

SEMANS: Yes.

GIORGIO: He did? . . . Well, he was right, because you know, now that we look back, we can really laugh [at] a few situations, but at the moment, you know, it was things that you cannot imagine—

SEMANS: Crises.

GIORGIO: We had crises. . . . My specific experience were quite, sometime, difficult because I had acquire in America a certain way to deal, a certain *trust* that you have among people of a certain level. You know, that if I tell you that I'll do something, I will do it, I don't have to sign a paper, I don't have to—but, you know, the old country is the very cautious. And I'd forgot this after so many years. I go to Italy, I used to go to Italy to play concert, see my family. But when officially you deal—for instance, we had some problem with the janitor of the theater that would promise to open the door for a rehearsal certain time, and then he wouldn't show up. And 120 student would be outside with instrument, in the sun, very hot,

waiting because he would have late evening and he
would have sleep late.

So, I would boil in situation like that, you see, and the
presence of Dr. Semans was very important to me because *calming me down*! It was a great team, you know,
because he said, "Well, let's find where he is and send—"
and of course, which I hate to do, I hate to do—to give
this what we call [blackmail] in Italian. The American,
they expect it, but I didn't felt this way, you see, I felt
that they had to do that, because they had been paid already, and they promise, and this was their word.

So, I had some problem, sometime, but I mean, as I
say, I see now from distance, this were absolutely
nothing because, you know, that could have been correct
easily.[28]

Anything that has to do with the arts is fragile. Any project or undertaking, any achievement, seems to rise to unlikely moments of beauty on the
quivering points of human stress. The payoff for the strain of the Siena
program was obvious and immediate. "It gave us right at the very start,"
says composer Robert Ward, who followed Vittorio Giannini as president
of the school of the arts, "a kind of national and international recognition
which we could not get any other way."[29] The payout behind the scenes,
however, was heavier, more complicated, more delicately balanced in design than even those involved in the program at first realized. The Siena
session was a veritable bumblebee of a program; the records of the first five
years prove scientifically and logically, beyond a doubt, that *the thing could
not fly*. And yet Jim and Mary Semans, captivated, it would seem, by the
impossible possibilities, plunged into the delicate task. And the nuts and
bolts of that plunge provide a fascinating lesson, in miniature, in the difficulties of international relations and the arts.

The plan, as Giannini had envisioned it and as the Semanses and
Giorgio Ciompi attempted to carry it out, was designed to enhance the
American image in Europe. These were not college students on a dilet-
tante's year abroad. "It seems to me," Jim Semans wrote thoughtfully to a
colleague at Duke Medical Center,

> that this is the type of imaginative intercultural exchange which is
> badly needed. It is not simply a Stanford or Sweetbriar campus trans-
> ferred to Italy, but a dedicated group of students living in the heart of
> a city and, for the most part, being taught by native teachers and

learning how all-consumed their lives are with their profession . . .
[the students] have taken this not as a sort of glamorous sightseeing
event, but a serious cultural enterprise.

The doctor described his own role in Italy as one of keeping to original
intentions: "I do not flatter myself that I am so terribly needed but I find
that the artistic people do like to rely on someone in my position to make
final decisions, especially since I am the only one, outside of the Italian
government people in Siena, who knows anything of those initial conversations setting this up." The difficulty of holding to original intentions had
become evident to Jim Semans the first time Giorgio Ciompi tried to write
a check on the joint Accademia–NCSA summer session bank account in
Siena. According to the agreements of October 1966, only the signatures of
the artistic directors of the program—Ciompi and Fabbri—could be honored on the joint account. As it turned out, only the signature of Danilo
Verzili, president of the Monte dei Paschi Bank, was honored that first year.
"We then began to experience," Jim Semans noted later, "the lack of attention paid on the Italian side to the original charter written out by Mr. Fanfani . . . it became a sort of Christian Bible in that everyone was sinning
and not following the recommendations of the charter, but at least we
knew explicitly whether something was committed in defiance of the
charter or in compliance with the charter! This is about as close as we
could say that the charter was followed. However," he continued ruefully,
"it was a very good charter and proved to be very valuable as an instrument
for reference."[30]

Classes had begun on July 17; on July 22 Jim Semans found himself in a
meeting with the Italians to discuss "the problem of finding a new seat for
the courses of the Summer Session." Some changes appeared to be necessary, "for the success of future terms," "on the basis of past experience"
(five days). The Italians stated five conditions for continuing the program:
retain Ciompi as the American artistic director; give a "permanent appointment with adequate compensation" to the Italian secretary—the
"general factotum"—for the program; standardize so as to simplify the
preparatory work involved in the session; increase the budget and the financial contribution from the American side; and find another building in
which to conduct the courses because "the noise of musical instruments
has provoked several complaints from the citizens and even more from the
nearby hospital." Dr. Semans anticipated the issue of greater American financial support; Fanfani had pointed out from the beginning that the contribution from the Italian government would be gradually decreased. To

the Italian suggestion that the students attend classes in the Villa Castel-
nuovo Berardenga, located a few miles outside Siena, however, Semans objected because it "did not seem to him to be completely in accordance with
the ideas of Dr. Giannini, who wanted the students to be in close contact
with the life of the city." While they awaited the arrival of Robert Ward in
August, without whom no decision could be made, another element was
added: "For every building taken into consideration it would be advisable
to prepare a budget . . . of the cost of necessary work. . . . It would also be
necessary to establish, for each one, assignment of new financial responsibilities (since this year the class-rooms were free)."[31]

By August 22, when President Ward could attend the meetings at the
Accademia, Mario Fabbri had come up with a solution. If the school of the
arts summer session could begin in June, early enough to get in five weeks
of work before the Chigiana session began in July, the Americans could use
the premises of the Chigiana provided they bore the cost of "janitors, dete-
rioration of pianos, electricity," and such things. This seemed fair enough
to Robert Ward, who observed that the additional revenue generated
"would perhaps be welcome" to the Chigiana (which was undergoing a
period of debt and uncertainty since the death of Count Chigi), as well as
the opportunity to extend the teaching period for its faculty, who could
contract separately with the North Carolina session. This entirely reasonable and efficient solution, so obvious to the straightforward American
mind, evidently did not seem simple to the Italians. The idea of using the
Chigiana, Mario Fabbri warned darkly, "must under no circumstances appear to originate with . . . himself."[32]

Plans for the 1968 summer session, arrived at in discussions "entirely
frank and friendly," Robert Ward took care to note, appeared to be something everyone could live with. The first five weeks of the NCSA session
would precede the Chigiana's, and the final three weeks would be divided
between concert-giving, touring, and some special classes with the Chigiana students. The number of American students would be reduced to
below a hundred so that all could be housed conveniently in the Hotel
Continental. The students would concentrate on orchestral work, which
the Chigiana did not do (the Accademia's summer "courses of perfection"
were in solo work only) and therefore would not give the appearance of
being in competition with the Chigiana. Further to enhance good relations, private lessons would not be taught by the American instructors but
instead would remain in the province of the Chigiana faculty. And most
emphatically, "the two institutions should in no circumstances give concerts on the same day." Because the Chigiana did not have an orchestra of

its own, Fabbri suggested that the ideal arrangement would be for the NCSA summer orchestra to serve as the Chigiana's, to be, in other words, the practice orchestra for the Chigiana's conducting students. This provision Robert Ward would not agree to.[33] It raised the threat of more problems than it would solve.

Thus under the new plan the NCSA session would overlap as little as possible with the Chigiana session, while providing instruction for the American students with a number of Italians, because "Dr. Giannini's original idea was to have Italian teachers." Accordingly, Giorgio Ciompi and Jim Semans went to Italy in January of 1968 to hire Italian teachers for the summer session. Because Maestro Fabbri himself had suggested on the previous August 22 that a good plan might be for the American students to "take two lessons a week with their own teachers and one with a Chigiana professor," Giorgio Ciompi and Dr. Semans were perhaps surprised to find that it was not going to be that simple. In Firenze, at the Hotel Villa Medici, they met with Mario Fabbri to discuss the summer faculty appointments. Fabbri had approached two pianists, but they were not available; Ciompi had already contacted a third artist, but Fabbri immediately vetoed the choice as "absolutely impossible for the reaction that this appointment would provoke in some of the members of the Accademia Chigiana." Ciompi then raised the name of a Chigiana professor. No, said Fabbri, the maestro "would never do it." It was becoming clear, Giorgio noted privately, "that Maestro Fabbri does not want to involve with our summer session any of the key position teachers of the Accademia, with the exception of their appearances as special events [for master classes]. The reasons for all this are quite obscure and complicated, and lay on very subtle politics and artistic jalousies [sic], going back to the times of Count Chigi."[34]

Faculties everywhere have their personality problems. It is, therefore, the issue of the employment of the secretary for the program in Siena that is perhaps most characteristically Italianate. For reasons "quite obscure" and undoubtedly complicated, a permanent position for this person had become, by the end of August 1967, a condition of equal importance with matters of financing, housing, and planning. The duties of this factotum were not artistic; he was to be concerned with practical necessities—the unlocking of doors to classrooms, the rental of instruments, the confirmation of business arrangements. He had been chosen by Fabbri, and in their last meeting in Siena, Robert Ward agreed "that an arrangement which would equitably divide [the secretary's] responsibilities to the Chigiana and the N.C.S.A. Summer Session shall be reached."[35] By December of

that year, the employment of the secretary was perceived as a major negotiating point of heartrending dimensions, as Mario Fabbri explained:

> The Chigiana cannot, at least for the moment, receive [the secretary]
> in its own staff. . . . The Chigiana is going through a very delicate pe-
> riod (after the death of Count Chigi Saracini). . . . How could it take
> on, even indirectly, another employee? . . . [The secretary] is here in
> Siena, having left *everything* in Trieste, with a wife and three small
> children; he lives, at least for the moment, on what the "Summer Ses-
> sion" gives him. . . . I understand, and so does he, that it is not logical
> to pay all year for the work of about four months.
>
> We all agree. But we must find a solution not so much for 1968, but
> for 1969, giving him a long time to find . . . honorable occupation,
> here or there . . . for the sustai[n]ment of his family.

The solution was for the NCSA summer session to agree to a twelve-
month contract with the secretary, including insurance and a thirteenth-
month "premium," with the understanding that the terms would not be
repeated. Why such an issue should escalate into what Giorgio Ciompi described as an "ultra-sensitive problem" is perhaps best explained by Luigi
Barzini, whose brother Ugo was replacing Vieri Traxler in the Foreign
Ministry in 1968. Barzini had written in his 1964 book, *The Italians*, of the
importance in the conduct of everyday Italian affairs of maintaining complex alliances within particular groups or cabalas (*consorterie*, as the Italians
call them). These political and professional *consorterie* are further complicated by the preeminence of family ties, to the point that those on the outside who attempt to understand what is going on "sometimes cannot un-
ravel apparently inexplicable situations unless they know the invisible ties"
that bind the various participants, "not as heads of internal factions, but as
fathers-in-law of each other's offspring." Along these lines we find a clue:
the secretary's father-in-law somehow became part of the package, to teach
Italian to the summer session students ("I had some difficulties," Ciompi
recorded later, "to convince him that we don't need more than five weeks
of Italian teaching"), and the father-in-law's son was on the faculty of the
Accademia.[36]

Giorgio Ciompi moved ahead, valiantly doing the tasks that had been
assigned to him and redoing the tasks that had been assigned to the secretary. Arrangements for room and board at the Hotel Continental "had
been confirmed previously by telephone," but when Ciompi arrived in
Siena in January, he found that they were not firm. In Florence he "found
out that the guarantee and promises of ALITALIA [to the secretary] for our

round-trip were not secure at all." He went to Rome, where he called on Ugo Barzini, and the two of them "faced the situation with some strength." Alitalia quickly bowed to pressure from the Foreign Ministry. Barzini was also able to reassure Ciompi that the Italian government's seven-million-lire contribution to the summer session for 1968 would be transferred to the Monte dei Paschi Bank in February. Nonetheless, Giorgio pondered, "It is interesting to remind ourselves at this moment that against all the agreements that date back to Giannini, Fanfani, Traxler, Semans, meetings in Italy, no one in the New World and in the Old World except Avvocato Verzili has the right to withdraw any amount of money from our account at the Monte dei Paschi for our summer school session." When Ciompi returned to the United States at the end of January, he had not been able to achieve his and Robert Ward's highest priority arrangement: a written and signed contract specifying the terms under which the NCSA summer session was to use the Chigi Palazzo.[37]

In the spring of 1968, in an effort to reach a better understanding with Mario Fabbri, Jim and Mary Semans invited him to visit them in Durham, North Carolina, and to lecture at Duke on his recoveries of lost music (which he did, on May 7, 11, and 14, and at the school of the arts on May 8, 1968). In a letter to Giorgio Ciompi detailing the arrangements for the visits, Fabbri provided a charmingly contradictory description of himself: "I am a 'lone wolf' . . . and I like family life." Ciompi remembered,

> We enjoy him very much because, of course, he knew inside the Accademia Musicale Chigiana and all the details that we need to know. And as a person, extremely warm and very special. . . . For instance, after a while that we met him, we find out he was alpinista—a mountain climber. He show us picture that you don't believe—crossing, for instance, a canyon on a rope, to tell you what kind of a guy he was, and very, very enthusiastic about this project. And he understood in full the spirit and it help us a lot . . . he was a musicologist, and brought music that he had discovered in Florence, and we play this music at Duke. And it was a great reunion here. Every time I go to Florence, we talk about. That was his first visit to America. In fact, for him, it was really more complicated than for our people to go to the moon. Oh, that was much easy than for him to come in this new world.

On his first night at the Semans's guest house, Pinecrest, Fabbri insisted that Giorgio Ciompi stay with him because he felt so lonesome. The conditions for calming this complex artistic personality must have been admirably met; more than a year later, Mario Fabbri still happily recalled his visit to America and "the wonderful days of Pinecrest." [38]

The 1968 summer session in Siena began classes on June 10 and ended with the students' departure July 26. One hundred students attended classes in chamber music and orchestra; piano, organ, and voice; composition and conducting; Italian language and art history, taught by faculty of both Italians and Americans. Once again, Piero Bellugi had been engaged to conduct the orchestra, and the students lived in the Hotel Continental, practiced in its lobbies, and walked to their classes at the Chigiana. The student orchestra toured, giving concerts at the Spoleto Festival, in Pisa, Poggibonsi, Florence, Trieste, and Fanfani's home town of Arezzo, a concert which the former foreign minister, now president of the Italian Senate, drove from Rome to attend. Fortunately, the performance, according to *La Nazione*, was "Il brilliante successo" of the "studenti americani," under the "Impeccabile direzione" of Maestro Bellugi. There were other triumphs. Governor of North Carolina Dan K. Moore and his wife visited Siena, garnering favorable publicity for the session back home, which Jim and Mary Semans hoped would help with requests for funding from the legislature and foundations. On July 4, the pope granted an audience to the Moores, the Semanses, and a group of students from the session. Jim Semans was most impressed by "the extreme clarity and simplicity of the Papal presence, as opposed to the incredible mystery and ignorance of the church ceremony in the chapel in the Park hotel." In the Vatican audience room, with its frescoes and sculpted ceiling decorated with gold brought back by Columbus, a tall monsignor in a floor-length cape arranged the group, "so that Il Papa could view the angelic faces of the girls from the second row back and be shielded from the effect, offensive to the celebatic eye, of the bare knees of the mini-skirted ladies." [39]

Practical difficulties, misunderstandings, and tantrums plagued the 1968 session. Concerts any distance from Siena presented problems of logistics and fatigue, exacerbated by elements of la dolce vita. After a long, hot bus ride in the afternoon to Spoleto or Arezzo or Pisa, the students would have to change clothes, attend a dress rehearsal, give a concert, change clothes again, eat a late supper, and finally ride back to Siena, where they arrived, Ciompi noted, "tired and depressed . . . so that the next day was entirely lost for work or rehearsals." Clothes and instruments followed to and fro somewhat perilously in a separate truck driven by men who "liked wine too much." Contracts for the use of theaters in Siena were forever scampering and metamorphosing, like sought-after creatures in bad dreams. Use of the Teatro dei Rinnuovati, for example, had been arranged through the mayor of Siena, Commissioner Padalino, who offered it free, save for a payment of 300,000 lire "to cover the expenses of cleaning, electricity, janitors etc." At the Rinnuovati, Ciompi had to pay the janitors 474,265 lire; long after the session was over, the town of Siena was still billing NCSA for the original 300,000 lire.[40] (It would appear that in Italy, janitors are fairly high up in the power structure.) The careful planning that had begun in the summer of 1967, intended to cut down on friction and calamity abroad, came not so much to naught as to reality: the cultural hydra in Siena was not for beheading. It was for living with. "The Italian habits of work," Jim Semans later noted privately after five years of experience, "are far from being a set structure. However, since the days of Machiavelli there has been a desire on the part of Italians to improvise and to act tangentially rather than follow the Anglo-Saxon technique of long range planning and the direct approach in organization. This requires a talent for which the Italian is famous, and that is mental alacrity. I have never seen a day-dreaming Italian." In light of the new arrangements in Siena— "the absence of the Accademia Chigiana and all the students and teachers and all controversial discussions that our playing brought on the scene"[41]— Giorgio hopefully began a diary on the first day of classes:

MONDAY, JUNE 10, 1968 — Opening of Session with Gen. Barbarulli, Fabbri, all faculty except Esposito and Vlad . . . Adriana Ciompi was translator. . . .

Giorgio, Bellugi, Fabbri, [A.—the secretary] meet for three hours to put together program and dates. First rehearsal cancelled by Bellugi. . . .

Auditions held—8 cellos, 8 violas, 16 violins. First class string section. Spirit is good.

Situation develops between two choral groups—one of children in Fiesole through pressure of Mayor of Fiesole. Trying to get in on our Bartok program with a Proko[f]ieff work. The other group in Siena . . . a local choral society[,] want an all opera choral program. Fiesole program liquidated. Siena had to be compromised [i.e., Giorgio agreed to the concert], because of local intrigue brought on by Fabbri and encouraged by himself, for us to play with this choral group.

Giorgio Ciompi accidentally finds out that the concert in Pisa and possibly the one in Viareggio would
be conducted by Cavallaro. This had never been
mentioned to Giorgio before, and he would never
have approved of this due to last year's experience
with Cavallaro, who with Bellugi's backing set up
these two concerts. [A.] forgot to mention these
facts to Giorgio . . . Giorgio will say, either Bellugi
conducts or one of our students, otherwise he will
cancel concerts.

TUESDAY,
JUNE 11

Difficulty at Chigiana with janitor. Kicked out before time was up. Decided to issue passes to students and faculty for admission to Chigiana.
Giorgio had to call Fabbri three times to get
Chigiana opened from 9–1 and 3–7. This would
include an extra hour at additional cost of $504 per
day not $500. We must pay L. 30,000 for every time
we use Teatro di Rinnuovati. This theater will not be
usable as originally promised. . . .

WEDNESDAY,
JUNE 12 &
THURSDAY,
JUNE 13

First rehearsal of orchestra. The pit of orchestra still
open. Can be closed only next Monday at a cost of
over L. 80,000. We decided to push the orchestra
back, and to try the first concert with the open pit.
We also decided that the Chigiana should close the
pit at their own expense, because they have to close
it in any case for their own concerts, and we did not
see any reason why we should pay for something
they have always paid for themselves these past
25 years.

We face some problems of missing parts and also
bad instruments that had been sent for the percussion section. We must change all of them. Big
trouble also with the double-basses. We don't have
any. [A.] had plenty of time, but somehow was
waiting for me. This is unfortunate. I had written
and prepared this situation months ago, due to similar experience last year. Now exactly the same has

happened . . . [A.] only does well when there are no real difficulties or problems to contend with.

Another problem is that of harps. Fabbri promised to have two harps for us at the Chigiana, but we only find one fit to play. This one may not be removed from the Palazzo Chigiana. Long conversation with Fabbri to convince him that we must have the use of this harp, at least in the theater. Our girl harpist is desperate.

After the rehearsal I had a long conversation with Bellugi about the concerts at Pisa and Viareggio, and the unexpected intrusion once again of Cavallaro. Bellugi said that this was not his doing, while I know that it is only his. I have been very hard on [A.] over this misunderstanding, and the only excuse for him is that he was so anxious to pin down the dates of the orchestra's performances out of town; and he seems quite incapable of standing up to their intrigues. . . .

FRIDAY, JUNE 14

9:30 meeting with Bellugi and Cavallaro. I am convinced that to cancel the concert in Pisa would have bad repercussions on our school and our organization. All the authorities of that town are involved in the concert. We face a 'fait accompli' [A.] has signed too many letters, and we have to go along with them. . . .

Another surprise from Bellugi is that we will be conducting another concert in Naples on the 28th June, which is the date of our concert in Siena. This is another 'fait accompli'. In this instance he even had Fabbri fooled, creating the impression that he would allow the Choral Group of Siena participate in half of our concert, with his assistant conducting the choral part. The truth is that he never intended being in Siena at that time. . . .

In his memoirs of the first years in Siena, Jim Semans has remarked on the artistic temperament of Piero Bellugi and the "maddeningly labyrinthine ways of his mind," generously balanced, however, by Bellugi's "contagious charm" and the way he "inspired our students to play so brilliantly." [42]

FRIDAY,
JUNE 21

The thought that this Diary would be a day by day record of the events of the Summer Session has proved impossible. It certainly would show the incredible change of decision that occurs from minute to minute. We will try to record some of the difficulties in the program—precisely the most important.

The people from the Choral Society are continually coming, making pressure for financial help that varies from $500 to $1,000 each time. I try to convince them that this is not our responsibility, that we are doing it for public relations purposes, and will not put any money into it because it has not been budgeted for and we do not have the funds. They then went to Fabbri for help, but met with refusal. At a luncheon meeting with Verzili, I explained the situation to him and he promised to make a contribution to help this group (Socialist). Now the people of the Choral Society are very happy, and we will be able to work in good harmony with them. . . . We will pay for the publicity for the evening, in the form of posters. I am quite sure it will be a great success.

The trouble with the double-bass continues. Most frustrating of all troubles. [A.] went to Florence to look for them. We found a couple of instruments here in very bad condition. I tried to fix them myself. Finally, we got one sent by last year's player, Ercole, a very kind man. He plays with the [chamber] orchestra of the Chigiana, and will let us use his bass.

Trouble continues with the harp player we brought with us. . . . Got in touch with . . . last year's harp teacher. The first student she suggested accepted, and then changed her mind at the last minute. We got in touch with the second . . . who seemed willing to come with her harp, to help in the emergency. She asked for L. 60,000 for the two appearances, which would include the transportation of her harp. On the evening of the concert in the presence of her fiancé (a very low grade type), she declared that she wouldn't play for less than L. 85,000 for this first appearance only. I felt very depressed and humiliated, but had to accept. Exchange of very harsh words between her, her fiancé and myself, in the presence of [A.]. Upset by all these goings on, she played very badly or not at all, and fainted after the concert. The fiancé now seems to understand the implications of his horrible actions, and promises that she will appear to play at the San Lucchese concert on the 22nd. I do not care. . . . This has been one of the hardest episodes of this Summer Session—so far!

WEDNESDAY, JULY 3   I shall continue today the diary I started at the beginning of the session. It was impossible to continue regularly, and this will be a resumé of the past weeks, in which we have faced an enormous amount of highly unusual problems. The concert in San Lucchese was most pleasant and a great success for the orchestra. The people who organized it were extremely kind and cordial. . . . Our first student concert was wonderfully received in the hall of the Accademia Chigiana. Most of our students were present and the local people . . . were very enthusiastic. . . .

The week from 24 to 30 June we had to leave the Theatre Rinnuovati to let the Piccolo Theatro di Siena move in. This is a local organization of ballet and comedy for children headed by Maestro Francini. This very kind and nice person was not previously informed that the Theatre would be occupied by us during his annual recital demonstration. Thus I decided to leave the Theatre for four days in order to help him. In the meantime, we moved into a large crypt under a church for our rehearsals.

It is impossible to describe the rehearsal of Friday evening, June 28th. We found ourselves in the presence of the Choral Society [of Siena], formed of local amature [sic] singers, headed by a very aggressive, emotional choral conductor, Maestro Ammannati, and four soloists who tried to out-do each other. After ten minutes, everybody was conducting, and everybody was singing. The young conductor [Alfred] Morris behaved beautifully. I stopped the rehearsal to calm down the spirits. We were accused of not knowing Italian traditions, and I tried my best not to offend these people who do not know better. The orchestra found the situation almost tragic-comic [sic]. Some were hysterical with laughture [sic]. The rehearsal ended better than it began, but I developed a tremendous resentment toward Fabbri who allowed and pushed us into such a terrible experience, which could have ended in an artistic disaster. . . . Bellugi appeared at the dress rehearsal, and with his help we cut some of the chorus soli, which provoked tremendous reactions from the directors of the choral group. We stood firm on our decision. [Afterward] Bellugi walked noisily out of the theatre [knocking the plaster off the wall, noted in JHS's handwriting on carbon of diary], demonstrating his disapproval of the whole affair. I later told him that he was partly responsible because he left the entire project for a week, and previously approved the choral cooperation with Fabbri. I know that this terrible experience was extremely valuable for our conducting students. Also the orchestra learned some of the dark side of Italian opera, as it possibly was done many years ago. I have no personal resentment with the choral group, which has already expressed to me the desire to repeat such a concert next year. . . ! I am going to suggest to Fabbri that the musicians, teachers, and students of the Accademia Chigiana should be the ones to take our place next time. Only then shall I forgive him. . . .

We were back in the Theatre for the concert with
the Choral Society of Siena and four soloists from
La Scalla [sic] (they said). The rehearsals were on
Friday evening and Saturday afternoon. The President of the Choral Society, Sig. Savelli, right to the
last minute was looking for money to cover the expenses of the concert, and even asked me to contrib-
ute in the amount of 300,000 lire, which, of course,
I refused. . . . [Some of our] orchestral parts were
lost on the way from Milano, but were finally re-
covered at the railroad station in Siena, where they
were waiting to be delivered. Meanwhile, we lost
two days of rehearsals. Bellugi being absent for a
concert in Napoli, I had to take a chance and use
two student conductors for the entire concert.

By July 11, Julia Mueller was reporting that their conductor had been in
residence only sixteen of the thirty-three days that NCSA had been in Siena. With regard to teaching, she noted wryly, "I am convinced . . . that
Maestro Bellugi, true genius that he is . . . has not the faintest notion of
what would be . . . involved." A major cause of the trouble lay in the
double nature of the session, which Giannini had designed as a true summer school, with a set curriculum, taught by master teachers in Italy, offering both advancement in musical skills and cultural sophistication through
daily contact with Italian language, art, and history. But because of the astonishing level of expertise the summer session orchestra demonstrated, a
kind of doppelgänger effect occurred: what were supposed to be recitals by
a student orchestra immediately escalated into major musical events. And
so the students found themselves accompanied in Siena by their ghostly
professional seconds. Sometimes they were allowed to be earnest students,
assumed to be immature yet as performers and in need of the guidance and
support of their teachers. At other times they were a concert-giving entity
under Bellugi's direction, expected to build, rehearse, and perform at the
highest professional level the maestro's choice of repertoire. The opportunity was extraordinary, the experience invaluable, the situation stressful.
"[Bellugi] has treated the orchestra, from the beginning, as a professional
group . . . I attribute much of the discontent and low morale [of the or-
chestra] to his absence, just as I attribute a large share of success to his
presence," Julia Mueller concluded fairly. She recommended a "clarifica-
tion of policy" for the next summer and a change in physical arrangements,

citing the "difficulties of being a 'guest' in a building not our own in which every move is subject to frustrating delays, special permissions, additional fees."[43] The janitors were continuing to be fractious—as Ciompi testified:

> I have recently been presented with a bill for the cleaning of the Chigiana of 260,000 lire. I informed Fabbri by telephone that after what we paid for being in the Chigiana, at least the cleaning should be included. . . . On this occasion I pointed out to him his unfortunate, continual postponement of the final contract, which is still missing. I have been through a great deal of worry in the last ten days regarding the seven million lire contribution from the Italian government for the summer session, for which I could not find a trace. Finally we discovered that the regular request had never been made, and we shall do it now. . . .
>
> I have already had a couple of long conversations with Dr. Semans and Mary. They are beginning to feel the terrific, invisible struggle which we are undergoing lies on the difficulty of communication with Fabbri, who is never here but in Florence (perhaps intentionally) and on the resistance we get from all of the Chigiana personnel and help, who definitely consider our presence there an intrusion.[44]

In July meetings with Robert Ward, Giorgio Ciompi, and Julia Mueller, Mario Fabbri actively offered suggestions for reorganizing the session so as to avoid difficulties. The meeting of July 17, Robert Ward noted, ended with "renewed assurances of friendship and good faith between all of us."[45] It was evident that despite apparently contradictory behavior, such as his absence during the session, difficulties in using the Chigiana, and the failure to provide a written contract stating the conditions for use of the Palazzo Chigi, the artistic director of the Chigiana bore no animus toward the summer session. On the contrary, what was gradually becoming clarified for the Americans was the unusual internal structure of the Chigiana and the uncomfortable position in which Fabbri found himself. Back in the United States, Giorgio reflected on the summer and concluded that Fabbri's friendship could be counted on, but that he could not "really be expected to promote our programs whole-heartedly, if this will jeopardize [those] of the Chigiana and antagonize their faculty."[46] The rapport that had been established at Pinecrest was by no means false. It was, therefore, that much greater a blow to the summer session when, on November 29, 1968, Mario Fabbri resigned as artistic director of the Accademia. For some months he had suspected that his files were being searched for evidence of communism. In addition, he was uncomfortable with the implications of a

20. *Siena, 1969: "People of the artistic quality of Gulli told us that . . . by* special intent *of the faculty* no one *was running the Accademia Chigiana." Franco Gulli, with a student (Archives of the North Carolina School of the Arts).*

bank running an artistic institution and feared that the board of the Monte dei Paschi Bank would soon be filled with communist-appointed representatives. Realizing that the carefully laid plans for the 1969 summer session were likely to go astray without the cooperation of whoever was in charge of the Accademia, Jim Semans determined to weather this latest crisis by discovering who that person was. He found out that, "by *special intent* of the faculty, *no one* was running the Accademia Chigiana":

> People of the artistic quality of Gulli told us that since World War II approximately twenty-five members of the faculty had remained staunch friends and joined hands each summer to carry on the master classes. All of these were men of unquestioned statu[r]e artistically, such as Brengola (chamber music), Guiliano (cello), Agosti (piano), and many others. . . . By attending the artistic sessions and talking with each other and by using the journal outlet of Dr. Moggi the younger, a physician who took care of our students . . . but at the same time wrote the music criticisms, it was possible for them to keep the situation in Siena under artistic control. They trusted Fabbri, but

as long as Fabbri felt like leaving, they were not in a hurry at all to have a new artistic director. This was because whomever the Monte dei Paschi Bank might choose to take Fabbri's place would have to be converted into their loyal fraternity. . . .

So, in this way the Accademia Chigiana remains a strong artistic structure in the face of the commercial sponsor, the Banco Monte dei Paschi, which is committed by contract to support it and keep it going.

I have only seen one similar organization and that is the Piedmont Hospital in Atlanta, Georgia, which had a structure only for tax purposes, and each member of the medical staff denied having any leverage over any other member, but professed himself the humble servant of the hospital. It resulted in each person in this institution feeling a strong sense of responsibility for his own particular duty to be done. Each had no one to be jealous of as far as power or leverage was concerned, and it seemed that the benefit of the patient turned out to be the only leverage that one sensed as he moved about in the hospital. I hope that it will always continue thus in both the Accademia Chigiana and the Piedmont Hospital.[47]

Certain practical improvements were made in the 1969 session. The students met first in Winston-Salem, where they lived and worked together from June 22 to July 11, developing camaraderie and discipline. The inept Italian secretary was replaced with a young, bilingual Italian law student, eager to work as advance agent for the summer session. A promising new conductor was engaged—Gaetano Delogu, a student of Franco Ferrara and assistant to Leonard Bernstein. The administrative staff was enlarged to include an assistant to the deans of men and women, H. Alan Sims, from California. The most daring change was the expansion of the international program to include dance (although Robert Lindgren had to scrape up his own financing), and perhaps the most useful was Jim Semans's idea to have an outside agency evaluate the Siena program and make recommendations.[48]

There were good omens for the 1969 session. Under the prodding of Governor Robert W. Scott, the North Carolina legislature appropriated $25,000 to help support the session. And twenty students from Juilliard enrolled in the session on the recommendation of their twelve Juilliard classmates who had attended the previous summer. Best of all, spirits among the 120 students were high, and the sun was shining in Pisa when

21. *Under the prodding of Governor Robert W. Scott, the North Carolina legislature appropriated $25,000 to support the 1969 summer session. Governor Scott, with Mary Semans (foreground) and Jim Semans (Archives of the North Carolina School of the Arts).*

they arrived. "Heavens, I was so surprised that such a great turnout was there," Alan Sims later recalled:

> There was Paolo [the new factotum] with the great banner out in front "Welcome North Carolina" and I don't know whether a band was there, I forget. If it wasn't then there was a band in my mind, and it was there and there was Doctor Jim and these various officials [including Vieri Traxler, now Italian consul general of New York] and men with cameras grinding away, the newspaper reporters with their pads . . . well, I thought my gracious, this must surely be Air Force No. 1 that has landed here.[49]

Paolo had worked diligently through the winter and spring to arrange concerts for the seventy-two-piece student orchestra, now identified in great red and yellow posters all over Siena as the "North Carolina Philharmonic." (The name change was in response to Mario Fabbri's practical suggestion that the Americans should shorten the name of their orchestra to one that could be easily remembered.) In addition to five concerts scheduled in Siena at the Teatro Rinnuovati, the students would be playing Rossini at Livorno; Hindemith at Lucca; Cherubini in the fifteenth-century Palazzo Pitti, "most monumental of the Florentine palaces," as the Bonechi guide to *The Wonderful Towns of Italy* tells us. (The Palazzo was built by Luca Pitti, "an extremely rich merchant belonging to a family antagonistic to the Medici.") After the concert the students could refresh and recreate themselves in the palace's sixteenth-century Ammannati courtyard, near the spray of the incomparable Artichoke Fountain of the Boboli Gardens. They played Stravinsky on the promontory above the sea at Castiglione della Peschaia and Moussorgski for the monks and about four hundred guests at the Basilica San Lucchese in Poggibonsi, where the good brothers served them spaghetti and roast veal and cakes. The North Carolina Philharmonic Orchestra: two of the four oboists were sixteen years old; two of the four bassoonists were seventeen; the *flauti* were nineteen, nineteen, twenty, and twenty-one; the tuba player was eighteen; the average age of the musicians was nineteen and a half, a figure somewhat inflated by the presence of several ambitious Japanese in their mid-twenties. The North Carolina Philharmonic Orchestra: now playing before a sixteenth-century della Robbia altar in the sanctuary of a thirteenth-century *convento,* in the hills of Tuscany, by way of Belmont, Benson, Sanford, Asheville, Pfafftown, and Winston-Salem, North Carolina, with connections to Augusta, Georgia; Newport, Tennessee; Auburn, Alabama; Smyrna Beach, Florida; General Delivery, Manset, Maine; and the Methodist Parsonage, New Matamoras, Ohio.[50] Vittorio would have loved it.

Surprisingly, the 1969 session, planned with Mario Fabbri's help, involved the Americans more directly with the Chigiana than in 1968. The NCSA session was to run concurrently with the Chigiana's (July 13 to August 31, with the students' departure scheduled for September 1), and up to twenty-five American students were to be accepted as regular students in the Chigiana's prestigious Corsi di Perfezionamento master classes for graduate students with such artist luminaries as Gino Bechi, Riccardo Brengola, Guido Agosti, Pietro Scarpini, and Franco Gulli. The idea seems to have been first discussed by the Semanses and Giorgio Ciompi in June of 1968, but it must have been in Jim Semans's mind ever since he received a letter of disappointment from a young flutist at the school of the arts who had attended the summer session in 1967. Ransom Wilson wrote to Dr. Semans to ask if something different could be worked out because the

22. *Severino Gazzelloni, Italy's "golden flute," giving a master class in one of the frescoed rooms of the Chigiana (Archives of the North Carolina School of the Arts).*

dates of the 1968 session would not permit him to study again with the Accademia's flute teacher, Severino Gazzelloni:

> Maestro Gazzelloni is recognized as one of the finest flute virtuosos in the world and is the finest flute teacher I have ever seen.
>
> If you will remember, there was quite a hassle over whether Summer Session students were to be allowed to attend Maestro Gazzelloni's master classes or not. It was finally decided that we could go, but that we could not play in the classes. However, Maestro Gazzelloni let us play once, liked us, and continued to teach us thereafter, unknown to the administration.
>
> By the time the summer session was over, I had learned quite a lot and he and I were very good friends.

The situation with Gazzelloni illustrates the difficulties and the possibilities of working with the Chigiana faculty, who operated independently of any policy or general regulation set down by the Chigiana "administration." Mario Fabbri had immediately accepted the idea of enrolling American students in the Chigiana but was never able to get the faculty to agree to accept the students on the basis of their audition in Winston-Salem for members of the North Carolina School of the Arts faculty, even though the students would be performing the same exam given by the Chigiana. Thus the students with the NCSA summer session had to audition twice, flying to Siena with no guarantee that they would be enrolled in the master classes for which the school of the arts had accepted them. Fabbri did offer a concession: NCSA students would be accepted as auditors at the Chigiana, as space permitted, for the modest fee of $15. In the end, all the students were accepted for the master classes, even by the great conductor Franco Ferrara, who, Jim Semans later reported to Robert Ward, was "truly enthusiastic" about them.[51]

Jim and Mary Semans hoped that such close personal involvements between members of the Chigiana faculty and individual American students would serve to diminish misunderstandings. And these interactions did prove to be remarkably successful. Riccardo Brengola, first violin of the Chigi Sextet (originally the Chigi Quintet) from 1939 to 1966, invited some of the students to play in a Chigiana performance. Franco Gulli, one of Italy's foremost violinists, was so impressed with the young concert mistress of the North Carolina Philharmonic Orchestra, Kathleen Lenski, that he coached her for the Paganini competition, held that fall in Genoa; she won second prize. Guido Agosti, the great Italian pianist and composer renowned for his playing of Beethoven and Debussy, was sufficiently pleased with his American students to look with warmth on the entire session, inviting the Semanses and Giorgio Ciompi to his home for coffee in spite of negative attitudes being expressed by some other members of the Chigiana faculty. For with the simultaneous presence of both groups of students and faculty—the Chigiana's and NCSA's—and Mario Fabbri's absence, opportunities for giving offense were multiplied. "As you know," Jim Semans later wrote to Guido Agosti, "after Mario Fabbri left we had no official spokesman with whom to communicate, so if there were misunderstandings about arrangements we are sorry." Indeed, at one point, there were some extremely annoying misunderstandings—"due to either accidents or intentional intrigue, we found ourselves performing within earshot of some of the classes conducted by the professors in the Accademia"—understandably irritating for both sides. Such details could destroy the relationship between the two institutions. The level of understanding reached its nadir, however, when Dr. Moggi the younger, a music critic for *La Nazione* close to the Chigiana faculty, published a curiously ambivalent review of an NCSA summer session chamber music concert. A student duo, guitarist and flutist, performed "with calligraphic correctness" but "without spirit"; the first soprano had a "pleasant" voice of "childish tenderness" but "inadequate in the upper register"; the next soprano was "more interesting and richer" but "technically immature"; a third, though "not always steady in pitch," sang with a "certain stylistic-expressive feeling." The most confusing evaluation of all was that of a trio performance of Brahms, "a Brahms not misinterpreted, but not deep enough. . . . A Brahms nevertheless, which did not lose all its fascination." Moggi, who had been a good friend to the session in previous years, was not interested in a merciless critique of a recital of "young, very young students to be admired unreservedly for their good-will and enthusiasm"; what he really wanted was an opportunity to raise questions about the relationship between the Accademia and NCSA: "It could be that we have not fully understood . . . the forms, the limits, the reciprocal situations—the exact meaning of the word 'sponsorship' . . . if some of our perplexities are not born of personal fantasies, the best thing is to understand one another well, with extreme clarity." Moggi closed with an old Italian proverb: *Patti chiari amicizia lunga,* "Clear agreements, long friendship."[52]

Moggi's meaning was clarified for Jim Semans when Guido Agosti, after a pleasant social evening during which he and Giorgio Ciompi had played the piano and violin together, stated that he was "confused": why was the North Carolina summer session in Siena, at the Chigiana? The faculty of the Accademia Chigiana, Jim Semans realized, suspected that the North Carolina Summer Session was there with the ulterior motive of eliminating the ideal situation which the professors had enjoyed ever since World War II. . . . The individual faculty members almost universally related very well to Giorgio Ciompi, the North Carolina Artistic Director, but they feared the destruction of their position if the summer session began to attract public attention and the money of the Banco Monte dei Paschi which might otherwise be theirs, and they saw a disease growing. They had a meeting and [Brengola] told Giorgio about it . . . and the name of the meeting was "la cura" which in Italian means "the treatment." . . . Moggi reflected the faculty's confusion that the North Carolina Summer Session might not be to their advantage when . . . he quoted the proverb, "Clear agreements make long friendships."

It is not without irony that just a year before, while riding the 1968 summer session roller coaster *ad astra per aspera,* Robert Ward had asked Danilo Verzili, president of the Monte dei Paschi Bank, to state again what "aspirations and motivations" had prompted the "very generous support" by the bank of the NCSA summer session. Verzili replied that "basically the interest was the same as originally expressed by Foreign Minister Fanfani": "a general cultural exchange between Italy and the United States, and the establishment of a situation in which talented young Americans would become familiar with the great heritage of Italian music. The hope was, of course, that they would take this knowledge and interest back to the United States."[53] The situation in Siena, in which a bank functioned as a foundation, one of whose beneficiaries was by legal agreement an academy of music, had provided the practical vehicle for a noble idea. The Americans now found themselves in the excruciatingly delicate position of trying to convince the Italians of an instance of Italian idealism. Never having been told any different, the Chigiana faculty naturally suspected intrigue on the American side. Furthermore, sponsorship of the North Carolina summer session by so powerful a political figure as Amintore Fanfani created "a feeling of pressure on Siena and on the Accademia Chigiana," Jim Semans observed, "since we were brought to them not by their particular invitation (they probably issue invitations to nobody!)." Semans decided that, in the absence of leadership within the Chigiana, the North Carolina staff would have to take on the Italian faculty one by one and establish personal relationships with them, "on their terms."[54]

Meanwhile, the question of continued Italian financing of the session was a legitimate concern; during the original negotiations in 1966, Dr. Semans and Minister Fanfani had agreed verbally that the Italian contribution would gradually diminish until, at the end of five years, the session would be on its own financially. (In fact, the grants from the federal Italian government and from the Monte dei Paschi for 1969 [$11,200 and $35,480] had decreased only slightly from the first grant of $50,000 for the 1967 session.) As part of NCSA's efforts to meet the goal of fiscal self-sufficiency (and to allay Sienese anxiety about the distribution of the Monte dei Paschi funds), Robert Ward had begun developing, in the summer of 1968, a plan for an international music festival that would attract a large number of cultured—and moneyed—tourists to Siena; and a winter consortium of North Carolina colleges to develop an academic year of study in Italy based in Siena at the Chigiana. This last was a particularly pleasing idea to the Monte dei Paschi Bank, which wanted to establish the Chigiana on a firmer economic footing by making use of its facilities on a twelve-month basis. To aid in developing the proposal, Jim Semans approached the Institute of International Education (IIE) in New York for expert advice. The IIE has operated since 1919 as a private, nonprofit agency which develops and administers educational and cultural exchange programs between the United States and other countries and provides information and consultative services on all aspects of such programs. The venerable institute "was at first rather cool and sceptical," Jim Semans remembers, "as if this were just another foreign program." Fortunately, NCSA's old friend Vieri Traxler was then serving as consul general of Italy in New York and was therefore able to call round and explain that "this was seriously considered as an Italian government program of international relationships outside our own State Department." This is how it came about that three members of the IIE staff were present to observe and evaluate the 1969 summer session, to make recommendations about it and about the possibilities for a festival and a winter program. The consultants encouraged the idea of expanding the summer session to include an international music festival, but they recommended that NCSA shelve the plan until the dust settled at the Accademia, which at the time of the IIE's August report was making plans for renovations and delaying artistic decisions until the appointment of a new director (the Accademia had been without an artistic director since Mario Fabbri's resignation in November 1968 some nine months before). About the winter program, the consultants were less hopeful. The undiluted Italianness of Siena—its chief charm and asset—made it a more difficult location than a city such as Rome or Florence, where the citizens "are used to Americans: they know what will be wanted and at what price; they comprehend the American demand for prompt action, and can accept the fact that in America business is conducted differently. . . . The administrators of a program [in Siena] . . . will at some time be tried to the limit of their patience and they must be prepared. . . . Local arrangements must be checked and double checked." The undisturbed antiquity of Siena's buildings made of her damp, windy, cold winters the obstacles to human life nature intended: "Floors are marble, rooms are vast, windows stretch from floor to very high ceilings. Often the whole is heated by one very small radiator which is usually turned off for the better part of the night, early morning and afternoon. . . . Italian and American concepts of heat differ radically." Both of the "operating" libraries in Siena had no heat at all, and many priceless collections of art were housed in buildings that had neither heat, nor lights, nor outlets for light plugs. But "the number of things to be seen [in Siena] staggers the imagination," the consultants noted. At the Accademia Chigiana alone, "the collection is overwhelming."[55]

Despite the obvious advantages to tourists and students alike of intensive treasure-hunting in Siena, the festival and the winter program were not worked out—but not because of inherent difficulties. Rather, as Dr. Semans notes wisely, because the city of Siena "has survived very nicely with the well thought out plan of the Monte dei Paschi Bank since its Halcyon days of the 15th century," the Sienese were "rather reluctant to have their pattern of life altered in any way."[56] The IIE survey, however, proved valuable. At the time, it was an act of good faith on the part of the Americans, demonstrating a willingness to work at making their presence in Siena beneficial to the city. And, too, the survey provided documentation of the program's standing after three years' development, as perceived by experienced, disinterested professionals, habitués of neither passionate camp. After observing the program and consulting with the Italians as well as the Americans, the IIE consultants made a number of practical, constructive suggestions, which seem, more than anything else, to lend additional authority to what Jim Semans, Giorgio Ciompi, and Robert Ward had already learned the hard way—for example, that the administrative staff needed to be expanded yet again: "At present Giorgio Ciompi is overburdened with trivial problems. He often is forced to work on printers' proofs, negotiate for busses, transportation of instruments, solve student problems. He should be free to do the work for which he is admirably suited; to spend more time with faculty and students, to supervise musical activities, and to consider artistic plans for the future." The consultants advised planning everything far in advance (though the Americans well knew that those plans could be counted on only so far in Italy, where the populace, Robert Ward has observed, prefer to keep "every moment of the scheduled day negotiable"). Relations with the Chigiana "must be handled with great tact": "The Accademia is an old and prestigious institution and extreme care must be taken not to step on its toes and to push plans about which it is reluctant. The fact that so much cooperation has developed over three years is . . . a tribute to the tact and constructive, patient attitude of Dr. Semans, Co-President of the Summer Session . . . it seems likely to us that in the present context potentials for great cooperation exist." It must have been gratifying for all those involved to read that the IIE's representatives judged the collaboration between the school of the arts and the Chigiana to have been "increasingly successful over the past three years"; rated the session "excellent" in contributing to "the students' musical growth" and to the broader objective of "furthering knowledge by Americans of Italian culture and arts"; and perceived faculty and student morale and spirit as "generally high, thanks in large part to the wisdom, energy, thoughtfulness and imagination brought to the Summer Session" by Jim and Mary Semans and Giorgio Ciompi.[57]

Although the IIE report advised that any expansion of the summer session step slowly, the consultants gave a cautious go-ahead to dance. The dance program that summer found an enthusiastic audience for ballet in Siena, Firenze, Vittorio Veneto, Venezia, Livorno, Portevenere—everywhere that Dean Robert Lindgren and his troupe performed. Although the logistics of a dance tour in Italy were, as the IIE put it, "a tricky business," the NCSA dance group impressed the experts as a plucky little band. "It appears to be quite self-sufficient," they commented.[58] Behind that reserved statement lies a three-week tour that contained all but one of the elements that characterized the Siena experience for the North Carolina School of the Arts. The dance group did not study ballet in Italy as the young musicians studied music, but they played Italy in the same funny, catastrophic, romantic, educational, concentrated, absorbing, exhausting way. Dean Lindgren recollects that summer in vivid voice:

> Because I loved Italy and had been there before, I thought it would be marvelous if the dancers could go too, not just on a performance basis but because that is where the ballet really started. Italy is really the home of ballet; that is where, at the courts of the Medici, it had its beginnings before going to France. Most of my education as a dancer has been through my experience in the theater. For instance, when I joined the ballet at eighteen, I had no idea who Marc Chagall or Matisse was, but as a dancer I saw the sets that they had designed for the ballet, I heard the music of Ravel and Stravinsky, and as I had

never learned about all these things, it was all by osmosis that I got my knowledge. . . . If I see things or hear things, then they leave a lasting impression on me. And I thought that an opportunity to see the beautiful churches, the landscape, the romanticism, the Renaissance—where it started—would be an education for the students.

We did not come under the same financial arrangement as the Siena group, but I had already talked about this in conversations with Dr. Semans, and he said that he would help us if we could find a reason for going. He thought that it would be of value to the students to go to Italy and . . . do some performances. A teacher at the school, Jim Moon, had been going to Asolo for fifteen years. He had a small home there and knew everybody in the area of Treviso and Vittorio Veneto, which is an area in northeast Italy, near Venice. So Jim Moon told me that he could get engagements near Venice and that we could see the "*pro locos*" [agents] in neighboring places and find out if they would like a dance company to come, and this is how it started.

Jim Moon went to Italy, arranged three dates, two in Asolo, one in Vittorio Veneto, and a benefit for Italia Nostra (Save Venice). Then through the agent that the music school was using, Paolo Olsoufieff, we arranged to play Spezia, Livorno, and Castiglione della Peschaia. These engagements didn't pay very much, only something like 350,000 or 250,000 [lire] an engagement. But we thought that if we could anticipate at least three or four thousand dollars of income in Italy and have some help that Dr. Semans offered, we could make it financially. I went to the students and asked them how they would like to go to Italy, at a cost to each and every one of them of only $450. I already had a company started in the school, and these were the students that I invited. Twenty responded—eight boys and twelve girls.

We already had a repertoire and costumes and enough money to buy our tickets. On my projected basis of ten dollars a day for room and board, we also had enough money to exist for the twenty-one days that our excursion ticket allowed us, so that even if we didn't have one engagement, we could stay in Italy for three weeks. Through Jim Moon, who had taken the Salem College group to Italy, we were allowed to have the benefit of the Villa Freya for nothing. The villa is in Asolo and was built by Freya Stark, an Englishwoman who wrote books like the *Bobbsey Twins* and became quite wealthy. She had since given it up and the Villa had become a city property. Jim Moon made arrangements for his Salem College group to stay there for six weeks, and then reserved two more weeks for us, which saved us much money. We made arrangements with a restaurant called the Due More to have our meals at a very reasonable rate, and the city of Asolo built a stage in the courtyard of the castle. Then we had to find a place where we could rehearse. Most places were unsatisfactory, and the matter was complicated because the schools didn't have gymnasiums. We ended up performing most of our rehearsals outside a school. So we had a time available to go, a certain number of engagements so that we could earn money, and with the financial help from Dr. Semans plus tuition from the students, I thought we had enough to take care of our budget.

We decided that we would go the first three weeks of August, but in order to make sure that we indeed had places to stay, I arranged to fly over with the Siena group on their chartered flight. I was there four weeks before the dancers arrived. In that period of time Jim Moon and I rented a car, and we drove all over Italy trying to commit all the local *pro locos,* or tourist bureaus, we possibly could. Each little city within the province can draw on money from their provincial capital to provide outside entertainment for tourists and local citizens. They might have an opera or a play, and then a ballet. This was how we were making all these arrangments. However, when you go to Italy and arrange a date to see somebody, it's give or take two hours from the appointed time whether they will or will not show up, and then they can't give you a decision right away and you have to come back, and that means sitting in cafés drinking wine or coffee and trying to decide, are you going to be able to play there or are you not? Then you have to work out some kind of agreement: Are they going to build a stage? What are they going to provide? Are they going to do the programs? Are they going to make the *manifestos* [posters]? Will they do the ads in the paper? At what hotel are we going to stay? What will be the rate? In what restaurant are we going to have our meals? There are all these preliminary arrangements that have to be made. I must say that it is a lot of fun, but it's frustrating work. You never really can pinpoint or finalize a contract with anyone. Jim Moon was marvelous because he was a real advance man. He spoke fluent Italian and arranged most of the things in Asolo. He got the carpenters to build barres, and organized all the people there to do the different jobs that had to be done. He found another young man, Claudio Gorini, to come on the road with me. Jim would stay in Asolo, but when the company went on tour, Claudio Gorini was supposed to be my interpreter and agent.

Of the four weeks in Italy before the company came, I spent two in

Asolo working with Jim Moon, and the other two with Claudio on the road. It was exhausting because two days after we had left a town with a contract in hand, we'd find out that they weren't quite so sure that they could have us after all. Meanwhile we had this whole company waiting, with plane reservations, all ready to come to Italy. My Italian was nil. I was saying "*bon giorno*," "*si*" and "*no*." . . .

We had decided to send our costumes, tapes, and all our equipment on the same plane with the [summer session] charter flight, but when I got to the airport in New York, suddenly these two great harp cases showed up that were being shipped over with the orchestra. When I got to the airport in Milan to check on my scenery and costumes, I had these same enormous harp cases that were put in with my equipment, and I couldn't do anything with them. I didn't have any money to send them anywhere. Whoever represented our school in Siena kept writing, telling me to send them on, but there was no way to get them there. Finally a truck was sent up to Milan from Siena, and I was at last rid of the harps. It was a real hassle getting all our costumes and scenery and everything through Italian customs, but Claudio was a great help with his Italian.

We also had to find a place in Italy where we could rent lights and a dimmer board and a cable. We looked around, and when we happened to be in the coastal city of Porto Venere, I noticed that there was a play being given by a summer stock company from Rome. When I saw on their boxes that their electric equipment came from a house in Milan, I contacted these people through Gorini. They said that yes, they would have lights and electrical equipment for us to rent. We had to go to Milan then and find this little Monte Bianci Electrical Supply Company and pick out all the instruments and transformers and cables and arrange for them to be picked up on a certain day. I went back to Asolo and through Jim found a man who rented buses and trucks. We rented a big bus from him and a small Volkswagen bus for all the electrical equipment, speakers, recorder, etc. . . . After everything was finally arranged, I just went back to Asolo and waited for the company. Dr. Semans came to Asolo to meet Jim and me, and I drove them down to Milan on the express highway. I had never driven a VW bus before in my life, and here I was driving on this *autostrada* down into the impossible traffic of Milan. We drove out to the airport where the kids arrived on a TWA plane. I was never so happy to see any group of people in my life as I was to see my students and the people who came with them! I knew that I could speak English, that they were familiar people, and that we could start rehearsing.

When the kids arrived they were very excited. We got on the bus, picked up the lighting equipment in the VW, and . . . then we started off to Asolo, which was about a four-hour trip. The kids arrived and saw the Villa Freya, and they thought, "My God, what is this?" because the villa is just a shell—there is nothing in it. We had, however, rented a lot of cots so that we could sleep four or five kids in a room, and I said all right, you can spend this day sleeping and the next day we'll start rehearsing because we have an engagement in three days.

The next day the kids all got up, and we all went up in the hills to a monastery that Jim Moon had arranged for us to rehearse in. It had very small rooms and was very dusty. As soon as the dancers started to jump, the whole building began to shake, and we thought the monastery would collapse. So we all went down the hill to look at the stage. I asked the students what they would rather do, rehearse in the old dusty monastery or outside? and they said, let's rehearse outside because there's fresh air and it's nicer. The Asolanis didn't know what had hit when they saw all these dancers arrive, walking around in leotards and tights and dancing on an outdoor stage right in front of the town's beautiful old church.

The first performance was in Vittorio Veneto. What they had done was to erect a beautiful stage right in front of the city hall. There was a lovely fountain directly in front of the stage, so while we were changing, the fountain played, lit with floodlights, and created an exciting scene. The admission was free, so anyone who wanted to come to the square could see the ballet. When we drove down to Vittorio Veneto on the bus, unfortunately it started to rain. The two gentlemen who had arranged for the ballet, Sebastiano, the *pro loco* and another, had been so happy to have the first ballet coming to Vittorio Veneto. They had placed beautiful flowers all around the stage, and it just rained, and rained and rained. They wanted us to make a decision about whether we could play in a movie house if the rain kept up. We got in a car and drove over to the movie house which was not a bad place but the stage was rather dirty now that it was no longer used, and just hadn't been kept up. The stage had a tremendous 3 percent rake which our dancers hadn't been used to, but I said O.K., if needs be, we can do it here.

But then Sebastiano said that it was so late (already 7:00 in the evening) that we couldn't possibly tell the audience we had changed the locale. So we went back and waited in the rain until about eight o'clock. The rain never let up, and those were the two unhappiest *impresarios* that I have ever seen! This poor man had tears in his eyes. We decided that we would cancel and come back the next day. We did come back the next day and had the performance, and these two men had beaming smiles on their faces. It was a big investment for them; we were the biggest expense that they had ever had, and certainly the biggest attraction that they were going to have the whole summer long. We had a tremendous success there. Behind the stage, draped out of the city hall windows, we had huge American and North Carolina flags and it was really an exciting performance. We probably drew about 2,000 people who just stood in the piazza and watched.

Our second performance was in Asolo itself. By this time the students and the Asolanis had begun to recognize each other. Every day the kids would go to the Bar Centrale and drink Coca-Cola, and the residents had seen us all around the city. I think it's a 15th century city, and it's still very small and looks just the same as it has during the last five centuries. All the city life takes place in the central piazza with an old fountain and church, and . . . there was a real curiosity about the performance. . . . In setting up the stage we had the usual problems of communicating with the Italians. We couldn't get our tape to work on their tape-recorders, which ran at a different speed. We finally found a local man with a Sony recorder that our tapes played on, and we were saved—we had sound. Again the opening was very elegant. They had rolled out a great red carpet from the square up the hill into the castle where the performance was to be held. They had the *Carabinieri* there in their uniforms and it was a big gala. Our opening ballet was Symphony 13 and our second ballet was "Raimonda" and our closing ballet was supposed to be "Screenplay." In Asolo it rains everyday in August. It's in the foothills of the Dolomites and clouds come over, there is thunder and lightning, a tremendous downpour, and then the sun comes out. Usually it comes in the early evening around four-thirty, five or six o'clock, and then after that happens, it's fine. On this particular night, however, with this quite elegant audience, the clouds began to assemble right at the beginning of the performance. We thought, "Oh, please, let us get through the first ballet." If we get through the first ballet, we have to be paid. If it rains and you cancel at a half hour then there is no obligation on the part of the *impressario* to pay. Every cent that we were earning in Italy is what we were living on, so we were all praying that it wouldn't rain. Well we got through the first two ballets fine, so we were home free, but the audience liked us, so we wanted to do the whole performance. But in the middle of the second movement of "Screenplay," the heavens opened and just drenched the audience. They tried to stand under a covered walk on the side and get the best protection they could. Finally everybody just fled to the café upstairs. All the dancers were rushing around, and we were trying to cover the lights, protect the stage, etc. We waited for about a half hour but the storm didn't subside and the performance was cancelled. . . .

The next day when we went back to the theater to see what had happened to the stage, we were quite surprised. In all the theaters we had insisted that they put a Masonite covering on the boards because some of the stages had spaces of two inches or knot holes, or nails. . . . But what happened in Asolo and was to happen again in other theaters, too, was that the rain soaked the Masonite and made tremendous bubbles in the stage. So that evening we did the performance, it had sort of mounds or bubbles. It is always rather precarious to perform outside because either the evening dew makes it slippery or occurrences such as this happen. . . .

[We] went down in the buses to Spezia, which has a beautiful castle also overlooking a harbor. It was an ancient ruin, beautifully located, but we had the same problems we often had. When we were playing in Spezia we couldn't get hotels there because it is an Italian resort and all the hotels are booked up way in advance, so when we arrived there in the afternoon, Gorini and I went to see what accommodations the *pro loco* had made for us. They replied that they were sorry but that they had no place for us to stay. I said that we had to have some place to stay, that we couldn't sleep in the streets. So I told the kids to take the bus and go to Porto Venere and swim until about 4 o'clock in the afternoon, and that when they got back we would have some place for them to stay.

We went to every hotel and every flea bag and god-knows-what in this town of about 150,000. During the war, it was Mussolini's main naval base on the Tyrrhenian coast. We tried to find rooms—any rooms. The rooms we finally found left a lot to be desired, but in desperation we got some rooms in one hotel and other rooms in what was really an Italian peasant's home. It was very clean, but very poor, and we had to go through many unpaved streets to get there. After I took the girls to the house, I told them that I would take them down to a tavern that I had seen from the taxi on the way up. I walked the girls down to the tavern about five minutes away where we finally had a seafood dinner which was delicious. We had "spaghetti con vengole," which is spaghetti with clams. The tavern was full of Italian sailors, and they saw these beautiful American girls—six of them—and they wondered what one man was doing with all of these girls. They were eyeing the girls and talking to me. I convinced the girls to smile but not encourage them. I felt like a mother superior trying to calm that group of girls. When we finished the meal, I walked back to the house with the girls, told them goodnight, and went back to the tavern to wait for Claudio Gorini who I thought was coming to pick me up in his car. I was relying on him for my ride. There were no taxis at this point because I couldn't telephone a taxi in Italian and there were none on the corner. I started walking toward town about three in the morning and I had a terrible time finding my rooming house. The only way I knew of getting there was to go to the center of the city to the statue of Garibaldi because then I knew that it was two streets left and one street up, etc. I finally found the house at about four in the morning, but in typical Italian fashion the door was closed. I rang and rang the bell and knocked on the door but I could not raise anything or anybody. Well, I just sat down on the ground in front of the door and slept there for about three hours. In the morning the man came to open the door, I went up to the apartment the family was renting to us. There was Claudio Gorini in the bedroom where we both were supposed to be sleeping. . . .

We drove down to Castiglione della Peschaia, which is down the coast from Spezia. We had a very enjoyable performance there. It took place in the middle of a pine grove on the beach, and the only complication was the lack of sanitary facilities. When dancers want to change costumes and are sort of nervous, a bathroom is a necessity, and here we were with absolutely no place to go. So we improvised behind stage as discreetly as we could. . . .

We started rehearsing again and played in Livorno. Then we had to take a trip all the way back to Venice for the Italia Nostra benefit. I had made reservations at a *pensione* in Venice a month earlier when I had been there with Jim Moon, so I drove on ahead with Claudio Gorini and the dancers all came on the bus. It was one of those long eight-hour trips, where the kids were exhausted and the road was through mountains, and the trip was just basically tiring. It was already toward the third week's end. Claudio and I went on to the hotel where we were told that they were sorry but that they didn't have the rooms that they had promised us. The hotel offered me a room and said that they'd find another *pensione* for the company. I told Claudio and the hotel people to please go down to meet the company and direct them to the local *pensione* and went to bed as I was exhausted, too.

When I went over to meet the company, I found this unhappy and very disgruntled group of dancers waiting for me. I asked what was the matter, and they replied that after a long and awful bus trip, they'd arrived at a hotel which was not the greatest, and had had to carry their own bags. I told them that this was Venice; that there was no transportation, that you have to carry your own bags or hire a porter and pay him. They said they had no money and were all very angry at me. I hadn't arranged for their bags to be carried and they were in tears. I guess that I was a little defensive, and said, "God, we've knocked ourselves green. We've been all over town trying to find these perfectly nice accommodations and are very tired ourselves." Well, this was the first time on the whole trip that we had had any dissension . . . and I was very upset because I thought, how could anyone come to Venice and be unhappy just to carry their bags! I had told the students in the first place not to bring anything that they couldn't carry comfortably, and of course, some of them had brought huge suitcases full of wardrobes that would have lasted a year! They were a little unhappy with me about that. After a night's rest, however, everything was completely different. Also, the next day we had a marvelous experience.

Claudio and I spoke to the lady who was arranging the performance in Venice. The evening was to be for the Italia Nostra, which was to raise money to save Venice. We weren't going to earn any money, but we thought that it would be fun to play in this little theater which is in an old monastery on the Isola San Giorgio. We still had to go through the whole process of trying to provide *manifestos* and arrange transportation for the audience who had been invited to come and see this. Claudio and I took Susan Moore and Rebecca McLain along with us to see the Contessa Maria Cicogna. The Contessa had a beautiful apartment in the Piazza San Marco in Venice, and I thought it would be fun to take the girls. They got all dressed up and we went down to see the Contessa who is a very elegant woman, very pleasant, very chic. We had a long conversation about how the performance would all take place, and the girls just sat there taking it all in. When the interview was over, she offered to send us back to the hotel in her *motoscafo*. We went down to the canal to find a great launch with a captain in a white uniform, and two sailors standing in the back. . . . We rode all down the Grand Canal and the smaller ones, until we came to our hotel. The experience of being with those two American dancers who had just been visiting a Contessa, and riding down the canals in a beautiful motor launch, was just like a—well it was just like a fairy tale for them.

We gave the performance the next day. Our boys had to get up at six o'clock in the morning and go down to the station where our bus was and take out all of our equipment. Claudio and I had arranged for gondolas in which we put all our lighting equipment, our tape recorder, and our costumes. At six o'clock in the morning, it was quite a sight to see all these dancers floating down the canal in gondolas with all our equipment, to the Isola San Giorgio, past an American battleship in the harbor. All these boats were going past and the waves were quite high that day. But they arrived and we gave the performance that night. . . . That was the last engagement that we had in that season, and Dr. Semans had come down to see it. Everytime that Dr. Semans came, it was a real morale booster because they felt that somebody from the school cared and had come out of his way to see them. He was always very generous and gave us an afterdinner party and everyone ate and drank themselves into oblivion and everyone was in a very happy frame of mind.

We had been in Italy for three weeks and the students had seen Rome, Florence, Venice, Asolo, Milano, Porto Venere, Castiglione, Livorno, and Spezia. We had given about nine or ten performances, we had studied in between, but what the students learned from the whole experience of being there and eating and seeing and absorbing is what was so incredible.[59]

"Is it not wonderful," Roger Hall (president of the North Carolina School of the Arts Foundation, January 19, 1970 to December 15, 1971) once remarked, "that a tee-shirted farm boy from western North Carolina suddenly finds himself . . . living and working for seven weeks in one of the treasured medieval cities of the Western World?"[60] It must be, for only a sense of wonder could keep ruffled artists, doubting budget-makers, and busy statesmen working together year after year, with remarkable tenacity, to support this complicated and enriching cultural exchange, through times convivial and not so convivial, in misunderstanding and in health, for richer or poorer, until exasperation in the service of a great ideal does its part, as it has every summer since 1967. Even Piero Bellugi came back; in 1970 he once again conducted the Summer Session Orchestra, brilliantly (as usual) and has continued to befriend the program through the years as flamboyant adviser and artistic liaison.

It may be that by surviving 1969, the summer session had proved that it could survive almost anything. On November 14, a new artistic director for the Chigiana was finally appointed. He was Luciano Alberti, "former music critic, man of letters (and non-musician!)," Mario Fabbri wrote Jim and Mary Semans in Durham. "He is a friendly person, of my own age (38 years)." Jim Semans and Robert Ward met with Alberti in Florence on January 18, 1970 and found him enthusiastic about continuing the program; while in Italy they also received the continued reassurance of a blessing from president of the Senate Fanfani. Italian support for the session was renewed (Monte dei Paschi $32,000, Italian federal government, $2,000), so that in 1970, ninety-three students attended the summer session in Siena, seventy-four of whom made up the symphony orchestra, which studied under Maestro Franco Ferrara. Governor of North Carolina Robert W. Scott brought his family to visit Siena that year (June 29–July 4), as did former Governor Terry Sanford and Margaret Rose (July 18–20). The session ended magnificently with a concert on the Capitoline Hill, presented under the patronage of the city of Rome in celebration of Rome's one hundredth anniversary as the capital of Italy. Three thousand Romans and tourists and the *New York Times* took note: "The student orchestra," wrote the *Times* correspondent, "made the rhythms of Aaron Copland and Gioacchino Rossini briefly dominate . . . the human commotion of a summer night in Rome." Halfway into the session of 1971, Jim Semans was able to report to Robert Ward that "we are now on a friendly working basis with the Accademia Chigiana in Siena, at last. . . . The remarkable thing is that there have been none of those crisis times, emergencies and panic sessions. . . . Almost miraculously after the first week, the old tensions and suspicions fell away." The session had acquired a way of making friends for itself, in spite of its turbulent and fluctuating nature ("movimentata e fluttuante," Luciano Alberti once characterized the program). Alberti himself became a friend, "full of compliments about everything." Equally important, the session won the wholehearted approval of NCSA's new dean of the School of Music, Nicholas Harsanyi, whose first experience with the program, in 1971, made him a convert:

> What [our students] learn here is invaluable and hard to put into words. To mention only the great difference in the way people feel

here toward the arts, the values to which they give priority should make us think twice. At the same time, I do not think that we need to apologize for what we show to them. Our orchestra, for instance, with young students, easily could be compared with their five top professional orchestras—which should make them think twice—[61]

Over the years the Siena session—now called the International Music Program—has changed and rearranged itself in response both to artistic experience and financial necessity. Eugene Rizzo, an American journalist living in Rome, took over publicity and the role of general factotum for the session in 1970. "Their man in Italy" recalls that in his first two years with the program, it repeated the established pattern, based on NCSA's relationship with the Accademia and the Monte dei Paschi Bank. But when financial support from the bank ceased (as agreed) after 1971, Rizzo's role changed from one of "organizing everything from scratch right down to counting soap bars—I used to say bitterly about the whole job, 'They even expect me to count soap bars'"—to putting the session on a different financial footing:

> We began to collect money from the cultural offices of the various cities where we were going to perform. . . . I [learned] that in Italy . . . the arts are pretty well taken care of through the regions. In other words, if you approach the regions, which are roughly equivalent to states in America, there are twenty of them . . . twenty regions. Each one of them has a pretty hefty budget for the arts, and what you do is approach them and tell them, "I can bring this type of entertainment, or that type . . . if you'll support us."
>
> And that was the first surprise, to realize that it was not that difficult, and sure enough, I started. . . . So, I'd go into the main office [of a region] and explain whom I was representing, and tell them about our concerts, and show them programs we'd already printed. . . . .
>
> One of the things I felt strongly about coming into the program, was that we had to have better programs and posters; we started to get individual, you know, beautiful posters. I would approach people who were graphic artists and get them to do it for free just out of friendship . . . and all of this increased our tone a little bit, and then once you have a little bit of program to show people, you can walk into anyone's office, spread them out on a table, and ask for

support. And I found I was getting it. As gradually we're moving into Umbria, we're also gradually getting more money . . . I think we discovered we could make it a paying proposition.

ZINN: Do you think the Italians are more receptive to an Italian person living in Italy, rather than an American coming over and trying to set logistics and financial affairs?

RIZZO: They're infinitely more disposed toward foreigners. I've found, in fact . . . the greatest card I have is being an American who is of Italian descent. Well, even that doesn't matter so much: the important thing is that you be an American that speaks Italian . . . they have so much suspicion of each other that they automatically open up to foreigners. . . . You have to live here as I have over the years to see this happen over and over again. . . .

And I must add to that, another irony and another paradox is that where we got our greatest support always turns out to be the regions that were most communistic. . . . The communists are very open. They want to prove how human they are . . . that they're very tolerant of everybody and everything. And so comes along an American proposing an American concert, and they always backed them. Some of our best friends were communist mayors.[62]

Financial support has continued to come from both private and commercial sources in North Carolina, and in 1979, a West German construction company (Philipp Holzmann, AG, parent company of J. A. Jones Construction Company of Charlotte) began making possible a yearly residency in Frankfurt-am-Main.[63] Robert Hickock, who became dean of the School of Music at NCSA on August 1, 1977, reflects on the growth and value of the program:

When I arrived here, I became aware of the existence of a thing called the International Music Program. . . . I discovered that this was a program of long standing, and an extremely important program, particularly in its potentialities, that needed reorganization, and that needed more support. And I was so convinced that it was an important program for the school that I felt that I had to become closely associated with it and do everything that I could to keep that program alive and improve it and put it on a more secure footing in terms of its policies, in terms of its personnel, and in terms of its budget.

I'm happy to say that I think that we've been able to accomplish a great deal of that, and the program is now—I think it's about as old as the school—it has expanded its activities to include not only orchestral music, but chamber music. . . . I've gone all the way from an orchestra of about eighty-eight with two trucks, buses, large staff, enormous deficit, to a small string orchestra of about twenty-five. It is obvious that the huge, grand symphony orchestra is, first of all, not feasible any more economically, and I think further than that, I think that the size militates against the nature of the experience that the students have. On the other hand, I think an orchestra of twenty-five is simply not adequate for the purposes of training, and certainly not adequate for extensive concertizing in Europe. This year [1984] we have taken an important step, I think, in terms of increasing the size of the orchestra to about 37. And in my view, once we get to between forty-two and forty-five, in terms of the orchestra, I think that that would be an ideal size, in setting the nature of the educational program we want to mount and concerning the very rigorous responsibilities that we have for concert-giving in Europe. Everybody, I think, has to relearn occasionally that this is not a sight-seeing trip with a few concerts spread around. This is a highly geared, professional tour, with very heavy performing responsibilities, with a little bit of sight-seeing spread around. Now, we are constantly in the business of trying to balance off those two aspects. . . .

We also, for two or three years, took along with us a jazz contingent, which was extremely popular in Europe. Some day I would like to reestablish that. Unfortunately, the problems of doing that are enormous. There is a great deal of equipment involved, even hooking up electrical instruments in Europe is unbelievably complex. So that there are problems in doing that, but I think eventually, and this may be pipe dream material, that eventually we'll have an orchestra of about forty or forty-five, and a chorus, let's say of thirty to forty and a small jazz contingent. I think that that would be an ideal format for the program. . . .

It has expanded its geographical route to include now very important locations in Germany as well as traditional sites in Italy. It has received important backing, not only from United States sources, but also European ones, particularly the Holzmann Construction Company in Frankfurt and now other companies such as the M.A.N. Company in Munich; it has been recognized by the various levels of the

Italian government as an important part of the fabric of the summer cultural scene in Italy, and it's even doing fairly well financially. I think that it has been an important thing for the School of Music in terms of establishing some kind of image beyond the United States. I think it has served the state extremely well in making it possible for both political and business connections to be formed between North Carolina and places in Europe . . . this is very good, for the state and allows for the state to . . . capitalize on something that is inherently good, for the benefit of making political and economic contacts.

I also think that it goes further than that. I think that the young people that we take there, both in terms of their own spirit and the good work that they do, very well represent the United States in areas which are not as friendly any more as one would care to wish. In particular, I think in West Germany, given the fact that the new generation is not mindful of the enormous contributions that the United States made towards the rebuilding of West Germany, I think a chance to experience our kids in this context is enormously helpful for our reputation and influence. . . . So I think that the International Music Program is a very potent preacher of the school, and one that represents the school, the state, and the country, extremely well.[64]

The International Music Program, the North Carolina Philharmonic Orchestra, "Sessione Estiva in Siena"—in whatever guise or naming, this adventure has survived because it is the proper child of the North Carolina School of the Arts, founded just as the school was founded, by men and women determined that the arts should not be a parochial vision in their state, but rather an opening out onto the whole world.

CODA

1962 – 1984

*The fugue usually concludes with a section
called the* coda . . . *in which the subject,
after all its tonal wanderings, reasserts
itself in the tonic key, return to which may
be emphasized by an insistent pedal.*

Bernstein and Picker,
An Introduction to Music

*John Le Doux, archivist at the
North Carolina School of the
Arts, has developed a chronology
of the school's history, on file at
the Semans Library, on the
NCSA campus. The following
version has been shortened and
edited by Leslie Banner.*

1962

Aug. 1
Encouraged by the commit-
ment of composer Vittorio
Giannini to serve as an artistic
adviser, Governor Terry Sanford appoints the North Carolina Conservatory Committee
to work for the establishment
of a state-supported conservatory of music. Martha
Muilenburg of Charlotte chairs
the committee, and Governor
Sanford's special assistant John
Ehle serves as secretary.

*Douglas Zinn began taping interviews for
the North Carolina School of the Arts Oral
History Project on October 19, 1981; the
project tapes and full transcripts are on file in
the Archives of the Semans Library. The following material from the Oral History has
been selected and edited by Leslie Banner.*

*Gordon Hanes served on Governor Sanford's
North Carolina Conservatory Committee,
appointed in August of 1962:*
And so this great artistic school . . . a
bunch of legislators wanted to get secondary roads paved, and Ben Roney was sitting in the balcony watching the vote, and
we got it. Now, in addition to that, it was
not in the budget. And the governor,
through his discretionary funding, money
left over from something, the governor
funded it the first year. But then in '65 we
had a new governor and we had to put it
through [*pro forma*], and we did, and by
that time, we had convinced enough
people that it was a good thing. And as it
turned out, it has succeeded far beyond
our wildest dreams.

Sept. 27
John Ehle broadens the original conservatory concept into a school for the performing arts, with the help of Vittorio Giannini and the unofficial encouragement of Ford Foundation Program Director McNeil Lowry.

1963

Mar. 21
The North Carolina Conservatory Committee reports both the need for and feasibility of a state-supported school for the performing arts and outlines additional recommendations.

June 21
North Carolina State legislature passes bill establishing the North Carolina School of the Arts, with a $325,000 appropriation to get the school started.

R. Philip Hanes, Jr., served on the first Board of Trustees of the North Carolina School of the Arts:

I almost immediately fell madly in love with [Vittorio Giannini]. He is just one of the most wonderful human, interesting guys I've ever met. He had an empathy about him. Everybody that went to him was Vittorio's best friend. I've never seen anything like it. . . but Vittorio always talked in dreams. He always, he always said that this is what's going to happen, and it wasn't going to happen necessarily. It was just a dream. And he always had that big old cigar—half the time it was dead, and he just loved to go out and drink red wine and eat a steak or some Italian food, and we'd just go out and talk together. He was just a very human being. Talk about anything. . . .

He was a visionary. When you talked to him, you knew his commitment was there. He had that whole thing all planned out. He didn't want a conservatory like you might find in Russia or one that you would find in England or certainly one that you would find in America. America is so totally different. He wanted a composite of the whole thing, and he had that whole picture in his mind, what kind of a thing he wanted. And he was so right. Gosh, he was right.

Robert Lindgren is dean of the School of Dance at the North Carolina School of the Arts:

We were only in the beginning of the second year when the telephone message came through . . . where was Dr. Giannini? We'd been calling his house for three

1964

Mar. 26
Governor Sanford appoints
Advisory Board of Artists:
Sidney Blackmer, actor; James
Christian Pfohl, conductor;
Richard Adler, musical comedy
writer; Agnes de Mille, chore-
ographer; Vittorio Giannini,
composer; Jan Peerce, tenor;
José Limon, dancer; Peter
Mennin, composer; Julius
Rudel, conductor; and Paul
Green, author.

Apr. 28–29
After investigating sites in several cities, the Advisory Board
of Artists selects Winston-
Salem, where more than five
thousand people have pledged
more than $850,000 in a two-
day telephone drive. Board
nominates Vittorio Giannini as
president and Giannini accepts.

days and no one knew where he was, and
so we went into his apartment and there
he was. So who was going to be head of
the school? He hadn't said anything. We
hadn't set up the school, we didn't have a
process of seniority. . . .

[Vittorio] was the one that got everybody inspired and put it together. Therefore, we all loved him. He was the one that
hired us specifically and came and said, "I
want you." So the love and devotion was
there. . . . The problems of the first year
of the school are unbelievable. There was
not one rule or one regulation, we had a
junior high school, high school and college all in one with two buildings—one
to house all the girls and one to house all
the boys and it was chaos. We were not
prepared and didn't have the proper staff
or proper people. We went out of our
minds but we managed and he was always
there. He would yell at me sometimes,
and other times he would say, "Bobby, re-
lax—you've got the enthusiasm but you
haven't got the patience." So I was sorry
to see him die because I loved him in that
very short time.

R. Philip Hanes, Jr.:
    Vittorio was there as the dreamer. We
needed to have somebody come in and
stabilize a lot of things. Because he promised everybody everything. And I know
when Robert Ward took over, everyone
would come and say, "But Vittorio promised me this, that, and the other thing,"
you know. And he always did. I mean
"You want it? you believe in it? it's your
dream? you really think you can handle it?
What are you going to do with it? Well, it

May 28
Governor Sanford names the
school's first Board of Trustees:
R. Philip Hanes, Jr., Smith
Bagley, and Wallace Carroll of
Winston-Salem; Sam Ragan,
E. N. Richards, Mrs. Everette
Miller, and Hugh Cannon of
Raleigh; James McClure
Clarke, Asheville; Mrs. Wilbur
Jolly, Louisburg; Dr. James H.
Semans, Durham; Mrs. James
Boyd, Southern Pines; Martha
Muilenburg, Charlotte.

June 24
Giannini moves into the
school's temporary offices in
the James G. Hanes Commu-
nity Center, with an administrative staff of one.

July 17
Board of Trustees holds its first
meeting and school is officially named the North Carolina
School of the Arts. Dr. James H.
Semans is chosen as chairman
of the board, and Vittorio
Giannini is named president of
the school.

sounds good to me, you can have it. I'll
see that you get it." That's the way he operated. And that's fine. He had a great
pyramid that was about ready to topple.

Robert Lindgren:

Bob Ward, I thought, came in and did a
very good job under very trying circumstances. Trying, I say, when the school
had very little money, very little support
from the legislature, very little support
anywhere but locally. He was also the
chancellor of the school when he had to
go directly to the legislature and make
his pitch for the school. It was a difficult
time in the 1960s and early 1970s when the
whole student revolution was happening,
and he took his knocks. . . . He had faculty coming and going and making demands, and he had no money to make
raises. They were talking about expansion
of buildings, and the foundation didn't
have the funds, so he had tremendous,
tremendous pressures. But like Giannini,
Bob Ward believed in me and gave me
freedom to do what I wanted and encouraged me in everything.

R. Philip Hanes, Jr.:

Of course, he was a very famous composer. He was very disciplined, and . . . as
I remember, he had one or two of his children already at the school . . . I believe he
had one of them there. And he was a parent, he knew the school, he was totally
enthusiastic about it, and I think he had
even recommended it to some other parents who had sent kids there and he was a
highly disciplined person and so forth. We
liked his wife.

23. *Left to right: NCSA President Robert Ward, with Sidney Blackmer, Dr. James H. Semans, and Dean of Drama Ronald Pollock (Archives of the North Carolina School of the Arts).*

Oct. 22
NCSA Foundation established at a meeting in Durham with Dr. Semans and state officials. R. B. Crawford named chairman of the foundation board. The foundation is charged with administering the nearly $1 million already raised by the citizens of Winston-Salem and soliciting contributions from other sources across the country.

Composer Robert Ward served as president of the North Carolina School of the Arts, 1967–1973:

The transition in many respects was made less difficult than it might have been by the very fact that the school was so new and in so many respects unformed. . . . There simply hadn't been the time. The two dormitories which had been built were still out in the middle of the field of mud when the kids moved in . . . the whole thing was still at that very beginning stage. So there was much to be done. There was not anything that had to be undone. And in one respect, I was almost glad it was that way because it was easier. . . . That experience, that Vittorio and I had, is one that will happen very

Dec. 9
Groundbreaking begins for
Sanford and Moore dormitories. The silver shovel used to
break ground is later presented
to Governor Sanford.

1965

Jan.
Robert Lindgren appointed
dean of the School of Dance.
Saul Caston appointed conductor of NCSA orchestra.

Apr. 8
William Ball named advisory
director of the School of
Drama. William Trotman appointed associate director.

Apr. 17–19
First auditions for prospective
NCSA students. Ballerina Alexandra Danilova, actor Sidney
Blackmer, and David Drew of
the Royal Ballet Touring Company are on hand to assist with
the dance and drama auditions.

rarely in any educator's life. . . . When I
came, one of the first interviews and conversations I had . . . was with the head of
education in the state government. . . .
He said "Look, we here are prepared to
support you . . . but we must tell you, we
know nothing about it, and it's entirely up
to you. We're going to be looking on,
we're going to be criticizing . . . but we
feel that essentially we've got to put it in
your hands entirely. . . ."

Well, the governors . . . could be very
influential. . . . For the budget director to
know that the governor was sympathetic
to what the school's needs were—he
could always bend things in your favor—
not dramatically, but enough to be very
helpful, and we also had on our board at
that time Hugh Cannon, whom I think
you have talked to, and Hugh, of course,
had been top administrative assistant to
Governor Sanford when the school was
set up, and Hugh knew the ins and outs
of Raleigh like no one else did, so that in
those ways the governors were very helpful. Some of them took more active interest than others; [Governor] Bob Scott
was very active. He'd come around the
school for performances. And you never
knew quite what to expect. For instance,
when Dan Moore became governor, everyone knew he had nothing to do with the
arts and . . . we thought oh no, this is
going to be a bad period. He turned out
to be one of the strongest supporters of
all, because he sort of took a rather states-
manlike view of the thing, that the arts are
important in a culture. . . . So he was
fine, very helpful. And as a matter of fact,
when a guy whom many people viewed as

May 22
Louis A. Mennini appointed
dean of music.

June 9
Renovations begin on Gray
Building.

Aug. 31
NCSA staff moves into Gray
Building.

Sept. 5
First NCSA students (high
school) arrive on campus and
occupy dormitories.

Sept. 7
NCSA begins classes (high
school, academic) for the first
time. Classes in the performing
arts and college academic
classes begin Sept. 21.

a rather stern, stiff person took this view
of the arts, and he was from the mountains—that quieted some of these people
out there who would have been inclined
to be very critical every chance they
could. So it was helpful. . . .

We had, I suppose, the normal problems of expansion because the school was
initially in this high school which had
been renovated very rapidly and rather
sketchily to take care of the needs of the
school. No buildings go up slower than
those which go to state institutions. . . .
We were always having to have makeshift
arrangements.

The second problem was . . . dealing
with the social life of the kids during what
was one of the most tempestuous periods
in this country. Now actually, if it was a
hard period, it was also a very interesting
period, because this was a very lively
bunch of students. . . . They were the first
ones to get into bizarre dress, and I remember that very well because some of
the older trustees and people involved in
the school were very disturbed by this,
and I was approached on a couple of occasions, and I said, "Look, we are not in a
situation here where I think it would be
wise for us to try to control the way people
dress. If they're clean and if they're de-
cently dressed, that's just fine." . . . The
whole drug situation was a different thing.
It was very new, there was no way of
keeping this from drifting from the older
students down to the young. . . . On the
other hand, that problem solved itself, in
some respects, more easily with the school
of the arts than it did in many schools,
because if a student became involved in

Sept. 21
Vittorio Giannini addresses the
school at opening convocation.

Dec.
The Corcoran Gallery of Art
lends four priceless Amati
stringed instruments to NCSA.

Dec. 10
Ronald Alexander, New York
playwright and writer for motion pictures and television,
speaks to NCSA students.

1966

Feb. 10
Governor Dan Moore an-
nounces the Ford Foundation
has awarded a $1.5 million chal-
lenge grant to NCSA.

drugs, you knew it the next morning . . .
you simply could not dance, you could
not play the piano, you could not function if you were under the effects of drugs.
So this came to our attention very rapidly.
Coping with it was something else . . .
you could get no information about it because the students were very loyal to their
peers. And it reached its rather dramatic
climax when we had a drug bust. . . .

A couple of high school students . . .
had decided to take off for a few days, and
I had a call one afternoon from the juve-
nile squad or one of the special units in
the Winston-Salem police, asking me
whether we had any list with the specific
addresses or room numbers of students on
it. I said, "Our dean of student affairs has
that in his office, and if you just call him
and tell him that I said you wanted the
addresses of some students, you can have
[them]." Well, the next morning about
7:00 A.M. I had this call . . . that they had
a drug bust at the school. Well, it went
through the school like wildfire, a great
consternation, and so we had a convocation at 11:00 that morning—I've never
had such a crowd in that auditorium, and
it was intense as could be, and meanwhile,
the word had gotten around that I had assisted the police in this. So we had some
speeches. The guy who was the president
of the student body got up and made a
speech about the police pigs, which was
the very conventional thing at that time.
Then it was my turn to take the floor, and
I said, "There are several things I think we
need to clear the air on. I understand that
it's been said that I assisted the police in
bringing this about," and I said, "I want

Mar. 24
Mme Eugenie Ouroussow, an official of the School of American Ballet and a member of the NCSA Advisory Board of Artists, visits NCSA for the first time.

Apr. 12–16, 18–22
Andrés Segovia gives master classes to twenty performing classical guitarists and fifty-six auditors.

Apr. 28
Dancer Daniel Nagrin performs his solo program "Path"; Nagrin also serves as a special observer and adviser to the School of Dance.

May 1
Rare Amati violin, used by the Claremont Quartet, stolen from a parked car in Brooklyn, New York.

you to know the facts." I told them exactly what had happened, but then I went on to say that I wanted them to know, however, "that had they told me they were going to pull a drug bust here to get rid of drugs in this institution, I would have assisted them to the hilt, and you must know that you will not receive the kind of protection and a haven in this school that no other young person outside the entrance of this school is going to have. We're not for drugs. We will assist in anything." God, you could have heard a pin drop in that place, and then there was a burst of applause because the students who were bothered by this and the highly responsible people on the faculty were very glad to hear this. . . . It was a tense period, but it was a lively bunch of students, and talented, and on the other hand, it was a hard time. . . .

I was the one that proposed . . . taking [design and production] out of the Drama Department . . . and the reasons for that were complex. In the first place, in this school, that group of people needed to be available, on a very equal kind of basis, to opera, modern dance and ballet, and drama alike. . . . So [we] needed . . . to separate them from any one school. I also felt that if they were involved, really, with all of the schools, it would be a better training for them. Then, the next reason was that in the theater particularly, directors had become so dominant and so controlling on productions, that very often . . . a good designer finds it very difficult to work because he's simply being dominated by the director. Well, at a time when we had more advances on the scenic

May 14
Osvaldo Riofrancos appointed
dean of drama.

June 8
Graduation of the first class of
fifty-five high school seniors.
President Vittorio Giannini is
principal speaker.

June 25
NCSA named North Carolina's
"pacemaker" in educational
improvement in a nationwide
school-recognition project
sponsored by the National
Education Association and *Parade* magazine.

Aug. 4
John Cone appointed academic
dean, replacing Julia Mueller of
Duke University, who served
as consultant, academic dean,
and acting dean from November 1964 to June 1966.

side than we've had in centuries, I felt it
was very important to give those people
their heads. . . . By setting [D and P] up
independently . . . we had the right person coordinating the complete scheduling . . . because they could only build so
many sets, and they had to do this in a
reasonable kind of rotation. So that
worked out, and that was good. And then
the last point here, and this came after
we'd established the School of Design and
Production, was that from the very start
there had been many inquiries . . . from
high school students who were painting
and in sculpture, and they said why
doesn't the school of the arts have something for them, too? . . . It occurred to
us that in the usual high school program,
a student whose gifts are in the visual
arts probably never gets close to the
theater. . . . So we decided that to make a
two-year program on the high school level
in the visual arts . . . might serve two purposes: if [the students] had the kind of
talent which would warrant development,
then they would go into the state schools
or any other school they wanted to at a
better level. [Second], they would be in
this ambiance where there was so much
theater, with the opportunity to go that
direction if they wanted to . . . at least to
have that as another avenue for their later
professional life. So we decided to put it
in, and indeed, it worked out exactly as
we'd hoped because this turned up a
number of designers who otherwise
would never have gotten close to the
theater.

Oct. 1, 5
In Siena and Rome, Vittorio Giannini and Dr. James H. Semans negotiate a five-year agreement with Italy's foreign minister, Amintore Fanfani; the artistic director of the Accademia Musicale Chigiana, Mario Fabbri; and the president of the Monte dei Paschi Bank of Siena, Danilo Verzili to establish an NCSA Summer Session in Siena; approximately one-half the expenses to be covered by a grant from the federal government of Italy and the Monte dei Paschi Bank.

Nov. 15–18, 30, Dec. 1–3, 7–9, 14–16
Camino Real, first major production of the School of Drama, is directed by Osvaldo Riofrancos.

Nov. 25
President Vittorio Giannini dies in New York City.

John Sneden is dean of the School of Design and Production at the North Carolina School of the Arts:

[We] train students to go into professional careers, either as scene designers or costume designers or lighting designers. . . . We make sure they have a basic understanding and some training in all the areas. And as they progress and want [specifically] to be a lighting designer [for example], then they take more and more courses in those areas, and then their crew assignments are geared more toward their area of specialty . . . we don't seek out [high school students] . . . but every now and then you find [some] that know this is what they want, and just say, "Look, if I stay another year in the high school, I'm just going to be wasting my time," and that's true. . . . In Design & Production . . . you need things, you need lighting equipment, you need shop equipment, if you're going to try to practice the art. If you want to be an actor, you can always do it in a room . . . but for us, we need tangible things, and many high schools simply don't have that. So a student will come, say this is what I really want. . . .

[At most schools, design and production], more often than not, [is a department] within the drama program . . . [here, it] has a sort of separate but equal structure within the organization of the entire school . . . [which] can have its problems. Sometimes you feel maybe you're not as close to the performance side . . . that sometimes students could forget that [in addition to] learning to be good craftsmen, the reason for our exis-

Dec. 2
Louis Mennini, dean of the
School of Music, named acting
president.
Governor Dan Moore and Italian ambassador Sergio Fenoaltea announce plans for a
summer session for music students to be held in Siena, Italy
(International Music Program).

Dec. 10–11
School of Dance gives its first
performance of *The Nutcracker*
ballet to a capacity house in
Reynolds Auditorium. *The
Nutcracker* becomes a highly
successful yearly tradition involving students from every
area of arts study at NCSA.

1967

Jan. 5
Giorgio Ciompi appointed artistic director of Siena summer
session.

tence is performance. However, I think
the good thing about it is that we have
the opportunity to work in music and
dance as well as theater, where most [other
schools'] programs might just be limited
to working with theater. . . . [For ex-
ample], all four schools [work] together
when we do a musical. And then you get
music, dance, drama and design all working together at the same time. More often
than not, if we do a ballet, we've got at
least three out of the four working together because you'll have music, dance
and D&P, or you might do a small musical just with the drama school, then you
have a bit of music, drama and D&P. . . .
It's a little easier working with the drama
school because you're working with scripts
. . . you're not writing the play as you go
along. When you're working with dance,
particularly on a new piece, it becomes
very complicated because you may not
know from one day to the next how it's
going to evolve. . . .

I think what makes the [design and
production] program unique is the school
itself, the students and faculty and our
situation and the atmosphere of the school,
in that we are here to train people for professional careers. And that's what, I guess,
really would make the difference. I can remember once when I was an undergraduate at [the university], several of the
faculty at Chapel Hill thought it was de-
meaning to think of going into theater
professionally. That kind of attitude is
strange, creates a strange atmosphere.

Feb. 24
Osvaldo Riofrancos resigns as
dean of drama.

Mar. 3
Governor Moore announces
the appointment of Robert
Ward as NCSA president.

Mar. 20
Five students from NCSA give
a concert for Governor and
Mrs. Moore and members of
the General Assembly.

Apr. 17
Clive Barnes, dance and drama
critic for the *New York Times,*
visits NCSA.

Apr. 28–29, May 2–4, 6, 10–13
William Woodman directs *Tar-
tuffe* for NCSA School of
Drama.

Robert Ward:

From the very start, we all had very
mixed feelings about [becoming a part of
the university]. On the one hand, we
knew that if all of the other [state] institutions merged . . . and we were left out,
this would aggravate our problem with
the legislature, and we felt that if there
were bad times economically or any sort
of recession in the state, we could imagine
[their] trying to close the school down,
and if we had to fight this all alone, it
would have been very difficult. So from
that standpoint, the umbrella of the university had certain advantages. . . . In the
recession in 1972, I think it's entirely possible . . . that the school might have been
closed down . . . just on a budgetary
matter, nothing else. . . . They did shut
down one of the other special schools, the
Advancement School, at that time.

Gordon Hanes:

Gosh, we were treading on thin ice for
years. . . . You see, [there] is another
problem with the legislature. The legislature says there are too many out-of-state
students. We are training out-of-state students. So I appeared before the Appropriations Committee and I said, "Gentlemen,
we will make a deal with you. We can only
recruit people of innate talent and skill,
people who are just born to be good in
the arts. The only comparable thing is the
football team at Chapel Hill and State,
and the basketball team. Now, we will
maintain the same percentage of in-state
students that you maintain on the football
and the basketball teams at Chapel Hill

Spring
John Cone, academic dean,
resigns.

and State." . . . Well, there isn't any
[response to that]. I mean, they go recruiting at Pennsylvania and everywhere
else. There has never been 50 percent of
the football or basketball team in-state
anywhere in any state institution. And it
is based on talent, and damn it, you can't
find that many good football and basket-

June 2
Second high school class and
first college seniors graduate.

ball players in the state of North Carolina
or any state. Sure. Now we have maintained it about 50-50 and I think that is
remarkable. . . . Now, now, it is safe in my
opinion because there is not one of the
hundred counties that hasn't had two or
three kids at the school and they go back
and they sell it and their parents sell it. I

June 22
Ira Zuckerman appointed dean
of drama.

think it is safe now.

*Sam Stone is director of development for the
North Carolina School of the Arts
Foundation:*

There is much dispute and argument
about [our going under the umbrella of
the university system]. The years here in-

June 26
First summer school opens.

volved are during [Governor Bob Scott's]
administration and the formal switch time
was July 1, 1972. . . . We actually had the
option to be in it or not to be in it. And
there are many people who argue . . . that
we ought to be standing as one—that we
ought not . . . to get swallowed up in that

July 4
First season of Festival Theatre
(professional summer theater)
in cooperation with NCSA
and the Winston-Salem Arts
Council.

new big monster and the political power
of the Chapel Hill campus and the state
campus, the number of legislators that
they have—and so all of that was just too
big, and Paul Green was especially strong
in arguing. He just regretted and regretted that we were going to be a part of
this. Jim Semans had some sentiments
with him on that and raised the questions

July 9–Sept. 1
First Siena summer session
(International Music Program)
begins.

July 22
John Iuele appointed conductor of NCSA Orchestra after
Saul Caston resigns.

Sept.
Marion Tatum Fitz-Simons appointed acting academic dean.

Oct.
Performers from the Schools of
Dance, Drama, and Music tour
state high schools.

very hard with us, and I think that question still sticks with Jim to a degree, as to whether it was the right thing. . . . I don't think many of our students or faculty really could comprehend the importance of doing it either one way or the other. The administrators here, right from the beginning—now this is in the Ward administration and not the Suderburg one— were pretty clear in thinking that their advantages weighed in favor of us being in. What we could see was that being a part of that structure would be a buffer. We were sorely pressed with the problems of fighting for budget considerations . . . being an oddball—the institution not having friends and advocates, no protection, no buffer. Ward himself would describe the circumstances of going before hearings of the legislative communities . . . and the school of the arts comes up after the Highway Department. Well, there's big yawns in the room. The Highway Department's a huge budget with many great consequences, many public works implications, employment freebies all over the place. School of the arts comes up next—"Well, we can really take a snooze now, this will be funny—ha, ha—what are the tippy-toe folks doing today?" And those are bad circumstances, and we couldn't get anybody to take us seriously, and our budget was so small relative to everybody else's. . . .

It looked like we had a lot to gain. I think it was the right move to make. Now you get what happens, being a part of this system . . . you get all locked in to all the line-item structures and the expectations of earned degrees. All that is something

Oct. 20–22, 24–26, 28–29
Paul Widner directs *The Importance of Being Earnest* for NCSA School of Drama.

Nov. 8
William Schuman, president of Lincoln Center for the Performing Arts, is featured speaker at NCSA "Evening with the Arts."

Dec. 8–10, 12–17
Englishman Malcolm Black directs *Enrico IV* for NCSA School of Drama.

1968

Jan. 26
Cellist Irving Klein and thirteen NCSA cello students leave for Puerto Rico to study for one week with Pablo Casals.

over which we have to fight at times because we want to plead always for exceptions. We don't fit everybody's expectations in all the indices that they use to measure institutions. We think that there are [other measurements] that are more important that apply to us, and so [for example] we always have more space per student than other campuses. . . .

Robert Ward:

There's no question in my view that the school has lost something. The board has none of the kind of authority it had then because at that time, the board chose the chancellor and approved all of the major staff positions and was a much closer board to the institution. . . . we knew that much of the power which at that moment was in the hands of our own Board of Trustees would get put into the hands of the Board of Governors [of the University of North Carolina], where, again, we would be the rather smallest school of all, and the most specialized school of all, having to try to get a little attention within that very big set-up. . . . Now all of the top positions have to go through the university where you're dealing with people who have close ties with one of the other institutions and [the school] simply does not get the [same] kind of attention. . . .

Sam Stone:

None of us are ever going to be happy until [the school is] more and better accepted, [is given] more attention. But historically, just by accident, one of the best things that ever happened to us was the

Mar.
Lawrence O. Carlson appointed academic dean.

Mar. 20
Rockefeller Foundation grant establishes Piedmont Chamber Players (Piedmont Chamber Orchestra), NCSA Professional Affiliate.

May 6
Governor Dan Moore and the Council of State officially accept the deeding of 14.8 acres of land to the state (Gray Building property) from NCSA Foundation.

May 12
Groundbreaking ceremonies for new college dormitories.

fact that President Friday's [William Friday, president of the Consolidated University of North Carolina] daughter was a student here in high school and college, and that gave him a reason to have interest in us, in a point of access that was exceptional, extraordinary. That may be one of the best things by chance that ever happened to us. Fortunately for us, Betsy has stayed with her career and has done very well. Of course, that meant, too, that he knew more about us than maybe he should have known, but he is a very civil, humane, tolerant, human being—a good politician and good educator, and he always seeks the best for us. We don't have any doubt about that. In a transition, there'll be questions, but the big item is simply the accomplishments and the achievements of the school. Nobody any longer can argue [about] our distinction or say that we're not paying our way—it would just be impossible to argue.

Robert Ward:
For instance . . . it will be a rare [dance program] in which, when you read the backgrounds of the dancers, some of them haven't come from the school of the arts. The list of those music students who have been at the school of the arts and now are in symphony orchestras around the country is a long one. . . . Our actors are appearing in films, broadway, and TV with some regularity, and our design and production school people are in demand all over the country because they come from the broadest training that you can get anywhere. And they all have had experience with straight drama, dance, opera,

24. NCSA dance faculty, left to right: Sonja Tyven, Dean Robert Lindgren, Agnes de Mille, Pauline Koner (Archives of the North Carolina School of the Arts).

June 5
Commencement exercises at
NCSA, with President Robert
Ward as speaker.

June 7–July 27
Siena summer session.

musicals and in a variety of different kinds of theater, so they are very well prepared. . . .

My personal view is that the budgets are never the problem—not the first problem. The first problem is whether there is a vision and creative excitement. . . . Despite budgetary problems which are hitting everything in the arts these days, those institutions which are coming up with exciting things . . . can expand. . . . That kind of thing means being very sensitive to those changing currents that are going on in the arts with audiences, with students, with everyone else. . . . My experience was that [going] back to foundations or agencies that had money to give, for

Aug. 4
Igor Buketoff to conduct first
series of concerts by Piedmont
Chamber Players.

Sept.
Ronald Pollock appointed
director of newly created
Department of Design and
Production.

Oct. 16
Sidney Blackmer visits NCSA,
speaks to student body.

Oct. 31
Dancer/choreographer José
Limon gives lecture/demon-
stration at NCSA.

more of the same thing that other places
were doing—no, you'd find it very difficult. But the exciting things that we did,
the creative things . . . there were no problems. The Ford Foundation grant came
through immediately on that basis. It was
because it was a stimulating, wonderful
new idea. And when those are around,
you find people that are interested.

*Agnes de Mille served on the Advisory Board
of Artists who selected Winston-Salem as the
site for the North Carolina School of the Arts:*
Oh, goodness me. I went down there
and lived there for a time [in 1973]. I lived
in Bob Ward's house . . . the head of the
school. He opened his home to me. He
and his wife, Mary, took me in, I lived
there. I launched my company from there.
It was made up largely of North Carolina
students and I used to work every evening
from 6 to 9, or 9:30. Those are difficult
hours to have, because the students are exhausted, and I had been exhausted waiting all day. But they were the only hours
they could give me. They had to do their
academics, and they had to do a certain
amount of routine dancing that was required to get through what they had to
do. But then they came to me, and
worked hard. I made [the dances] up on
the students, right there in the gymnasium. They were all Americana. That
was the nature of the thing. I taught them
how to do the square dances, and all that.
I did a big piece called Texas Fourth in
which they learned all the dances of the
thirties, the Big Apple, which was a
dance, long before it was a city. . . .

Nov. 21
Violinist Yehudi Menuhin visits
NCSA.

When I took the company out for six to eight weeks the first time, they all got school credit for that time. [Bob Ward] said to me, "We're in the business to train these people to be professionals. They're going to learn and be baptised in fire with you. You're paying them."

I paid them Equity wages. They nearly went mad, they didn't have money like this. Equity wages are very good. I know when they went to California, they went up one day for an afternoon in San Francisco from Santa Barbara, paying their own way, and having a high old time. They'd never dreamt of life like that. It was quite wonderful. But Ward said, "They are learning."

1969

Feb.
Dancer/actress Valerie Bettis works with NCSA dance students for two weeks.

Mel Tomlinson, who was the great treasure boy of this school, he's a star, a real, true one. When he first came to New York to rehearse with me, he got off the bus and saw what it was like in New York City, and burst into tears, went to a phone, and called Gyula Pandi, who was acting as my registrar. "Gyula, I cannot go alone to the rehearsal hall. Come get me." He was eighteen, six-foot-four, and Gyula had to go down there and take him like a baby by the hand, lead him to a taxi and get him to the rehearsal hall. He is now one of the stars of the New York City Ballet, and has been all over the world. I get postcards from him from Tokyo, Oslo, Istanbul, you name it.

Feb. 17
NCSA's production of Oliver Goldsmith's *She Stoops to Conquer* one of ten finalists in American College Theatre Festival. The ten finalists perform at Ford's Theatre in Washington, D.C., in May.

Feb. 22
Dancer/choreographer Ron Davis conducts master classes at NCSA.

Most ballet students are simply not educated at all. They get just enough to get past the state examination and not go to jail. They really don't know a thing, don't care, and never read a book. I don't

Mar. 19
Ira Zuckerman, dean of the
School of Drama, resigns effec-
tive June 30.

Mar. 25
Ronald Pollock, director of the
Department of Design and
Technical Production, ap-
pointed acting dean of drama
effective July 1.

June 6
Commencement exercises at
NCSA, with William Trotman
(actor, director, designer, and
former associate director of
drama) as the commencement
speaker.

July 13–Sept. 1
Third Siena summer session.
First summer session for dance
students in Asolo, Italy.

think that's true of the students of North
Carolina. They are taught things.

The fact that they're rubbing elbows in
the hall, in the cafeteria, and everywhere,
with young musicians, who think just as
highly of their trade, and young artists
who think just as highly, and are rabidly
enthusiastic about what they're doing.
They then meet on the stage and pool
efforts and resources. Now that is enlarg-
ing and it is spiritually very, very beneficial. These are going to be cosmopolitan
students. When I was there, from time to
time, things would happen that affected
the whole school. I remember Marcel
Marceau came. They stopped the school.
They stopped every class, and emptied
them out into the big gymnasium. Marceau gave them a three-hour talk and
demonstration. Now, you wouldn't find
that in every school. They'd still be practicing football somewhere. I don't think
you have a football team yet, do you?

I think the most significant thing about
the school is that the students are living in
a very pleasant environment, learning to
read and write and something of history,
mathematics, some smattering of sciences,
all that's good. And also they're learning
that there are several arts, all equally important—that is, that there are several disciplines of the mind toward expression of
ideas and emotions—that there isn't just
one. [Many ballet students] are medical
wrecks, and they haven't got an idea in
their heads. Their idea of dancing is to
keep a perfect *pointe*, keep a perfect line,
to stay in line. But the idea of going on
the stage and expressing something that

Fall
Work begins on Commons
Building (Student Union).

Oct.
Lower campus housing
completed.

1970

Jan. 22
John Iuele resigns as conductor
of the NCSA Orchestra.

Feb.
Valerie Bettis returns to the
school to work with modern
dancers.

means something to an audience, they
wouldn't know what you are talking
about. But I think the North Carolina
students would.

Robert Lindgren:
    [Vittorio Giannini] spelled out to me
very clearly the objectives of the school
. . . to train people when their talent
manifested that that training should take
place. In other words, here was a school
that could take twelve-year-old dancers
and not eighteen or nineteen-year-old college people. . . . Here was a school that
basically was going to start dancing at a
time when [the students] were young
enough to really be trained, and that was
the simple thing. . . . Could you train
young people who have no cultural background in dance, who have very little
training or no training? and could you set
up a program that would train people?
That was it.
Dance was never offered in the . . . secondary or elementary schools. . . . You
had to do it through private teaching and
then go to college. Well, a lot of trouble in
the training is that anybody can teach.
There's no license or law which says you
have to pass certain criteria to teach. So a
lot of people are receiving inferior training. People in colleges are being taught
[dancing] by people who have come out
of physical education departments . . . if
you wanted your daughter taught the arts,
you'd want to have [her] taught by an artist . . . who knows it from every angle,
not just from some books. . . . A coach of
a basketball team or football team isn't
usually somebody that doesn't know any-

Mar.
NCSA Foundation purchases
the home of the late Mrs. Fred
F. Bahnson, Sr., at 28 Cascade
Avenue for use as the home of
the school's president.

Mar.
Lawrence O. Carlson, aca-
demic dean, to leave NCSA
effective March 31.

May 8–16
Englishman Barry Boys directs
A Midsummer Night's Dream at
NCSA, with original music
and choreography.

May 21
William H. Baskin appointed
academic dean. Ronald Pollock
appointed dean of the School
of Drama.

thing about the sport other than from
learning it in college. You have done it,
you know all aspects of it . . . how much,
how severe, when times are to put girls on
point, when not to put them on point,
when boys can lift. I mean, it just is something only a professional knows, and how
can you explain to young people what
being in a dance company is like if you've
never been in a dance company? what
kind of energy you have to have, what
kind of intelligence you have to have,
what kind of an attitude you have to have
to get along with the choreographer, what
a choreographer is, how he works. I
mean, there are just all these questions.
[Many] ordinary dancing schools are just
physical, just for physical exercise or grace
or poise or for whatever reason, but
they're not to train dancers, many of
them. . . .

No other school in America . . . has the
facilities for educating academically or for
boarding students. That was the big thing
here. All the students were here on campus, they were captive. They didn't go
home at night and . . . they could receive
their education and their arts at the same
time. One of the problems of young people
going to New York now, even [to] the
School of American Ballet, is whether
they can get into professional children's
school, and whether that works out, and
how expensive it is for parents to send
their children there, and then again, living, for young people, in New York is impossible—very difficult to find a place to
live in New York City for a young twelve-
or thirteen-year-old. . . . The fact that
they could parallel their education and

May 30
Commencement exercises,
with Agnes de Mille as commencement speaker.

Summer
NCSA Theater undergoing
renovations.

June 15–Aug. 13
Fourth Siena summer session
enrolls ninety-three student
musicians. Dance students
make their headquarters in
Asolo for the second con-
secutive NCSA Summer Dance
Tour in Italy (Aug. 3–24), with
Jacques d'Amboise, premier
danseur of the New York City
Ballet, to perform and teach.
Camerata Chamber Singers de-
but in both Italy and Austria
July 30–August 9.

arts growth was extraordinary, because if
you go to the American School of Ballet,
you usually say, okay, we're going to give
up academics and practice just dance, and
concentrate on that, and live the best we
can in an unsupervised situation in New
York City. . . .

We also could put the best dancers with
the best dancers, and select them by audition. You see, we weren't going to be a
school that was just paying overhead and
therefore the amount of students that
came in to us was important. How many
times a week they studied—that's a commercial concern and [for] the school of
the arts, that wasn't a concern at all. . . .

We're the only conservatory I know of
that reauditions every single year and
sometimes says no, you can't come back.
That's maybe tough on some of the students, but in the long run a football player
doesn't hang around if the coach thinks
he's no good . . . or you don't make it to
medical school if you can't make the grade
average, so why do it in the arts? People
that are not meeting that higher standard
. . . you have to weed them out and make
room for the people who can.

*Composer Robert Suderburg served as chan-
cellor of the North Carolina School of the
Arts, 1974–1983:*
[Elizabeth and I] were leaving Philadelphia in 1966–67 . . . and at that time,
there was a lot of talk about this new
school starting with Vittorio, and a lot of
people were looking at it for jobs, and so
on, from the Philadelphia/New York area,
in music, which of course I knew the
most. . . . I only met [Vittorio] when we

June 28
Governor Robert Scott and
family attend NCSA Orchestra
concert in Siena.

July 16
School of Drama begins first
summer session in England in
conjunction with Rose Bruford
College. Dame Sybil Thorn-
dike to be guest of honor at
opening dinner.

Aug. 3
Robert Lindgren, dean of the
School of Dance, and four of
his dancers appear on NBC's
"Today Show" with Jacques
d'Amboise.

Aug. 5
Martha Hill Davies, head of
the Juilliard School dance department, holds choreography
workshop.

were in Philadelphia, and one of my
friends in Philadelphia was one of his students way back at Manhattan. And, of
course, I had heard a lot about him because the person who was head of my
School of Music at Washington . . . and
Vittorio were office-mates at Juilliard for
years. . . .

Well, Vittorio was an enthusiast, and he
had an 85% con level in the sense that he'd
convince you of anything, even if it were
totally impossible, because he believed it,
and he also . . . he was a vitalizer in life.
And he just really made things alive. And
I think that was such a nerve-firing part of
this whole process . . . that in no way can
you qualify or criticize it. There was
a great deal of con in it, because anybody who wants to have a school with all
of the performing arts together—that's in
the area of starry wish fulfillment, and
anybody with any practical sense would
never try to do anything like this. But Vittorio . . . Vittorio, at least as seen
through the eyes of his students that I
knew, was this light quotient. He was a
vitalizer. And in that sense he was absolutely a unique force in the founding of
the institution. Only one of the many
forces, however. I mean, he wasn't the
sole reason that it happened, but he sure
made it live. I mean, for example, last
week I was out in San Francisco to see
the final performances of "Jazz Is" at the
Bohemian Club. This is the tour that is
sponsored by R. J. Reynolds. And a
couple of the students, who are now
alumni, who were in the show as musicians, and I were sitting down and talking. . . . They remembered when they

25. NCSA Chancellor Robert Suderburg (Archives of the North Carolina School of the Arts).

Aug. 31
John A. Sneden accepts post of dean of the School of Design and Production.
New Student Commons Building provides site for registration.

Sept.
NCSA inaugurates high school Visual Arts Program.
North Carolina Dance Theatre formed by Dean Robert Lindgren.

Oct. 22
World premiere of Agnes de Mille's ballet *A Rose For Miss Emily*.

Nov. 2
City-county school board agrees to sell Gray Building to the state of North Carolina.

were new students, a lot of them from the rural South, and Vittorio was wandering around here keeping everybody alive and happy—they were first-year students—stimulated and so on. And they really not only treasure, but regard that as a source of vitality to this day. And a goal to this day. And the reason they brought it up is they thought this whole thing was so representative of what they found at the school to begin with. . . . So those are my impressions of Vittorio. . . . He was the saintly kind of person that everybody talks about. And to be a saintly person and also on a scam . . . is really quite an accomplishment.

Well, Bob [Ward] was here at a time when you really had to face a lot of not only fiscal but operational management issues which were not faced at the opening of the school. I mean . . . the school was started and "let's have a school" and no one thought how much it would cost, what kind of positions you would need to run it, and you know, you just went ahead and did it. Which if they hadn't done, it wouldn't have been here. So Bob was left with—you know when Vittorio died so unexpectedly, Bob was left not only with a fireman's job in terms of trying to keep things going, but in a sense, of putting together, operational, from all the way down, the levels of the school, personnel, things that would make it work. And also there was an expansion from roughly two hundred to five hundred-some students over those seven years that Bob was chancellor. And that was one part of it that was so difficult. . . . Then there was the problem of the school becoming part of

1971

Jan. 3
Nicholas Harsanyi named dean
of the School of Music, after
Louis Mennini resigns.

Jan. 8
Camerata Chamber Singers
leave for Israel to participate in
the Jerusalem Festival of
American College Choirs.

Feb. 23
Andrés Segovia conducts a
master class at NCSA.

Mar. 11–14
Composer Aaron Copland attends Copland Festival held
at NCSA.

the university or not. And this was something that put another level of political,
bureaucratic process and responsibility on
the chancellor and on the institution. And
he was really faced with a situation where
the school had expanded and expanded
beyond bounds for which either the state
or the foundation was willing to pay for
it. . . . So part of that had a mythical quotient in it because the school was run on
rubber bands and virtually pittance of actual operation money. And that, of course,
had something to do with the politics,
who wants a school of the arts? and particularly because the school, those years,
which were years of controversy all over
the country as far as college students, had
to be kept low profile. It couldn't go out
and be aggressive politically. So on one
hand, your hands are tied there and on
the other, they're tied because the resources are not available. So that it was
really quite an accomplishment to get the
school to the point that it was in
1974. . . .

[I had learned about the school] from a
lot of sources . . . I remember reading an
article about Agnes de Mille's Heritage
Dance Theatre in the *Saturday Review*.
Then some people that I knew in the
business sent their kids to the International Music Program. . . . That
was one of the things that worked very
well in establishing [the school's] reputation in the music business, which is probably one of the harder places. . . . And as
far as the Drama School, I learned a little
bit about it much later, because I ran into
a couple of graduates who worked in Act
Theatre in Seattle. . . . about what was

Mar. 18
Conductor André Previn visits
NCSA.

Apr. 28
New York violin dealer announces he has found the rare
Amati violin stolen from a
parked car in New York City
while on loan to the Claremont Quartet.

May
Cellist Janos Starker and violinist Josef Gingold present
monthly repertory seminars
at NCSA.

May 10–12
Pianist Anthony di Bonaven-
ture conducts master classes.

happening, and then secondarily, through
reading about it. . . . There was a fair
amount of publicity in those early years
primarily related to Agnes. And then
knowing some of the people who were
here, and that [was] a major part of it, because you pretty well, in the professional
schools around the country in your discipline, pretty well know who is where. . . .

[So, we came here] because of the nature of this institution, which is that it
deals with talent young and in a serious
way, and with serious performers from
the real world, not from some make-
believe world . . . and the individuals who
make it up were worth working with and
for . . . it was a chance for us to get back
East . . . to be with the most exciting
group of people you're ever going to run
into. . . .

The flexibility [of a chancellor] is defined very often by the quality of individual that you work with. And . . . if there
is any kind of basic aim in terms of the
last eight years here, [it's been] to get the
best, strongest, most qualified people in
this institution we possibly could. . . .
That, in a sense, does cut down on your
own flexibility because you have so much
strength around you, and very often, they
are in areas that they are better at, or
hopefully better at, than you are. In a
sense, they begin to define what you do,
rather than the other way around. And of
course, without that kind of development,
you don't have a healthy institution . . .
because I think the administration is supposed to support the deans. . . . One
of the things that we tried to do immediately . . . [was] to make sure that the per-

May 19
North Carolina Dance Theatre
established as a professional affiliate of the School of Dance
through a matching grant from
the Rockefeller Foundation.

June 5
Commencement exercises,
with speaker Joseph Papp,
founder and producer of New
York Shakespeare Festival Public Theatre.

June 14–Aug. 30
108 student musicians in Italy
for Siena summer session.
Third session in Asolo for
dance students (leave July 18
for one month). Second summer session of study for drama
students at Rose Bruford College near London (leave July 15
for six weeks).

son who is head of an area is head of it,
and doesn't get mucked around in by the
chancellor. And . . . you have to have the
resources to get that kind of person, and
that was one of the main distinctions between the first eight years and the last
eight years of the institution—because of
the state, and so on and so forth, there
were more resources to get that quality
level of person. . . . Well, my job, after I
can convince that kind of person to take
this institution as his own, is not only to
motivate him, but support him, and that's
not altruistic. Because the more I support
what they want to do, the better their area
is going to be run, and of course, I have a
conscience function and a review function, but in the long run, it's a matter of
stimulus and support and conscience if
you get the right kind of people. The
hardest thing is getting the right kind of
people. And they have to believe in you,
and they have to want to give as much as
you do, and they have to be professionally
competent and those are big orders. . . .
I'm obviously very proud of this staff, and
the faculty, and so on, because most of
them are new in the last eight years, and
in a sense, I have paternal ownership. But
the point is, I try to get people who are
better than I am and who know, in their
areas, what to do. I am supposed to support them. I'm not going to tell them
what to do. . . .

The newness of our institution is, of
course, one of the problems [that we have
with the university]. I mean . . . we have
to consistently make cases of exceptions
because we are exceptional, whether they
like it or not. And they have been very re-

Oct. 13
Piazza Artom and geometric
sculpture "The Elephants" (by
NCSA instructor Robin Cos-
telloe) dedicated.

Oct. 14
After feasibility study, NCSA
drops immediate plans to buy
the Carolina Theatre.

Oct. 30
Bill restructuring state-
supported colleges and universities under UNC governing
board enacted into law.

ceptive over the years to helping us solve
rather serious problems and not only solving the problems, but helping to provide
funding for them. I think that there will
always be a fair amount of strain because
of the unit-cost measure of this institution. [The university allots each member
institution X number of dollars per student for maintenance, and so on.] . . . We
cannot play the enrollment-increase-to-
gain-positions game, because we deal in
such small numbers. . . . The way the
standard division is within the university,
you get two extra faculty for X number of
students. Well, you get like one-sixth of a
[secretary] . . . and it really doesn't work
for us . . . that unit-cost measure. You
don't have the size and it means that inevitably you are always working under
this onus of one foot in the slums and one
foot in the stars. Which may be a good
stance for life, I don't know. But it makes
it difficult when the roofs are in ill repair.
. . . The university hasn't put much in
here at all in the way of facilities. Now
granted, we have the Workplace. But . . .
there has been far more private money put
into here than public money, and their argument, of course, is the unit-cost thing.
. . . You know, Bill's daughter was here,
and Bill [Friday] knows the school very
well. I mean, they all know it very well at
this point, and they're great advocates because outside of Chapel Hill, this is the
one nationally creditable, quality place in
the system. Now that's not saying anything against the other institutions. But
we do have a national stature, and this reflects well on the university and all of the
way down the line. And we do get the

Nov. 10
Mime artist Marcel Marceau
conducts lecture/demonstration
at NCSA.

1972

Apr. 21
NCSA School of Drama
presents *The Little Foxes* at the
Kennedy Center in Washing-
ton, for the American College
Theatre Festival.

June 1
NCSA announces overhaul of
the school's main auditorium
and drama theatre.

best students in the arts in the system,
and in the region, and in certain areas of
our school, in the country. So in that
sense, it's very good. They believe in it,
and of course, we've tried to broaden the
base far beyond the university. But they
always get to a point where they have to
unit-cost it, and therefore it's got to be a
special political movement to get this for
the school or that for the school, and we
end up always scraping to put operations
together. Now, I think that they understand the mission of the school, and they
have responded to all of the various problems we have had over these eight years,
and I think that a great deal of the credit
for the school now getting to a stable,
creditable point in its fiscal operations had
a lot to do with the university's help. . . .
But the problems now are going to be
pecking order. And Chapel Hill has always got to be first. . . . I think that this
school has to continue to make its case
both within and without the university,
because they will respond to political
pressure like the rest of the world. One is
always frustrated in the placement of the
school with regard to how much money
comes for this area or that area or that
area. But you always have to deal with
that argument.

Speaking of goals . . . one of the things
that I tried to make happen the first
couple of years I was here [is better exchange among the departments]. Each of
them has a very strong, independent discipline. . . . For example, the orchestra
hadn't really accompanied the dance
school prior to 1975–76 because that was
regarded as a "pit" job. Well, there have

June 10
Commencement exercises,
with speaker Jean Dalrymple,
producer emeritus of the New
York City Center of Music and
Drama and member of NCSA
Advisory Board of Artists.

June 12–Aug. 1
Siena summer session enrolls
ninety-nine students.

June 21
Visual arts students leave for
four weeks of study in Ireland.

July 1
Sixteen North Carolina institutions of higher education
merge under new UNC sys-
tem. NCSA now a component
of UNC.

been gains in that, but there will always
be a motion forward/backward depending
upon what the show is, what the situation
is, what the attitude at this particular time
with this particular group of students or
faculty is, to a musician playing in the pit,
or a dancer dancing in a theater production or—it's highly encouraged by some
of the members of the school. And, of
course, I strongly believe in this, because I
think musicians should know how to
move, dancers should know music, and
actors should regard speeches as gestures
in sound the same way musicians do. I
mean the common ground is the individual and his perceptive apparatus and the
way he thinks. I mean, that's given to all
the disciplines. . . . This is the way you
communicate, through this means—dancing, singing, whatever. And one can learn
from the other very well, but that already
assumes a sophistication level that sometimes is not present because you are training young students. . . . The whole
touring concept, the whole putting a
major winter dance on [*The Nutcracker*]
with the orchestra, has been very beneficial to the kids. They've liked it, they've
enjoyed it. We've gotten to a point now
where the conductor of the orchestra, and
the kids in the orchestra in these circumstances, they do not complain like they
used to five years ago. . . . And that's
fairly healthy, because a lot of them will
get jobs doing that.

Dean Robert Lindgren:
    Musicians only want to play on the con-
cert stage within the school. They always
think of themselves as concert artists who

July 13
Drama students leave for London for their third annual summer session at Rose Bruford College.

Oct. 24
NCSA's student employment bureau, "Applause," is formed.

Nov. 17–18
NCSA presents William Schuman Festival, with composer in attendance.

Dec. 1
NCSA Foundation purchases the South Main Street Church of Christ to be used initially as a recital hall.

specifically play on the stage. . . . But they don't know whether they're going to be pit musicians or combo musicians or quartets or quintets or play for the opera or ballet or for what. They may have great dreams of playing in the New York Philharmonic or the Philadelphia Symphony—that's their goal. But they don't want to play accompaniment, and Bob [Suderberg] at least was a strong believer that the school orchestra should accompany dance. And also he's encouraged me in my choice of choreographers and music. You know, he's always looking for something as a musician himself, he realizes that choreographers use his music, and probably it is played sometimes as much to choreography as it is with orchestras.

Robert Suderburg:

[Our] goal is to provide a place for the artist in society which is supportive, and also takes more responsibility than simply giving him a degree, but the entrance into the profession. And that's one of the things that attracted me about the school. Because I knew it was networked with the various professions in one degree or another, and that's really totally important. I mean, you can't go to some small college in any state and then expect to get into the profession. You have to go somewhere that's already networked in the profession. . . . Now we are under eight students per faculty member, and that student/teacher ratio is something we have to keep. And if you get more than thirty drama students a year, you completely destroy the basis of the curriculum which

1973

Jan. 27
Film actress Jean Arthur appears as guest artist with the NCSA Orchestra, narrating *Peter and the Wolf.*

Feb. 14–18, 20–24
Albert Millaire directs *The Misanthrope* for NCSA School of Drama.

Mar. 1
NCSA's main auditorium to be named Crawford Hall in honor of the first president of the NCSA Foundation, R. B. Crawford, Jr. Renovations on the hall completed later in the year.

ends up with this number of highly motivated, talented actors going out on the road in their last year and have been getting jobs. This year [1982] we had between five hundred to six hundred applications for that one class of thirty people, new students. So we're not going to have any trouble with applications. . . . And I think the quality level—the basic goal is to get absolutely the best students you can possibly get to apply to this school, pick the best of those and train them the best way you can, and also provide them with the kind of support necessary, and the kind of support the faculty needs. And this is not only salary, scholarship, and facilities, but this is the kind of emotional aura that *this* is where it can happen. Because we really believe in what you are doing, and we're going to work our tails off to make sure that society believes it also.

Malcolm Morrison is dean of the School of Drama at the North Carolina School of the Arts:
    Yes, originally I was a policeman . . . I left school at sixteen. I found that the British educational system . . . was entirely inappropriate for my particular ambitions . . . I wanted to go into the theater, but my father would not allow it. He did not quite see how one could portray life if you've never seen it. So, to get a slice of life, I guess, I turned up in the police force, and I stayed there until I was twenty-one. And then, I went to the Rose Bruford College of Speech and Drama, which is one of the top six drama schools in the country, and at that time, it was run by Rose Bruford herself, who was quite a

Apr. 9
Helen Hayes, acclaimed actress
and member of NCSA's Ad-
visory Board of Artists, visits
the school.

Apr. 13–14
NCSA presents opera by
Chancellor Robert Ward, *He
Who Gets Slapped.*

Apr. 26–29
Choreographer Agnes de Mille
stages Heritage Dance Theatre
at school.

June 2
Commencement exercises held,
with modern dancer and actress Carmen deLavallade as
speaker.

remarkable teacher . . . we had classes
from John Gielgud and Dame Peggy Ash-
croft and innumerable sort of luminaries
of the British theater. And through these
connections, actually out of drama school,
I was offered directing assignments in regional theaters and quite a few acting jobs
as well. . . . [When I came over to do *The
Caucasian Chalk Circle* as a guest director]
. . . it seemed to me that this was a quite
remarkable institution, and I had had the
benefit of floating all over the world, and I
hadn't really come across anywhere that
was quite like this. It was so exhilarating
. . . just the general sort of ambiance or
the kind of vision of the place and the
commitment of the community to the
place. If you work in London or any of
those major metropolises and do theater,
you don't really contact your audience at
all. You have no idea who they are—and
the idea of doing theater for people that
you could actually know seemed to me to
be very exciting. So, when I was offered
the job, you know, I had to really think
deeply because it was quite a dramatic
change. Most of my friends thought I
was nuts. You know, "Why do you want
to go to Winston-Salem? That's where the
witches were." And it was incredible, the
sort of misinformation and the lack of information and you know, they had no
idea that it was a place like this and neither did I. . . . The British theater . . . is
very institutionalized and there is something that diminishes the creativity in it.
And I just feel that the American theater
is about to blossom. I don't think it has
reached its peak yet, and I think that it's
finding its own indigenous form, and it's

June 14
Seventeen NCSA dance students leave for four-week program in Italy.

June 17–Aug. 18
International Music Program (formerly the Siena summer session) holds period of residence on campus before touring Italy and Switzerland.

July 13
Crawford Hall dedicated at intermission of a North Carolina Summer Festival Concert by the Festival Orchestra and its guest artist, Janos Starker.

finding its own playwrights, and its own actors, and its own style. And . . . I just felt that it would be exciting to be part of something, you know.

They had very limited facilities. I mean, my office was in the high school dorm. And I had innumerable sort of baby ballerinas of twelve and thirteen years of age sort of drifting by the door calling in "hi" in squeaky voices. There was one secretary who quit when I came . . . I mean, before I came, I am happy to say. So, I arrived the first day, standing in a dorm room, with no secretary, nobody with any kind of past association administratively with the School of Drama with the exception of Lesley Hunt. . . . The studios frankly, were pretty awful. One had been an old shower room and it was very clear that that was exactly what it was, with the pillars in the middle of the room so that every actor sort of had to peer around the pillars at each other. And then, about four studios, two with concrete floors, which is just great for movement classes, and that was about it. . . . The plans were extant for the new work place. And I had obviously looked those over very closely, and . . . I remember Bobby Lindgren and I—it was like the war of the worlds, because Bobby had made a deal with Ron Pollock to take over about half of the offices that were given to the School of Drama, for the Dance School. And we stood on the site one Sunday afternoon and I swear you could hear our voices reverberating down in Wachovia. Where I was staking a claim for the return of the drama offices. I can tell the story because Bobby and I actually get on very well to-

Sept. 14
Chancellor Robert Ward announces his resignation effective January 15. Ward takes
leave from school beginning
October 15 to work on his
opera. Martin Sokoloff named
acting chancellor.

Oct. 14–15
Dorothy Delay, professor of
violin at Juilliard, conducts
master classes.

Oct. 22
UNC Board of Governors approves request from NCSA for
a multipurpose building on the
school's campus.

Oct. 30–Nov. 2
Hungarian violinist and con-
ductor Tibor Varga conducts
NCSA Orchestra.

gether and admire each other and now it's
a matter of humor between us, but then it
was of extreme intensity. The facilities
were pretty well taken care of but there
were some grave mistakes. For example,
there was no provision of showers, which
is preposterous if you've got an intensive
movement program for actors. But of
course, [back] then it was postulated on
the program as it was being run, and there
was not really a hefty movement component to the training. . . .

It seemed that everybody was so eager
to develop the drama school. We were
very conscious that maybe it was lagging
behind the School of Music and the
School of Dance. . . . I first of all made
each of the four years of training very discrete. There was no interaction. I stopped
the interaction between years because it
seemed to me, first of all, we had to halt
the attrition. Secondly, we had to show
clear progress of training. It was possible
to come to this school and, although performances are a very important part of the
training experience, it was possible to
come to this school and never appear in a
main stage production. Mainly because
the casting was competitive. It was mainly
done by the faculty and they could choose
whomever they liked out of the school,
so, you could come in here as a freshman
and take a main stage role and the guy
who'd been here for four years was still
playing servants, and that to me is unac-
ceptable. So, I gave no performance at all
to the freshmen until they had a basis in
technique; that they got training in movement, in voice and speech and textual
analysis. In fact, prepared their minds,

Dec. 3–14
Duncan Noble's "A Cavalcade
of Music Theatre" tours state
high schools.

1974

Mar. 8
Robert Suderburg named
chancellor of NCSA.

May 18
Ceremony unveiling a portrait
of Vittorio Giannini is held.
The portrait was a gift to
the school from Dr. James H.
Semans.

June 1
Commencement exercises held
at NCSA, with speaker Na-
nanne Porcher, lighting director for the American Ballet
Theatre in New York.

bodies and emotions to be actors. The
second year, I did their performance experience in studio productions, where they
perform only for the School of Drama,
for their colleagues and faculty. And those
are without costumes. The actor[s], I believe, [are] responsible for the transforma-
tion of the space and the experience, so
they only have themselves as a resource.
The workshop productions, which are
mounted and given to the public, are
done at the moment in the church, which
is a beautiful black box space, really, it is
terrific to work in. I think it's the best
space that we've got. That was the juniors'
responsibility and then, in your final year,
you perform in the major productions
which were given in the de Mille [Theater]
and now with the Stevens Center, some of
them are done there as well. That did two
things. First of all, it established a progress and it halted the attrition because
people could see that there was a career
carrot at the end of this. That there were
certain things that you did at certain
stages of the program for which you have
no experience in the first place. The
fourth year was formed into a company,
and we developed a repertory system
where they play three plays in repertory.
Then those plays are taken on the road
and they go on a six-week tour up and
down the east coast. So, that by the time
they've left, they've had the experience of
playing in major houses, like the Stevens
Center, they've had the experience of playing repertory, they've had the experience
of touring and being responsible for their
own work. The other thing that I did was
to define the area of theater that we would

June 17–Aug. 21
International Music Program.
Dance students study in
Portugal.

July 16
Licia Albanese, former principal soprano with the Metropolitan Opera, is the guest
soloist at the NCSA Festival Orchestra Concert in Crawford Hall.

Sept.
Robert Barnett, artistic director of the Atlanta Ballet, conducts master classes.

Sept. 12
State Budget Office notifies
NCSA it will receive funds to
build a new library-classroom-
administration building.

be working on. You can't be an actor in
this present day and age, I think, without
being a reasonably literate individual. And
you need to know what the repertoire
available to you is, so I defined the first
year as basically inductive. The second
year, we work on a trimester, so each
term has a specific theme. And so, the first
term of the sophomore year was Modern American, the second term was
nineteenth-century realism, the third term
eighteenth-century and the Restoration;
then in the junior year modern/absurd, experimental and new plays, Shakespeare
and the Elizabethan theater, and then a
free choice. And then, finally, we dealt
with the seniors as a company, and chose
their repertoire accordingly. That seems to
work very well. That guarantees that those
students have had direct hands-on experience with material of each of those important genres, and I know it's not everything
that one could do, but they do seem to
me, looking across the basic repertoire of
the regional theaters in this country and
the basic fare that is available, it does seem
to me that they have experience in the
practical areas of the theater. I mean, sure
we could all go off and do, you know,
German Expressionism, but how often are
they going to need to do that? But they
will certainly probably do a Molière play.
Or they'll certainly have to do a Chekhov
or an Ibsen or a Shakespeare and certainly
they should know how to work with new
plays and playwrights, because that is
where the future of the American theater
is going to be. . . .

Since I've been here, we've set up a series of master classes and had some ex-

Sept. 18
Robert Suderburg formally installed as chancellor of NCSA.

Oct. 1
Twenty drama students leave for England for the School of Drama's first full school year of study abroad.

1975

Jan. 8
Ronald Pollock, dean of drama, resigns, effective August 1976.

Jan. 29
New NCSA scholarship named in honor of former North Carolina Governor Terry Sanford.

traordinary people during the intensive arts period, which is the final two weeks of the fall term. The general studies classes do not take place, and there are exclusively arts classes. So, I set up a program wherein we had a lot of the alumni that have done well for themselves in theater and films and television, and various other guests. . . . So it was an endless procession of people from ABC television, casting directors, and agents, and managements and actors and directors. Just connecting the students with the whole sort of background and the whole sort of network of theater. For some reason or another, you know, they watch things like "Fame" and it's about, you know, screaming your lungs out and bashing your feet all over the place, and being terribly exciting and "on" all the time. And then, as a result of that somebody sort of suddenly walks in one day and says "You are going to be famous." Well, of course, it's much more of a business than that. We have to make sure that they understand that and that they know how to deal with it. So one of the other things that we do in the fourth year is their résumés, how to write them, the kind of information that is good on them, good and bad résumés, there are photographs that have to be sent, what's a good photograph—you know, you can't send a snapshot of yourself with Auntie Lill in the back garden, you know, the last time she visited. It's quite extraordinary, the kind of misinformation, or the uncertainty that people have going into this business just because they don't get the information. You see, I think that it is interesting that in the American educational

Feb. 3
Classical guitarist Andrés
Segovia receives first honorary
Doctor of Fine Arts degree
awarded by NCSA.

Feb. 7
Agnes de Mille Theatre dedicated at black-tie affair by invitation only, featuring Miss
de Mille restaging her ballet
Three Virgins and a Devil.

May 31
Commencement exercises at
NCSA, with producer Peter
Zeisler delivering the address.

June 15–Aug. 8
International Music Program.

system, to my mind, there is much more
preparation for music and other forms of
art. The nearest that most of the people
get is the high school musical. . . . I mean,
it's too parochial—it doesn't really give
any one of them an experience of the
sheer grind of developing a voice. It takes
us four years of solid training with three
voice teachers here to get our students up
to a standard. Not only where the voice is
pleasant to listen to and the diction is
such that you can understand it, but where
you have developed enough stamina in
that physical instrument to play tough
roles nightly and not lose it. We talk about
their preparation . . . they have only seen
a kind of superficial view of what the
whole process is about, and we have to let
them know all those other areas.

One of the things that I think I drew
from [Rose Bruford's] which I think has
been most helpful for me here, is the connection between the actual training, the
drama school itself, and the actual profession. . . . You know, on that golden day
when everybody is given their little diploma and told they are actors, what was
the next step? Where were they to go? . . .
Whether you be a lawyer or a doctor or a
surgeon or an actor, quite often those sort
of affiliations, those sort of little networks
that emerge between the educational process and the actual practice, are very, very
important for the establishment of a career. I guess that I learned that out of
drama school. It was through Rose Bruford's. . . . So that I think I made it my
first mission, when I came here . . . [to]
set myself targets in certain areas that I
wanted to see development in. And one of

July 8
Four international summer
programs leave for Italy: International Music Program; fifteen piano students (also
IMP); visual arts students; and
dance students.

Sept. 30
NCSA announces the purchase
of the old Pierce Laundry
Building on Waughtown Street
(across from the school's main
entrance) for use by the School
of Design and Production.
Two other buildings, the old
Salem Spring Company and
the old Bilt-Rite Parts, Inc.,
used by NCSA since 1968, were
bought by the state in January 1975.

my prime targets was the League of Professional Training Programs because it did
mean a certain kind of national recognition. . . . We made the application in 1977,
and normally they do not allow a program
into the League of Professional Training
Programs unless it's been in existence for
at least three years. We did it in two,
which was sort of epoch-making for
them. And we were the only new program
who had been admitted in something like
seven or eight years. . . .

Well, the League of Professional Theater Training Programs was set up originally because of the unhappiness that
certain people in America had with the
quality of training that actors were getting. They felt that they had certain common goals, and that they wanted to form
a league that could establish guidelines
about what is appropriate for the training
of an actor. And they were schools like
Carnegie Mellon, Yale, Brandeis, I believe,
several of the major schools that got together and formed this league. And it was
an extraordinary move, I think, in the history of American theater. First of all, it
made a bold statement that recognized the
value of training for the actor. Secondly, it
set extremely stringent guidelines about
what was felt to be appropriate—the
amount of hours that were to be spent in
the studio, the quality of the teachers, the
vision and leadership of the programs by
experienced master teachers—all sorts of
conditions, and that had a tremendous
impact on theater in this country. . . . You
could only become a member of the
league by unanimous vote. Indeed, we got
that. And that has been tremendous for us

Oct. 18
Groundbreaking ceremony for
new Workplace building.

Oct. 22
Former NCSA President
Robert Ward presented with
North Carolina Award.

Oct. 25
NCSA module performs at the
Kennedy Center for the Conference of the Alliance for Arts,
as an extension of the high
school tour program.

Nov. 21
Malcolm Morrison named
dean of the School of Drama,
to assume duties August 1,
1976.

because one of the reasons I wanted us to
get in was not only the assertion of being
particular or elitist and the notion that
this had to do with the quality of training,
but also that there were certain benefits.
One is that all of the schools do a national
tour together, where they audition students for the program. That helped our
recruiting enormously. The first year I was
here, we saw eighty-six people for thirty-
five places. Now we see something like
five hundred to six hundred people for the
thirty-five places. Which means obviously
that you are elevating the quality of your
work if the selection is that scrupulous.
Then, the other thing that the league
does, is that each year, each of the schools
makes a presentation to agents, management, and casting directors from films,
television, and the theater. There is an audience in the Juilliard theater every year
for the league presentation, probably two
hundred and fifty to three hundred of the
most influential people in films, theater
and television in this country. And each
school has to make a presentation of their
students. Now that is used as an evaluation process, too, that all of the rest of the
schools are marking them.

*Lesley Hunt is assistant dean of the School
of Drama at the North Carolina School of
the Arts:*
    There are only eleven schools in this
country in that league, and you can be
dropped if your standard drops. Being a
member of the league allows us to present our Senior graduating class to the
agents, producers, directors in New York
City, so in April we will take the current

1976

Feb. 5–8, 11–14
Barnet Kellman directs *A Streetcar Named Desire* for the School of Drama.

Mar. 9
Nicholas Harsanyi, dean of the School of Music, resigns effective August 1, 1977.

Mar. 10–11
Pianist Claude Frank presents master classes at NCSA.

Apr. 7
Paul Green, well-known North Carolina author and playwright, awarded Doctor of Fine Arts degree.

Senior class and they will have all of forty-five or fifty minutes to present their wares, and that's not very much time, but if you have it they can see it, and if it's what they want, then they hire you. Actually, what happens is they do a series of call-backs and things like that, and your name goes up as to which company or which producer is interested in you, and then they interview you.

Malcolm Morrison:
And we have done remarkably well with those presentations. I mean, we've had highlights like, one boy got forty-two offers out of the league presentation and promptly had a nervous breakdown because he didn't know how to deal with it.

Lesley Hunt:
I don't think you can ever really prepare someone for the competitiveness. I think one of the major things . . . that gives our students an advantage over some of the others, is that they leave here with an incredible sunny naiveté. And it's been commented on so many times by people in New York . . . that the students are fresh, that they're excited about their work, that they want to go to work, and that they're really open and ready to go . . . because we don't really encourage our students to work in the summertime . . . not in theater. We ask them to go out and do what we call "job jobs." To get to know about life, because that's what they've got to have in theater. So they don't get a rather sort of jaded view of theater by having to work in maybe weekly rep, and I don't mean to imply that weekly rep is jaded,

May 14
Max Rudolf, music director emeritus of the Cincinnati Symphony and former conductor and artistic administrator of New York City's Metropolitan Opera, conducts NCSA Orchestra.

May 29
Commencement exercises with Grace J. Rohrer, secretary of the North Carolina Department of Cultural Resources, delivering the address.

June 14–Aug. 6
Tenth International Music Program opens at Reynolda Hall, Wake Forest University, because of construction at NCSA. IMP to study and perform in Italy July 19–August 6.

July 17
Crawford Hall closed until mid-fall for acoustic renovations.

but you have to work fast, it's very tiring, and you lose some of that joy of working, in that you cannot do it well. Completely well. . . . So they do leave here with this wonderful thing, going out and saying "O.K. world, here I am." And the world tends to respond with "Wow, that's refreshing." And so they do work, our students go out and work, and I sound as though I'm surprised, and I suppose, in a way, I am, and it's wonderful.

Malcolm Morrison:

What I did see [here] was the virtue of a place that has a few trees and some grass and just one single purpose. I have been offered jobs other places, like New York University, California Institute of the Arts, and so on. One of the things I found daunting about accepting those positions, apart from the fact that I like this place too much, is that the students are tired, pale, quite often late for classes, and just the problem, I think, of competing with everyday life to make yourself present in the classroom in those places is a real problem to them. We don't have that problem. Most of our students here are fresh, ready when we need them. So [in regard to not being located near New York or San Francisco], what you lose on the swings you gain on the round-about. I guess we get more value, or our students get more value for their money out of their training here, because they do not have to deal with and compete with those pressures. It seems to me that it is entirely appropriate in life to—after all, you know, what is it, four years? It's just a moment anyway, that you might reasonably pause

July 26
By invitation of the American embassy, NCSA's International Festival Orchestra officially represents the U.S. Bicentennial in Italy with a concert in Rome.

Oct. 1
Joan Mondale, wife of the vice-president of the United States, visits NCSA.

Oct. 8
Piedmont Opera Theatre (NCSA Professional Affiliate) incorporated.

Nov.
Latest renovations complete for Crawford Hall.

and put yourself into a reflective situation and find out really what your job is before you then go on to the next thing, which is dealing with it in life.

William Tribby is director of general studies at the North Carolina School of the Arts:
I'd known about the school since it started; in fact, I'd followed it very closely from a distance and had recommended a number of students that I had worked with in Maryland to audition, and several of them had, and of course had recorded really wonderful experiences. I was the head of a theater department at Western Maryland College and had been there for twenty years and was not particularly eager or actively searching for a job. But in the back of my mind as others', there's always certain places that you're fascinated with and you figure if ever anything came up, you would owe it to yourself to at least apply—and I did, and of course visited the place, and I knew when I left the interview that if there were an offer, I wouldn't think twice. . . . I had found in my own educational interests—I was still actively teaching and directing and acting theater—I was becoming more and more excited about developing interdisciplinary humanities programs, and the opportunity to come here, to work in an arts environment in a program that almost by its very nature has to have a lot of interdisciplinary humanities approach to knowledge and to have this age group from seventh grade through college—it's all right here. . . .
We've put in, with the help of various teams of faculty . . . a course called foun-

1977

Jan. 4
Nomination of Robert
Hickock as next dean of music
approved by the UNC Board
of Governors. Hickock to begin duties August 1.

May
North Carolina Shakespeare
Festival (NCSA Professional
Affiliate) formed. High Point
Theatre and Exhibition Center
to become the base for the
festival.

May 20
Max Rudolf, former conductor
and artistic administrator with
the Metropolitan Opera and
musical director of the Cincinnati Symphony, returns to conduct NCSA Orchestra.

dations of values in the arts and humanities. It's required of all degree students.
Its glue is philosophy. It deals with classical thinkers . . . since the cave times in
the Western and Eastern world. It's a
three-term course, and students who go
through that have at least been exposed to
some things that we, and certainly other
people, would regard as something any
educated person should have been introduced to. . . . And the last term of that
course particularly focuses on the modern
time, but also the modern in relation to
works of art that have been somewhat
controversial, which have raised questions
about, is this thing really a play or a
poem? whether it's the "Rites of Spring"
as a dance . . . whether it is *Six Characters
in Search of an Author* by Pirandello as a
play—many people wonder is this a play
or not? T. S. Eliot's "Wasteland," other
documents like this. . . . The progress of
the two semesters, the first two terms, has
been one of getting some foundation in
what the values are and then applying
them as they must do as individual artists.
They are not going to be in some little
closet or attic someplace. They're going to
have to get out and function as political
and, hopefully, alive individuals other
than just being excellent artists, and not
wait for a lawyer to fight in a censorship
case, for example. They should have some
opinions of their own as artists and such a
thing as censorship gets hit, which most
of them will face at some point. So there's
that one. Another course we've put in . . .
is an arts in context course. . . . The
glue of that one is history. We had found
that . . . these students come in here re-

May 29
Commencement exercises at
NCSA, with speaker Valerie
Bettis (stage, screen, and tele-
vision actress/dancer/choreog-
rapher).

June 3
Frank G. Dickey accepts appointment as interim dean of
academic studies.

July 11–Sept. 2
International Music Program.

Sept. 20
Israeli-born violinist Itzhak
Perlman visits NCSA students
before giving concert at Wake
Forest.

membering very little in regard to history,
having no idea of sequence. And we get
complaints from the person who teaches
dance and art history—it's all one com-
plaint. And that is, that they have to
spend 90% of their time teaching history,
and "it leaves me only 10% to deal with
theater or art or music and I simply can't
do that. I have got to deal with the history of this art form."

Lesley Hunt:

Now, I teach period and style within
the School of Drama, so they learn the
dances of the period. They learn all about
the everyday tasks that people have to do
in a certain period. So they get that kind
of education and it also goes along with
what they are doing in general studies. We
try to balance their learning the literature
of the period at the same time as they are
performing plays of that period. They are
looking at the history and the philosophy.

William Tribby:

So what we are proposing . . . is that
they take either art history or preferably
the arts in context course which . . . goes
through the major periods of history, it's a
chronological approach. It doesn't attempt to cover the whole world in three
terms, but basically goes from cave to
space dealing with some primitive and
highly technological societies, some rural
as well as highly urbanized societies. So
that at least if they've gone through and
gotten that, they've gotten the tools for
dealing with a society. . . . And I'm very
happy about that. We also did quite a
change-around in the already required

Oct. 10
Dance writer Jack Anderson at
NCSA for two weeks as guest
lecturer in dance history.

Oct. 21
Sergio Luca, virtuoso Israeli
violinist, gives a master class
and concert with NCSA pi-
ano faculty member Anne
Epperson.

Dec. 3
Sarah Graham Kenan Memo-
rial Organ dedicated in
Crawford Hall.

freshman English program, which we now
call critical perspectives. Again, the emphasis on that thing is writing, writing,
writing, through all three terms. . . . The
first term . . . it's primarily introducing
them to short fiction and essays and as
I say, writing. The second term is more
writing, and dealing with poetry, which is
essential for any educated person . . . but
also particularly useful for an artist since
poetry has been such a source for all the
arts, and then, the third term is one focus-
ing on the artist's life and it deals with
biography. And they also do a major research project. We decided, why not tap
something that they're already interested
in? and every one of those students is interested in another person who lived and
breathed in their art form . . . and so this
is something that we knew they would do
anyway. . . . And of course, in that classroom you've got dancers and musicians
and drama students and D&P students,
and they're learning about the artists from
each area, too, which is a help. . . .

We do not have English majors here,
history majors, philosophy majors, physics majors—we've got to offer stuff that is
for that nonmajor and still have a fine
program, but not attempt to be the traditional undergraduate program. So we have
topics courses that change each term. For
example, we feel that each year we should
have at least one history course offered
each term, at least one philosophy course,
at least one literature course. . . . And we
also have, of course, already a science
course offered, a social studies course. So
the area is being covered, in addition to
the languages.

1978

Jan. 9
William H. Baskin III, academic dean, resigns while on leave of absence as dean of the American College in Paris.

Feb. 1
NCSA granted federal funds to study the feasibility of renovating the Carolina Theatre in downtown Winston-Salem.

Feb. 18–19
School of Drama hosts the southeastern regional meeting of the International Mimes and Pantomimists.

Apr. 25–26
Guido Agosti, distinguished Italian pianist and teacher, conducts a series of piano master classes.

I was warned and told that one of the reasons they wanted me to come in . . . was to make stronger the ties between general studies and the arts. . . . I was made to feel totally welcome by the arts areas, the arts deans and their assistants and their students. I guess probably one of the advantages I may have brought was the fact that I had spent twenty years fighting for the arts on a predominantly liberal arts campus. So I think . . . they realized they were getting somebody who had not been primarily academic even though I had the credentials in that area. . . . But I have found them to be, the arts areas, tremendously cooperative, they work very closely with us and they give me curricular revisions, very supportive. Of course, you're still going to get, no matter what happens, a number of students who will say when pressures get tough, "I didn't come here to study general studies. I came here to be in arts." And of course, they did. This is an arts school and I think our faculty and staff in general studies has to keep reminding itself that they did not come to teach in a traditional liberal arts college or high school. They came to work in an area where you've got a room full of artists whose primary purpose for being here and staying here is the arts training they're getting. And a number of the arts faculty do not have a traditional academic training and shouldn't. Sometimes they will say things to a student that can either help or hinder us—they'll say, "Oh, look, I never even graduated from high school— look where I am." And the student will say, "Wow, I could drop out right now."

Apr. 26-29
Four-day celebration including a street parade, a campus carnival, special exhibits and visiting dignitaries (actress Helen Hayes and Bess Abell, executive assistant to Joan Mondale) mark the formal dedication ceremonies of the Workplace.

Apr. 27-29
Pas de Deux, Concerto Barocco, and *Petrouchka* presented by the Schools of Dance, Music, and Design and Production. Yurek Lazowski, who danced the title role of Petrouchka with the American Ballet Theatre, supervises NCSA's revival of the ballet. Sara Leland, principal dancer with the New York City Ballet, stages other ballets.

But I think the opposite is more often the case, and that is, they'll walk into a music class, a private lesson, and the teacher will be sitting there reading a novel. The student will be amazed that the teacher does anything but sit in there and teach trumpet all day, and the teacher will say something like "I've just been reading this novel. Are you familiar with this writer? I've read everything that this person has written." And the student is amazed that the trumpet teacher also reads. Some of the so-called uneducated—I mean some of the arts faculty seem to be somewhat unnecessarily sensitive about not having some sort of formal education. Some of those very people are the most beautifully educated people around here. . . . And I think students, when they look for that, see that—that these are highly intelligent, motivated people and that perhaps in the years when they came up, not having that high school diploma or not having that college degree was not regarded as important as it tends to be now. But I have found certainly a willingness to cooperate, always keeping in mind that we have to realize that the school is the School of the Arts.

[The objective of the General Studies Department] is to provide as strong a liberal arts education as we possibly can for the person who is a practicing artist, but also primarily a human being who is going to exist politically, religiously, socially and all those other ways, in addition to being an artist. And that is fundamental to the founding of this school; they were determined not to be just some conservatory. I think we have to keep re-

May 8
Choreographer Agnes de Mille joins prominent educator, lecturer, and author Harold Taylor in a conference with the theme "The Humanities and the Performing Arts—Problems and Prospects."

June 3
Commencement exercises at NCSA, with Interim Academic Dean Frank G. Dickey as speaker.

June 6
Carolina Scenic Studios (NCSA Professional Affiliate) incorporated.

June 13
League of Professional Theatre Training Programs, an alliance of America's major acting schools, accepts NCSA as a member.

minding ourselves of that charge in the founding of the school. It is a place where students can come and get some of the best arts education they are ever going to receive anywhere, and also get next to an education that is important for any artist, any human being. . . . We don't have to sit here, I think, and offer courses that are constantly relating to the arts. It's sometimes a relief to the student just to be able to go into a philosophy class that is a philosophy class. But I think also, at the same time, we have to keep in mind that we have full-time practicing artists, and that can be quite an advantage in terms of the way you approach a class. So our objective is to keep true to that goal, and to keep adapting to better ways to do it. . . .

I guess the thing that constantly is exciting to me . . . is what it is to work in an environment of truly highly motivated students, and how much I realized I had not been next to that sort of student as a constant, day-to-day thing, and the difference it makes walking down the halls, in the classrooms. . . . [The students are] so different . . . just before I came here, the primary guitar teacher had left and evidently there had been some sort of little undercover story around here about classical guitar is just one of the finest intellectual students you'll ever have here, you know. That tended to be sort of a generalization made . . . the generalizations [are] about different strengths. I guess you hear constantly that the drama students are certainly very articulate, and you won't have a quiet class with drama students. They will all talk to you. But the music students tend to be much more re-

June 25–Aug. 17
International Music Program.

June 28
Former President Robert
Ward, on leave from the School
of Music faculty, to retire
effective fall 1979.

Oct. 5
NCSA trustees and NCSA
Foundation board members
agree to accept the Carolina
Theatre building as a gift from
the Piedmont Publishing Company (deeded March 12, 1979).
Restoration and renovation
cost to be raised primarily
from federal and out-of-state
private sources.

flective and quiet, but also very good students. And that the D&P students, you'll
always know where you stand with them
because they won't stand back on pro-
tocol—they'll say I don't like something.
And the dance students, of course you
hear more about their activity in the high
school.

Sam Stone:

Class scheduling was always [a] severe
[problem] . . . in each of the disciplines,
they all have a different rhythm and a different pattern. Dancers wanted early class
in the morning and then a late class in the
afternoon, which forces their academic
work into the middle of the day. Drama
students would rather have the whole afternoon for their acting classes and all of
their academics in the morning. Technical
theater would rather not do anything until
noon because they like to work late at
night. So trying to accommodate all those
interests back and forth was hard, and
they're all different physical reasons, and
their own body development and so on—
it's different. So a lot of the accommodations just have to be worked out and I'd
have to say that it's only been in the last
few years since Bill Tribby has been director of general studies . . . that the daily
[scheduling] of the hours has been worked
out in a satisfactory way. . . . The calendar
for the year, Marion Fitz-Simons and . . .
Bill Baskin, who was the dean then, we
worked on it together. What we were trying to do is to get the school year into
units that made more sense as far as the
performance calendar, that is, the performance cycle. And what we could see was

Oct. 7
Carolina Theatre to be chris-
tened the Roger L. Stevens
Center upon renovation.

Dec. 6
UNC Board of Governors approves the appointment of
Richard H. Miller, as acting
dean of academic studies
effective January 1979.
Israeli concert violinist Sergio
Luca, with pianist Anne Epperson, presents recital.

1979

Mar. 2
French organist Louis
Robilliard in recital on the
Sarah Graham Kenan Memo-
rial Organ in Crawford Hall.

that the productions quite naturally sort
of fell into a fall, winter, and spring season—three different cycles that way. We
could not begin classes before Labor Day
because many of the students were involved in summer theater or summer stock
or some other work of some kind that went
through Labor Day. So we couldn't go the
route that colleges were going at that time,
starting before Labor Day and finishing
with exams before Christmas. If you start
after Labor Day, there's no way to get fifteen weeks scrunched into that time. And
on the other end of the year, we couldn't
run too late into June because of the same
reasons—employment started in the summer. So we were kind of boxed in from
something shortly after Labor Day to
something by June 1. Another factor was
that of the habit we were in of producing
The Nutcracker in a big fashion, and that
took a lot of the time of the students, and
there was a disruption from one point of
view and that had to be accommodated
and recognized. We were also, though, at
the same time, interested in the plan that
many colleges had adopted called 4-1-4 . . .
which was four months, then one intense,
and then four more months. . . . And we
were interested in some month adaptation
of that idea to this school, hearing the arts
people saying, wouldn't it be wonderful
to have some time in which we did only
arts and wouldn't be bothered with all
this academic business?

Lesley Hunt:
   It's very difficult because every art in its
time table takes full time, so there is very
little time to overlap. In the intensive arts

Apr. 1
Organist Robert Burns King
in guest recital at school.

May 10
Randy Jones, member of the
disco group Village People and
former modern dance student
at the school, returns for a
visit. Jones later establishes
a scholarship in his name
at NCSA.

June 2
Commencement exercises,
with Representative Carl J.
Stewart, Speaker of the
North Carolina House of
Representatives.

period, which is coming up just after
Thanksgiving, we do overlap. We have
two people from the dance department
will come and work with the drama students, and a person from the music department will come and work with the
drama students, and some of our faculty
will go into their departments and work.

Sam Stone:

So we played around with the calendar
and decided to chop the thirty-week year
to two fifteen-week semesters and divide
it by three rather than two and make three
ten-week terms—not quite a quarter system, what some schools call a quarter system with eleven-week terms, but three
ten-week terms. And as we found that we
could fit that between sometime after Labor Day and end by Thanksgiving, and
then start the first of January and run to
the middle of March, and have a Spring
break and start right after that and run to
the first of June and have another ten
weeks. Well, that left us with some time in
December after Thanksgiving and . . .
feeling that the students, for their money,
deserved two more weeks of education.
So we said, well, let's have an intensive
arts time, let's do this one part of the
4-1-4 idea in December, and do it for two
weeks between Thanksgiving and the
Christmas break, and during which time
very happily or conveniently is the height
of *The Nutcracker* production time and the
students are involved in *The Nutcracker*
and that's what they'll do for intensive
arts, and the other students such as the
modern dance students and the other students in music and drama, they'll do

June 24–Aug. 18
International Music Program.
Concert on July 23 marks the
program's first performance in
Germany.

Oct. 11
World-famous ballet star Edward Villella conducts master
class and informal workshop.

1980

Jan. 19
Violinist and teacher Dorothy
Delay holds master classes.

Feb. 8
Internationally acclaimed violinist Itzhak Perlman awarded
an honorary Doctor of Music
degree at school convocation.

something else in their own field quite
apart from the academics. So that's the
calendar we have, and that's the reason it's
worked that way.

*Robert Hickock was dean of the School of
Music at the North Carolina School of the
Arts, 1977–1985:*
I think that I heard about the school
when it was formed. I was in New York at
that point, so that would have been 1965,
and I remember reading in *The New York
Times* of the founding of the North Carolina School of the Arts, and my recollec-
tion is that I thought at the time it was a
terrific idea. . . . Then I lost track of it
completely until one day I received a telephone call from Martin Sokoloff whom I
had known for many years in New York.
. . . And he told me that the deanship of
the School of Music here was going to be
vacant, and asked if I would be considered
as an applicant. At that time I had been in
New York for almost twenty-five years,
and had decided more or less that some
time I was going to remove myself from
the city because it was becoming a very
difficult place to live and to work. The
costs, for instance, of getting a concert on
the stage in New York at that point were
prohibitive, and the City University had
suffered major crises financially, and it was
clear to me that my aspirations for the
Brooklyn College School of Performing
Arts of which I was the dean at that
point—those aspirations simply were not
going to come to fruition. So I was ready
to leave New York, but I was hardly ready
to go to North Carolina. And I remember
that my original response was something

26. Left to right: Dean Malcolm Morrison, Trustee Gordon Hanes, Dean Robert Hickock (Archives of the North Carolina School of the Arts).

Apr. 12
Workplace receives Award for Excellence in Architecture from North Carolina Chapter of the American Institute of Architecture (Newman-Calloway-Johnson-Van Eteen-Winfree, architects).

Apr. 24–25
La Sylphide ballet presented by the School of Dance, with the assistance of Danish ballet master Hans Brenaa. Brenaa to work with NCSA ballet students.

like, Come on Martin, I'm not going to North Carolina. . . .

During the first year the faculty and I reviewed the entire curriculum of the School of Music from the point of view of its well-defined mission, which is that of producing professional performers. I was very happy that the school had such a pure mission because in almost every other school where I have been employed, there were inevitably schisms between musicologists and performers and education persons and that always, even with the greatest good will, was divisive. Here, we all understand and agree on our mission, and any disagreements that come about revolve around differences of opinion as to how best to pursue the agreed-upon objectives. At any rate, we spent a great deal of time. The faculty put out an

Apr. 25

NCSA publicly honors seven with honorary doctoral degrees: Agnes de Mille (choreographer, author and director), José Ferrer (actor and director), Gordon Hanes (longtime arts supporter and patron; member of Governor Sanford's North Carolina Conservatory Committee), Rosemary Harris (English-born actress, now a North Carolina resident), Nananne Porcher (lighting designer and theater consultant), William Schuman (composer and president emeritus of the Juilliard School and of Lincoln Center), and Oliver Smith (Broadway scenic designer and co-director of the American Ballet Theatre).

enormous effort during that first year, and as a result, we revised the curriculum quite completely. . . .

And the basic tenets of the new curriculum were that we were going to make sure that we allowed for adequate time. . . . for the student to be in the practice room, and to allow also for a great deal of performance activity. This meant culling from the curriculum of the School of Music . . . many traditional courses that you will find at any standard college music department or professional conservatory. But we thought that that was essential because if in fact we were in the business of training professional performers, then the major thrust of what we do has to be in that direction. That is not to say that we constructed a situation in which all they do is play the violin or the clarinet or the tuba. We have a very, I think, sound series of courses in music style, music literature, music theory, so that our students are in fact well educated. But the great bulk of their term is spent in the performance situation, either in their lessons, in their master classes, their group rehearsals, and in the hard business of being in the practice room by yourself for long periods of time. . . .

What impressed me immediately about the school were [three] factors: One—the school contains very good units in dance, in design and production, in drama, in addition to music. I think the fact that all of those disciplines are located on the campus is one of the major strengths of the school. The second thing that impressed me was the fact that the School of Music—and I learned later the School of

May 31
Commencement exercises,
with Schuyler Chapin, dean of
the School of the Arts at Columbia University.

June 3
Mack Trucks, Inc., accepts an
offer from NCSA to buy Mack
Truck property on Waughtown
Street. Administrative offices to
move into Mack Truck office
building.

Dance—has not only college students but
high school and even younger. I think
that's a great strength of the school. The
third thing that I found to be extremely
valuable, and I am convinced that this has
to be maintained, is the size of the school.
That is to say, it is small. That really does
allow the faculty and the dean to know
each student, to give particular attention
to the students, to constantly be evaluating each student, ascertaining the needs of
the student, and to hopefully providing
them. In larger schools such as Brooklyn
College, which had, at the time I left it,
something like thirty-five thousand students—obviously not all music students
or dance students but nevertheless—just
the sheer bulk of humanity militated
against the kind of intimate knowledge
that we have of our students here at the
school. And the thing I'll add to the three
things I've already mentioned, the fourth
thing that pleased me very much is the
fact that while the school of the arts is indeed a unit of the University of North
Carolina, it is not embedded in a huge
campus surrounded by Schools of Medicine, Engineering, Science, etc., so that
while obviously the school of the arts is in
competition with other units, the arts on
this campus are not in competition with
the other schools of endeavor. And I think
that this is a great strength both psychologically and spiritually. Our students, as
an entire student body, have a unity of
purpose and a camaraderie that you do
not find in similar schools when they are
surrounded by many other disciplines.
    [As compared to Manhattan and
Brooklyn], the main [difference at the

June 10
Louis Robilliard, teacher of organ at Conservatory National in Lyons, France, and guest teacher at the Summer Organ Academy of Salem College and NCSA, presents a recital on the Kenan Memorial Organ.

June 23–Aug. 18
International Music Program. Two choral groups from West Germany to join IMP orchestra in concerts in four North Carolina cities. IMP to move preparatory sessions to Pinehurst Hotel and Country Club in Pinehurst, North Carolina, beginning in 1981.

Sept. 2
George Trautwein appointed conductor of NCSA Orchestra, music director and conductor of the Piedmont Chamber Orchestra, and principal conductor of the International Music Program effective at the beginning of the 1981 academic year.

North Carolina School of the Arts] is the atmosphere the students meet when they get here . . . a very concentrated potent atmosphere in which everybody hits the ground running, knowing exactly what they want to do. Almost no students come to the North Carolina School of the Arts to sample things; to decide whether they want to be a physics major or a Romance language major or a piano major. They come here having a very good idea of how they want to spend their energies and what they want to do. And they are surrounded by other people who feel exactly the same way. In other words, it is a much more concentrated environment in which they exist. They are, almost without exception, extremely talented. And it is our responsibility to challenge that talent, to discipline it, and to allow them to discover how to work, how to practice, how to learn, how to consolidate their resources, how to deal with the pressures that are inevitably involved in any of the performing arts. That is a psychology that one has to learn to deal with, both internally and externally. And I'm happy to say that the great majority of our students do in fact successfully deal with that. So I think that the environment that our students meet when they get here and their own internal organization and strength and desire across the board are the things that make our students and this school quite unusual. I'm not saying that these things don't exist at the other schools, but I think that in many of them, even the conservatories, they are diffused in comparison to the atmosphere here.

There are also many more performing

Nov. 25
Dean of Dance Robert
Lindgren awarded state's high-
est honor at North Carolina
Awards in Raleigh.

1981

Jan. 21
Pulitzer Prize-winning composer and percussionist
Michael Colgrass leads a workshop and rehearsal of his
works.

Apr. 2–5
American College Dance Festival held at NCSA. Three
internationally known choreographers (Murray Louis, Clay
Taliaferro, Pauline Koner) serve
as judges.

opportunities for our students here. . . .
For instance, the Manhattan School, where
they have, let's say thirty-five percussion
majors—well, there's no way you can educate thirty-five percussion majors the way
they should be educated. They have to get
private instruction, they have to work on
all of the percussion instruments, they
need chamber experience, and they need
orchestral experience. Here, we limit very
much the number of students that we take
in a department like percussion, in order
to be able to give all of them the kind of
training that they need. . . .

[The students] are evaluated every
term, and at the end of each year. Then
they are considered in terms of their progress to date and what the faculty estimates
their potential is, and on the basis of that
very careful analysis and estimate, they are
either invited to return next fall or they
are advised to either seek some other institution in the arts or to consider some
other life's work. . . . I don't think [this
practice is] absolutely unique, but I think
that it is applied [here] with a thoroughness and a humanity that is, if not unique,
very unusual. The last thing we want to
do is encourage a student in the area of
music if we do not in fact hold the conviction that that student has a fighting
chance to be successful. And so we spend
quite a bit of time considering each student on that basis. And if we find one
who we feel simply does not have the potential of becoming a successful performer,
then we try to advise that person to seek
other avenues. . . .

When I arrived here [in 1977], the only
important performing organization was

Apr. 27
Robert Joffrey, founder of the
Joffrey Ballet in New York, vis-
its dance classes at NCSA.

May 5–26
Acclaimed English actress
Rosemary Harris conducts
master classes for senior drama
students.

May 7–8
Helen Hayes awarded Doctor
of Fine Arts degree May 7;
School of Drama presents
benefit performance of *Rosen-
crantz and Guildenstern Are
Dead* (under direction of noted
actress/director Rae Allen) for
Helen Hayes Scholarship fund.
Workshops given by Miss
Hayes May 8.

the orchestra. And as you and I sit here now, we have a full symphony orchestra, chamber orchestra, a very active chamber music program, the wind ensemble, a chorus, a percussion ensemble, etc.—a very large increase in the amount of music making on the part of our students. Not only on campus, but our students, through the Applause Agency on campus, do a great deal of work off the campus. In addition, many of them perform in Winston-Salem's symphony, some in the Salisbury Symphony, the Greensboro Symphony, occasionally even substituting in the North Carolina Symphony. So that both on and off campus there is a great deal of performance activity, and of course, this is very important for our students, because that's actual professional experience. . . .

I think that the major change in the school is one of adopting the responsibility of preparing our students for the profession as it actually exists in the cold, cold world. Not as we would like for it to exist, hope it would exist, but as it actually exists. And that has actually become a part of our curriculum. In other words, we've assumed the responsibility of not only making the best musician technically and educationally out of each of our students that he or she can become, [but] we have assumed the additional moral responsibility of giving them as much experience and as much information and as much savvy about the professional world as possible. We have a steady stream of guests that participate in our Phase III seminars (Phase III is the preprofessional phase of our curriculum). We send our

May 8
Conductor and violinist
Milton Katims conducts
NCSA Orchestra and gives
master classes for violin and vi-
ola students.

May 15
Composer Ezra Laderman
conducts three of his works
at NCSA.

May 15–16
"Ritual/Habitual," an original
modern dance choreographed
by NCSA faculty member Di-
anne Markham and performed
by six NCSA dancers, pre-
sented at Kennedy Center as
part of the National College
Dance Festival.

May 16
David Baker, internationally
recognized jazz composer/art-
ist/teacher/conductor, works
with NCSA Jazz Ensemble and
offers public workshop.

students off campus to engage in activities
as close to professional conditions as possible. We construct for our last year students in Phase III individual curriculum
based upon what their professional aspirations are. In other words, we do everything within our capability to prepare the
student to go off this campus ready to
succeed in the profession. That is unique
in the North Carolina School of Arts.
And in one way or the other, that attitude
and that mission manifests itself in each of
the arts schools on this campus. . . .

We have had, in the School of Music—
and I believe across the board—a vast increase in the number and in the role of
[guest] performing artists. . . . For instance, this year we had four major conductors as guests with our orchestra . . .
we were able to bring the composer
Robert Ward to the campus as part of that
program, and we have had, I would say,
twenty or thirty other guests, just this
year. . . . And we are very adept at squeez-
ing the last bit of juice out of each one of
these visits. If a pianist comes in, we have
the pianist play for our students, and we
have that person visit with our Phase III
students talking, not about how to play
the piano, but about how to get a job.
How do you operate in the profession. So
that we feel that we derive the greatest
benefit out of each one of these persons.
For instance, a guest orchestra conductor
not only comes in and rehearses the orchestra and performs the concert, but
does mock auditions on the campus for all
of our orchestra players. As if he were
hiring for a professional orchestra. And he
provides a critique for each of the stu-

May 30
Commencement exercises at
NCSA, with J. Michael Miller,
associate dean of the School
of the Arts at New York
University.

June 17
Organist Rene Saorgin, professor of organ at the Conservatory in Nice, France,
performs in Crawford Hall
during the Salem (College)
Organ Academy.

June 21–Aug. 18
International Music Program
in residence at Pinehurst for
the first time.

June 23
Comedian Jerry Lewis visits
NCSA.

dents that he hears so that they have an understanding of where they stand. That sort of ability to take advantage of all of the various aspects of a visiting artist is enormously helpful. . . .

The professional record of our gradu-ates . . . manifests itself in different ways among the schools. For instance, Design and Production, which is, you know, a unique school in a unique school. It turns out people who are really so well trained and have had the kind of experience that any professional company is just dying to have, with little competition among other schools of its kind, so that it has some-thing like a 95 percent employment record. Terrific. The School of Dance is lucky if it can keep its students, because year after year professional companies swing through here and just take them. Well, that makes sense, because the life ex-pectancy, the professional life expectancy of a dancer, is incredibly short, it's like a football player's. So that both in terms of its students leaving to go into the profes-sion and its students getting into the pro-fession after graduation, I think the employment rate for dance is also quite healthy. . . . The School of Drama is in many respects in a very good position by virtue of being in the League of Schools of Professional Theater, which makes it possible for our entire graduating class to go up to New York and to receive really quite remarkable exposure in front of cast-ing directors . . . an impressive number of drama graduates show up from time to time in good plays, good television, etc. Music is an entirely different situation, and I think that we have a very good

July 9
Dr. James H. Semans, retired longtime member of the Board of Trustees and founding chairman, is voted an honorary member of the board.

Oct. 9
Twenty members of the James A. Gray family gather to help NCSA rededicate the Gray Building after renovations on second floor.

Oct. 29–Nov. 1, Nov. 3–7
Michael John McGann directs *Philadelphia, Here I Come* for NCSA School of Drama.

Nov. 6
North Carolina author John Ehle (a major figure in the founding of NCSA) and Arthur Mitchell, founder and artistic director of the Dance Theatre of Harlem, receive honorary doctorates from the school.

record, and I think that it is improving primarily because of the new attitude that we've taken toward the preparation of our kids to go into their profession. The shining lights go straight from here into the National Symphony Orchestra or the Detroit Orchestra, and we have one now that has a good chance of getting into the Boston Orchestra, but many more of them than in drama or in dance or in D & P, go into graduate studies. That's something in music which—I'm afraid that's part of it. So they go into Juilliard or they go on to Manhattan or they go someplace else, because, unfortunately, we don't have a graduate degree. But even there, we have a very good placement record. . . . A few years ago they did a study of the entire school, and the overall employment record was something like 77 percent, which is outlandishly successful. That represents, however, a 90-some percent in D & P. . . . But I would say that our kids go out of here better prepared to take auditions and to succeed in those auditions than the average student at places like Manhattan, even Juilliard. And that most of them have gotten much more performance opportunities than students at those institutions. . . .

The mind set among a large percentage of kids who want to become musicians is that you've got to be in a big city like Boston, Chicago, Philadelphia, New York, because that's where the action is. And to an extent, they're quite right. A student in New York in one week can hear two or three of the greatest orchestras in the world, opera, etc. Of course he doesn't have the money or the time to do it, but . . . it's there. And the atmosphere is

Nov. 7
Roland Bader, guest conductor
for the Berlin Philharmonic,
conducts NCSA Orchestra.

1982

Jan. 8
Chuck Davis, dancer/teacher,
visits NCSA for week of master classes.

Jan. 29
NCSA and officials of R. J.
Reynolds Industries, Inc., with
Governor James B. Hunt pres-
ent, announce "Jazz Is" com-
pany to tour cross-country.

Feb. 3
Susan Landale, a member of
the faculty at the Conservatory
of Rueil-Malmaison in France,
gives organ recital at NCSA.

there. So that that is a problem for us in
terms of recruitment because obviously
Winston-Salem is not one of those towns.
Now you and I know that Winston-Salem
is a great place to be, and there are lots
of activities going on, but that's a little
hard to compare to New York or Chicago.
So that that puts us at a recruitment dis-
advantage. However, anyone who looks
carefully (and the problem is that a lot of
them don't look carefully) at the actual
performing possibilities here as opposed
to let's say Stony Brook in New York, or
Oberlin, I mean it's three or four times as
great when you take into account the activities of the school, the Winston-Salem
Symphony, the Piedmont Opera, all of
that. . . . The quality of the faculty . . . is
certainly on a par, and the fact that [the
students] are not in a hostile atmosphere,
is very important . . . one of the things
that has always surprised me about this
situation, is that the students are incredibly supportive of each other. . . . There
are many advantages to being in this
situation: The fact that your teacher
knows you, the fact that your teacher isn't
always off on tour, the fact that the administration knows you, the fact that there
are lots of performing activities, the fact
that for the most part you are safe—that's
pretty important. I think—I think it's
really a balancing-off situation. There are
many, it is *undeniable,* that there are many
advantages in going to school in New
York City, not because of the schools, but
because of everything else. Actually, very
few people go to Juilliard to get educated.
They go there because that's the way to
get a job. Many of them go to Juilliard

Feb. 5
Dancer Bill Evans conducts master class.

Mar. 26
First NCSA graduate program—in design and production—approved by UNC Board of Governors, to begin in fall 1982.

May 6–9, 11–15
Richard Edelman directs *The Devils* for NCSA School of Drama.

May 29
Commencement exercises, with former governor of North Carolina and current Duke University President Terry Sanford.

and study with another teacher outside the institution. . . . We've had kids go to Juilliard, Oberlin, Boston University, Peabody, transfer out of here to go there, and they came back. They say, "All we did was take our lessons, and that was great, but nothing else to do. Never played in the orchestra." . . .

There is no question that the Stevens Center provides for the School of Music an important performance place. In terms of its size, of its stage, the acoustical properties, the nature of the house, its location, its glamour, it is an extremely important thing for the School of Music. Our performance location prior to that was Crawford Hall on the campus and we were confined to that. . . . I think that the presence of the Stevens Center, the attractiveness of it to audiences, the atmosphere that is possible there—a real professional house as opposed to a school auditorium—and the acoustical benefits are enormously important . . . it presents all kinds of logistical problems for us such as transporting people and equipment. In order to make the house itself successful, there is going to have to be some attitude towards the occupation rate, and if you're not careful, the house can get so busy that you don't have enough time. For instance, we are not now putting into Stevens all the concerts in the School of Music that should be there. We are still performing some of them here. We're not doing that because we don't want to go to Stevens; we're doing that because the hall is occupied by the School of Drama, the School of Dance, and then you have to take into account the availability of the

June 24–Aug. 19
International Music Program.
First year of residency at
Davidson College, Davidson,
North Carolina.

July 23–Aug. 12
Premier ballerina Alexandra
Danilova to join NCSA dance
students in Bassano del
Grappa, Italy.

Oct. 22
Robert Denvers, Belgian dance
teacher in New York, teaches
master class at NCSA.

1983

Apr. 19
Piedmont Chamber Orchestra
to suspend operations because
of financial difficulties.

hall and the justifiable availability of the
hall to the various affiliates of the school,
the North Carolina Dance Theater, the
[North Carolina] Shakespeare [Festival],
and other important institutions in the
town such as the Piedmont Opera Theatre
and the Winston-Salem Symphony. All
those organizations which are related to
us either very tightly or very loosely are
important to the town and are important to the school. But it means that the
schedule tends to be very tight and also
needs to become more rigid because in a
house of that sort you have to plan at least
three years in advance. When you take
into account, in addition to all of those
events, and many of them, particularly
dance and opera and drama, are very time-
consuming because there's a great deal of
set-in time, not just the rehearsal and the
performance, but two weeks solid of getting the scenery in, getting the rehearsals,
etc. When you take into account the necessity on the part of the people who are
running the house to minimize their
losses by scheduling popular events into
the house, then you're going to inevitably
come up against difficult schedule
crunches. But that's a situation that other
institutions have to live with. And there's
no reason why we can't learn to live with
that either.

John Sneden:
    Well, I'm sure we'll be asked to do big-
ger shows. I mean, the need for filling up
that large theater, that large stage, is
going to impact on how much money
we're going to need to produce shows . . .
but I like the idea of a theater downtown.

Apr. 22–24
Gala performances celebrate
the opening of the Stevens
Center.
April 22: Benefit in tribute to
Roger L. Stevens with Gregory
Peck as master of ceremonies;
Leonard Bernstein as con-
ductor; Isaac Stern as soloist;
with performances by Hume
Cronyn, Zoe Caldwell, Jean
Stapleton, Gianna Rolandi,
Jessica Tandy, Mel Tomlinson,
Heather Watts, and NCSA stu-
dents, alumni, and faculty. Also
participating in the tribute are
Agnes de Mille, Sir Anton
Dolin, Cliff Robertson, Gover-
nor James B. Hunt, and Oliver
Smith. Attending the tribute
and chairing the national Hon-
orary Committee for the gala
opening are President and Mrs.
Gerald Ford and Mrs. Lyndon
Baines Johnson. Also among
those attending are Joan Mondale, Selwa Roosevelt, and former North Carolina Governors
Sanford, Moore, Holshouser,
and Scott.
April 23–24: Fully staged performance of Cole Porter's *Kiss
Me Kate* performed by the
school.

Some don't, I like it. I like the idea of getting off the campus, out of the educational surroundings and into a more
professional context. Personally, I think it
would be fun to go to a theater downtown. Since the beginning of the school,
we have done so many performances off
campus anyway. We were always using
Reynolds Auditorium or oftentimes we
were using the little auditorium at Sum-
mit School. That's been a great experience
for our program in having to deal with
building the scenery in a shop in such a
way that you put it into trucks and take it
to the theater, you do a load-in, etc., like
they do in the professional world. It's very
rare that . . . you have your scene shop
next door to your theater, and all you do
is open the doors and shove it in. I think
this is a much more realistic method of
dealing with scenery, or training students
to view the whole technical side as something which you take and do a load-in.
And, as I say, yeah, there will be problems, I'm sure. Carting people downtown.
But there were problems carting people to
Reynolds.

R. Philip Hanes, Jr.:

And I said I want to name it the Stevens Center because I think an arts building ought to be named after people in
the arts. Helen Hayes Theatre or Agnes
de Mille Theatre or something like that,
and Roger represents everything that we
want to represent. He is the greatest
producer of drama in England and America. He is Sir Roger Stevens by the way.
He was knighted in England for his work
in theater. He created the National En-

May 28
Commencement exercises held
at Stevens Center, with
William C. Friday, president of
the Consolidated University of
North Carolina.

June 10–Aug. 17
International Music Program.
North Carolina Governor
James B. Hunt joins orchestra
June 29 in Stuttgart and at-
tends concerts in Frankfurt and
Amarbach as part of inter-
national trade mission to
Germany.

July 12
Eldridge C. Hanes, chairman
of the Board of Trustees, announces the formation of the
Board of Visitors, a board of
national leaders in the arts,
business, and civic affairs
formed to assist in the school's
development.

dowment for the Arts. It was all his creation. He built the Kennedy Center. He
represents all the arts. . . .

Well, he said, "You're crazy." And I told
him why I wanted to do it, and I told him
what I thought. And he said he was very
flattered, and he said he had been asked
twice before and had turned it down, but
he felt that we were quality enough that
he wouldn't be embarrassed by it. Well,
the next day after—you know he went to
the dedication night and then he went to
Kiss Me Kate, and the morning after *Kiss
Me Kate,* he was sitting there and he was
still teary-eyed. I have never seen him that
emotional, and he said, "Phil, you don't
know what has happened to me." And I
said, "What's that?" He said, "After I had
agreed to let you name it the Stevens Center, I got to thinking, just suppose that
this is a two-bit operation? Just suppose
that that school is just not at all what you
say it is? Just suppose I've been hyped
into this thing, and then I have to go
down to this dedication, and you pull
out—you know, you do a real dumb job
on that dedication, and it just looks like
amateur night, and then I have all my
friends there watching the first performance of the school of the arts, and it's
amateur night then." He said, "I almost
had an ulcer thinking of those two
nights." He said, "Let me tell you what
you did." He said, "The Kennedy Center
waited something like eight years, I think
it was, before they did their first gala, and
you opened on a preview night before you
had even formally opened the building,
with a gala that was better than the third
one that we did. The timing was perfect.

July 18
Eighteen ballet and modern
dancers leave for Vicenza, Italy.

Aug.
George Trautwein, NCSA Orchestra conductor and director
of orchestra programs, leaves
the school.

Aug. 31
Robert Suderburg begins one-
year leave of absence. Lawrence
Hart appointed acting
chancellor.

Sept. 26
"Where Dreams Debut: The
North Carolina School of the
Arts," videotape documentary,
first broadcast nationally on
public television.

The length of it was perfect. Every single
thing about it was perfect, and you had
the top people involved. I don't believe it.
Second," he said, "the house is pristine. I
was worried about that. The acoustics are
superb. The sight lines are superb. Everything works. The lighting and everything
is just perfect. Thirdly," he said, "of all the
musicals that I know, *Kiss Me Kate* is perhaps the most difficult, complex musical
I've ever seen." And he said, "That production was better than I have seen a professional company do in its whole first week,
and these were amateurs," and he said,
"but when you think that a professional
company has—" I think he told me two
months of rehearsals—"and you had ten
days of rehearsals, for me to say that, and
also I am saying the first week of performance, they have two weeks of previews
before they even do that, and you open
with it just like *that,* and it was perfect."
And he says, "I am dumbfounded." . . .

Isaac Stern was so excited by our kids,
he said, "I want to come back and teach a
master class." And I said, "You're kidding." And he said, "No, I want to come
back for a day of master classes." I said,
"When you going to do that?" and he
said, "The minute I can find an opportunity." Two days later he called me back
and said, "I am going to be down there
next Friday," and he came back the following Friday, and gave a day of master
classes. Well, now, that's a testimonial. But
he would never have come if we had
named [the theater] the Phil Hanes Auditorium or whatever. . . . He came because of Roger Stevens, but he came, and
now he'll come back.

Oct. 8
Distinguished German con-
ductor and Yale instructor
Otto-Werner Muller conducts
NCSA Orchestra.

Nov. 5
At NCSA, international artists
David Shifrin, clarinet, and
William Doppman, piano,
present a preview of their Lin-
coln Center recital.

Dec. 9
Resignation of Chancellor
Robert Suderburg announced,
effective August 31, 1984.

1984

Jan. 17
NCSA announces the member-
ship of the first Board of
Visitors.

Robert Suderburg:

First of all, it will finally and once and
for all in this particular city and in this
region, give a credibility to the institution, which it has not enjoyed in any
sense. Because you know, we are in a
throw-away high school. And this credibility in the presentation downtown, and
actually having done something which
most of them said the school couldn't do,
gives a credibility to the institution which
provides the traditional foundation for
further fund raising for the institution . . .
having [the Stevens Center] there and
having it as a place which is first-class . . .
means that the performances and the uses
of the building of the school and the at-
tribution of all of this quality and so on
and so forth for the school, will be a
stimulus to greater fund raising. . . . It is
not that the building is important. Because they were never important. It's what
happens inside of them. But you have to
have a place that something happens . . .
it will be a place for the performances of
the school of the arts to flower . . . because that hall is going to affect the
quality of performances. It's going to be
better. The orchestra is going to sound
better because they will have a hall they
can really hear in. In fact, in terms of an
orchestra, the hall *is* part of the instrument, and the great orchestras have great
halls. There *are* no great orchestras in bad
halls. It's just a given. And the same thing
works with . . . dance and drama. It just
works that way.

Robert Lindgren:

Oh, being off campus doesn't make any

Feb. 19
Former President Robert Ward
returns to conduct NCSA
Orchestra in two of his
compositions.

Feb. 24
Joan Lippincott, virtuoso
organist, performs a guest recital at NCSA.

Mar. 1—4
Evening of ballets by August
Bournonville, staged for student dancers by Hans Brenaa
of the Royal Danish Ballet.

Mar. 10
Roland Bader, conductor and
choirmaster of St. Hedwig's
Cathedral in Berlin, conducts
NCSA Orchestra.

difference because for years we've been
going to Reynolds Auditorium. We did
The Nutcracker down there . . . a lot of
big ballets—down there, and musicals, so
that's just going to give us our own theater to do that. I don't think it's going to
create any problems. Maybe a few in the
beginning, but you'll accept that and grow
into that and everything will grow with it.
I mean, it's the same thing with clothes—
you get rid of short pants and put on long
pants and they feel strange at first and
pretty soon you're used to that, and then
you want a suit. . . . You soon forget what
you had before because you've gotten
used to what you have now, and you're
looking for something more. . . . I'm a
Depression child. When you ain't got, you
tighten your belt. When you've got, you
expand. I mean, I can't look at it any
other way, and here we are trying to make
a school. If depression comes and times
are tough, corporate, federal and state
funds—you do the best that you know
how. All I asked for when I came here was
space, a piano, and good teachers. As long
as you've got that, you've got a program.
Whether you have a beautiful theater or
whether everything is glamorous and
glorious and we all have tape recorders or
telephones or television or scholarship
money or funds—we're always going to
be doing what we set out to do . . . teach
people how to dance.

Robert Hickock:
    I think that the people who were here
on the scene [at the beginning]—I don't
know whether they were good administrators or not, I don't care. But they pro-

Apr. 18
Ransom Wilson, virtuoso flutist (with French pianist Jean-
Phillipe Collard), in concert at
the Stevens Center. First concert in the center by a graduate
of the school.

June 2
Commencement exercises at
NCSA, with dancer/choreogra-
pher Ruth Page.

June 13–Aug. 9
International Music Program.
Dance students study in Rome.

July 27
Jane E. Milley appointed chan-
cellor, to assume her duties
September 1.

vided the philosophical and spiritual
gridwork for this school, and as one who
came to it later, it is *that* foundation
which has made it possible for me to do
anything good that I have done. Giannini
was so much on target and the people remarkable who supported him and the
original faculty who set the school up,
who set the aims, who resisted lots of
temptations such as "Why shouldn't
we have music education here? Why
shouldn't the school be a lot broader?" I
appreciate that very much. . . . It's those
early years and the original conception
that have allowed the school to become
everything good that it has become.
Whether they would even recognize the
place or not is another question. I didn't
know Giannini. I never met him personally. So, if he were here, for all we know,
he'd be tearing his hair out. "This isn't
what I had in mind at all!" I doubt that.
But I must say, a school this young, to
have such a well-formed tradition,
[principles] that are so sound and that
constantly inspire efforts from the faculty
and from the students far beyond any normal expectations, I mean, that's, that's a
remarkable achievement. And somewhere
in this history of the school, I'm sure
you're going to get to the essence of that.
This school has a spirit, this school has an
energy, has an approach that, sure, is the
result of the people here, and all that, but
that wouldn't be enough. It had to be, it
had to come directly from the original inspiration of the school and the way those
early guys went about doing it. And I
think it's really a remarkable achievement.
Somewhere that's got to get in, okay?

NOTES

ABBREVIATIONS

DAH   Division of Archives and History of the North Carolina Department of Cultural Resources, Raleigh

NCSA   Archives of the North Carolina School of the Arts, Winston-Salem

CHAPTER I

1. Ragan, ed., *New Day*, frontispiece, facing a portrait of Terry Sanford.
2. Mitchell, ed., *Messages, Addresses, and Public Papers of Terry Sanford*, p. 115.
3. The election of 1960 in North Carolina was closely contested (Sanford, 735,248 to Robert L. Gavin's 613,975), reflecting the national contest (in North Carolina, Kennedy over Nixon by 713,318 to 655,648). After Sanford had received the Democratic nomination for governor, he endorsed John F. Kennedy, a controversial move at that time as North Carolinians were suspicious of Roman Catholicism.
See pp. 14–19, in Sanford, *But What about the People?* for an informal account of the campaign. Sanford points out that although his campaign covered important issues other than education, it was the Quality Education Program on which "we built our hopes for the state's growth" (p. 19).
4. Mitchell, ed., *Messages of Sanford*, p. 118.
5. Ragan, ed., *New Day*, p. 15.
6. Graham Jones, biographical sketch of Terry Sanford, in Mitchell, ed., *Messages of Sanford*, p. xxviii; Winfred Godwin, interview with Bruce Stewart, March 5, 1979, NCSA.
7. Ragan, ed., *New Day*, pp. 49, 55.
8. Sanford, *But What about the People?* pp. 5, xiv; see also Sanford, address to the American Symphony Orchestra League and Community Arts Councils, Detroit, Michigan, 1964 (Mitchell, ed., *Messages of Sanford*, pp. 440–49) and the bill that created the North Carolina School of the Arts (Article 4, Chp. 116 of the General Statutes), which declares that it is "the policy of the State to foster, encourage and promote, and to provide assistance for, the cultural development of the citizens of North Carolina."
9. James Christian Pfohl, interview with Douglas Zinn, December 22, 1981, NCSA; "President's Remarks," Mrs. Kennedy's First Young People's Concert, August 22, 1961 (Pfohl's transcript); "President Hears Brevard Orchestra," *Journal and Sentinel* [Winston-Salem], August 23, 1961.
10. President Lyndon Johnson's determination that his administration should also recognize the place of the arts in the "Great Society" resulted in the formation of the National Council on the Arts and the National Foundation on the Arts and

the Humanities Act of 1965, which created two endowments, one for the arts and one for the humanities (Lowry, ed., *Performing Arts*, pp. 17–18, 21). John Ehle was appointed a member of the National Council on the Humanities, 1966–70, and R. Philip Hanes, Jr., whose influence was crucial in locating the school of the arts in Winston-Salem, was named a member of the National Council of the Arts, 1965–70.

11. The law was changed in 1977, during the administration of Governor James B. Hunt; Joe Doster, interview with Bruce Stewart, March 9, 1979; Hugh Cannon, interview with Douglas Zinn, October 27, 1981, NCSA; Sam Ragan quotes from interviews with J. A. C. Dunn (*Chapel Hill Weekly*, September 1964), and Joe Doster and Jay Jenkins (*Charlotte Observer*, August 16, 1964) in *New Day*, pp. 105–9. Sanford, in talking to Dunn, expressed his disappointment at the state's inaction on slum housing and the apparent ineffectiveness of his highway safety program and the Crescent 2000 Commission (meant to provide for orderly growth in the Piedmont Crescent, the arc extending from Raleigh to Charlotte). "These are examples of what this office could have done if I had realized the influence the office has, regardless of its occupant, just the name itself carried a lot of weight."

12. Andrew Jones, interview with Douglas Zinn, February 17, 1982, NCSA; Cannon interview; Sanford, *But What about the People?* p. 51.

13. "One-Man Rand," pp. 77–78. The Rand Corporation, founded in 1948 in Santa Monica, California, is an independent, nonprofit research organization funded by federal, state, and local governments, private corporations, foundations, and its own fees and endowments. Rand maintains a large staff of research professionals who study—among other things—problems in American society such as education, communication, racial discrimination, poverty, and so on. John Ehle would seem to fit the description. Cannon interview; see also Joel Fleishman interview with Douglas Zinn, January 4, 1982: "It was, in fact, John [Ehle] who did virtually all of the development of the work on the school of the arts . . . basically, John always carried the initiative."

14. *Move Over, Mountain* and *Kingstree Island* were published by William Morrow and Company, New York, and *Lion on the Hearth* by Harper and Brothers. Ehle also wrote biographies in the 1950s and 1960s: *The Survivor* (New York: Holt, 1958); *Shepherd of the Streets* (New York: Sloane, 1960); and *The Free Men* (New York: Harper & Row, 1965), an account of the 1963 civil rights struggle in Chapel Hill, which is surely one of the earliest examples of what has since come to be called the "New Journalism." Ehle was awarded North Carolina's Mayflower Society Cup in 1965 for *The Free Men*, and for his fiction, the Sir Walter Raleigh Prize, 1964, 1967, 1970, and 1975. Ehle's six North Carolina novels following *Lion on the Hearth* are *The Land Breakers* (1964), *The Road* (1967), *Time of Drums* (1970), *The Journey of August King* (1971), *The Winter People* (1982), and *Last One Home* (1984), all published by Harper & Row. In 1974 Random House published Ehle's novel *The Changing of the Guard*, a tour de force in which Ehle not only tells the story of a motion picture company shooting on location in Paris but writes the movie his characters appear in as well (a tale of the French Revolution, told—in typical Ehle fashion—from the unexpected point of view of the unhappy King Louis XVI). *The Cheeses and Wines of England and France, with Notes on Irish Whiskey* (New York: Harper & Row, 1972) is a charming disquisition (with recipes) on two of Ehle's

hobbies. Biographical information on John Ehle can be found in *Who's Who in America* and *Who's Who in the South and Southwest* (Chicago: A. N. Marquis Co.) from 1952 to the present. Newspaper articles about Ehle are too numerous to cite. For easy reference, see the Clippings File in the North Carolina Collection, Wilson Library, University of North Carolina, Chapel Hill. For a thorough critical reading of Ehle's mountain novels, see Banner, "The North Carolina Mountaineer in Native Fiction."

15. John Ehle, speech delivered at a national meeting on gifted students, sponsored by the Sid Richardson Foundation of Fort Worth, Texas, June 10, 1981 (hereafter cited as Texas speech); Ehle, "What's the Matter with Chapel Hill?" *News and Observer* [Raleigh], May 14, 1961; Ehle, interview with Leslie Banner and Douglas Zinn, December 8, 1983.

16. Robert Frost, speech, March 3, 1961, at Memorial Hall, on the campus of the University of North Carolina at Chapel Hill, tape recording in the North Carolina Collection, Wilson Library, University of North Carolina, Chapel Hill.

17. Ehle interview.

18. Ehle, Texas speech.

19. Lowry, ed., *Performing Arts,* p. 5.

20. Lowry, "The University and the Creative Arts," pp. 102–3, originally delivered before the Association of Graduate Schools, New Orleans, October 24, 1961.

21. Ibid., p. 104.

22. Ibid., p. 112.

23. Ehle proposed the North Carolina science high school in 1972 to Democratic gubernatorial candidate Hargrove "Skipper" Bowles. When Republican James Holshouser was elected, Ehle shelved the project for four years, until the election of James B. Hunt, who determinedly supported the school in spite of early opposition from the Department of Public Instruction and educators from the state's major colleges and universities (Ehle, Texas speech).

24. Sanford, *But What about the People?* pp. 55, 144.

25. Terry Sanford, interview with Douglas Zinn, January 22, 1982; Tom Lambeth, interview with Douglas Zinn, March 19, 1982; Fleishman interview; Ehle, "A Letter about Vittorio Giannini," p. 7.

26. Ehle interview. Sam Ragan remembers that John Ehle consulted him about the governor's job offer, "and I said, 'Well, jump at it—you're the right man for it.'" Ragan credits Sanford for having recognized that "John was a good spokesman, he was really a first-rate writer, and he also was a person who wasn't afraid to look at ideas or to entertain new ideas" (Sam Ragan, interview with Douglas Zinn, March 5, 1982). See also Sanford's reference to this dinner in *But What about the People?* pp. 50–51, and Ehle's *Newsweek* interview of June 1, 1964, in which he erroneously places the famous dinner in August rather than April of 1962: "I had taken a leave from the university and was on my way to New York to begin a novel when I got a call from the governor. He asked me to have dinner. That was 21 months ago. Helluva long dinner" (p. 78). *Newsweek* captioned the accompanying photo of Ehle, "The man who came to dinner."

27. Ehle, "A Letter about Vittorio Giannini," pp. 7–8; Ehle, Texas speech; see also Fleishman interview: "It was [John Ehle] that got in touch with the foundation and set up a meeting with McNeil Lowry at the Ford Foundation."

28. Ehle, "A Letter about Vittorio Giannini," p. 8; W. McNeil Lowry, interview with Douglas Zinn, December 6, 1982; Cannon interview. The exact date of the first "Governor's Weekend" at Transylvania Music Camp does not appear on the day-by-day calendar of the governor's activities, kept in Terry Sanford's press secretary's files for 1961–64. In a 1965 interview with Dorothy Nesbitt for *Dance Scope* magazine (see "North Carolina Leads the Way—A State School for the Arts," *Dance Scope,* Spring 1965, pp. 15–18), Hugh Cannon recalled going to Brevard with the governor on a Friday morning. The governor's schedule for July 1962 shows that on Friday, July 13 and Friday, July 20, he had appointments in Raleigh, but the week of July 22–28, the governor was taking a short week off, dividing his time between Raleigh and his family home in Fayetteville. Since records at the Brevard, North Carolina, hospital show that Vittorio Giannini was an in-patient there July 13–30, 1962, it is evident that Governor Sanford decided on the spur of the moment to extend his working vacation to include a trip to the mountains on Friday, July 27 (see "Governor Terry Sanford's Schedules," DAH).

29. Pfohl interview; Sanford, *But What about the People?* pp. 59–60.

30. Pfohl interview; see Joseph E. Maddy, "Gifted Child," *New York Times,* March 8, 1964. Maddy opened his privately supported, expanded Interlochen—the dream of a lifetime—only two months or so after Terry Sanford's 1962 visit to Brevard galvanized the North Carolina governor into action for a state-supported conservatory. On November 21, 1962, John Ehle, by then secretary of the North Carolina Conservatory Committee, wrote to Maddy requesting information about the school and a print of Maddy's film, *The Three R's and the Arts,* which Ehle hoped to show at the third meeting of the North Carolina Conservatory Committee, December 6, 1962 (DAH).

Letters in the DAH and newspaper reports about the meetings do not indicate that the film was used or even received, nor does Interlochen seem to have been mentioned at the meeting or visited by committee members. But because Pfohl and Ehle were obviously knowledgeable about Interlochen, the other members of the conservatory committee must have been informed about it as well. Walter E. Ross, director of libraries, National Music Corporation, sent Ehle a black and white print of the film, but it may not have arrived in time for the meeting (Ross to Ehle, November 28, 1962, DAH).

31. Pfohl interview.

32. Ibid.

33. Sanford interview.

34. Cannon interview.

35. Ehle, "A Letter about Vittorio Giannini," p. 8.

36. Pfohl interview.

37. Ehle interview; Ehle, "A Letter about Vittorio Giannini," p. 15. Giannini was married to Lucia Avella from June 1, 1931 until their divorce in 1951 (David Ewen, "Vittorio Giannini," in *American Composers: A Biographical Dictionary* [London: Robert Hale, 1983], p. 256).

38. de Schauensee, "The Gianninis," p. 14–16.

39. Ibid., p. 16; Marracco, "Vittorio Giannini," p. 349.

40. Among Giannini's principal works are four (numbered) symphonies (1950–

60); three divertimentos for orchestra (1953, 1961, 1964); two violin sonatas (1926, 1945); *Lucedia,* opera (1934); *Requiem,* for vocal soloists, chorus, and orchestra (1936); *The Scarlet Letter,* opera (1937); *Beauty and the Beast,* radio opera (1938); *Blennerhasset,* radio opera (1939); *Frescobaldia,* for orchestra (1948); *The Taming of the Shrew,* opera (1950); *Canticle for Christmas,* for baritone, chorus, and orchestra (1951); *Canticle of the Martyrs,* for vocal soloists, chorus, and orchestra (1957); *The Medead,* monodrama for soprano and orchestra (1960); *The Harvest,* opera (1961); and *The Servant of Two Masters,* opera (1966) (partial listing, taken from Ewen, "Vittorio Giannini," p. 257).

41. Marracco, "Vittorio Giannini," p. 349.

42. Ewen, "Vittorio Giannini," p. 25.

43. M. L. Mark, "The Band Music of Vittorio Giannini," 77–80.

44. The Giannini sisters, Christina, Maura, and Evadne, interview with Douglas Zinn, November 12, 1982.

45. Lowry interview. Determining what those concepts and principles should be proved more troublesome than perhaps even McNeil Lowry bargained for. When the Ford Foundation announced in December 1963 its award of $7,756,000 to strengthen professional ballet, adherents of modern dance such as Martha Graham and José Limon were outraged that all the money was given to support the development of classical ballet, with the lion's share going to George Balanchine's School of American Ballet. Albert Goldberg, writing in the *Los Angeles Times,* quoted angry pronouncements from Martha Graham, Juilliard's Martha Hill, and impresario Sol Hurok, pointing out that for the moment, modern dance in America had had "the door slammed on its toes." Hill expressed fear that, given the frail financial footing on which American dance had balanced itself for decades, the injection of a massive amount of money by Ford solely into classical ballet would effectively create "a monopoly unhealthy to the full development of American dance." Goldberg accused Ford of entering into "the dangerous field of aesthetic discrimination"—a most unfair criticism, it would seem, because the parceling out of so much money on any other basis is difficult to imagine. It is no wonder that, as Philip Hanes recalls, Lowry later told an early meeting of the National Endowment for the Arts that "nobody is ever grateful for giving away money. . . . They all treat you as though you're the worst guy in the world" (Albert Goldberg, *Los Angeles Times,* January 5, 1964; R. Philip Hanes, Jr., interview with Leslie Banner and Douglas Zinn, December 8, 1983). See also, "Ford Dance Grants Assailed in Letter," *New York Times,* January 7, 1964.

The Ford Foundation commissioned three major works by Giannini: *The Medead,* a monodrama for soprano and orchestra, based on Euripides (premiered October 20, 1960, by Irene Jordan and the Atlanta Symphony); *The Harvest,* libretto by Giannini and Karl Flaster, a tragic opera set on an American farm at the turn of the century (premiered November 25, 1961, by the Lyric Opera of Chicago); and *The Servant of Two Masters,* an opera buffa, libretto by Bernard Stambler, adapted from Goldoni (commissioned by the New York City Opera with a grant from the Ford Foundation, and premiered in New York March 9, 1967, some three months after the composer's death) (Ewen, "Vittorio Giannini," p. 257).

46. Sanford, *But What about the People?* p. 60. In his January 22, 1982, interview

with Douglas Zinn, Sanford recalls writing the memo to Tom Lambeth, but interviews with both Joel Fleishman and Lambeth (January 4, 1982, and March 19, 1982) indicate that the order to set up the North Carolina Conservatory Committee went first to Fleishman. The original memo, which is not in the DAH, has apparently been lost. In a note dated July 15, 1963, John Ehle wrote to Joel Fleishman that he could not "locate in any file the Governor's memo to you of last summer pertaining to the conservatory. I do think a copy should be found and put with the school records. Please do all you can" (DAH).

47. [Ehle], *A Statement Concerning the Proposed Performing Arts School in North Carolina* (Raleigh, N.C.: The Governor's Office, April 6, 1964), n.p., DAH (hereafter cited as *Governor's Book*).

48. Fleishman interview. Also see Sanford interview: "Your friends and supporters, as you're looking [at] various boards and positions in the government, put together several thousand [names]. So you keep a book on people that ought to be put on something, and that's one way of doing it; and other people think of names, and that's another way names emerge. . . . [For example, Martha Muilenburg] had been very much interested in music. She was also one of my political supporters . . . I thought Martha, one, had an interest. I thought two, that she had a lot of energy and could get things done, and she was a very remarkable lady."

49. Biographical information on the members of the North Carolina Conservatory Committee has been summarized from pp. 5–32, Bruce B. Stewart, "The Politics of Art: The Origin of the North Carolina School of the Arts," NCSA.

50. *Governor's Book*; Cannon interview.

51. "A Performing Arts School?" *Greensboro Daily News,* May 12, 1963; E.M.Y., "Tar Heel Talk: Mr. Ehle's Feather," ibid., May 14, 1963.

52. Sanford interview.

53. Ehle interview; Ehle, "A Letter about Vittorio Giannini," pp. 7–8; Lowry interview.

54. Lowry interview.

55. Lowry, ed., *Performing Arts,* p. 5.

56. John J. O'Connor, "Performing Arts: Dropping the Bricks," *Wall Street Journal,* August 12, 1969.

57. Rockefeller Panel, *Performing Arts,* pp. 204–5.

58. Kirstein, "The Performing Arts and Our Egregious Elite," pp. 195, 189.

59. Ibid., 185–86.

60. Ehle interview.

61. Minutes of initial meeting, March 29, 1961, Cultural Advancement for North Carolina, Chairman, Rachel Davis, [North Carolina] House of Representatives, attached to a letter from Davis to Ehle, February 12, 1963, DAH.

62. Ibid.

63. Siebolt Frieswyk to Ralph Andrews, January 4, 1963, DAH.

64. Derived from Sanford's reply to Andrews, January 22, 1963; Andrews to Ehle, January 24, 1963. See also Ehle to Andrews, January 22, 1963. On May 7, 1963, Davis wrote to Ehle pledging to support the conservatory bill in the legislature "in every way" (DAH).

CHAPTER 2

1. Ehle interview.

2. Ibid.

3. Lambeth interview.

4. Ehle interview.

5. Ibid. Sanford essentially confirmed this interpretation of Ehle's role in 1966, in his own account of the establishing of the school of the arts: "I appointed a group of knowledgeable citizens, with Mrs. Martha Muilenburg of Charlotte as chairman. Actually, this was another part of John Ehle's idea, so I assigned him to bird-dog the committee" (*But What about the People?* p. 60).

6. Ehle, "A Letter about Vittorio Giannini," pp. 8–9; Ehle interview.

7. Ehle to Muilenburg, September 19, 1962; Ehle to Lowry, September 22, 1962, DAH.

8. Ehle interview; Fleishman interview; Ehle, "A Letter about Vittorio Giannini," p. 10.

9. Ehle to Muilenburg, October 4, 1962; minutes of the September 27, 1962 meeting of the NCCC, DAH.

10. Giannini's presentation derived from Ehle's minutes of the September 27, 1962 meeting, sent to Martha Muilenburg for approval on October 4, 1962 (DAH).

11. Ragan, Weaver, and Wilson were absent; Younts and Cone had not yet been appointed (minutes, September 27, 1962, DAH). It soon became clear that the three performing arts belonged together because of their interrelationship; the School of Design and Production eventually emerged as the necessary support for the performing arts.

12. Minutes, September 27, 1962.

13. Ehle to Lowry, September 28, 1962, DAH.

14. Norris L. Hodgkins, Jr., to Mrs. Carl Durham, October 26, 1962, DAH. Hodgkins thanks Durham for visiting the Boyd property, a 165-acre tract owned by the late author's widow. The Boyd home, Weymouth, was later opened as a center for artists.

15. Ehle to Cone, October 29, 1962; see also Cone to Joseph M. McDaniel, October 25, 1962, DAH.

16. Louis K. Wechsler, "A Statement on the History, Aims, and Program of the High School of Music and Art, New York City," June 28, 1960, DAH.

17. Lowry interview.

18. Muilenburg to Ehle, November 6, 1962, DAH. My account of the November 2 meeting of the NCCC is taken from Ehle's notes, DAH, and from newspaper accounts in the 3 November editions of the *Greensboro Daily News,* the *News and Observer* [Raleigh], and the *Charlotte Observer.*

19. A few months after the *Journal's* November 6 editorial, Gramley told Ehle that "the reports had not been accurate": "He told me he was for it [the conservatory], had never been against it, in fact . . . and that he hoped it would be put right across the street from him. Now, there's a man who really had gotten the word" (John Ehle, reading from his Raleigh journal during the December 8, 1983 interview); Gene Strassler to Ehle, September 23, 1962; string instruction proposal

from Earl Beach, filed with October 1962 DAH material; Arnold E. Hoffman to Ehle, September 25, 1962, DAH.

20. Pete McKnight's report in September 1962 folder, DAH; also see Ehle's memo of November 19, 1962 to McKnight, Weaver, Giannini, Durham, and Muilenburg re: the subcommittee's itinerary in New York, DAH; McKnight's memories of the committee's work taken from his February 10, 1979, interview with Bruce Stewart at the News and Observer Building in Charlotte, North Carolina (NCSA).

21. Snyder to Ehle, December 2, 1962, DAH.

22. Martha Muilenburg enclosed a copy of Governor Sanford's original letter to each member of the North Carolina Conservatory Committee and of Vittorio Giannini's presentation at the NCCC's first meeting with each letter of invitation. Arts leaders were asked to limit their comments to ten to fifteen minutes and to provide a written summary. Judging from the list appended to the undated draft of Mrs. Muilenburg's letter in the DAH, the invitations were accepted by representatives of every institution and organization approached.

23. Lowry interview; Cannon interview.

24. Ehle, "A Letter about Vittorio Giannini," pp. 10–11.

25. Lowry interview.

26. Ehle, Texas speech.

27. "Conservatory Group Has Closed Meet," *Raleigh Times,* December 6, 1962.

28. Lowry interview.

29. Ehle interview.

30. Dycke traced the genesis of the High School of the Performing Arts, not to a great ideal but to "a few boys cutting classes." When principal Franklin Keller found some of his boys at the Metropolitan Vocational High School in the boiler room, cutting class to make music, he agreed to let the music teacher try a vocational music class. Eventually, Keller enlisted the aid of Margaret Lewisohn, president of the Public Educational Association, who persuaded a number of New York artists to ask the Board of Education to establish a performing arts school. This was in 1948; today (1962), Dycke said, PA is part of the High School of Music and Art (founded by Mayor LaGuardia), but although HSMA has an academic format, PA's has remained vocational, with four periods a day devoted to the student's arts specialty (as opposed to HSMA's three-period maximum).

Acceptance at PA is by audition only, and students must progress in performance achievement or they will be dropped from the school. The program is equally divided between academics and arts training, and Dycke pointed out that in her experience there is a high correlation between academic and artistic achievement. Although some talented students do not do well academically, it is not because they are unintelligent but because their focus and interest are different. Thus PA makes allowances for the highly talented who do not perform academically, though the school does not give license. Arts progress is what retains the student.

Dycke did not feel qualified to go into details about financing, but she did cover some of the other important administrative matters: the school day lasts from 8:30 to 3:00, with eight periods of forty minutes each; the student body is around six hundred, of whom 50 to 60 percent graduate; salaries are the same for PA teachers as for teachers at New York's other public schools, but as PA's faculty members are all professionals living in a major city, they are able to supplement their incomes by practicing their craft, which, of course, is to the benefit of the school (minutes, December 6, 1962 meeting of the North Carolina Conservatory Committee, DAH).

31. My account of the December 6, 1962, open meeting of the North Carolina Conservatory Committee is based on the following accounts: Ehle, "A Letter about Vittorio Giannini," pp. 11–12; Sydney M. Cone, "Committee Work Told," *Greensboro Daily News,* May 12, 1963; Vince Horner, *News and Observer* [Raleigh], December 7, 1962; Harriet Doar, *Charlotte Observer,* December 7, 1962; *Herald* [Sanford, N.C.], December 13, 1962. Minutes of the December meeting are incomplete because a tape was made of the day's testimony, which was to be transcribed. No transcription could be found in the DAH, but the schedule of speakers at least was written down (without notation of their comments): 11:00 A.M. to noon— Benjamin Swalin, John Lehman, Lee Rigsby, Henry Janiec; noon to 1:00 P.M.— Paul Green, Ed Loessin, Harry Davis; 2:00 to 3:00 P.M. —John T. Caldwell, Glen Haydon (chairman, Music Department, UNC–Chapel Hill), James Christian Pfohl; 3:00 to 4:00 P.M. —Allan Bone (chairman, Music Department, Duke University), Earl Beach (chairman, Music Department, East Carolina College), Robert W. John (chairman, Department of Music, North Carolina College, Durham); 4:00 to 5:15 P.M.—James Frank West (head, School of Music, St. Andrews College), Clemens Sandresky (dean, School of Music, Salem College), M. T. Cousins (director, Asheville Symphony), William Spencer (chairman, Department of Music, Appalachian State Teachers College), Richard M. Renfro (director of education, Western Carolina College). Recognized from the floor were Carlyle Sitterson (dean of the College of Arts and Sciences, UNC–Chapel Hill), Arnold Hoffman (director of music, Department of Public Instruction), Wilton Mason (professor of music, UNC–Chapel Hill), and Romulus V. Linney (director of fine arts, Student Union, North Carolina State College, Raleigh).

32. Ben Swalin, interview with Douglas Zinn, January 25, 1982.

33. Mrs. G. V. Lawrence to Ehle, January 4, 1963 (DAH); Ehle, "A Letter about Vittorio Giannini," pp. 11–12.

34. Ehle interview; Ehle to Lowry, December 20, 1962 (DAH). On December 14, Ehle also gave Marjorie Dycke an update and told her that her appearance before the NCCC had given the school "a good shove forward" (DAH).

35. Sanford to Cone, December 17, 1962; Cone to Muilenburg, December 22, 1962, DAH.

36. Sanford to Mereb Mossman, January 22, 1963, DAH.

37. Ehle to Mrs. George C. Eichhorn, February 5, 1963, DAH.

38. Memo from Hargrove Bowles, Jr., to Ehle, February 12, 1963, DAH.

39. Muilenburg to Sanford, February 4, 1963, DAH.

40. Cone to Ehle, February 11, 1963, DAH.

41. Cone to Gordon Hanes, February 19, 1963, DAH.

42. Ehle to Sanford, February 14, 1963, DAH; Lowry interview.

43. Godwin interview.

44. Ehle to Sanford, February 14, 1963; Sanford to Babcock, Reynolds and Company, Winston-Salem, March 14, 1963; Ehle to Lowry, March 18, 1963; Ehle, yellow pad notes for Ford visit, March 12, 1963, all in DAH.

45. Muilenburg to Ehle, February 4, 1963, DAH; Ehle interview.

46. NCCC minutes, March 15, 1963, DAH.

47. All quotations and summaries are based on the text of the NCCC report of March 21, 1963, as reproduced in *The Governor's Book*.

48. Winston-Salem now argues it has become such a cultural center, as innumerable articles in the popular press conspire to affirm.

49. McKnight to Muilenburg, March 14, 1963, DAH; McKnight interview; Ehle to Henry Hall Wilson, March 18, 1963; Ehle to Gordon Hanes, March 18, 1963, DAH.

50. NCCC Report, *The Governor's Book*.

51. See, e.g., Sanford to Steed Rollins, *Durham Morning Herald;* H. W. Kendall, *Greensboro Daily News;* David Whichard, *Reflector* [Greenville]; Henry Belk, *News-Argus* [Goldsboro], March 27, 1963; Ehle to Bill Snider, *Greensboro Daily News,* March 27, 1963, DAH.

52. *The Governor's Book,* p. 11 of the committee report.

53. Sanford to Cone, March 27, 1963; Ehle to Lowry, March 18, 1963; Ehle to Rigsby, March 28, 1963; Rigsby to Ehle, April 2, 1963, all in DAH.

54. Ehle interview.

55. Ehle, reading from his 1962–63 Raleigh journal during the December 8, 1963 interview.

CHAPTER 3

1. Letter texts as reproduced in *The Governor's Book*.

2. Brooks Atkinson, "Critic at Large: North Carolina Looks toward Developing Special School for the Arts," *New York Times,* May 21, 1963.

3. Ehle, Texas speech.

4. Sanford to Cannon, April 30, 1963; Cannon to Sanford, May 1, 1963, DAH; Cannon interview.

5. Ehle added a seventh "Whereas" in the final draft of the bill: "WHEREAS, one or more North Carolina communities stand ready to provide land and buildings for the campus of the school." My analysis of John Ehle's influence on the NCSA bill is based on a comparison of the drafts in the DAH with the final version passed by the legislature. I have not discussed all the alterations, but only those that seem to me to be the significant changes and additions in Ehle's hand.

6. Ehle, Texas speech.

7. Ehle interview; Giannini to Ehle, April 6, 1963, DAH.

8. Cannon interview; *Journal of the Senate of the General Assembly of the State of North Carolina, Session 1963,* p. 339; *Journal of the House of Representatives of the General Assembly of the State of North Carolina, Session 1963,* p. 542; "Bill to Create Arts School Wins Approval," *Greensboro Record,* May 7, 1963; "Committee OK's Arts Center Bill," *Raleigh Times,* May 7, 1963; *Journal of the Senate,* p. 346; *Journal of the House of Representatives,* p. 600; Ehle, Texas speech; Ben Roney and Judge David Britt, interview with Douglas Zinn, October 7, 1982.

9. John Ehle, reading from his 1962–63 Raleigh journal during the December 8, 1983 interview. See also note, "Dear John—Will you please be at Higher Education meeting 9:00 AM tomorrow Friday, House.—Rachel Davis," penciled in date May 10, 1963, DAH.

10. "Bill to Create Arts School Wins Approval," *Greensboro Record,* May 7, 1963;

Harold Luce to Cannon, May 7, 1963; Ehle to Sanford, May 8, 1963; Sanford to Luce, May 8, 1963, all in DAH.

11. William Hilbrink to Cannon, May 10, 1963; Sanford to Anita Patterson, Juanita Jones, Jean Spencer, Mary Ida Hodge, Heath Ellis, Nancy Gray Riley, May 16, 1963, DAH.

12. Ehle's 1962–63 Raleigh journal, read during the December 8, 1983 interview.

13. As indicated on the copy of the governor's answer to Luce in the DAH.

14. Raymond Lowery, "Onward and Upward with State's Arts," *News and Observer* [Raleigh], May 19, 1963.

15. Ehle interview.

16. Ibid.; Ehle to Miles Wolff, May 14, 1963 (not sent); Ehle to Wolff, May 14, 1963 (sent); Wolff to Ehle, May 10, 1963, DAH.

17. Ehle interview.

18. Ehle to Wolff, May 14, 1963, DAH.

19. An unsigned and undated memo in the May 1963 material from Ehle's office in the DAH. It is clearly a point-by-point refutation of the *Greensboro Daily News* articles. The name "Gene Strassler" is written in pencil in the upper right-hand corner, and John Ehle has confirmed that he did not write the memo.

20. Mrs. Frank Starbuck to Sanford, May 12, 1963; Sanford to Mrs. Frank Starbuck, May 21, 1963, DAH.

21. E. M. Y., "Tar Heel Talk: Mr. Ehle's Feather," *Greensboro Daily News,* May 14, 1963.

22. "Gut-Shot Aimed at the University," *Chapel Hill Weekly,* May 23, 1963; "Keep the Aspidistra Flying," ibid., May 26, 1963.

23. Editorial, "A Technical School for the Arts," *Twin City Sentinel* [Winston-Salem], May 14, 1963; Raymond Lowery, "Onward and Upward with State's Arts," *News and Observer* [Raleigh], May 19, 1963; Harriet Doar, "School of Performing Arts," *Charlotte Observer,* May 19, 1963; Ehle, Texas speech.

24. Agenda notes for open hearing in committee in the General Assembly, May 23, 1963, DAH; Ehle, Texas Speech.

25. Sanford to E. H. Anderson, Hickory, N.C., Jack H. Campbell, Morganton, N.C., Thomas A. Henson, Greensboro, N.C., John B. Russell, Greensboro, N.C., all letters written May 20, 1963; Sanford to Joseph R. Morton, Greensboro, N.C., and Paul Hickfong, Greensboro, N.C., both written June 6, 1963, DAH.

26. Ehle to Sanford, June 6, 1963; Ehle to Harriet Doar, May 23, 1963; Ehle to Sanford, May 15, 1963; Ehle to Cannon, June 11, 1963 [apparently sent June 17, 1963]; Ehle to Cannon, June 4, 1963, DAH.

27. McKnight to Ehle, April 26, 1963; Ehle to James Rush, *Winston-Salem Journal-Sentinel* executive news editor, April 9, 1963; (the Raleigh writer was probably Raymond Lowery); Lois Haswell to Sanford, May 17, 1963, DAH.

28. Ehle interview; Ehle to Louise Esteven, May 30, 1963; A. H. Reiss, associate editor, *Arts Management,* to Ehle, June 6, 1963; Ehle to Reiss, June 10, 1963; Ehle to Richard Coe, June 11, 1963, DAH.

29. "Cart before the Horse," *News and Observer* [Raleigh], June 10, 1963; Cannon interview; Roney and Britt interview. See State of North Carolina, *1963 Session Laws and Resolutions* ([Raleigh, N.C.:] Published by Authority), pp. 1014–15, 1018–19, 1309, 1422. Matching funds for community colleges were set aside "pursuant to the

provisions of Chapter 115A of the General Statutes of North Carolina" (Session Laws of 1963), which was the charter for the state's new system of community colleges, technical institutes, and industrial education centers. Governor Sanford's program to help the retarded was specifically identified in the bill: to UNC to establish a child development center, $390,000, and to establish a training program for teachers for the retarded, $240,600; to Murdoch School for training, $155,960; for teacher scholarships and curriculum development, $190,000; for vocational training for the retarded, $222,000; for vocational rehabilitation in residential schools, $230,092; for the establishment of evaluative clinics to identify the retarded, $354,000; to the Council on Mental Retardation for studies, $40,000.

30. *Journal of the Senate,* p. 650; William A. Shires, "Around the Square—School for Arts Seems Assured in Fund Grant," *Raleigh Times,* June 12, 1963.

31. Ehle to Wilbur Jolly, June 17, 1963, DAH, emphasis added.

32. Roney and Britt interview; Ehle interview.

33. Ehle, "A Letter about Vittorio Giannini," p. 15; "Senate OKs Fund for Arts School," *News and Observer* [Raleigh], June 18, 1963; "On Dix Hill and 'Toe-Dancers,'" *Charlotte Observer,* June 21, 1963; Giannini to Lowry, telegram, June 18, 1963, DAH.

34. H.B. 1395, Chapter 1207, "An Act to Regulate Visiting Speakers at State Supported Colleges and Universities," ratified June 26, 1963 (State of North Carolina, *1963 Session Laws and Resolutions* [Raleigh, N.C.], Published by Authority).

35. Terry Sanford, speaking on the occasion of the presentation of a bust of Dr. James H. Semans, December 5, 1981; Cannon interview.

36. Joe Doster, interview with Bruce Stewart, March 9, 1979; Roney and Britt interview; Ragan, presentation speech, December 5, 1981; Gordon Hanes, interview with Douglas Zinn, October 14, 1983; Doster interview; Sanford interview; Ehle, "A Letter about Vittorio Giannini," p. 16.

37. Sam Ragan and Terry Sanford, presentation speeches, December 5, 1981; Sanford, *But What about the People?,* pp. 61–62.

38. *Journal of the House of Representatives,* pp. 1152–53; "Assembly Okays N.C. Arts School," *Charlotte Observer,* June 22, 1963; Roney and Britt interview; Cannon interview; Tom Inman, "Arts School Bill Enacted," *News and Observer* [Raleigh], June 22, 1963; Bill Connelly, "Performing-Arts School Approved," *Winston-Salem Journal,* June 22, 1963.

39. Roney and Britt interview.

40. "Assembly Okays"; Connelly, "Performing-Arts School Approved."

41. Others who spoke for the bill were Ned Delamar (Pamlico) and Martha Evans (Mecklenburg) (Inman, "Arts School Bill Enacted"; Connelly, "Performing-Arts School Approved").

42. Roney and Britt interview.

43. "Assembly Okays"; Inman, "Arts School Bill Enacted"; Connelly, "Performing-Arts School Approved"; Ray Parker, Jr., "State's Politics Still Breed Hearty Lot of Individualists," *News and Observer* [Raleigh], July 7, 1963.

44. Roney and Britt interview.

45. Voting in the affirmative were Representatives Badgley, Bahnson, Bailey, Baker, Barbee, Bebber, Bennett of Yancey, Britt of Johnston, Britt of Robeson, Brooks, Burden, Carroll, Chase, Coggins, Daniels, Davis, Delamar, Dolley,

Drummond, Eagles, Euliss, Evans of Chowan, Evans of Mecklenburg, Forbes, Galiafianakis, Garinger, Green, Greenwood, Gregory, Hamrick, Harding, Hargett, Harriss, Hawfield, Henley, Hicks, High, Hill, Horton, Hunter, Jernigan, Johnson of Duplin, Jones, Kerr, Lane, Leatherman, Leatherwood, Lupton, Mabe, Martin, McFadyen, McMillan of Robeson, Moody, Owens, Palmer, Pope, Quinn, Ragsdale, Ramsey of Person, Roberson, Rodenbaugh, Sawyer, Saxon, Sermons, Snyder, Speed, Strickland, Swann, Tate, Taylor, Thornburg, Venters, Wallace, Watkins, White, Whitehurst, Wicker, Wilson, Woodard of Wilson, and Zollicoffer—80.

Voting in the negative were Representatives Bennett of Carteret, Calder, Garner, Godwin, Holshouser, Johnson of Alleghany, Kiser, Lacy, Leonard, Messer, Newman, O'Hanlon, Osteen, Randall, Simpson, Uzzell, Vaughn, and Woodard of Northampton—18. The following absent members were paired: Rep. Story, aye, Rep. Ramsey of Madison, no (*Journal of the House of Representatives*, pp. 1178–79).

46. Arthur Johnsey, "Conservatory Gets Approval of House," *Greensboro Daily News*, June 22, 1963; Ehle to McKnight, June 22, 1963, DAH.

CHAPTER 4

1. Ehle to Lowry, August 13, 1963; Lowry to Ehle, August 8, 1963, DAH.

2. McKnight interview; Ehle, Texas speech; Ehle, "A Letter about Vittorio Giannini," p. 17.

3. Sanford to Muilenburg, July 2, 1963; Ehle to Lowry, July 4, 1963; Sanford to Lowry, August 12, 1963 (not sent), August 16, 1963, DAH.

4. Ehle to Joe Robinson, Department of Economics and Sociology, University of Cologne, Cologne, Germany, July 2, 1963, DAH.

5. "They Seek a Climate for Arts," *Charlotte Observer*, December 30, 1963; Alex Coffin, "Is Arts School Coming Here?" *Charlotte News*, December 30, 1963.

6. Ehle interview.

7. Sanford to Lowry, August 12, 1963, not sent; Sanford to Giannini, September 27, 1963, DAH.

8. Giannini did not send Ehle a copy of this curriculum, however, until August 8 (DAH).

9. Giannini to Ehle, July 16, 1963, DAH.

10. Ehle to Sanford, September 23, 1963, not sent; Ehle to Giannini, October 22, 1963, DAH.

11. Giannini to Ehle, November 9, 1963; Ehle to Giannini, December 5, 1963; Eric Salmon to Ehle, January 1, 1964; Ruth Mayleas to Ehle, February 3, 1964, DAH.

12. Ehle to Giannini, November 5, 13, 1963; Giannini to Ehle, November 12, 1963, DAH.

13. Lowry to Ehle, August 8, 1963, DAH; "Under the Dome," *News and Observer* [Raleigh], November 15, 1963; Coffin, "Is Arts School Coming Here?"; Ehle interview.

14. Ehle interview.

15. Ibid., reading from his Raleigh journal, an entry from the late spring of 1963.

16. John Ehle, interview with Leslie Banner, October 26, 1984; "One-Man

Rand," p. 78. See also Ehle to Arthur Gelb of the *New York Times,* February 20, 1964: "Governor Sanford will be in New York City March 9th. . . . Suspect we'll move Tower of Light Building from New York World's Fair. He can discuss that" (DAH).

17. July 1963 file, notes on Ridgecrest and Lake Junaluska; Ehle to James Fowler, July 29, 1963; Fowler to Ehle, August 12, 1963, DAH; Clifford Bair to Ehle, March 31, 1964, DAH.

18. Mary Semans to Ehle, January 15, 1964; Ehle to Mary Semans, January 17, 1964, DAH; Pat Carter, "Bids for New State Schools Proposed Here," *Durham Morning Herald,* February 13, 1964; "Durham as Site for Arts School," ibid., February 15, 1964; "Under the Dome," *News and Observer* [Raleigh], November 15, 1963.

19. Advisory Board Site Selection Committee, Conference with Terry Sanford, April 29, 1964, tape recording, NCSA. The Research Triangle is primarily a scientific and industrial community although it is the home of the National Humanities Center.

20. Ehle, interview, October 26, 1984.

21. James Ross, "Hillsborough Seeking New Arts School," *Greensboro Daily News,* March 29, 1964; Ehle, Texas speech; "Orange Pealings," *News of Orange County,* October 24, 1963; "Will Hillsborough Try to Get Performing Arts Institution?" ibid., October 31, 1963; notes on a conversation with Bob Murphy, re: Hillsborough, November 12, 1963, DAH; Advisory Board tape (NCSA).

22. Sanford interview.

23. Ehle interview.

24. Ehle, "A Letter about Vittorio Giannini," p. 18.

25. Ehle to Sanford, ca. June 18, 1963, not sent, DAH.

26. "Raleigh Pushed as Arts Center," *Raleigh Times,* March 14, 1963; Cannon to Ehle, May 20, 1963, memo re: Mansion Park Building from F. B. Turner to Cannon, forwarded to Ehle; Ralph Reeves, Holloway-Reeves, Associates, Architects, Raleigh, N.C., to Sam Ragan, May 7, 1963; Ragan to Cannon, May 8, 1963; Ehle to Sanford, ca. June 18, 1963, not sent, DAH.

27. Mrs. T. Winfield Blackwell to Muilenburg, November 30, December 14, 1962, DAH; Lowry interview.

28. R. Philip Hanes, Jr., interview; Hanes to Ehle, February 27, 1963, DAH.

29. R. Philip Hanes, Jr., to Sanford, May 16, 1963, DAH; "Winston-Salem and the Arts School," *Twin City Sentinel,* May 15, 1963; "Arts School Committee Appointed," *Winston-Salem Journal,* May 22, 1963; "Philip Hanes Named Head of Committee," *Winston-Salem Journal,* May 23, 1963. In addition to Mayor Benton and Philip Hanes, the paper listed as members of the committee James B. I. Rush, executive news editor, *Winston-Salem Journal* and *Twin City Sentinel;* Mrs. Winfield Blackwell, president, Arts Council of Winston-Salem; Dale H. Gramley, president, Salem College; Katherine Bahnson, member, North Carolina Conservatory Committee; Harold W. Tribble, president, Wake Forest College; Ralph M. Stockton, Jr., trustee, Winston-Salem State College; James A. Gray, executive director, Old Salem, Inc.; William C. Herring, executive secretary, Arts Council of Winston-Salem; Sebastian C. Sommer, executive director, Winston-Salem Foundation; and Charles H. Babcock, Jr., senior vice-president, Mary Reynolds Babcock Foundation.

30. R. Philip Hanes, Jr., to Ehle, May 23, 1963; R. Philip Hanes, Jr., to Senator

Gordon Hanes, May 29, 1963; R. Philip Hanes, Jr., to Marvin Barrett, *Show* magazine, June 27, 1963, DAH. See also "Atlanta: Some Pros and Cons of Culture in the South": Ralph McGill, "As It Was"; Barbara Wyden, "As It Is," *Show,* June 1963, pp. 9–11, 104–6.

31. Ehle to Sanford, June 6, 1963, DAH; Franklin J. Keller to M. C. Benton, Jr., July 30, 1963, NCSA.

32. "Proposal of Winston-Salem as a Site for the School for the Performing Arts," August 8, 1963, DAH.

33. R. Philip Hanes, Jr., to Ehle, August 1, 1963; R. Philip Hanes, Jr., to Ehle, August 27, 1963; Ehle to R. Philip Hanes, Jr., September 4, 1963, DAH.

34. Ehle to Sanford, September 23, 1963, not sent, DAH.

35. R. Philip Hanes, Jr., to Ehle, October 19, 1963, DAH.

36. Ehle to Giannini, November 13, 1963, DAH. John Ehle may or may not have gone to Charlotte and Winston-Salem the following week, but he did travel to Washington, D.C., during this time. In a letter dated November 26, 1963 to his young friend Celeste Brouse, Ehle described his visit to the capitol as a way of comforting the child in her distress over the assassination of President Kennedy. Ehle's description gently and whimsically suggests that the president had now passed by the time of violence, into the place of peace and memory in American history: "I was in Washington last week, and was in the Capitol on Friday morning. I remembered that visit with particular concern when I heard on Friday afternoon that Mr. Kennedy had been shot. To tell you the truth, I entered the Capitol at dawn and without permission. There is a door on the East side of the building which opens onto a construction project of some sort, and I got in through that way. The building was then almost deserted; only the Negro janitors were there. They were sweeping and dusting. I walked along the hollow halls and heard them talking, the Negro voices. The place is owned by the Negroes early in the morning.

"A Negro woman in a rose-brown dress was sweeping down the marble steps with a yellow-straw broom such as one buys in a grocery store. I was really surprised, for I expected something finer.

"After wandering about at length, at last I found the rotunda. I was alone in the room, the same room which was so crowded this morning when Mr. Kennedy's body was left there. There are angels, or maybe they are heralds, at the very top of the dome, and they are painted in pastel colors. There must be thirty of them. What they signify I can't say, but they were silent, and the only noise at all was from the birds chirping outside.

"Near the top of the dome is a great circle of ivory figures, of explorers, Indians, builders, soldiers, horses, miners, scouts, artillerymen, and, finally, an aeroplane pilot. Below, all around me, were the statues of great leaders, some of them black marble. Washington and Jefferson are black. There are paintings, too, of DeSoto, of Pocahontas being baptized, of signers of the Declaration of Independence. There is a statue of Lincoln, who looks tired even in marble; he is offering a paper of some sort, a scroll. I suppose it's the Emancipation Proclamation. There is a painting of General Cornwallis surrendering, and Washington, as he resigns his commission, has his vest too tight—as usual.

"Andrew Jackson is a brown statue. He is proud and booted. There are some pilgrims in the room, and they, of course, are praying. One gathers in watching pilgrims that America was cleared and populated and constructed in a state of prayer.

"There is a head of Lafayette which someday you will want to see, and a painting of Columbus landing.

"The floor of the place is stone, a tan and brown stone, laid in a circular pattern. And over one doorway, when I left, a beautiful clock said it was 7:08, and beyond the clock I saw a smaller room and a long row of marble columns.

"There is another room beside this domed room, and in it are statues of other great Americans, and they stand at this hour of the morning very much like figures in a wax museum. Behind them the four Negro women were having a hushed conversation. As I recall, they were meeting behind Henry Clay and Mr. Calhoun.

"I went out of there and back into the rotunda, where a Negro woman was humming as she dusted the feet of Mr. Hamilton. I went on through the rotunda and was going toward the Senate chamber, anxious to get out now, somewhat moved by the sights I had seen, when a guard appeared, walked up behind me and asked me who in the world I was and how I had gotten into the place. I explained mildly, simply that I was a writer and got into all sorts of locked places. He was officially irritated and showed me out. I went away convinced that the Capitol is as fine a place to see dawn come as I have yet found anywhere in our country."

37. George L. Hall to Bill Joslin, cc John Ehle, Sam Ragan, Wesley Wallace, December 18, 1963, DAH.

38. Ehle, Texas speech.

39. Wolff to Ehle, December 18, 1963; Ehle to Wolff, December 20, 1963, DAH.

40. "They Seek a Climate for the Arts," *Charlotte Observer,* December 30, 1963; Alex Coffin, "Is Arts School Coming Here?" *Charlotte News,* December 30, 1963; "Charlotte, Winston-Salem Eyed for Performing Arts Facility," *News and Observer* [Raleigh], December 31, 1963; "Report of the Sites Selection Committee for the School of Performing Arts—Charlotte," January 22, 1964; memorandum, phone call from McKnight to Ehle, January 24, 1964, DAH. The Charlotte committee recommended the purchase of available acreage on which to build a campus at the following locations, in order of preference: Coliseum Drive, Briar Creek Road, and Randolph Road. For temporary housing it suggested Chantilly School or the Coddington Building, with the adjoining Mecklenburg Hotel. In addition to Chairman Stenhouse, committee members were W. T. Harris, Benjamin S. Horack, J. Scott Cramer, B. H. Whitton, E. L. Vinson and John R. Knott.

41. Ehle, Texas speech; R. Philip Hanes, Jr., interview.

42. Ehle, telephone memorandum (apparently a note to himself), January 22, 1964; R. Philip Hanes, Jr., to Ehle, January 24, 1964, DAH.

43. James Gray to Ehle, telephone memorandum, January 24, 1964, DAH; Ehle interview, December 8, 1983; Ehle, telephone interview with Leslie Banner, December 1, 1984. Graylyn eventually became a conference center, administered by Wake Forest University.

44. Ehle to Lowry, February 5, 1964; Ehle to Robert Smith, Tallahassee, Florida, January 31, 1964; Ehle to Edward Pilkington, Columbia, S.C., January 31, 1964; Ehle to Cannon, February 25, 1964; R. Philip Hanes, Jr., to Ehle, February 14, 1964; R. Philip Hanes, Jr., to Ehle, February 20, 1964, all in DAH.

45. Ehle's suggestions for the Board of Trustees were Mrs. James Boyd, Southern

Pines, per Cliff Blue; Sam Ragan, Raleigh; John Schinnan, past president of the North Carolina State Ballet, Chapel Hill; Dale Gramley, Winston-Salem, per Charles Babcock; David Crumer, superintendent of schools, Tryon; Robert Lee Humber, Greenville; Mrs. John Henley, per Ben Roney; Louise Durham, Chapel Hill; Ben Roney; John Ehle, Chapel Hill; Mrs. McNeil Smith, Greensboro; James Gray, Winston-Salem; Eva Stott, Spring Hope; Martha Muilenburg, Charlotte; Hugh Cannon, Raleigh; John Caldwell, Raleigh, "if you need somebody from the University" (Ehle to Sanford, December 9, 1963, memo, not sent, DAH).

46. Ehle to Sanford, ca. June 18, 1963, not sent; Ehle's notes, July 2, 1963; Ehle to Lowry, July 4, 1963; Sanford to R. Philip Hanes, Jr., September 4, 1963; Sanford to Giannini, September 27, 1963; Ehle to Giannini, November 13, 1963; undated, un-identified newspaper clipping from Winston-Salem paper, ca. third week in November 1963, all in DAH.

47. "Under the Dome," *News and Observer* [Raleigh], November 15, 1963; Ehle, telephone interview, December 1, 1984. Ehle consulted his journal for the period December 1963–January 1964.

48. Ehle, telephone interview, December 1, 1984.

49. Ibid.

50. Ehle, memorandum of telephone conversation with Giannini, January 7, 1964; Giannini to Ehle, January 16, 1964; Giannini to Ehle, January 17, 1964, DAH. Giannini's list included for dance, Barbara Weisberger, Pennsylvania Ballet; Eugenie Ouroussow, American Ballet; Jeanne Erdman, New York, Modern; Paul Taylor; Agnes de Mille; José Limon; for drama, Oliver Rea, Guthrie Theater; Zelda Fichandler, Washington; Paul Green; Sidney Blackmer; Andy Griffith; Theodore Hoffman; Elia Kazan; Richard Adler; Clancy; Schneider, New York; for music, Jean Morel, conductor, Juilliard Orchestra; Julius Rudel; Phyllis Curtin; Leontyne Price; Ben Swalin; Vittorio Giannini.

51. Lowry interview.

52. Sanford to Lowry, draft, February 19, 1964; retyped and sent February 21, 1964; Lowry interview.

53. Sanford to Advisory Board, March 2, 1964, DAH.

54. Julius Rudel to Sanford, March 10, 1964; Blackmer to Sanford, March 16, 1964; Sanford to Pfohl, March 24, 1964 re: Pfohl's March 12 acceptance; Eugenie Ouroussow to Sanford, March 24, 1964; Sanford to Ouroussow, July 23, 1964, August 3, 1964, with commission, DAH.

55. Sanford to Leontyne Price, April 17, 1964 re: her letter of April 3; Sanford to Zelda Fichandler, March 25, 1964 re: her letter of March 16, DAH.

56. Agnes de Mille, interview with Douglas Zinn, June 9, 1982.

57. Sanford's letter of invitation to Peter Mennin seems to be missing from the DAH. Sanford wrote to Jan Peerce on March 25 and followed with a telegram, March 26, 1964, DAH.

58. Press release in DAH. Musical comedy writer Richard Adler graduated from the University of North Carolina in 1943; with Jerold Ross he wrote *The Pajama Game* and *Damn Yankees*. Sidney Blackmer of Salisbury, North Carolina, was a distinguished actor who appeared in more than a hundred films and plays; he was perhaps best known for his performance in the Broadway production of *Come Back, Little Sheba*, for which he won a Tony Award for Best Actor in 1950. Agnes

de Mille's father, William C. de Mille, was a native of North Carolina; Miss de Mille's choreography in *Oklahoma* revolutionized the use of dance in American musical theater. Dramatist Paul Green, born in Lillington, North Carolina, won the Pulitzer Prize for his play *In Abraham's Bosom* (about the struggles of rural southern blacks) and created the outdoor drama. José Limon is one of America's leading figures in the development of modern dance. Peter Mennin is a composer and was in 1964 president of the Juilliard School of Music. Jan Peerce was a world-renowned tenor of the Metropolitan Opera; his son graduated from the University of North Carolina. Julius Rudel became the conductor of the New York City Opera Company in 1943; in 1964 he was the opera's general manager as well.

59. Ehle to Lowry, March 26, 1964, DAH.

60. Ehle to Milton Esterow, March 25, 1964; Ehle to Coe, March 27, 1964 re: previous mailing of release; Richard L. Coe, "One on the Aisle," *Washington Post,* March 27, 1964, DAH.

61. Letters went to Robert Murphy, Hillsborough; James Stenhouse, Charlotte, cc C. A. Pete McKnight; Smith Bagley, Winston-Salem; R. Philip Hanes, Jr., Winston-Salem, bc James Gray, Anne Forsyth; Miles Wolff, Greensboro; William Joslin, Raleigh, cc Sam Ragan; all March 25, 1964; Bill Joslin to Ehle, phone message, April 6, 1964, DAH.

62. Ehle to Celeste Brouse, March 24, 1964, DAH.

63. Smith Bagley to J. Forrest Pete Barnwell, cc John Ehle, March 20, 1964, re: plans of Gray High School, to be forwarded by Stinson-Hall-Hines and Associates of Winston-Salem, DAH.

64. "Board Named for School for Performing Arts," *Winston-Salem Journal,* March 27, 1964; Jackie Owen, "Gray Sought as Arts School," *Twin City Sentinel,* March 27, 1964; "Not Much Time to Act," ibid., March 28, 1964; Marvin Cable, "State School Can Use Gray," *Winston-Salem Journal,* April 3, 1964; Arlene Edwards, "Change in School's Name Expected," *Winston-Salem Journal,* May 1, 1964; R. Philip Hanes, Jr., interview.

65. "Performing Arts School in U.N.C. Framework," *Greensboro Daily News,* April 1, 1964; "Performing Arts School Asked as Part of UNC-G," *Greensboro Record,* April 8, 1964; Ehle to Sanford, ca. June 18, 1963; Ehle to Sanford, April 7, 1964, DAH.

66. "No Education in Isolation," editorial, *News and Observer* [Raleigh], April 1, 1964; Joslin to Ehle, phone call, April 6, 1964, DAH; Jack Kneece, "Hotel Is Offered as School Site," *News and Observer* [Raleigh], April 30, 1964; "Meeting Held to Lure State Art School Here," *Greensboro Record,* April 7, 1964.

67. Phyllis H. Kramer (secretary to W. McNeil Lowry) to Ehle, April 15, 1964; Julia Ribet to Advisory Board, April 7, 1964; Mennin to Sanford, "available by phone," April 27, 1964; Ehle to Sanford, April 24, 1964; Pat Carter, "Bids for New State Schools Proposed Here," *Durham Morning Herald,* February 13, 1964; Charles Norton, phone call to Ehle, April 9, 1964; Wolff to Ehle, April 10, 1964; George Eichhorn to Ehle, April 13, 1964; Ehle interview, October 26, 1984; "Arts School Bid 'Off-Again,'" *News of Orange County,* April 30, 1964 re: April 28 decision; Ehle to Sanford, April 24, 1964; Ehle to Mrs. Terry Sanford, April 6, 1964, DAH. Ehle's suggested candidates for the Board of Trustees and the dinner party were Mrs.

James Boyd, Mrs. Wilbur Jolly, Ben Roney, Dr. James Semans, Louise Durham, Martha Muilenburg, Hugh Cannon, Joel Fleishman, Senator Gordon Hanes, and Alden Baker.

68. R. Philip Hanes, Jr., interview.

69. Ibid.; Ehle, Texas speech.

70. Ehle, telephone memorandum re: Smith Bagley, April 22, 1964, DAH.

71. Ehle, telephone memorandum re: Jim Stenhouse, April 22, 1964, DAH; Harriet Doar, "Queen City Bid for Arts School Appears Dead," *Charlotte Observer,* April 22, 1964; Ehle to Sanford, April 29, 1964; Governor's Conference with the NCSA Advisory Board, April 29, 1964, on tape, DAH.

72. "Clearer Sailing," *Winston-Salem Journal,* April 23, 1964; Ehle, telephone memorandum re: Phil Hanes, April 24, 1964, DAH; Ed Campbell, "Funds Are Sought for Arts School, *Twin City Sentinel,* April 24, 1964; Ehle to Sanford, two memos, April 24, 1984, DAH.

73. R. Philip Hanes, Jr., telephone memorandum, April 27, 1964, message possibly taken by Ehle's secretary, DAH; Jan Witherspoon, "Funds Sought to Get School," *Winston-Salem Journal,* April 27, 1964; "Phones to Start Ringing," ibid., April 28, 1964; "$214,729 Pledged in Telephone Drive," ibid., April 29, 1964.

74. Sanford to the Advisory Board, April 7, 1964, DAH; Ehle, "A Letter about Vittorio Giannini," p. 19.

75. Rose Post, "Film Role Won't Keep Blackmer from More Vital Role in State," *Salisbury Post,* April 26, 1964.

76. Ehle to Sanford, April 24, 1964; "The Schedule of the Advisory Board for the 18th and 20th of April North Carolina Performing Arts School," n.d. but evidently the final schedule, DAH; Ehle, Texas speech; de Mille interview.

77. De Mille interview; Beverly Wolter, "Arts Jury Will View City," *Winston-Salem Journal,* April 28, 1964; Schedule of the Advisory Board, DAH; Beverly Wolter, "Arts Jury Is Shown City's Cultural Fare," *Winston-Salem Journal*, April 29, 1964.

78. Wolter, "Arts Jury Is Shown"; Schedule of the Advisory Board, DAH; de Mille interview.

79. "Key Decision on School Site," *Greensboro Daily News,* April 28, 1964; de Mille interview; "Arguments on School Heard," *Greensboro Daily News,* April 29, 1964; "Give Us the School," *Winston-Salem Journal,* April 28, 1964; "$214,729 Pledged."

80. "Arts School Committee Visit Here Tomorrow," *Durham Morning Herald,* April 28, 1964; "Local Advantages for Arts School," ibid., April 29, 1964; Jon Phelps, "Prominent Artists Consider Durham Bid for Arts School," ibid., April 30, 1964.

81. Phelps, "Prominent Artists"; "Arts School Bid 'Off-Again,'" *News of Orange County,* April 30, 1964; Ehle interview, October 26, 1984.

82. Phelps, "Prominent Artists"; "Arts School Advisors to Tour Three Cities," *News and Observer* [Raleigh], April 28, 1964; "Invitation to the Arts," ibid., April 29, 1964; "Hotel Is Offered as School Site," ibid., April 30, 1964.

83. "A Different and Better Approach," *Chapel Hill Weekly,* June 12, 1963; William Friday, interview with Leslie Banner, April 9, 1985; Ehle, Texas speech.

84. Schedule of the Advisory Board, DAH; de Mille interview; "Arts School Word Today," *Winston-Salem Journal,* April 30, 1964; "'Dial for Dollars' Campaign Ends in Victory," *Twin City Sentinel,* April 30, 1964.

85. Advisory Board tape, NCSA. All references to the events and comments at this meeting are to this tape, except when otherwise noted.

86. Ehle, "A Letter about Vittorio Giannini," p. 20.

87. De Mille interview.

88. "Statement by Governor Terry Sanford," press release from the Governor's Office, April 30, 1964, DAH.

89. The Durham, North Carolina, afternoon paper reported the story on page 2A and gave Ehle credit for being "chief idea man for the governor's educational and anti-poverty projects" and "a key force in development of the North Carolina Fund, the administration's foundation-backed agency which is leading the state's war on poverty." The paper made no mention of the arts school (*Durham Sun,* April 29, 1964).

90. Ehle to Celeste Brouse, October 8, 1963, DAH.

CHAPTER 5

1. Jackie Owen, "Leaders Say 'It's a Great Day,'" *Twin City Sentinel,* April 30, 1964; "Arts School Word Today," *Winston-Salem Journal,* April 30, 1964; "'Dial for Dollars' Campaign Ends in Victory," *Twin City Sentinel,* April 30, 1964; "Statement by Governor Terry Sanford," April 30, 1964, DAH; yellow note re: conversation with Smith Bagley, May 5, 1964, signed by Ehle, DAH; North Carolina School of the Arts Foundation, Inc., History of Giving, confidential report prepared for Mrs. James Semans, January 14, 1971, Semans Files.

2. Beverly Wolter, "Arts School Fund Solicitors Attend Victory Celebration," *Winston-Salem Journal,* May 1, 1964; "Open Letter" from R. Philip Hanes, Jr., to Governor Sanford, April 30, 1964, DAH.

3. Sanford to R. Philip Hanes, Jr., May 12, 1964, DAH.

4. "Winston-Salem Action Puts Charlotte Effort to Shame," *Charlotte Observer,* May 5, 1964; "Winston-Salem Wins N.C. School for Arts," *Raleigh Times,* April 30, 1964; "Site for School," *Durham Morning Herald,* May 2, 1964; Jim Clotfelter, "By Site Seekers, Twin City Choice," ibid., May 3, 1964; "A School That Is Yet to Perform," *Greensboro Daily News,* May 2, 1964.

5. R. Philip Hanes, Jr., interview; "Ford Foundation Promotes Lowry," *New York Times,* June 22, 1964; Lowry to Giannini, July 8, 1964, NCSA; Ehle to Cannon, May 13, 1964, DAH. During June, July, and August of 1964, Giannini worked full-time as the school's president and halftime the following nine months, at a salary prorated on the basis of $20,000 a year. Up to this time, Giannini had worked without compensation (except for expenses) to develop the school (Ehle to Mattie Keys, budget officer, State Department of Administration, March 27, 1963, DAH).

6. "Terry Picks Trustees of Arts School," *News and Observer* [Raleigh], May 29, 1964.

7. Governor Sanford had announced on May 13 that he would recommend Gian-

nini to the Board of Trustees ("Vittorio Giannini Named Head of North Carolina Arts School," *New York Times,* May 14, 1964; "Giannini to Head Arts School," *News and Observer* [Raleigh], May 14, 1964). "Dr. Semans Named to Head New N.C. Arts School Board," *Durham Morning Herald,* July 18, 1964; "V. Giannini President of School of Arts," *News and Observer* [Raleigh], July 18, 1964; Dr. James H. Semans, interview with Douglas Zinn, October 19 and 21, 1981; Mary Semans, interview with Douglas Zinn, November 4, 1981.

8. "Davidson College Gets $500,000," *News and Observer* [Raleigh], May 24, 1964; Ribet to Keys, December 10, 1964, NCSA.

9. "Dr. Semans Named," *Durham Morning Herald,* July 18, 1964; "Art School Trustees Set Oct. 1965 as Target Date," *News and Observer* [Raleigh], August 15, 1964.

10. Bagley, note to Ehle on March 20, 1964 letter to J. Forrest Barnwell, DAH; "Art School Trustees Set . . . Date"; Duberman, *Black Mountain,* pp. 281–86.

11. Dr. Semans interview; Minutes of the Board of Trustees Meeting, November 14, 1964, Stanhope Hotel, New York City, NCSA.

12. Minutes, Board of Trustees, November 14, 1964, NCSA; R. Philip Hanes, Jr., interview; "Winston's 'Great Builder' Dies," *Winston-Salem Journal,* July 30, 1984; Bill East, "R. B. Crawford Dies at Age 83," *Twin City Sentinel,* July 30, 1984; Dr. Semans interview.

13. "Arts School Dormitories to House 254," *Twin City Sentinel,* January 15, 1965; Minutes, Board of Trustees, November 14, 1964, NCSA; Dr. Semans interview; R. Philips Hanes, Jr., interview; Bruce Stewart, interviews with Douglas Zinn, January 23 and April 24, 1982; Tom Kenan, interview with Douglas Zinn, March 9, 1982. Tom Kenan took his father's place on the Board of the North Carolina School of the Arts Foundation near the end of 1966 and has served three times on the NCSA Board of Trustees.

14. Minutes, Board of Trustees Meeting, November 14, 1964, NCSA. Other members of the first Foundation Board were Cliff Cameron, vice-president; Katherine Bahnson, secretary-treasurer; Dr. James H. Semans, chairman ex-officio; Professor John Scott; Frank Kenan; Mrs. Terry Sanford; and Joel Fleishman.

15. Andrew Jones, interview with Douglas Zinn, January 17, 1982.

16. Philip Dunigan, interview with Douglas Zinn, August 29, 1984.

17. Roney and Britt interview; Dr. Semans interview; Andrew Jones interview.

18. Gordon Hanes interview; Mary Semans interivew; Ehle, Texas speech.

19. Minutes, Board of Trustees Meeting, November 14, 1964, NCSA; Joe Goodman, "Arts School Need for Funds Stressed," *Journal and Sentinel* [Winston-Salem], February 28, 1965; "State School of Arts Plans Told at Meet," *News and Observer* [Raleigh], March 16, 1965; "Open Forum," Vittorio Giannini, interviewed by Velma Jean Clary, WTOB radio, December 13, 1964, NCSA.

20. Lowry to Cannon, November 25, 1964, NCSA.

21. Press release, November 2, 1965, NCSA; Dr. Semans interview; Joseph M. McDaniel, Jr., to Dr. James H. Semans, December 27, 1965, letter and Terms of Grant, NCSA; R. Philip Hanes, Jr., interview.

22. Press release, November 14, 1964, NCSA; announcement of the school's first faculty appointments would almost certainly have been on the agenda of an Oc-

tober 29, 1964, meeting at the Ford Foundation between McNeil Lowry and Giannini and Cannon (Lowry to Cannon, November 25, 1964, NCSA); press release, January 3, 1965, NCSA; Dunigan interview.

23. Press release, January 16, 1965, press release on appointment of Lindgren, [January 1965], NCSA; "Dance Dean Picked for NC School of Arts," *News and Observer* [Raleigh], January 28, 1965; Lowry interview.

24. Robert Lindgren, interview with Douglas Zinn, April 22, 1982. In December 1963 Ford made its controversial awards (totaling $7,756,750) to support classical dance in America. The foundation also voted to continue its funding of scholarships for advanced training of students selected from local schools across the country. The students were chosen by professionals from the School of American Ballet and the San Francisco Ballet School (Lowry, *Performing Arts,* pp. 11, 61).

25. Rose Bampton, interview with Douglas Zinn, June 10, 1982. See also "Opera Star Named Head of Voice Department," *News and Observer* [Raleigh], February 8, 1965.

26. Press release, hand-dated March 19, 1965, press release, April 1, 1965, NCSA; "N.Y. Director, Ex-Twin Citian Joins Arts School Drama Staff," *Twin City Sentinel* [Winston-Salem], April 8, 1965. Trotman had been the first director of the Institute of Outdoor Drama at UNC–Chapel Hill (1963) and was directing the drama department at the Governor's School in Winston-Salem. He had spent two seasons as a member of the Ford Foundation Acting Company at the famous Alley Theatre in Houston, and he had numerous appearances on television and radio to his credit, including NBC's "American Adventure Series," for which Ehle wrote twenty-six plays from 1954 to 1956. William Trotman went to school with Ehle at Chapel Hill, and the two had "acted together many, many times."

27. William Trotman, interview with Douglas Zinn, January 29, 1982. *The Servant of Two Masters* was written by Carlo Goldoni (1707–93), an Italian dramatist who chronicled the social life of his native Venice in a series of comedies written in the manner of Molière. Goldoni has been called the father of modern Italian comedy. It is not surprising that Giannini would have based an opera buffa on one of this playwright's zesty satires.

28. Lowry interview. At the November 14, 1964, meeting of the Board of Trustees, Giannini pointed out that in the field of drama, "the salaries that we can offer are not at all sufficient because an outstanding person in drama makes a very good living" (NCSA).

29. Trotman interview. From the beginning, Dr. Semans emphatically presented the position of the Board of Trustees, that the school was to be "a cooperative effort with equal importance assigned to each [department] . . . what kind of medical school would you have if medicine outstripped surgery and all of the other departments of the school?" (Dr. Semans interview).

30. Press release, April 14, 1965, NCSA; Olegna Fuschi, interview with Douglas Zinn, June 9, 1982.

31. Cannon interviw; Giannini sisters interview; press releases, dated as noted, NCSA; Pauline Koner, interview with Douglas Zinn, June 16, 1982. As of May 17, 1965, the school's academic department consisted of Julia Mueller, academic dean; Bruce B. Stewart, dean of student affairs; Robert T. Kimzey, principal of the high

school division; Marion Foster Fitz-Simons, director of English studies in both divisions and associate of the drama department; Mary Vann Wilkins, director of social studies, high school division; Mary Cartwright, director of foreign languages, high school division; William S. Greene, Jr., director of science and mathematics, both divisions; Gerd Young, English instructor, high school division, history instructor, college division, and associate of the drama department. Seven additional academic appointments were announced on July 20, without specifying division. They were William Van Hoven, librarian; Dorothea Bell, mathematics and physics; Adrianna Ciompi, Italian and French; Raina Fehl, German; Scherer James, English and Spanish; Lois Raff, social studies; Marjorie Randolph, foreign languages; and Reginald F. Spaulding, English. On June 17, Giannini announced three appointments in the school of drama: Christina Giannini, scenic and costume designer; Paul Tremaine, technical director; and Bentley B. Anderson, to teach speech and acting. On July 28 three more artists joined the music faculty: Selma Amansky, dramatic soprano; Frederick Bergstone, replacing Clarendon Van Norman, French hornist with the Clarion Wind Quintet; and Sherwood Shaffer, composer and former faculty member at the Manhattan School of Music. Ewald V. Nolte of Salem College joined the music department as choral conductor September 1, 1965, completing the roster of resident and regular faculty (as opposed to visiting faculty) for the school's first semester (press releases, NCSA).

32. Duncan Noble, interview with Douglas Zinn, March 6, 1982.

33. Minutes of the Joint Meeting of the Advisory Board and Board of Trustees, November 14, 1964, NCSA; Lindgren interview; "Semi-Annual Report—First Semester—1965–66 North Carolina School of the Arts," NCSA.

34. "Target: Artistic Oasis at Winston-Salem," WBT radio, Charlotte, N.C., October 1965.

35. Press release, April 14, 1965, NCSA; Trotman interview; Sanford, *But What about the People?* p. 65; Dr. Semans interview.

36. Press release, April 14, 1965, NCSA; Ed McHale, "For Youth, a Nervous Audition," *News and Observer* [Raleigh], April 18, 1965; Fuschi interview; Carroll, presentation speech; Bampton interview; Dr. Semans, presentation speech; Sanford, *But What about the People?* p. 65; Sanford, presentation speech.

37. Press releases of May 13, June 7, June 24, and September 1, 1965, NCSA; Fuschi interview; Dunigan interview; "Semi-Annual Report," 1965–66, NCSA.

38. Giannini sisters interview; Joe Goodman, "New School Is Taking on Sights, Sounds of the Arts," *Journal and Sentinel* [Winston-Salem], September 12, 1965.

39. Dr. James H. Semans to Wallace Carroll, telegram, December 9, 1964, NCSA; "Noted Musician Seeking Faculty for School of Arts," *Greensboro Daily News*, September 27, 1964; Jackie Owen, "A Theater for the Drama School," *Twin City Sentinel*, September 9, 1965.

40. Giannini sisters interview; Lindgren interview; Koner interview.

41. Dunigan interview; Bampton interview; Fuschi interview; Giannini sisters interview.

42. Giannini sisters interview; Dunigan interview. By January of 1966 Giannini had relented sufficiently to authorize the purchase of a harpsichord for the school from George Lucktenberg of Converse College. The Sperrhake 260, which Luck-

tenberg had been using since 1957 for concert tours, was to be used for recitals at the school and for students who were to study the harpsichord with Mrs. Clemens Sandresky of the music faculty (NCSA press release, January 20, 1966).

43. Bampton interview; Fuschi interview.

44. Koner interview.

45. Dr. Semans interview.

46. Trotman interview.

47. Giannini sisters interview.

48. Arturo Ciompi, interview with Leslie Banner and Douglas Zinn, November 21, 1984.

49. Giannini sisters interview; Ciompi interview.

50. Julia W. Mueller, acting dean of academic studies, "Report of Academic Department of North Carolina School of the Arts, First Semester, 1965–66," in "Semi Annual Report"; Bruce Stewart interview, January 23, 1982; Dr. Semans interview; J. Winthrop Young to Bruce B. Stewart, January 14, [1966], in "Semi Annual Report," NCSA.

51. Ciompi interview.

52. Marion Fitz-Simons, interview with Doulgas Zinn, January 20, 1982.

53. Trotman interview.

54. Ciompi interview.

55. Giannini sisters interview.

56. Stewart interviews; press release, NCSA.

57. Fitz-Simons interview; Kate Erwin, "A Day at the School of the Arts," *News and Observer* [Raleigh], April 10, 1966; de Mille interview; Giannini sisters interview; Trotman interview; Minutes of the Academic and Arts Faculty Meeting Called by Dr. Giannini on Friday, October 14, 1966, NCSA.

58. Ciompi interview; faculty meeting minutes, October 14, 1966; Giannini sisters interview.

59. Press release, June 5, 1966; graduation ceremony, tape, June 8, 1966, NCSA.

60. Ehle, "A Letter about Vittorio Giannini," p. 21; Giannini sisters interview; commemorative service for Vittorio Giannini, tape, December 1, 1966, NCSA.

CHAPTER 6

1. John Ehle, conversation with Leslie Banner, March 30, 1985; Mary Semans, speech to the Junior League of Winston-Salem, 1971; Dr. James H. Semans, speech (unidentified), April 16, 1970; Dr. Semans, "Fortuitous Circumstances Adding to the Success of the North Carolina School of the Arts Summer Session in Siena, Italy," notes forwarded to Beverly Wolters, *Winston-Salem Journal and Sentinel*, September 23, 1967. Most of the material relating to the history of the International Music Program of the North Carolina School of the Arts comes from the combined private files of Dr. and Mrs. James H. Semans and Giorgio Ciompi, hereafter cited as Semans Files.

2. Press release, December 2, 1966, NCSA; Semans, *Siena*, p. 1; Dr. Semans to Mr. and Mrs. Sigmund Koch, letter drafted aboard the SS *France*, October 13, 1966, Semans Files.

3. Semans, *Siena*, pp. 2–4; Dr. Semans, "History and Anecdotes of the Summer Session of the North Carolina School of the Arts in Siena, Italy, 1967," ms. memoir, p. 3; Dr. James H. Semans, personal memo, October 1 and 5, 1966, "Verbal agreement of the 1st session . . ."; Dr. Semans to Ehle, letter drafted aboard SS *France*, October 13, 1966, Semans Files.

4. Dr. Semans, personal memo, 1966; Semans, *Siena*, p. 3; "Minutes of the Meeting Held in the Prefettura of Siena, Saturday, October 1, 1966," Semans Files.

5. Mary Semans, Junior League speech, 1971.

6. Sargeant "Profiles," pp. 37–77.

7. Sargeant, "Profiles," p. 38 and passim; Danilo Verzili, "The Great Contributions to Classical Music of Count Guido Chigi Saracini," speech delivered in Raleigh, North Carolina, at the Governor's Mansion when Governor Moore announced the summer session in Siena, December 2, 1966, Semans Files.

8. Vieri Traxler, "Remarks," speech delivered at the International Banking Convention, Chapel Hill, N.C., October 13, 1970, Semans Files.

9. Dr. Semans, personal memo, 1966; Sargeant, "Profiles," p. 63; Mary Semans, Junior League speech, 1971.

10. Dr. Semans, personal memo, 1966; Barzini, *The Italians*, p. 51; George R. F. Baker, "Summers in Siena," ms. mailed to Dr. Semans, November 19, 1971, Semans Files.

11. Traxler, "Remarks."

12. "Minutes of the Meeting, October 1, 1966"; Giannini to Mario Fabbri, November 1, 1966; *Summer Session at Siena, Italy* (pamphlet), North Carolina School of the Arts, 1967, Semans Files; Jane Hall, "N.C. School Sets Session in Italy," *News and Observer* [Raleigh], December 3, 1966.

13. Fabbri to Giannini, "Rough translation of last letter from Mr. Fabbri," November 1966, Semans Files.

14. Dr. Semans, "Fortuitous Circumstances"; Mary Semans, Junior League speech, 1971; Adriana and Giorgio Ciompi, interview with Dr. James H. Semans and Douglas Zinn, November 16, 1981.

15. Hall, "N.C. School Sets Session."

16. Giannini sisters interview.

17. Semans, *Siena*, p. 7; Dr. Semans to Stewart ——, January 31, 1967, Semans Files.

18. Dr. Semans, "Notes on preparatory work carried out in FLORENCE, SIENA AND ROME, ITALY between January 22, 1967 and February 6, 1967," dictated February 15, 1967, Semans Files.

19. Dr. Semans, "Notes," February 15, 1967; Dr. Semans, "Memorandum of Conversation JHS had with Giorgio Ciompi," February 1967; Dr. Semans to Franco Agostini, April 22, 1967; Dr. Semans to Ernest Brooks, not sent, February 1967, Semans Files; Earl W. Wolslagel, "U.S. Youngsters Shine in Italy," *Durham Morning Herald*, September 24, 1967.

20. Dr. Semans to Ernest Brooks, not sent, [January] 1967, Semans Files; William Herring, interview with Douglas Zinn, March 14, 1985; Dr. Semans, "The next episode . . . July 1967," ms. memoir, Semans Files.

21. Semans, *Siena*, p. 6; North Carolina School of the Arts, *Handbook Summer Session in Siena*; Dr. Semans to Stewart ——, January 31, 1967, Semans Files.

22. Dr. Semans to Ernest Brooks, August 12, 1967, Semans Files.

23. "Foreign Minister Fanfani Attends Opening of Summer Session," ms. page, July 17 [?], 1967; Dr. Semans to The Honorable Governor Dan K. Moore and Mrs. Moore, July 27, 1967, Semans Files.

24. "Minutes of a Meeting Held on August 22nd, 1967 in Maestro Fabbri's Office at the Accademia Chigiana, Siena," Semans Files.

25. Dr. Semans to R. Philip Hanes, Jr., July 25, 1967; Dr. Semans to William Herring, July 31, 1967, Semans Files.

26. Giorgio Ciompi interview; "Minutes, August 22nd, 1967," Semans Files; Giannini sisters interview. Eugene Rizzo, an American expatriate journalist living in Italy, served as publicity director and then as "general factotum" for the summer session in later years.

27. "N.C. School of Arts Making Big Hit during Italian Summer Study Recitals," *Durham Morning Herald,* August 20, 1967; Brunetto Moggi, "Eighth North Carolina Concert," *La Nazione* [Florence, Italy], August 17, 1967 (translation); Giorgio Ciompi interview.

28. Giannini sisters interview; Giorgio Ciompi interview.

29. Robert Ward, interview with Douglas Zinn, January 14, 1982.

30. Dr. Semans to James Glenn, July 25, 1967; Dr. Semans, "1967—The incident of the establishment of credit," ms. memoir, n.d., Semans Files.

31. Vieri Traxler, "Résumé of a conversation in Siena Saturday, July 22, 1967, about the future of the N.C.S.A. Summer Session in Siena," Semans Files. In addition to Semans and Traxler, Fabbri and Verzili were also present and Valdettaro of the Foreign Ministry.

32. "Minutes, August 22nd." Also present were Alfredo Antonini, Dr. Semans, and Giorgio Ciompi. Robert Ward, "Memorandum, 24th August, 1967"; Fabbri to Giorgio Ciompi, December 18, 1967, Semans Files.

33. Ward, "Memorandum, 24th August, 1967"; "Minutes, August 22nd, 1967"; "Minutes of a meeting held on Tuesday, 29th August [1967] at the Accademia Chigiana, at 4 p.m." (Semans Files).

34. "Minutes of a meeting held August 30th, 1967, at the Accademia Chigiana, Siena, at 9:30 A.M." Present were Fabbri, Ward, Mueller, Ciompi, and Agostini. "Memorandum of a Trip to Italy January 15–January 28, 1968 by Giorgio Ciompi"; "Minutes, August 22nd, 1967," Semans Files.

35. Dr. Semans, personal memo, 1966; "Minutes of the Meeting held in Rome the 5th of October, 1968"; Fabbri to Giannini, November 21, 1966 (translation); "Minutes, August 30th, 1967," Semans Files.

36. Fabbri to Ciompi, December 18, 1967 (translation); "Memorandum by Giorgio Ciompi"; Barzini, *The Italians,* pp. 198, 214–33; note in handwriting of Dr. Semans, on "Memorandum by Giorgio Ciompi," p. 2, Semans Files.

37. "Memorandum by Giorgio Ciompi"; [Giorgio Ciompi], "Diary," June 10–July 3, 1968; Ward to Ciompi, November 22, 1967. Italian support for the second summer session was about the same as for the first year: $10,000 from the federal government and $40,000 from the Monte dei Paschi Bank.

38. Semans, "Fabbri's Visit to the United States," ms. memoir, n.d.; Fabbri to Ciompi (translation), April 4, 1968; Julia Mueller, "Calendar with Reference to

Fabbri Visit," attached to March 18, 1968 memorandum to Ciompi, Semans Files; Giorgio Ciompi interview; Fabbri to Dr. Semans (translation), November 17, 1969, Semans Files.

39. Julia Mueller, memorandum to students and staff of the NCSA Summer Session in Siena, May 20, 1968, Semans Files; Earl Wolslagel, "Duke to Inaugurate Summer Session in Arts in Italy," Office of Information Services, Duke University, June 2, 1968; Earl Wolslagel, "Young Americans Play in Siena," *Daily American* [Rome, Italy], June 27, 1968; "Il Brillante Successo degli Studenti Americani," in section "Cronaca di Arezzo," *La Nazione* [Florence], July 12, 1968; Dr. Semans, "Our Visit to the Vatican, July 4, 1968," ms. memoir, Semans Files. The 1968 summer session brochure lists as teaching faculty Piero Bellugi, orchestra and conducting; Giorgio Ciompi, Julia Mueller (chair of the Duke Music Department), Irving Klein (NCSA), Frederick Bergstone (NCSA), and Paul Berl (Mannes, Manhattan, and Yale), chamber music; Vincenzo Vitale, piano, and Alessandro Esposito, organ (Italian—no bio available when the brochure was published); Norman Farrow (NCSA), voice; Roman Vlad (Rome Philharmonic Academy), composition; Marianna Jenkins (Duke), history of Italian art; Frances Rello (New York City public schools), and Francesco Gulli (Italian, no affiliation listed), Italian language classes. In addition, special master classes were to be arranged with the faculty of the Chigiana. NCSA granted college credit to participants (chosen by audition); tuition and fees were raised to $690, still only a fraction of the program's cost, which was being supported, the brochure notes, "by subsidies from Foundations and private sources in the United States and by a generous subsidy from the Italian Government." As in 1967, approximately half the students came from NCSA and the rest from a number of outstanding schools, including Oberlin, Mannes, Eastman, Columbia, Brandeis, Temple, Vassar, and Princeton (among others), with an impressive six from Manhattan and twelve from Juilliard ("Siena Summer Session 1968," list of students).

40. Ciompi, memorandum to Dr. James H. Semans, Robert Ward, Paolo Olsoufieff, H. Alan Sims, undated, but internal evidence clearly places it in the fall or winter of 1968; "Important Details for Advance Agent and Manager to the North Carolina Conservatory Summer Session in Siena—1969," [December 7, 1968] [JHS handwritten note], Semans Files.

41. Dr. Semans, "Modus Operandi," October 15, 1971, ms. memoir; "Memorandum by Giorgio Ciompi," Semans Files.

42. Semans, *Siena*, pp. 24–27.

43. J. Mueller (signature), "Siena—July 11, 1968," undirected report, Semans Files.

44. Ciompi, "Diary."

45. "Points Arising from Preliminary Meeting between Mr. Robert Ward & Mr. Fabbri—7/15/68"; [Robert Ward], "On Friday Morning, July 19th, the meeting between Maestro Fabbri, Giorgio Ciompi, J. Mueller and myself," Semans Files.

46. "Summer Session in Siena, Notes on Meeting at 1415 Bivins Street, Durham, North Carolina, Tuesday, August 11, 1968," Semans Files. Present at the meeting were Dr. and Mrs. Semans, Mr. and Mrs. Robert Ward, Giorgio Ciompi, Jim Rush, Tom Kenan, Julia Mueller, and Robert Lindgren.

47. Fabbri to Dr. Semans, November 13, 1968 (translation). A handwritten note

by JHS confirms the resignation and date; Ciompi, "Résumé of telephone conversation between Giorgio Ciompi and Mario Fabbri on May 11, 1969"; Dr. Semans, "Modus Operandi," Semans Files.

48. Julia Mueller, "1969 Season," calendar, curriculum, student, staff, and budget lists, with notations in Julia Mueller's handwriting; "Notes for Meeting Bivins St. 8/13/68"; Ward to Dr. Semans, January 14, 1969; "Siena Summer Session Bulletin [1969]—Part II"; Dr. Semans to Richard B. Myer, Institute of International Education, April 30, 1969, Semans Files.

Deans of men and women, from the NCSA faculty, were William H. Baskin III and Gerd Young. Teaching faculty who went to Italy from the school that year were Rose Bampton (voice), Jerry Horner (viola), Irving Klein (cello), Robert Listokin (clarinet), and Jesús Silva (guitar). Donal Nold, of Manhattan and the Philadelphia Academy, came as vocal coach. Giorgio Ciompi, once again, was artistic director.

49. "Students' Love Is Italian Music," *Durham Morning Herald*, August 10, 1969; Dr. Semans to Dr. Luciano Alberti, Florence, Italy, December 24, 1969; Dr. Semans to The Honorable Lindsey C. Warren, Jr., August 11, 1969; H. Alan Sims, "1969 Siena Summer Session," ms., apparently a transcription, Semans Files.

50. "On Friday morning, July 19th [1968]"; Bonechi Guide, *The Wonderful Towns of Italy* (1965), p. 75; "North Carolina Philharmonic Orchestra," 1969 concert dates and programs, ms. listing; "Students' Love"; Mary Semans to Dirk Dawson, July 22, 1969; "Componenti dell'Orchestra (in ordine alfabetico)," in "Concerto Sinfonico" (concert program), North Carolina School of the Arts III Summer Session at Siena Sotto Il Patrocinio della Accademia Musicale Chigiana, Siena. Teatro dei Rinnuovati, 21 Agosto 1969; Mary B. Ward to Dr. Semans, June 9, 1969, enclosure, "Siena Summer Session 1969," list of students with instruments, ages, schools, school years, and home addresses, Semans Files.

51. "1969 Season"; "Notes, 8/13/68"; Fondazione Accademia Musicale Chigiana, *Programa Della XXXVIII Annata Corsi di Perfezionamento*, Palazzo Chigi Saracini, Siena (Italia), 15 Luglio–10 Settembre 1969; "Draft Prospectus as discussed between Dr. & Mrs. Semans and Maestro Ciompi on Sunday, June 23, 1968"; Randy Wilson to Dr. Semans, n.d. [internal evidence suggests early 1968]; "Points Arising, 7/15/68"; "On Friday Morning, July 19th"; "Tentative Revision of Plan for North Carolina School of the Arts Siena Summer Session," attached to July 20, 1968 memorandum, Ward to Ciompi; Ward to Dr. Semans, January 14, 1969; Dr. Semans to Ward, August 18, 1969, Semans Files.

52. Dr. Semans to Verzili, April 14, 1969; Dr. Semans to Ward, August 18, 1969; Doe Volz, "Ojai Violinist Wins Major Prize in Italy," photocopy, n.d., source not identified; James H. Semans or Mary Semans, "Unique Experience of the Summer Session in Italy," ms. speech, n.d.; Dr. Semans to Guido Agosti, October 14, 1969; James H. Semans, "North Carolina School of the Arts Italian Program in Siena, January 14, 1970," Semans Files; [A. Moggi], "Concerto di Musica da Camera della North Carolina School," *La Nazione* [Florence], August 21, 1969 (translation).

53. James H. Semans, "Problems in the Accademia Chigiana and NCSS Relationship," ms. memoir, n.d.; "Luncheon Meeting, Siena—July 16, 1968," Semans Files; present at this meeting, in addition to Ward and Verzili, were Dr. Semans and Mr. and Mrs. Giorgio Ciompi.

54. [JHS], "Survey by the International Institute of Education, United Nations, New York, 1969," ms. memoir, n.d.; [JHS], "Problems," Semans Files.

55. "Meeting Notes," [Siena], luncheon, July 12, 1968; present were Dr. and Mrs. Semans, Mr. and Mrs. Giorgio Ciompi, and Verzili; Dr. Semans to Ward, December 7, 1968; "Luncheon, July 16, 1968"; Semans to Senator Fanfani, draft attached to a note from Vieri Traxler, November 6, 1969; Institute of International Education, *This Is IIE,* brochure, 1969; "Survey"; Margaret F. Jory and Randolph A. Kidder, "Report for North Carolina School of the Arts," August 1969, Semans Files. The consultants were Margaret Fairbank Jory (July 23–August 17), Randolph A. Kidder (August 5–12), and Lansing Collins (August 11–12).

56. Semans, "Survey."

57. Jory and Kidder, "Report"; James H. Semans or Mary Semans, "Unique Experience."

58. Jory and Kidder, "Report."

59. "Robert Lindgren, 1969—Dance Group to Italy," edited dictation, n.d. (Semans Files).

60. Roger Hall Re: Siena to Ward, August 17, 1970, Semans Files.

61. William Weaver, "A Cross-Pollination with America," *Paris* [France] *Herald-Tribune,* July 21, 1970; Fabbri to Dr. Semans, November 17, 1969; James H. Semans, "North Carolina School of the Arts Italian Program in Siena January 14, 1970," ms. memoir; "Notes dictated at the end of the exploratory trip to Italy made by JHS and Robert Ward from January 10 to January 22, 1970," ms. memoir; "North Carolina School of the Arts Summer Session in Siena, July 2, 1970, Financial Survey of North Carolina Summer Session—1970," Semans Files; "North Carolina School of the Arts to Send Musicians, Dancers and Singers to Italy This Summer," NCSA press release, June 10, 1970, NCSA; "Americans to Honor Italy in Outdoor Rome Concert," mimeographed press release (no source), August 6, 1970, Semans Files; Alfred Friendly, Jr., "Arts in Italy a Magnet for U.S. Youth," *New York Times,* August 14, 1970; Dr. Semans to Ward, July 22, 1971; Alberti to Ward, April 22, 1971; Ward to Herbert Handt, February 11, 1971; Nicholas Harsanyi to Ward, July 5, 1971, Semans Files.

62. Eugene Rizzo, interview with Douglas Zinn, August 13, 1983.

63. See, for example, "The Summer Export of Culture from the New World to the Old," *North Carolina,* March 1984, pp. 28, 30, 62.

64. Robert Hickock, interview with Douglas Zinn, February 21, 1984.

BIBLIOGRAPHY

MANUSCRIPT SOURCES

Division of Archives and History of the North Carolina Department of Cultural Resources, Raleigh, North Carolina (DAH)

Agenda notes for open hearing in the General Assembly. May 23, 1963.
Andrews, Ralph. Letter to John Ehle. January 24, 1963.
Bagley, Smith. Letter to J. Forrest Barnwell, cc John Ehle. March 20, 1964.
———. Letter to John Ehle. March 20, 1964.
Bair, Clifford. Letter to John Ehle. March 31, 1964.
Beach, Earl. String instruction proposal. October 1962 file.
Blackmer, Sidney. Letters to Terry Sanford. January 24, March 16, 1964.
Blackwell, Mrs. T. Winfield. Letters to Martha Muilenburg. November 30, December 14, 1962.
Bowles, Hargrove, Jr. Memorandum to John Ehle. February 12, 1963.
Cannon, Hugh. Letter to Terry Sanford. May 1, 1963.
———. Memorandum to John Ehle. May 20, 1963.
Cone, Sydney. Letter to John Ehle. February 11, 1963.
———. Letter to Gordon Hanes. February 19, 1963.
———. Letter to Joseph M. McDaniel. October 25, 1962.
———. Letter to Martha Muilenburg. December 22, 1962.
———. Letter to Frances Wrape. October 25, 1962.
Cultural Advancement for North Carolina. Minutes of initial meeting. March 29, 1961.
Davis, Rachel, M.D. Letters to John Ehle. February 12, May 7, ca. May 10, 1963.
Dycke, Marjorie. Speech on the history and philosophy of New York's High School of Performing Arts. December 6, 1962.
Ehle, John. Letters to:
Ralph Andrews. January 22, 1963.
Smith Bagley. March 25, 1964.
Celeste Brouse. October 8, November 26, 1963, March 24, 1964.
Hugh Cannon. June 4, 11, 1963, February 25, May 13, 1964.
Richard Coe. June 11, 1963, March 27, 1964.
Sydney Cone. October 29, 1962.
Harriet Doar. May 23, 1963.
Marjorie Dycke. December 14, 1962.
Mrs. George C. Eichhorn. February 4, 1963.
Milton Esterow. March 25, 1964.
Louise Esteven. May 30, 1963.
James Fowler. July 29, 1963.

Arthur Gelb. February 20, 1964.
Vittorio Giannini. October 22, November 5, 13, December 5, 1963.
Gordon Hanes. March 18, 1963.
R. Philip Hanes, Jr. September 4, 1963, bc James Gray, Anne Forsyth. March 25, 1964.
Wilbur Jolly. June 17, 1963.
William Joslin, cc Sam Ragan. March 25, 1964.
Mattie Keys. March 27, 1963.
W. McNeil Lowry. September 22, 28, December 20, 1962, March 18, July 4, August 13, 1963, February 5, March 26, 1964.
Joseph E. Maddy. November 21, 1962.
Pete McKnight. June 22, 1963.
Martha Muilenburg. September 19, October 4, 1962.
Robert Murphy. March 25, 1964.
Edward Pilkington, January 31, 1964.
A. H. Reiss. June 10, 1963.
Lee Rigsby. March 28, 1963.
Joe Robinson. July 2, 1963.
James Rush. April 9, 1963.
Terry Sanford. February 14, May 8, 15, June 6, September 23 (not sent), 1963, April 7, 24, 29, 1964.
Mrs. Terry Sanford. April 6, 1964.
Mary D. B. T. Semans. January 17, 1964.
Robert Smith. January 31, 1964.
Bill Snider. March 27, 1963.
James Stenhouse, cc Pete McKnight. March 25, 1964.
Henry Hall Wilson. October 9, 1962, March 18, 1963.
Miles Wolff. May 14 (not sent), May 14 (sent), December 20, 1963, March 25, 1964.
————. Memorandums and Notes:
Memorandums to Joel Fleishman. October 3, 1962, July 15, 1963.
Memorandum to Pete McKnight, Fred Weaver, Vittorio Giannini, Mrs. Carl Durham, and Martha Muilenburg. November 19, 1962.
Memorandums to Terry Sanford. December 9 (not sent), ca. June 18, 1963 (not sent), April 24, 1964.
Notes from telephone conversations with Smith Bagley. April 22, May 5, 1964.
Notes from a telephone conversation with Vittorio Giannini. January 7, 1964.
Notes from a telephone conversation with James Gray. January 24, 1964.
Notes from telephone conversations with R. Philip Hanes, Jr. April 24, 27, 1964.
Notes from a telephone conversation with Bill Joslin. April 6, 1964.
Notes from a telephone conversation with Pete McKnight. January 24, 1964.
Notes from a telephone conversation with Bob Murphy. November 12, 1963.
Notes from a telephone conversation with Charles Norton. April 9, 1964.
Notes from a telephone conversation with Jim Stenhouse. April 22, 1964.
Personal notes for Ford Foundation visit on March 12, 1963.
Personal notes. November 2, 1962, May, July, July 2, 1963, January 22, 1964.

Eichhorn, George. Letter to John Ehle. April 13, 1964.

Fleishman, Joel. Memorandum to John Ehle. October 2, 1962.

Fowler, James. Letter to John Ehle. August 12, 1963.

Frieswyk, Siebolt. Letter to Ralph Andrews. January 4, 1963.

"Governor Terry Sanford's Schedules." Press Secretary's Files. 1961–64.

Giannini, Vittorio. Letters to John Ehle. April 6, July 16, August 8, November 9, November 12, 1963, January 16, 17, 1964.

———. Telegram to W. McNeil Lowry. June 18, 1963.

Hall, George L. Letter to Bill Joslin, cc John Ehle, Sam Ragan, Wesley Wallace. December 18, 1963.

Hanes, R. Philip, Jr. Letters to:
Marvin Barrett. June 27, 1963.
John Ehle. February 27, May 23, August 1, 27, October 19, 1963, January 24, February 14, 20, 1964.
Gordon Hanes. May 29, 1963.
Terry Sanford. May 16, August 16, 1963, April 30, 1964.

Haswell, Lois. Letter to Terry Sanford. May 17, 1963.

Hilbrink, William. Letter to Hugh Cannon. May 10, 1963.

Hodgkins, Norris L., Jr. Letter to Mrs. Carl Durham. October 26, 1962.

Hoffman, Arnold E. Letter to John Ehle. September 25, 1962.

Journal of the House of Representatives of the General Assembly of the State of North Carolina, Session 1963.

Journal of the Senate of the General Assembly of the State of North Carolina, Session 1963.

Kramer, Phyllis H. Letter to John Ehle. April 15, 1964.

Lawrence, Mrs. G. V. Letter to John Ehle. January 4, 1963.

Lowry, W. McNeil. Letter to John Ehle. October 9, 1962, August 8, 1963.

Luce, Harold. Letter to Hugh Cannon. May 7, 1963.

Mayleas, Ruth. Letter to John Ehle. February 3, 1964.

McKnight, Pete. Letter to John Ehle. April 26, 1963.

———. Letter to Martha Muilenburg. March 14, 1963.

———. Report on NCCC Program Committee visit to New York City Conservatories, November 27–29, 1962.

Mennin, Peter. Letter to Terry Sanford. April 27, 1964.

Muilenburg, Martha. Letters to John Ehle. November 6, 1962, February 4, 1963.

———. Letter to Terry Sanford. February 4, 1963.

North Carolina Conservatory Committee. Minutes of meetings. September 27, November 2, December 6, 1962, March 15, 1963.

North Carolina School of the Arts Bill. Drafts of May 2–4, 1963.

Ouroussow, Eugenie. Letter to Terry Sanford. March 24, 1964.

"Proposal of Winston-Salem as a Site for the School of the Performing Arts." August 8, 1963.

Ragan, Sam. Letter to Hugh Cannon. May 8, 1963.

Reeves, Ralph. Letter to Sam Ragan. May 7, 1963.

Reiss, A. H. Letter to John Ehle. June 6, 1963.

"Report of the Sites Selection Committee for the School of Performing Arts—Charlotte." January 22, 1964.

Ribet, Julia. Letter to Advisory Board. April 7, 1964.

Rigsby, Lee. Letter to John Ehle. April 2, 1963.

Ross, Walter E. Letter to John Ehle. November 28, 1962.

Rudel, Julius. Letter to Terry Sanford. March 10, 1964.

Salmon, Eric. Letter to John Ehle. Janaury 1, 1964.

Sanford, Terry. Letters to:

    Richard Adler. March 2, 1964.

    Advisory Board. March 2, April 7, 1964.

    E. H. Anderson. May 20, 1963.

    Ralph Andrews. January 22, 1963.

    Charles H. Babcock, Reynolds and Company. March 14, 1963.

    Henry Belk. March 27, 1963.

    Sidney Blackmer. January 17, March 2, 1964.

    Jack H. Campbell. May 20, 1963.

    Hugh Cannon. April 30, 1963.

    Sydney Cone. December 17, 1962, March 27, 1963.

    Agnes de Mille. March 2, 1964.

    Heath Ellis. May 16, 1963.

    Zelda Fichandler. March 2, 25, 1964.

    Frederick Franklin. March 2, 1964.

    Vittorio Giannini. September 27, 1963, March 2, 1964.

    Paul Green. March 2, 1964.

    R. Philip Hanes, Jr. September 4, 1963, May 12, 1964.

    Thomas A. Henson. May 20, 1963.

    Paul Hickfong. June 6, 1963.

    Mary Ida Hodge. May 17, 1963.

    Juanita Jones. May 16, 1963.

    H. W. Kendall. March 27, 1963.

    José Limon. March 2, 1964.

    W. McNeil Lowry. August 12 (not sent), August 16, 1963; draft, February 19, 1964; retyped February 21, 1964.

    Harold Luce. May 8, 1963.

    Joseph R. Morton, June 6, 1963.

    Mereb Mossman. January 22, 1963.

    Martha Muilenburg. July 2, 1963.

    Eugenie Ouroussow. March 2, July 23, August 3, 1964.

    Anita Patterson. May 16, 1963.

    Jan Peerce. March 25, 26, 1964 telegram.

    James Christian Pfohl. March 2, 24, 1964.

    Leontyne Price. March 2, April 17, 1964.

    Nancy Gray Riley, May 16, 1963.

    Steed Rollins. March 27, 1963.

    Julius Rudel. March 2, 1964.

    John B. Russell. May 20, 1963.

    Jean Spencer. May 16, 1963.

    Mrs. Frank Starbuck. May 21, 1963.

    David Whichard. March 27, 1963.

———. "Statement by Governor Terry Sanford." Press release from the Governor's Office. April 30, 1964.
"The Schedule of the Advisory Board for the 28th and 29th of April North Carolina Performing Arts School." N.d.
Semans, Mary D. B. T. (Mrs. James). Letter to John Ehle. January 15, 1964.
Snyder, Allegra Fuller. Letter to John Ehle. December 2, 1962.
———. Résumé. n.d.
Starbuck, Mrs. Frank. Letter to Terry Sanford. May 12, 1963.
A Statement Concerning the Proposed Performing Arts School in North Carolina. [Governor's Book]. Raleigh, N.C.: Governor's Office, April 6, 1964.
State of North Carolina. *1963 Session Laws and Resolutions.* [Raleigh, N.C.]: Published by Authority.
Strassler, Gene. Letter to John Ehle. September 23, 1962.
———. Memorandum to John Ehle. May 1963.
Wechsler, Louis K. "A Statement on the History, Aims, and Program of the High School of Music and Art, New York City." June 28, 1960.
Wolff, Miles. Letters to John Ehle. May 10, December 18, 1963, April 10, 1964.
Wrape, Frances. Letter to Sydney Cone. October 22, 1962.

Archives of the North Carolina School of the Arts, Winston-Salem, North Carolina (NCSA)

Advisory Board Site Selection Committee. Conference with Terry Sanford at the Governor's Mansion. Tape recording. April 29, 1964.
Commemorative Service for Vittorio Giannini. Tape recording. December 1, 1966.
Doster, Joe. Interview with Bruce B. Stewart. March 9, 1979.
[Ehle, John.] *A Statement Concerning the Proposed Performing Arts School in North Carolina.* Raleigh, N.C.: The Governor's Office, April 6, 1964.
Giannini, Vittorio. Interview with Velma Jean Clary. "Open Forum," WTOB radio, December 13, 1964.
Godwin, Winfred. Interview with Bruce B. Stewart. March 5, 1979.
Graduation Ceremony. Tape recording. June 8, 1966.
Keller, Franklin J. Letter to M. C. Benton, Jr. July 30, 1963.
Kennedy, John F. President's Remarks, Mrs. Kennedy's First Young People's Concert. August 22, 1961.
Lowry, W. McNeil. Letter to Hugh Cannon. November 25, 1964.
———. Letter to Vittorio Giannini. July 8, 1964.
McDaniel, Joseph M., Jr. Letter to Dr. James H. Semans. December 27, 1965.
McKnight, Pete. Interview with Bruce B. Stewart. February 10, 1979.
Minutes of the Academic and Arts Faculty Meeting Called by Dr. Giannini on Friday, October 14, 1966.
Minutes of the Board of Trustees Meeting. Stanhope Hotel, New York City. November 14, 1964.
Minutes of the Joint Meeting of the Advisory Board and Board of Trustees. Stanhope Hotel, New York City. November 14, 1965.
Mueller, Julia W. "Report of Academic Department of North Carolina School of

the Arts, First Semester, 1965–1966." In "Semi-Annual Report—First Semester—1965–1966 North Carolina School of the Arts."

North Carolina School of the Arts. Press Releases: November 14, 1964, January 3, 16, 1965, [January 1965], March 19, April 1, 11, 14, May 13, 23, June 7, 24, July 4, August 8, September 1, November 2, 1965, January 20, June 5, December 2, 1966, June 10, 1970.

Ribet, Julia. Letter to Mattie Keys. December 10, 1964.

Semans, Dr. James H. Telegram to Wallace Carroll. December 9, 1964.

"Semi-Annual Report—First Semester—1965–1966 North Carolina School of the Arts."

Stewart, Bruce B. "The Politics of Art: The Origin of the North Carolina School of the Arts." Typescript, n.d.

"Target: Artistic Oasis at Winston-Salem." WBT radio (Charlotte). October 1965.

"Terms of Grant." December 27, 1965.

Young, J. Winthrop. Letter to Bruce B. Stewart. January 14, 1966.

Zinn, Douglas. Oral History Interviews:

Rose Bampton. June 10, 1982.

Hugh Cannon. October 27, 1981.

Arturo Ciompi. November 21, 1984. With Leslie Banner.

Giorgio and Adriana Ciompi. November 16, 1981. With Dr. James H. Semans.

Agnes de Mille. June 9, 1982.

Philip Dunigan. August 29, 1984.

John Ehle. December 8, 1983. With Leslie Banner.

Marion Fitz-Simons. January 20, 1982.

Joel Fleishman. January 4, 1982.

Olegna Fuschi. June 9, 1982.

Giannini sisters, Christina, Maura, and Evadne. November 12, 1982.

Gordon Hanes. October 14, 1983.

R. Philip Hanes, Jr. December 8, 1983. With Leslie Banner.

William Herring. March 14, 1985.

Robert Hickock. February 21, 1984.

Lesley Hunt. November 6, 1981.

Andrew Jones. February 17, 1982.

Tom Kenan. March 9, 1982.

Pauline Koner. November 11, 1982.

Tom Lambeth. March 19, 1982.

Robert Lindgren. April 22, 1982.

W. McNeil Lowry. December 6, 1982.

Betty Masten. September 26, 1984.

Malcolm Morrison. August 29, 1984.

Duncan Noble. March 6, 1982.

James Christian Pfohl. December 22, 1981.

Sam Ragan. March 5, 1982.

Eugene Rizzo. August 13, 1983.

Ben Roney and Judge David Britt. October 7, 1982.

Terry Sanford. January 22, 1982.

Dr. James H. Semans. October 19 and 21, 1981.

Mary D. B. T. (Mrs. James H.) Semans. November 4, 1981.
John Sneden. April 22, 1982.
Martin Sokoloff. August 16, 1982.
Bruce B. Stewart. January 23 and April 24, 1982.
Sam Stone. March 19, 1982.
Robert Suderburg. August 16, 1982.
Ben Swalin. January 25, 1982.
William Tribby. April 22, 1982.
William Trotman. January 29, 1982.
Robert Ward. January 14, 1982.

Semans Files, Durham, North Carolina

Alberti, Luciano. Letter to Robert Ward. April 22, 1971.
"Americans to Honor Italy in Outdoor Rome Concert." Mimeograhed press release, no source. August 6, 1970.
Baker, George R. F. "Summers in Siena." Ms. mailed to Dr. James H. Semans, November 19, 1971.
Bonechi Guide. *The Wonderful Towns of Italy.* 1965.
Carroll, Wallace. Speech on the Occasion of the Presentation of a Bust of James H. Semans, M.D. Hotel Europa, Durham, N.C., December 5, 1981.
Ciompi, Giorgio. "Diary." June 10–July 3, 1968.
———. Memorandum to Dr. James H. Semans, Robert Ward, Paolo Olsoufieff, H. Alan Sims. [Fall/winter 1968].
———. Memorandum of a trip to Italy, January 15–28, 1968.
———. "Résumé of telephone conversation between Giorgio Ciompi and Mario Fabbri on May 11, 1969."
"Concerto Sinfonico" (concert program). North Carolina School of the Arts III Summer Session at Siena Sotto Il Patrocinio della Accademia Musicale Chigiana, Siena, Teatro dei Rinnuovati, 21 Agosto 1969.
"Draft Prospectus as discussed between Dr. & Mrs. Semans and Maestro Ciompi on Sunday, June 23, 1968."
Ehle, John. Speech delivered at a national meeting on gifted students, sponsored by the Sid Richardson Foundation of Fort Worth, Texas. June 10, 1981.
Fabbri, Mario. Letters to:
Giorgio Ciompi. December 18, 1967, April 4, 1968.
Vittorio Giannini. November, November 21, 1966.
Dr. James H. Semans. November 13, 1968, November 17, 1969.
Fondazione Accademia Musicale Chigiana. *Programa Della XXXVIII Annata Corsi di Perfezionamento.* Palazzo Chigi Saracini, Siena (Italia), 15 Luglio–10 Settembre 1969.
"Foreign Minister Fanfani Attends Opening of Summer Session." Ms. page. [?] July 1967.
Giannini, Vittorio. Letter to Mario Fabbri. November 1, 1966.
Hall, Roger. Memorandum Re: Siena to Robert Ward. August 17, 1970.
Harsanyi, Nicholas. Letter to Robert Ward. July 5, 1971.

Institute of International Education. *This is IIE*. Brochure. 1969.

Jory, Margaret F. and Randolph A. Kidder. "Report for North Carolina School of the Arts." August 1969.

Lindgren, Robert. "Dance Group to Italy." Edited dictation. [1969].

"Luncheon Meeting, Siena—July 16, 1968."

"Meeting Notes" [Siena]. Luncheon, July 12, 1968.

"Minutes of a Meeting Held on August 22nd, 1967 in Maestro Fabbri's Office at the Accademia Chigiana, Siena."

"Minutes of a meeting held on Tuesday, 29th August [1967] at the Accademia Chigiana, at 4 P.M."

"Minutes of a meeting held August 30th, 1967, at the Accademia Chigiana, Siena, at 9:30 A.M."

"Minutes of the Meeting Held in the Prefettura of Siena, Saturday, October 1, 1966."

"Minutes of the Meeting held in Rome the 5th of October, 1966."

Mueller, Julia. "Calendar with Reference to Fabbri Visit." Attached to March 18, 1968 memorandum to Giorgio Ciompi.

———. Memorandum to students and staff of the NCSA Summer Session in Siena. May 20, 1968.

———. "1969 Season." Calendar, curriculum, student, staff, and budget lists.

———. "Siena—July 11, 1968." Undirected report.

"North Carolina Philharmonic Orchestra." Ms. listing, 1969 concert dates and programs.

North Carolina School of the Arts. *Handbook Summer Session in Siena*. 1967.

North Carolina School of the Arts. *Summer Session at Siena, Italy*. Pamphlet, 1967.

North Carolina School of the Arts Foundation, Inc. "History of Giving." Confidential report prepared for Mrs. James Semans.

"North Carolina School of the Arts Summer Session in Siena, 2 July 1970, Financial Survey."

"Notes for Meeting Bivins St. 8/13/68."

"Points Arising from Preliminary Meeting between Mr. Robert Ward & Mr. Fabbri—7/15/68."

Ragan, Sam. Speech on the Occasion of the Presentation of a Bust of James H. Semans, M.D. Hotel Europa, Durham, N.C., December 5, 1981.

Semans, James H. "Fortuitous Circumstances Adding to the Success of the North Carolina School of the Arts Summer Session in Siena, Italy." Notes forwarded to Beverly Wolters, Winston-Salem *Journal and Sentinel*, September 23, 1967.

———. Letters to:

Stewart ———. January 31, 1967.

Guido Agosti. October 14, 1969.

Franco Agostini. April 22, 1967.

Luciano Alberti. December 24, 1969.

Ernest Brooks. January 1967 (not sent), February 1967 (not sent), August 12, 1967.

John Ehle. October 13, 1966.

Senator Fanfani. Draft attached to a note from Vieri Traxler. November 6, 1969.

James Glenn. July 25, 1967.

R. Philip Hanes, Jr. July 25, 1967.

William Herring. July 31, 1967.

Mr. and Mrs. Sigmund Koch. October 13, 1966.

The Honorable Governor Dan K. Moore and Mrs. Moore. July 27, 1967.

Richard B. Myer. April 30, 1969.

Danilo Verzili. April 14, 1969.

Robert Ward. December 7, 1968, August 18, 1969, July 22, 1971.

The Honorable Lindsey C. Warren, Jr. August 11, 1969.

———. Ms. memoirs:

"Fabbri's Visit to the United States." n.d.

"History and Anecdotes of the Summer Session of the North Carolina School of the Arts in Siena, Italy, 1967."

"Modus Operandi." October 15, 1971.

"The Next Episode . . . July 1967."

"1967—The incident of the establishment of credit." n.d.

"North Carolina School of the Arts Italian Program in Siena January 14, 1970."

"Notes dictated at the end of the exploratory trip to Italy made by JHS and Robert Ward from January 10 to January 22, 1970."

"Notes on preparatory work carried out in FLORENCE, SIENA AND ROME, ITALY between January 22, 1967 and February 6, 1967." Dictation of February 15, 1967.

"Our Visit to the Vatican, July 4, 1968."

"Problems in the Accademia Chigiana and NCSS Relationship." N.d.

"Survey by the International Institute of Education, United Nations, New York, 1969." N.d.

———. Important Details for Advance Agent and Manager to the North Carolina Conservatory Summer Session in Siena—1969 [December 7, 1968].

———. Memorandum (personal). "Verbal agreement of the 1st Session." October 1 and 5, 1966.

———. "Memorandum of Conversation JHS had with Giorgio Ciompi." February 1967.

Semans, James H., *Siena: Six Summers of Music; Sketches of an American Program Abroad*. Ed. Eugene Rizzo. Burlington, N.C.: Meredith-Webb Printing Co., 1973.

———. Speech, unidentified, April 16, 1970.

———. Speech. On the Occasion of the Presentation of a Bust of James H. Semans, M.D. Hotel Europa, Durham, N.C., December 5, 1981.

Semans, James H. or Mary. "Unique Experience of the Summer Session in Italy." Speech, not identified.

Semans, Mary. Letter to Dirk Dawson. July 22, 1969.

———. Speech to the Junior League of Winston-Salem. 1971.

"Siena Summer Session 1969." List of students with instruments, ages, schools, school years, and home addresses. Enclosure with Mary B. Ward to Dr. James H. Semans, June 9, 1969.

"Siena Summer Session Bulletin [1969]—Part II."

Sims, H. Alan. "1969 Siena Summer Session." Ms., apparently a transcription.

"Summer Session in Siena, Notes on Meeting at 1415 Bivins Street, Durham, North Carolina, Tuesday, August 12, 1968."

Traxler, Vieri. "Remarks." Speech delivered at the International Banking Convention, Chapel Hill, N.C., October 13, 1970.

———. "Résumé of a conversation in Siena Saturday, July 22, 1967, about the future of the N.C.S.A. Summer Session in Siena."

Verzili, Danilo. "The Great Contributions to Classical Music of Count Guido Chigi Saracini." Speech delivered in Raleigh, North Carolina, at the Governor's Mansion, on the occasion of Governor Dan K. Moore's announcement of the North Carolina School of the Arts Summer Session in Siena, December 2, 1966.

Volz, Doe. "Ojai Violinist Wins Major Prize in Italy." Photocopy, source not identified, n.d.

Ward, Mary B. Letter to Dr. James H. Semans. June 9, 1969.

Ward, Robert. Letter to Giorgio Ciompi. November 22, 1967.

———. Letter to Herbert Handt. February 11, 1971.

———. Letter to Dr. James H. Semans. January 14, 1969.

———. "Memorandum, 24th August, 1967."

———. "On Friday Morning, July 19th, the meeting between Maestro Fabbri, Giorgio Ciompi, J. Mueller and myself."

———. "Tentative Revision of Plan for North Carolina School of the Arts Siena Summer Session." Attached to July 20, 1968 memorandum to Giorgio Ciompi.

Wilson, Randy. Letter to Dr. James H. Semans. [Early 1968.]

Wolslagel, Earl. "Duke to Inaugurate Summer Session in Arts in Italy." Office of Information Services, Duke University. June 2, 1968.

OTHER SOURCES

Atlanta Journal/Constitution. December 13, 14, 1981.

Banner, Laura Leslie. "The North Carolina Mountaineer in Native Fiction." Ph.D. dissertation, University of North Carolina at Chapel Hill, 1984.

Barzini, Luigi. *The Italians.* New York: Atheneum, 1964.

Chapel Hill Weekly. May 23, 26, 1963.

Charlotte News. December 30, 1963.

Charlotte Observer. November 3, December 7, 1962, May 19, June 21, 22, December 30, 1963, April 22, May 5, 1964.

Daily American [Rome, Italy]. June 27, 1968.

de Schauensee, Max. "The Gianninis: A Portrait of a Prodigious Philadelphia Family." *Opera News,* April 11, 1964, pp. 14–16.

Dorian, Frederick. *Commitment to Culture.* Pittsburgh: University of Pittsburgh Press, 1964.

Duberman, Martin. *Black Mountain: An Exploration in Community.* New York: E. P. Dutton, 1972.

Durham Morning Herald. February 13, 15, April 28, 29, 30, May 3, July 18, 1964, August 20, September 24, 1967, August 10, 1969.

Durham Sun. April 29, 1964.

Ehle, John. "A Letter about Vittorio Giannini." In *Giannini's Dream: A Tribute to Dr. Vittorio Giannini.* Winston-Salem: North Carolina School of the Arts Foundation, 1974.

———. "What's the Matter with Chapel Hill?" *News and Observer* [Raleigh, N.C.], May 14, 1961.

"Ehle, John." Clippings File. North Carolina Collection, Wilson Library, University of North Carolina at Chapel Hill.

Ewen, David. "Vittorio Giannini." In *American Composers: A Biographical Dictionary.* London: Robert Hale, 1983.

Frost, Robert. Speech given in Memorial Hall on the campus of the University of North Carolina at Chapel Hill, March 3, 1961. Tape recording, North Carolina Collection, Wilson Library, University of North Carolina at Chapel Hill.

Gale, Joseph. Review. "Agnes deMille's Heritage Dance Theatre," North Carolina School of the Arts, April 26–29, 1973. *Dance Magazine,* August 1973, p. 21.

Gates, John D. "The North Carolina School of the Arts." *Southern World,* December 1980.

Getlein, Frank. "Where Homework Might Be Dance or Music or Theater." *Smithsonian,* March 1981.

Gingrich, Arnold. *Business and the Arts.* New York: Paul S. Erickson, 1969.

Greensboro Daily News. May 12, 14, 1963.

Greensboro Record. May 7, 1963, April 7, 8, 1964.

Herald [Sanford, N.C.]. December 13, 1962.

Hering, Doris. "A World for the Lonely Piper." *Dance Magazine,* March 19, 1965, pp. 38–41.

———. " 'The Leisure to Learn': Dance at the North Carolina School of the Arts—An Interim Appraisal." *Dance Magazine,* October 1967.

Jones, Graham. "Biographical Sketch of Terry Sanford." In *Messages, Addresses and Public Papers of Terry Sanford, Governor of North Carolina, 1961–1965.* Ed. Memory F. Mitchell. Raleigh: Council of State, State of North Carolina, 1966.

Journal and Sentinel [Winston-Salem, N.C.]. August 23, 1961, April 30, 1964, February 28, September 12, 1965.

Kirstein, Lincoln. "The Performing Arts and Our Egregious Elite." In *The Performing Arts and American Society.* Ed. W. McNeil Lowry. Englewood Cliffs, N.J.: Prentice-Hall, 1978.

La Nazione [Florence, Italy]. August 17, 1967, July 12, 1968, August 21, 1969.

Los Angeles Times. January 5, 1964.

Lowry, W. McNeil, ed. *The Performing Arts and American Society.* Englewood Cliffs, N.J.: Prentice-Hall, 1978.

———. "The University and the Creative Arts." *Educational Theater Journal* 14 (1961): 99–112.

Mark, M. L. "The Band Music of Vittorio Giannini." *Music Educators Journal* 55 (April 1969): 77–80.

Marracco, W. Thomas. "Vittorio Giannini." In *The New Grove Dictionary of Music and Musicians.* Washington, D.C.: Grove's Dictionaries of Music, 1980.

McGill, Ralph. "Atlanta. Some Pros and Cons of Culture in the South: As It Was." *Show,* June 1963, pp. 9–11.

McKinzie, Richard D. *The New Deal for Artists.* Princeton, N.J.: Princeton University Press, 1973.

Mitchell, Memory F., ed. *Messages, Addresses, and Public Papers of Terry Sanford, Governor of North Carolina, 1961–1965.* Raleigh: Council of State, State of North Carolina, 1966.

New York Times. October 5, 1962, May 21, December 3, 1963, January 7, March 8, June 22, 1964, August 14, 1970.

News-Argus [Goldsboro, N.C.]. March 27, 1963.

News and Observer [Raleigh, N.C.]. November 3, December 7, 1962, May 19, June 10, 18, 22, 30, July 7, November 15, December 31, 1963, April 1, 28, 29, 30, May 24, 29, July 18, August 15, 1964, January 28, February 8, March 6, 16, April 18, 1965, April 10, December 3, 1966.

News of Orange County [Hillsborough, N.C.]. October 24, 31, 1963, April 30, 1964.

"North Carolina School of the Arts Graduates—On the Road to Success." *Arts Journal,* April 1982.

"One-Man Rand." *Newsweek,* June 1, 1964, pp. 77–78.

Paris [France] *Herald-Tribune.* July 21, 1970.

Ragan, Sam, ed. *The New Day.* Zebulon, N.C.: Record Publishing Co., 1964.

Raleigh Times. December 6, 1962, March 14, May 7, June 12, 1963, April 30, 1964.

Reiss, Alvin H. *Culture and Company.* New York: Twayne, 1972.

Rockefeller Panel. *The Performing Arts: Problems and Prospects.* New York: McGraw-Hill, 1965.

Salisbury Post. April 26, 1964.

Sanford, Terry. *But What about the People?* New York: Harper & Row, 1966.

Sargeant, Winthrop. "Profiles: Torna! Torna! Torna!" *New Yorker* 36 (3 September 1960): 37–77.

"The Summer Export of Culture from the New World to the Old." *North Carolina,* March 1984, pp. 28, 30, 62.

Toffler, Alvin. *The Culture Consumers.* N.p.: St. Martin's Press, 1964.

Troxler, Howard. "Art and Ambition." *Tarheel,* January 1982.

Twin-City Sentinel [Winston-Salem, N.C.]. May 14, 15, June 25, 1963, March 27, 28, April 24, 30, 1964, January 15, April 8, September 9, 1965, July 30, 1984.

Wall Street Journal. August 12, 1969.

Washington Post. June 13, 1963, March 27, 1964.

Winston-Salem Journal. May 22, 23, June 22, 1963, March 27, April 3, 4, 23, 27, 28, 29, 30, May 1, 1964, April 23, 1983, July 30, 1984.

Wyden, Barbara. "Atlanta. Some Pros and Cons of Culture in the South: As It Is." *Show,* June 1963, pp. 104–6.

INDEX